The System of
Criminal Justice

The System of Criminal Justice

N. Gary Holten
Melvin E. Jones
FLORIDA TECHNOLOGICAL UNIVERSITY

Little, Brown and Company
BOSTON TORONTO

Drawings by David Omar White. For the protection of privacy and of the innocent all illustrations in this text were drawn, rather than photographed, from real life.

Copyright © 1978 by Little, Brown and Company (Inc.)

All rights reserved. No part of this book may be reproduced in any form or by any electronic or mechanical means including information storage and retrieval systems without permission in writing from the publisher, except by a reviewer who may quote brief passages in a review.

Library of Congress
Catalog Card No. 77-86631

Second Printing

Published simultaneously in Canada by Little, Brown & Company (Canada) Limited

Printed in the United States of America

For
our wives Carolyn and Cara Lee
and our children
Scott and Jamie Holten
and
Rusty and Kristy Jones

Preface

The System of Criminal Justice is a comprehensive introductory text that examines the history, functions, structures, processes, and interactions of the four components of American criminal justice: law enforcement, prosecution, trial courts and corrections. Unlike most other criminal justice texts, we have separated the office of prosecution from the courts and given to it the status of a major criminal justice component. The role played by prosecutors in the criminal justice system clearly demonstrates the necessity of such an approach. Also, unlike most other texts, we approach the study of criminal justice from a systems standpoint. It is not only a useful analytical tool but also reflects the interrelatedness and interdependence of criminal justice components and the existence, however imperfect, of a criminal justice "system." In addition, we have furnished the reader with a number of study aids. These include an outline, chapter objectives, and a list of key terms and concepts at the beginning of each chapter, and "test yourself" questions at the end of the chapter, plus an extensive glossary of criminal justice terms and bibliography at the end of the text.

We open Part I with an introduction to the systems approach; discussion of the key concepts of crime, law, and justice; and an overview of the functions, structures, and process of the entire criminal justice system. In Parts II through V we describe the history, functions, structures, and processes of each criminal justice component. We also discuss the relationships among the components and to the environment within which each operates. We treat juvenile justice in Part VI and close with a discussion of recent trends and innovations in the criminal justice system in Part VII. Throughout the book we have taken no ideological stand but have simply attempted to present an objective and balanced description of the criminal justice system.

Writing a book requires the assistance, cooperation, and encouragement of many people. We would like to thank those who have given us these things. All or portions of the manuscript were read by a number of scholars, including Warren Barnes, Mark Bennett, Richard Farmer, Matthew Fitzgerald, Hal Kane, Edward Mandt, and Robert Taylor. We found their comments to be helpful, and many of their suggestions were incorporated into the book. Lawson L. Lamar, Chief of Criminal Intake in the State Attorney's Office of Florida's Ninth Judicial Circuit, offered valuable guidance in writing the section on prosecution. Special thanks must go to Susie Weiss, who not only typed the manuscript many times over but worried with us over such things as grammar, lost footnotes and ever-approaching deadlines. The people at Little, Brown deserve special recognition for the way in which they guided two new authors through the long path from rough drafts to published text. Frank Graham helped get the book off the ground and well under way. Rick Boyer, Jane Robbins, and Cynthia Chapin were each instrumental in the development and polishing of the final text.

Naturally, we could not have spent the many months this project required without the understanding and encouragement of our wives. They worked hard at providing the time, place, and proper atmosphere that we needed to get the job done. Hopefully, they already know the extent of our appreciation.

N. G. H.
M. E. J.

Introduction to the Student

An increasing number of people believe we are failing to cope with crime. A very recent Harris poll found that enforcement agencies and criminal courts are not enjoying the same confidence they enjoyed in the past. Louis Harris writes:

> At the federal level, law enforcement officials get a 49–39 percent negative rating on their job performance, the lowest recorded by the Harris Survey since 1967.
>
> At the state level, law enforcement officials come up with a narrow 47–42 percent positive rating, down from 51–39 percent two years ago.
>
> At the local level, the public gives police forces a relatively good 52–46 percent positive rating. However, this is down from the much higher levels of 57–40 percent positive in 1975 and 64–33 percent positive in 1970.

Harris notes that a 67–16 percent majority believe that law enforcement "does not really discourage people from committing crimes," and 8 percent feel that the system actually "encourages" it. He observes that courts, too, come under public attack, as 74 percent indicate courts are too lenient with criminals. This is up from 49 percent who felt that way a decade ago.

Such indications of the attitudes of citizens are very sobering to those working in criminal justice agencies. On the other hand, much of the adverse public opinion could be based on people's unreasonable expectations of what police, courts, and other agencies can do about crime and criminals. Many people may misunderstand the functions or purposes of the various agencies and the limits placed on them by their environments. They may have only a vague notion of the structures and relationships that exist among the various government departments, agencies, offices, institutions, and programs that play some part in criminal justice. There are, unfortunately, many criminal justice officials who do not really see the whole picture either. They may know their own jobs thoroughly but not understand how these jobs fit into the criminal justice process in general.

The purpose of this text is to examine the functions, structures, and process of criminal justice. It will do so in clear and straightforward terms. We take no ideological position. We do not, on the other hand, avoid commentary. We deal with controversial issues by trying to present contrasting positions.

We have provided a number of aids to learning: for each chapter there is an outline, list of key terms, statement of objectives, and list of questions to help measure comprehension. At the end of the text there is a bibliography and glossary of terms. We hope that you as a student will find this text informative, thought provoking, and enjoyable to read.

Contents

**PART 1
THE CRIMINAL JUSTICE
SYSTEM** 2

**CHAPTER 1
A SYSTEM OF CRIMINAL JUSTICE** 4

    A Systems Approach 6
    Application of the Systems Approach
        to Criminal Justice 7
    Functions of a System 8
    Interdependence of System
        Components 9
    System Dynamics 11
    Criticisms of the Systems Approach
        to Criminal Justice 15
    Reasons for Viewing Criminal
        Justice as a Nonsystem 16
    Trends Toward a System of
        Criminal Justice 17

CHAPTER 2
FOUNDATIONS OF THE CRIMINAL JUSTICE SYSTEM: CRIME, LAW, AND CONCEPTS OF JUSTICE 20

Crime 22
  Classifying Crimes 22
  Levels of Crime 28
Law 33
  Nature of Law 33
  Forms of Law 34
  Types of Law 34
Justice 36
  Justice as a System Input 36
  Justice Defined 37
  Uses of Justice 37
The Constitution 39
  Provisions in the Original Text 39
  The Bill of Rights 40
The Supreme Court and
    Constitutional Law 42
Application of the Bill of Rights to
    States 42
  Appellate Courts and the Criminal
    Justice System 45

CHAPTER 3
AN OVERVIEW OF CRIMINAL JUSTICE: FUNCTIONS, STRUCTURES, AND PROCESSES 50

System Functions 52
  Perceptions of Criminal Justice
    Functions 52
  Criminal Justice Functions 53
System Structures 57
  Law Enforcement 57
  Prosecutors 58
  Courts 60
  Corrections 61
Basic System Processes 65
  Stages of the Criminal Justice
    Process 65
  Juvenile Justice 73

PART II
LAW ENFORCEMENT 78

CHAPTER 4
LAW ENFORCEMENT FUNCTIONS AND STRUCTURES 80

   Municipal Police 82
      Historical Development 83
      Municipal Police Functions 86
      Police Organization 90
   The Office of Sheriff 98
      Historical Development 98
      Functions 99
      Organization 100
   State Law Enforcement Agencies 101
      Historical Development 101
      Functions 102
      Organization 103
   Federal Law Enforcement 104
      Department of Justice 104
      Department of the Treasury 108

CHAPTER 5
LAW ENFORCEMENT PROCESSES 112

   Police Authority 114
      Arrest 114
      Search and Seizure 115
   Crime Detection 117
      Methods of Crime Detection and Crime Stages 117
      Steps Taken by Patrol 119
      Proactive Crime Detention 122
   Crime Investigation 124
      Investigative Functions 124
      Preliminary Investigations 125
      Follow-up Investigations 126
      How Crimes are Solved 129
   Case Preparation 130
      Crimes Cleared Versus Prosecutable Cases 131
      Investigative Thoroughness and Case Disposition 131
      New Emphasis on Case Preparation 132
   The Environment of Law Enforcement 133
      Organizational and Individual Behavior 133
      Internal Environmental Influences on Departmental Behavior 136
      External Environmental Influences on Departmental Behavior 137
      Environmental Influences on Individual Behavior 144

PART III
PROSECUTION 148

CHAPTER 6
PROSECUTION FUNCTIONS AND STRUCTURES 150

Importance of Prosecution 152
    Wide Discretion in Prosecution Decisions 152
    Scope of the Office 153
    Consumer of System Resources 154
History of Prosecution 154
Functions of the Prosecutor 155
    Charging 155
    Trial Advocacy 157
    Civil Responsibilities 157
    Other Functions 157
Structure and Organization 158
    Federal Level 158
    State Level 159
    Local Prosecutors 160

CHAPTER 7
THE PROSECUTION PROCESS 170

The Charging Stage 172
    Case Intake 173
    Case Screening 173
    Charging Decision 174
    The Grand Jury 180
    Precharge Hearings 182
The Adjudication Stage 183
    Arraignment 184
    Pretrial Activities 184
    Trial Activities 188
    Standards of Trial Practice 190
The Sentencing Stage 191
Postsentencing Activities 191
Environmental Impact on Prosecutors' Behavior 191
    The Impact of Government 192
    The Impact of the Community 193
    The Impact of Interagency Relations 194

PART IV
THE COURTS 200

CHAPTER 8
CRIMINAL COURT FUNCTIONS AND STRUCTURES 202

    Historical Development 204
        English Origins 205
        American Development 207
    Functions of Criminal Trial Courts 208
        Provision of Justice 208
        Adjudication of Defendants 209
        Sentencing of Those Adjudicated Guilty 209
        Principles of Justice 210
    Structure of the Court System 213
        Key Concepts and Principles 214
        State Court Systems 215
        Federal Court System 218

CHAPTER 9
COURT PARTICIPANTS 222

    Judges 224
        Judicial Recruitment and Selection 225
        Quality of Judges 230
    Defense Attorneys 233
        The Right to Counsel 233
        Defense Attorney Functions 233
        Selection of Defense Counsel 235
    Citizens as Jurors 239
        Knowledge About Juries 240
        Selection of Jurors 241
        Conditions in Jury Service 243
    Witnesses 244
    Court Support Personnel 245

CHAPTER 10
COURTS: PRETRIAL ACTIVITY AND PROCESS 250

    Arrest and Charging Stages 252
        Determining Probable Cause 252
        Assuring Appearances by the Defendant 256
    Adjudication: Pretrial Activities 264
        Arraignment 264
        Hearings on Motions 265
        Pretrial Conferences 269
        The Court and Negotiated Pleas 269

CHAPTER 11
COURTS: TRIAL AND SENTENCING 276

    Pretrial Decisions 278
        Place of Trial 278
        Trial Date 278
        Trial by Judge or Jury? 279
        Trial by Jury 280
    Trial Procedure 282
        Opening Statements 282
        Presentation of the State's Case 283
        Presentation of the Defense's Case 286
        Rebuttal and Surrebuttal 287
        Closing Arguments 287
        Jury Charge and Deliberations 288
        Court Adjudication 289
    Sentencing Stage 290
        Purposes of Criminal Sanctions 290
        Sentencing Alternatives 292
        Sentencing Procedures 296
        Sentencing Disparities 298
        Sentencing Reform 298
    Environment of Criminal Courts 299
        Impact of the Community 300
        Impact of Government 300
        Impact of Other Criminal Justice Components 302

PART V
CORRECTIONS

CHAPTER 12
CORRECTIONS: FUNCTIONS AND STRUCTURE 308

History of Corrections 310
    Criminal Treatment in Ancient Times 311
    Criminal Treatment in England 311
    Development of Criminal Treatment in the United States 312
Functions of Corrections 317
    Traditional Functions 317
    Recently Emerging Functions of Corrections 324
    Corrections Goals: Mixed Purposes 325
Structure of Corrections 326
    Institutions 326
    Community-Related Corrections 335

CHAPTER 13
CORRECTIONS: PROCESSES AND ENVIRONMENT 348

Pre-sentence Activities by Corrections Agencies 350
    Diversion from Formal Criminal Justice Processing 350
    Pre-sentence Investigations 351
Probation 352
    Restrictions on and Conditions of Probation 353
    The Role of the Probation Officer 354
    Revocation of Probation 356
    Termination of Probation 357
Institutionalization 357
    Reception 358
    Classification 358
    Treatment 359
    Informal Processing of Inmates 363
    Rights of Prisoners 365
Parole 367
    Parole Selection 368
    Period of Supervision 369
Community Corrections 371
    Institutional Programs 371
    Halfway Houses 372
    Intensive Intervention Programs 373
Environmental Influences on Corrections 375
    Physical Environment 375
    Community Influences 376
    Government Influences 377
    Relations with Other Components 378

PART VI
JUVENILE JUSTICE 384

CHAPTER 14
THE JUVENILE JUSTICE SYSTEM 386

   Historical Treatment of Juvenile
      Offenders 388
     Adult Status for Juvenile
      Offenders 388
     Parens Patriae 389
     Due Process for Juvenile
      Offenders 390
   The Process of Juvenile Justice 396
     Juvenile Justice System versus
      Juvenile Court 396
     Juvenile Delinquency Defined 397
     Law Enforcement and
      Juveniles 399
     Juvenile Court 400
   Juvenile Corrections 404
     Probation 404
     Juvenile Institutions 406
     Juvenile Aftercare (Parole) 408

PART VII
TOWARD A TRUE SYSTEM 412

CHAPTER 15
INNOVATIONS IN CRIMINAL
JUSTICE 414

   The Partial Nationalization of
     Criminal Justice 416
     The Warren Court and Criminal
      Justice 416
     The President's Crime
      Commission 417
     Federal Legislation Since 1968 417
     The LEAA: Progress and
      Controversy 419
     The National Advisory
      Commission on Criminal Justice
      Standards and Goals 424
   Innovations Within Criminal Justice
     Components 427
     Law Enforcement 427
     Prosecutors 434
     Courts 436
     Corrections 439
   Toward a True System of Criminal
     Justice 442
     Criminal Justice Information
      Systems 443
     Legislation and Code
      Revisions 444

The System of
Criminal Justice

PART I
The Criminal Justice System

CHAPTER 1
A System of Criminal Justice

OUTLINE

A SYSTEMS APPROACH

APPLICATION OF THE SYSTEMS APPROACH TO CRIMINAL JUSTICE
   Functions of a System
      Criminal Justice Functions
      Criminal Justice Components
   Interdependence of System Components
   System Dynamics
      Inputs
      Outputs
      Feedback
      Environment

CRITICISMS OF THE SYSTEMS APPROACH TO CRIMINAL JUSTICE
   Reasons for Viewing Criminal Justice as a Nonsystem
      System Imperfection
      System Fragmentation
   Trends Toward a System of Criminal Justice

OBJECTIVES

After reading this chapter the student should be able to:

Describe the characteristics of a system.

Relate the criminal justice system to the larger political and social systems.

List the functions of the criminal justice system.

List the components of the criminal justice system and relate each to the functions performed.

Explain the concept of the interdependence of the parts of the criminal justice system.

Discuss reasons why some object to viewing criminal justice as a system.

KEY TERMS

system
system components
interdependence of system components
system environment
system inputs
system demands and supports
system outputs
system feedback
system structure
system functions
law enforcement
prosecution
criminal trial courts
corrections
system fragmentation
vertical and horizontal fragmentation

☐ There is a "system" of criminal justice in the United States. The law enforcement agencies, offices of prosecution, criminal trial courts, and correctional institutions and programs are all components, or integral parts, of a criminal justice system.

Many scholars and criminal justice officials object to this claim, however, and refer to the present collection of institutions and programs as a criminal justice "nonsystem." Some do so because they believe that, in fact, a real system does not exist—at least, not yet. Others do so because they believe there should not be a system—that a true system of criminal justice would violate the basic principles of our Constitution and amount to a police state.

A SYSTEMS APPROACH

Whether the reader chooses to agree with us that criminal justice is a system will depend on the meaning he or she attaches to the term. In simplest terms a **system** consists of several parts that interact with each other to produce some result, serve some function(s), or meet some objective(s). From this and other complex definitions, we can make the following observations about system characteristics:

1. Systems have identifiable **components.** These are its parts or elements, structures that perform certain functions that contribute to the functioning of the system.

2. Each system constitutes an identifiable whole. This means that we can distinguish one system from another. Each has a boundary generally defined by the nature of its activities and outputs, its overall function. For example, a political system is defined by activities related to its output of public policy.

3. The system's components are **interdependent.** The elements of a system affect each other and depend on each other. Quite often one element cannot function without input from another. Thus criminal courts would have no purpose without input from police (arrests) and prosecutors (decisions to prosecute).

4. Each system operates within an **environment.** No system operates in a vacuum. An environment consists of any element outside the system's boundary. In the environment of each system there are many elements that can affect the system and its output. For example, America's economic and social systems—as well as those of every other society—are part of the political system's environment and certainly affect its operation.

5. For every system there are **inputs** into its decision-making area. They keep the system going as they flow into it from the environment. Inputs are of two types: (a) **demands:**—that is, what is wanted or expected from the system (e.g., citizens demanding that government halt inflation and lower unemployment); and (b) **supports**—that is, anything that serves to undergird or buttress the system (e.g., citizens supporting a government policy or obeying laws).

6. For each system there is **output.** Simply put, this is what the system produces, whether it be energy from an electrical system, movement from a mechanical system, or public policy from a political system.

7. Anytime there is output from a system, reaction in the environment produces what we can call **feedback.** Whenever there is an output from the system, it affects something or someone and a reaction generally occurs. This consequently may generate new input into the system.

While the preceding list of statements oversimplifies systems theory, it gives us a general grasp of its nature.[1] It is fairly obvious that such an approach can be applied to the field of criminal justice. Criminal justice does have identifiable parts or elements that perform various functions—police, prosecutors, courts, and corrections. These elements do constitute an identifiable whole. Together they engage in activities producing a primary output of justice. The elements are interdependent. The output of each element does affect the other elements. And, in fact, any element would be useless without the others. Whether or not the various elements always work together smoothly toward the same goal, they are highly interrelated. Criminal justice does operate within an environment from which it receives inputs consisting of demands (e.g., do something about crime) and supports (e.g., citizen participation, budget allocations). In short, criminal justice *is* a system and systems theory is a useful and natural framework for analysis. Some objections to its usage will be discussed later in this chapter.

APPLICATION OF THE SYSTEMS APPROACH TO CRIMINAL JUSTICE

Let us now examine more closely the criminal justice system and the value of a systems approach for understanding it. We will begin at the broadest level with society as a whole (social system) and work down to the level of the criminal justice system.

Functions of a System

Recall our mention of the concepts of **structure** and **functions.** Within any society, including that of the United States, there are functions that must be performed if the needs of its citizens are to be met and if the society itself is to survive or prosper. Among people's needs are those for shelter, food, services (such as health care), and physical security and safety. For each of these needs, a structure or structures exist to meet them.

A broad category of functions that must be performed for society as a whole has been described as "the authoritative allocation of values," which simply means making basic decisions about who gets what, when, and how. Now, some of these decisions are made by the economic system of the United States, especially if we take the word "values" to mean goods and selected services. But the word "authoritative" and the broadest meaning of "values" (to include, for example, personal security) mean that we are talking about the political system of the nation.

The political system includes subsystems designed to perform specific political functions. For example, the function of nominating candidates for office in the United States is performed by our political parties. The functions of ensuring that the views of specific social and economic groups in our nation are expressed to officeholders are performed by political interest groups, sometimes called pressure groups.

Some political functions are supported and reinforced by what is said to be legitimate resort to coercion or force. These are the functions performed by government in the United States. Thus government is the central and most important subsystem of the political system. But it too is made up of subsystems, such as those that function basically as rule makers (legislative bodies), rule enforcers (executive and administrative bodies), and rule interpreters and adjudicators (the judicial bodies). Within government (more specifically, within executive branches and a portion of the judiciary) we find the subsystem we call the criminal justice system.

Criminal Justice Functions The criminal justice system serves the general functions of (1) protecting citizens' lives, safety, property, and other rights as law provides; (2) preserving social and public order; (3) preventing crime by denying opportunities for crime and deterring would-be offenders; and (4) enforcing the law, with justice, by apprehending and prosecuting suspects, adjudicating the accused; and administering sanctions to those convicted. These functions may be summarized as *protection, order maintenance, law enforcement,* and *crime prevention.* To some they may also be seen in combination as *crime control.*

Criminal Justice Components The system is subdivided into four components, each of which has its own specific functions:

1. law enforcement, which involves the keeping of peace (order maintenance), the detection of crime and the arrest of suspected violators, and the provision of a wide variety of other services
2. the offices of **prosecution,** which involve the proper charging of suspected offenders and their prosecution
3. criminal trial courts, which involve the adjudication of cases to determine guilt or innocence and the proper sentencing of those found guilty, all within the broader function of providing justice
4. corrections, which involve the administration of appropriate sanctions in keeping with the sentence handed down

These functions and their corresponding structures comprise the major components or elements of the criminal justice system. There are, in addition, other agencies and actors who become involved in the criminal justice process on either an ad hoc or regular basis depending on the situation, jurisdiction, type of case, and other factors. These include social service agencies that become involved in juvenile cases, medical and psychiatric agencies, and the like. Illustration of the structural arrangement of society, the political system, and the criminal justice system appears in Figure 1.1.

Interdependence of System Components

Up to this point the picture of the relationship between the various systems and subsystems is incomplete. We have not stressed the interdependence that exists in this set of relationships. It is clear, for example, that the functions of law enforcement could not be performed without the other criminal justice agencies performing their respective functions. Arresting violators would be pointless if the process ended at arrest and if there were no possibilities of prosecution and sentencing. Just as pointless would be the existence of correctional facilities if there were no agencies to determine the guilt of suspected violators.

This illustrates the interdependence of the components of the criminal justice system, but a similar interdependence exists between the criminal justice system and the political system of which it is a part. As one scholar has characterized it, "Decisions are made in the politi-

FIGURE 1.1 Relationship between the Criminal Justice System and Social and Political Systems

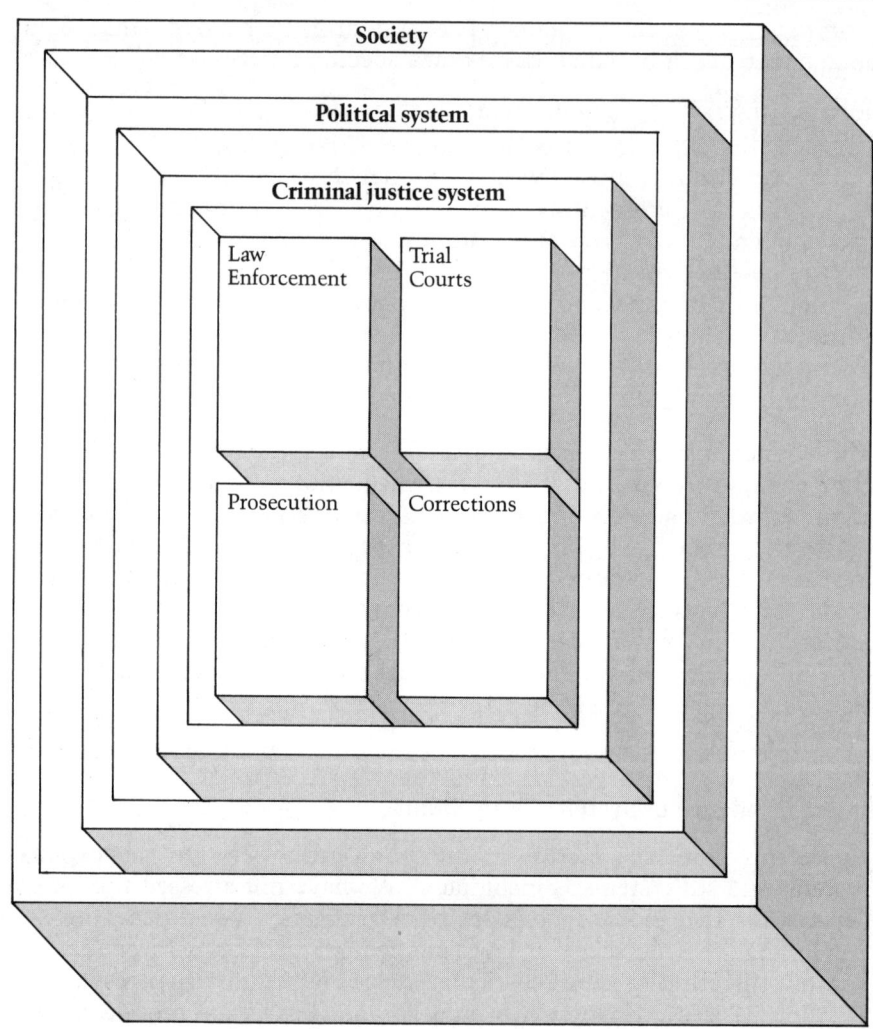

cal process which allocate resources to the criminal justice system and thus determine the scope and the intensity with which the law will be enforced."[2] Conversely, the political system would not long survive without the protection afforded to it and to the citizens by the criminal justice system.

System Dynamics

The interdependence of system components leads to a discussion of the dynamics of systems theory, or what we have previously referred to as processes and outputs. Simply put, neither the system nor its components are rigid and static but both are moving, acting, and interacting. The action can be seen as flow, and this flow can be expressed in terms of inputs, outputs, and feedback. Inputs are of fundamental importance for any system such as criminal justice. They furnish the moving force for decisions made within the system. Outputs flow from the criminal justice system and have an impact on society and the political system. As noted earlier, the impact of a system's output on subsequent input is called feedback.

Inputs Recall that inputs are of two kinds: supports and demands. We made reference earlier to a kind of input from the political system into the criminal justice system—the allocation of resources. This type of input can be labeled support. Further supports from the political system may include selection, appointment, and promotion of personnel. Direct citizen participation in the criminal justice system through such avenues as jury duty and crime reporting can also be viewed as system supports. Supports are sometimes material, as in citizens' approval of a bond issue for expansion of the police department, or symbolic, as in the election or reelection of the mayor or city councilman (political system) or the prosecutor (criminal justice system).

Another kind of input is demands. These are the things that are desired or expected from the system. Let us use an example: The behavior of a prosecutor in pushing for a conviction in a pornography case can be understood in light of input demands from several sources. From another component of the criminal justice system—law enforcement—comes the input of the arrest of an adult book shop employee or owner. From the mayor or city council may have come an input to both prosecutor and police: demands to crack down on "smut" dealers in general, or a specific demand to arrest and prosecute a particular book dealer. From society at large, perhaps a citizens' group concerned with morality or decency in literature, comes the input of demands for elimination of smut from the community. Such demands from citizens may be viewed as input into both the political and criminal justice systems.

Outputs Outputs of a system can take many forms. They stem from the performance (or nonperformance) of system functions. We noted earlier, for example, that the function of a political system is the authoritative allocation of values for a society—deciding who gets what, when, and how. The basic output related to governmental attempts to fulfill this function is public policy. Recall that the criminal justice system's functions were defined to be protection (lives, safety, property, rights), order maintenance, law enforcement, and crime prevention. Associated with these functions are a variety of outputs, most of which are unique to specific components of the system. Thus we can speak of such outputs as patrol and arrests (law enforcement), charges, pleas, and trial prosecutions (prosecution), setting of bail, disposition of cases, and sentencing (courts), and persons released (corrections). Both functions and outputs will be discussed in more detail in subsequent chapters.

Feedback Outputs are important to people who are part of a system's environment and some reaction from them is usually forth-

Citizen reports of crime are a major form of input into criminal justice systems.

coming. This reaction, if communicated back into the system, is called feedback. The concept is important because it recognizes that the flow of activity (in the criminal justice system or in any system) is not just in one direction: INPUTS → OUTPUTS. That is, what the system does (output) will at least partially determine subsequent inputs. It may, in fact, result in changes in the system. To return to our smut dealer example, if the prosecutor decides to prosecute and fails to obtain a conviction—due perhaps to mistakes on his part or to other reasons—citizens may express outrage. They may vent their expressions toward the criminal justice system directly or indirectly through the political system. An unsuccessful prosecutor thus might find himself the subject of citizen criticism and perhaps the recipient of a budget cut from the political system. A successful prosecution, on the other hand, may result in varying kinds of support, such as reelection or budget increases. It should also be noted that specific decisions or patterns of behavior by a decision maker may be influenced, partially or completely, by his or her awareness of possible consequences.

To the diagram of social, political, and criminal justice systems, we may now add the depiction of the concepts of inputs, outputs, and feedback, which express the dynamics of these systems. See Figure 1.2.

Environment One other concept remains important to the understanding of the systems approach to criminal justice. As discussed before, each system operates within an environment. From the environment come inputs into the system. The environment provides conditions under which the system operates. For a system such as the human body, the environment is complex and includes such obvious things as air, food, and human relationships. Each person also operates within the confines of the criminal justice, political, and social systems. The political system of any society also has an environment, and this includes not only that society's own economic and social systems but also the economic, political, and social systems of other societies.

The criminal justice system also has its environment. As we have noted, this environment contains many elements that provide input into the system. Crime, of course, is the major input into the criminal justice system. It is, in fact, the very reason for its existence. Law, as created by the political system, is another major input. It provides the very foundation for the criminal justice system by defining those acts that are to be labeled "crimes" and by stipulating the rules under which the system attempts to cope with crime.

An additional input is the variety of notions about and expectations of justice from those in the system's environment. Nearly everyone,

FIGURE 1.2 System Dynamics

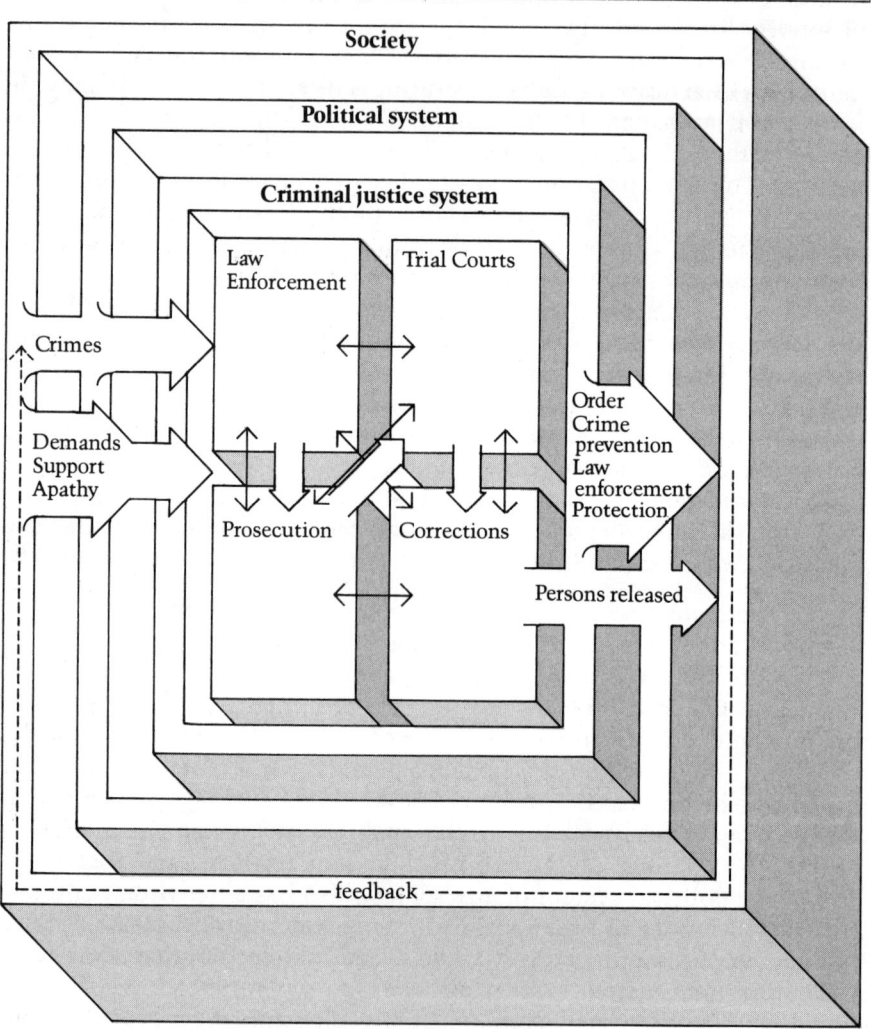

from private citizen to public official, has a feeling about what constitutes justice. Whatever our notion of justice is, there are great expectations that it will be a primary output of the criminal justice system. Further environmental inputs may include system resources, policy directives and guidance, and various citizen supports and demands.

Law, crime, and justice will be discussed in more detail in Chapter 2. Environmental influences on each system component will be examined throughout the text.

CRITICISMS OF THE SYSTEMS APPROACH TO CRIMINAL JUSTICE

As we have said, not all who follow the activities of criminal justice agree with the utilization of a systems approach. In fact, as Felkenes notes, some would say "that the concept of a system is a complete fallacy; that each step in the criminal process is dealt with by a completely independent agency owing no allegiance to anyone but itself"; that each agency "cares little about how its activities affect other offices that also were organized to assist in coping with illegal activities by prosecuting or rehabilitating those individuals through the system."[3] Perhaps this line of thought has been most succinctly expressed by the American Bar Association:

> The American criminal justice system is rocked by inefficiency, lack of coordination, and an obsessive adherence to outmoded practices and procedures. In many respects, the entire process might more aptly be termed a nonsystem, a feudalistic confederation of several independent components often working at cross purposes.[4]

We, of course, reject the notion of a nonsystem. While it is true that there has been a tendency for many criminal justice agencies to think and act independently of others, this in no way justifies the label of nonsystem. As we have indicated, criminal justice does have the essential qualities of a system. Probably the most important of these is component interrelatedness and interdependence. There is no question but that this quality is found in the criminal justice area. As one author puts it:

> In spite of operating independently, whatever one agency does affects the others. For example, if corrections does not correct, a recidivist may be created. The police will stand a good chance of having to rearrest; the courts will have to retry, and corrections once again will have the task of rehabilitation. Likewise, if there is an attempt to modify the functions or activities of one agency, the others will feel the change. Should the police, by the addition of more manpower and better scientific investigational aids, be able to apprehend 25 percent more suspects, the effects of this increase on the casework of the prosecutor and courts could very well be staggering. Assume also that out of an extra 20 percent who go to trial, 80 percent are convicted. How will the corrections components be able to assimilate the additional workload in terms of probation, institutionalization, and parole?[5]

Reasons for Viewing Criminal Justice as a Nonsystem

While contending that a criminal justice system does exist, we recognize the difficulty of some in visualizing this. There appear to be several reasons for this difficulty: (1) the confusion of an "imperfect" system with the absence of any system and (2) system "fragmentation."[6]

System Imperfection What critics of the systems approach really appear to be focusing on is the imperfection of the system. That we have failed to achieve a perfect system in which all components consciously and harmoniously work toward a common goal is, indeed, not debatable. Recognition of this, however, only leads us to conclude that there exists an imperfect system, instead of a nonsystem. And, as we will discuss later, recent years have seen an increasing effort by government and criminal justice personnel to move toward a more well-defined, less imperfect system.

System Fragmentation We can speak of two kinds of **fragmentation: horizontal** and **vertical.** In the first instance we refer to the existence of different criminal justice components—police, prosecution, courts, and corrections. We can also point to a vast multitude of criminal justice agencies, departments, offices, bureaus, and facilities that exist within each of these four criminal justice components. For example, law enforcement at the national level is shared by a variety of agencies including the FBI, the Drug Enforcement Administration, the Secret Service, the Internal Revenue Intelligence Division, the Bureau of Customs, the Immigration and Naturalization Service, the Coast Guard, postal inspectors, and even the U.S. Forest Service (rangers). States, too, often have multiple agencies in law enforcement ranging from state police to fish and game officers.

The term vertical fragmentation is used to denote the criminal justice components that generally operate at multiple levels of government. For example, there are federal, state, county, and municipal judges; federal law enforcement agencies, state police, and local police (county sheriff, city police); federal, state, and local courts, and on and on. In short we can say that we have a federal criminal justice system, fifty state systems, and a seemingly endless number of local (city and county) systems. Since at each level there are a large number of agencies within the general umbrella of criminal justice, it is no wonder many tend to view the area as a nonsystem.

Before leaving the subject it is interesting to note that fragmentation has undoubtedly been rooted in at least two related historical factors. The first is the rather piecemeal fashion in which different criminal justice elements developed during the nation's early history. Within most states (or prerevolutionary colonies), criminal justice agencies first appeared at the local level, that is, in counties or towns. Not only was the origin largely local, but the individual components emerged independently of each other. Fragmentation was the rule.[7]

The second factor is the history of our Constitution. The Founding Fathers were, by and large, fearful of creating centralized authority, since they believed centralization and authoritarianism went hand in hand. Thus the constitution they produced was filled with obstacles to centralization of power and authority. For one thing, the separation of national and state governments was maintained. The system of federalism they created gave the national government primary responsibility for some overriding political and economic matters; but the bulk of functional power and responsibilities was originally left to the states.[8] For example, one of the areas of public concern clearly left to the states was the exercising of police powers. Here the term "police powers" refers to all powers a government may use to protect the health, welfare, and safety of its citizens.[9] This includes those matters covered by criminal justice. In other words, concern with criminal matters and the capture, trial, and punishment of accused offenders were almost entirely state affairs. The states, in turn, left these matters almost entirely to counties and towns. Thus fragmentation was virtually assured.

Trends Toward a System of Criminal Justice

Fragmentation certainly has not yet been overcome, and many criminal justice components continue to act as agencies independent of one another. However, there have been several trends propelling criminal justice increasingly toward a well-defined system.

First, some state governments have moved to decrease vertical fragmentation. For example, they have integrated their trial courts and offices of prosecution into statewide agencies. They have encouraged consolidation of local police departments into metropolitan or countywide departments, and they have broadened the powers of state police agencies.[10]

Second, the federal government has been involved in several separate but parallel efforts that attack both vertical and horizontal fragmentation. It may even be claimed that the total effect of these actions is an attempt to nationalize criminal justice. These efforts include the following:

1. decisions by the Supreme Court over the past fifteen years that have made a major impact on the criminal justice process, including an increasing standardization of policies and procedures[11]

2. new criminal laws enacted by Congress, especially over the past decade, which have expanded federal jurisdiction over criminal activities formerly left to states[12]

3. establishment of the Law Enforcement Assistance Administration (LEAA) with its grants process, which encourages local agencies to overcome horizontal fragmentation in applying for and administering federally funded projects[13]

4. creation of a set of standards and goals by a national advisory commission and the subsequent linking of LEAA grants to the parallel establishment of systemwide standards and goals within each state[14]

For those who see criminal justice as a nonsystem, perhaps further developments of the nature discussed above may force a change in thinking. If a criminal justice system has not existed—a position we reject—the trend would clearly be in that direction. We agree with the statement by Chamelin, Fox, and Whisenand, who also contend that there is a criminal justice system:

The criminal justice system, is, in reality, if not in appearance, a system. A system is a series of component parts that possess common interrelationships. You are most likely to accept the criminal justice system as a system if you recognize that society is in the process of imposing the system concept on an existing criminal justice apparatus that for years has been loosely tied together.[15]

TEST YOURSELF

Here is a sample of key terms and concepts. Can you define or discuss each of them? If not, you should carefully read the chapter again. For a further test of your understanding of the material, refer to the complete list of objectives, key terms and concepts at the beginning of the chapter.

system component interdependence
system inputs
system feedback
system fragmentation

Answer the following questions:

1. Can you describe the four functions of the criminal justice system?

2. Give a couple of examples of input into the criminal justice system, a couple of examples of output of the system, and an example of feedback that results in a change within the system. Write them down.

3. Explain the two historical factors that contributed to the fragmentation of the criminal justice system.

NOTES

1. For more complete discussions of systems theory, see David Easton, *The Political System* (New York: Knopf, 1953); "An Approach to the Analysis of Political Systems," *World Politics* 9 (April 1957), pp. 383-84; Harold Lasswell, *Who Gets What, When, How* (New York: World Publishing, 1958); Carl J. Friedrich, *Man and His Government, an Empirical Theory of Politics* (New York: McGraw-Hill, 1963); Gabriel Almond, "Political Theory and Political Science," *American Political Science Review* 60 (Dec. 1966); and Marian D. Irish and James W. Prothro, *The Politics of American Democracy*, 5th ed. (Englewood Cliffs, N.J.: Prentice-Hall, 1971).
2. George F. Cole, *Criminal Justice: Law and Politics* (North Scituate: Duxbury Press, 1972), p. 1.
3. George T. Felkenes, *The Criminal Justice System* (Englewood Cliffs, N.J.: Prentice-Hall, 1973), p. 3.
4. American Bar Association, *New Perspectives on Urban Crime*, spec. 31, Committee on Crime Prevention and Control (Chicago: American Bar Association, 1972), p. 7.
5. Felkenes, *Criminal Justice System*, pp. 4-5.
6. For a discussion of the overall problem, see President's Commission on Law Enforcement and Administration of Justice, *The Challenge of Crime in a Free Society* (Washington, D.C.: Government Printing Office, 1967), pp. 7-12.
7. Ibid.
8. For example, see Samuel Eliot Morrison, *The Oxford History of the American People* (New York: Oxford University Press, 1965), pp. 304-12.
9. Rosco J. Tresolini and Martin Shapiro, *American Constitutional Law*, 3d ed. (New York: Macmillan), p. 119; and Alphens T. Mason and William M. Beany, *The Supreme Court in a Free Society*, 3rd ed. (New York: Norton, 1970), p. 193.
10. See National Advisory Commission on Criminal Justice Standards and Goals, *Courts* (Washington, D.C.: Government Printing Office, 1973), pp. 164-67. Florida unified its court system in 1972.
11. The many and varied Supreme Court decisions with the greatest impact on criminal justice processes will be discussed later, especially in the chapter on the judiciary.
12. We will have a good deal to say about this in later chapters. The "implied powers" clause, also known as the "elastic" clause of article I, section 8, grants Congress the authority "to make all laws which shall be necessary and proper for carrying into execution the foregoing powers. . . ." One of the foregoing powers provided in that section is the power "to regulate commerce with foreign nations, and among the several States, and with Indian tribes."
13. See, for example, Law Enforcement Assistance Administration, *Guideline Manual: Guide for Discretionary Grant Programs*, M 4500.1c (Washington, D.C.: Government Printing Office, 1974), esp. pp. i-xiii.
14. Ibid.
15. Neil C. Chamelin, Vernon Fox, and Paul Whisenand, *Introduction to Criminal Justice* (Englewood Cliffs, N.J.: Prentice-Hall, 1975), p. 2.

CHAPTER 2
Foundations of the Criminal Justice System: Crime, Law and Concepts of Justice

OUTLINE

CRIME
    Classifying Crimes
        Mala en Se and *Mala Prohibita* Crimes
        Felonies and Misdemeanors
        FBI Crime Categories
        Blumberg crime classifications
    Levels of Crime
        "Uniform Crime Reports" Data
        Victimization Surveys

LAW
    Nature of Law
    Forms of Law
        Common Law
        Statutory Law
        Case Law
    Types of Law
        Civil Law
        Criminal Law

JUSTICE
    Justice as a System Input
    Justice Defined
    Uses of Justice
        Substantive Justice
        Procedural Justice

THE CONSTITUTION
    Provisions in the Original Text
    The Bill of Rights

THE SUPREME COURT AND CONSTITUTIONAL LAW

APPLICATION OF THE BILL OF RIGHTS TO STATES
        The Warren Revolution
        The Burger Court Consolidation
    Appellate Courts and the Criminal Justice System

OBJECTIVES

After reading this chapter the student should be able to:

Discuss several different ways in which crimes are divided by type.

Explain what the "Uniform Crime Reports" are, how they are produced, and some of their inherent weaknesses.

List and define the crimes included in the "Crime Index" and identify some major crimes that are excluded from this list.

Discuss some recent trends in the data on Index crimes.

Describe various types and forms of law, identifying the distinctive characteristics of criminal law.

Describe varying perceptions of justice and explain the basic differences between substantive and procedural justice.

Explain the importance of the U.S. Constitution to criminal justice, identifying some of the most important provisions found in the first ten amendments (Bill of Rights).

Discuss the special role played by the Supreme Court in the American system of constitutional law.

Describe the impact of the Warren Court on criminal justice, citing some important cases.

KEY TERMS

mala en se crimes
mala prohibita crimes
felony and misdemeanor crimes
"Uniform Crime Reports"
part I crimes
part II crimes
FBI "Crime Index"
offenses known
cleared crimes
clearances by exception
Blumberg crime classifications
crime victimization surveys
legal norms
law
forms of law
common law
statutory law
case law
civil law
criminal law
sanctions
justice
legal justice
justice of dispensation
substantive justice
procedural justice
Bill of Rights
constitutional law
judicial review
preferred position theory
selective incorporation

☐ Having provided a framework for the study of the criminal justice system, we now turn our attention to certain key elements in the environment within which the system operates. You will recall that we noted the importance of three specific environmental elements: *crime, law,* and concepts of *justice*. The importance of these elements is that they provide the criminal justice system with its major inputs, and they also impose constraints on the operation of that system.

As to whether to begin the discussion of key elements with the concept of crime or with the concept of law, we find ourselves in the classic dilemma posed by the question, "Which came first, the chicken or the egg?" It is obvious that human behavior that posed a threat to social order or harmed individuals in society existed long before laws were enacted. Thus it would appear that crime came first. On the other hand, many modern scholars like to assert that crime is that behavior that a society outlaws—or, in other words, that crimes are defined by law.

We choose to examine crime first for two reasons. The behavior we label as crime came first, and crime is a primary concern of citizens which moves them and their government to make new laws or amend existing ones.

CRIME

Behavior considered criminal has been with us since the emergence of humanity. However, in recent years many people believe that the crime problem has reached proportions that could be called a crisis. Statistics on crime indicate that a virtual explosion has occurred within the past fifteen years or so. The United States and nations all over the world seem to be gripped in an unprecedented struggle with criminal behavior on the part of rapidly increasing numbers of people. In this country crime has become a hotly debated social and political issue, and even presidential candidates have taken to capitalizing on the fear of crime and criminals.[1]

Classifying Crimes

Before we examine the extent of crime in the United States, as reflected in statistics, we need to look at some of the ways in which crimes are separated by type. Obviously not all crimes are considered equally harmful or serious, and different crimes are committed by various persons or groups using widely disparate methods. Even the reasons for committing crimes vary.

Mala en Se and Mala Prohibita Crimes Various typologies of crime have been proposed over the years. One of the oldest is the distinction made between offenses said to be *mala en se,* or evil in and of themselves; and *mala prohibita,* or criminal only because society has outlawed them in the interest of social order. Among the *mala en se* offenses are those of murder, rape, arson, and most thefts—acts that endanger human life or property directly. *Mala prohibita* acts include vagrancy, drunkenness, and some traffic offenses. This distinction was originally made in Great Britain to channel offenses to the proper court, but it has been carried on in our Anglo-American legal tradition. Cole notes that there have been recent additions to the *mala prohibita* list in three categories: "crimes without victims, political crimes, and regulatory offenses."[2]

Felonies and Misdemeanors Another distinction between serious and less serious crimes is that made between **felonies** and **misdemeanors.**

Felonies may result in a year or more in prison, while misdemeanors are generally punishable by up to a year in a local jail.

There are several bases upon which this distinction can be made, but the universal basis is the punishment deemed appropriate for the crime. Felonies are crimes that are considered serious enough to warrant punishment, in most jurisdictions, of a year or more of confinement in a penitentiary. Misdemeanors are offenses that are generally punishable by less than one year of incarceration and usually mean sentencing to a county or city corrections facility. This distinction is primarily a legal one, and each state determines which crimes belong in which category. The states also provide different courts and somewhat different procedures for the two classes.[3]

FBI Crime Categories The most widely adopted classification scheme is the one devised by the Federal Bureau of Investigation for purposes of gathering statistics on crime in the United States. The scheme consists of a list of twenty-nine categories of crimes, with most of the items based on common law concepts. These categories are used by law enforcement agencies throughout the country to record their crime statistics. The data are then turned over to the FBI, which annually publishes the **Uniform Crime Reports** (UCR).[4]

The list is subdivided into **Parts I and II**, with those crimes in part I designated as "serious." The Part I crimes comprise what is known as the FBI's **"Crime Index,"** and the data in this group are reported by the press as the index to serious crimes committed during the preceding year. The list of Part I and II crimes is as follows:[5]

Part I Crimes

1. Criminal homicide: *Murder and nonnegligent manslaughter, all willful felonious homicides as distinguished from deaths caused by negligence. Excludes attempts to kill, assaults to kill, suicides, accidental deaths, or justifiable homicides.*
2. Forcible rape: *The carnal knowledge of a female forcibly and against her will in the categories of rape by force, assault to rape, and attempted rape. Excludes statutory offenses (no force used—victim under age of consent).*
3. Robbery: *Stealing or taking anything of value from the care, custody, or control of a person by force or violence or by putting in fear, such as strong-arm robbery, stickups, armed robbery, assault to rob, and attempt to rob.*
4. Aggravated assault: *Assault with intent to kill or for the purpose of inflicting severe bodily injury by shooting, cutting, stabbing, maiming, poisoning, scalding, or by the use of acids, explosives, or other means. Excludes simple assaults.*
5. Burglary—breaking or entering: *Burglary, housebreaking, safecracking, or any breaking or unlawful entry of a structure with the intent to commit a felony or a theft. Includes attempted forcible entry.*

6. Larceny—theft *(except auto theft): The unlawful taking, carrying, leading, or riding away of property from the possession or constructive possession of another. Theft of bicycles, automobile accessories, shoplifting, pocket picking, or any stealing of property or article of value which is not taken by force and violence or by fraud. Excludes embezzlement, con games, forgery, worthless checks, and the like.*
7. Motor vehicle theft: *Unlawful taking or stealing or attempted theft of a motor vehicle.*

Part II Crimes

8. Other assaults: *Assaults that are not of an aggravated nature.*
9. Arson: *Willful or malicious burning. . . .*
10. Forgery *and* counterfeiting.
11. Fraud: *Includes bad checks except forgeries and counterfeiting.*
12. Embezzlement.
13. Stolen property.
14. Vandalism.
15. Weapons: *Carrying, possessing.*
16. Prostitution *and* commercialized vice.
17. Sex offenses *(except forcible rape, prostitution, and commercialized vice): Statutory rape, offenses against chastity, common decency, morals, and the like. Includes attempts.*
18. Gambling.
19. Offenses against the family and children: *Nonsupport, neglect, desertion, or abuse of family and children.*
20. Narcotic drug laws: *Offenses relating to narcotic drugs, such as unlawful possession, sale, or use. Excludes federal offenses.*
21. Driving under the influence.
22. Liquor laws: *State or local liquor law violations, except drunkenness (class 23) and driving under the influence (class 21).*
23. Drunkenness.
24. Disorderly conduct.
25. Vagrancy.
26. All other offenses: *All violations of state or local laws except classes 1 through 25.*
27. Suspicion: *Arrests for no specific offense and released without formal charges being placed.*
28. Curfew *and* loitering laws *(juveniles).*
29. Runaway *(juvenile).*

Using the categories in parts I and II, the FBI gathers statistics from police departments throughout the United States. For part II offenses only one statistic is used: the number of arrests. For part I offenses, however, three statistics are used: (1) the number of **offenses known**—that is, the number of crimes verified as having been committed in each category; (2) the number of arrests; and (3) the number and percentage of crimes in each category **cleared.** Crimes cleared are those for which a specific culprit is known to be responsible. A crime is cleared by the arrest of a suspect, or by what is called **exception.** A clearance by exception occurs whenever the identity of a suspect is known but he or she is not arrested for this particular crime. This situation can occur when a suspect arrested for one crime confesses to—thus clears—other crimes or when the method of operation for a crime is matched up with that of a known offender.

There are many problems with the "Uniform Crime Reports". While some of them are too complex to go into here, we can mention at least five major problems:

Many crimes are never reported to law enforcement agencies by their victims or witnesses, thus they never become offenses known. This very clearly underestimates the actual crime rate.

Police departments do not always record or report the data accurately. Some distortion is even deliberate with a few departments.

Many, if not most, arrests do not result in convictions. Nevertheless, the crimes continue to be listed as cleared.

The distinction made between serious part I crimes and the less serious ones in part II is often specious. A petty larceny is counted equal to a murder in the index, while an embezzlement or fraud of thousands of dollars is not included among these serious crimes at all.

Since the data are collected from police departments, and only the crimes that come to police attention are included, many crimes are excluded. Some of these excluded crimes, such as embezzlements and consumer frauds, would fit into UCR part II categories. Others, such as kidnapping, antitrust violations, and some forms of political offenses, would not fit in any category except "other." The problem is that even when prosecution occurs it is usually the result of an investigation by a grand jury or some administrative agency, that is, one that does not involve the police.[6]

Nevertheless, despite all the weaknesses and gaps in the "Uniform Crime Reports," they are the major source of official crime data. We will have a look at some of the data later on because they can at least provide an insight into trends within certain categories, especially those within the Index.

Blumberg Crime Classifications The last classification pattern we will examine is one suggested by criminologist Abraham Blumberg, known as the **Blumberg crime classifications.**[7] He writes that "modern crime may be said to exist at seven broadly distinct levels." These levels are as follows:

1. *Upperworld crime:* Blumberg describes this crime as that which is "planned like a military campaign in the walnut-paneled executive suites of corporations with billions of dollars in assets, in state houses, and in country clubs." This sort of crime has also been called "white collar crime" by Edwin Sutherland and others.[8]

2. *Organized crime:* The most difficult of all types to define, these are certainly crimes that "cut across state lines and national boundaries and range from legitimate enterprises such as labor unions to activities which cater to appetites and pursuits forbidden by penal codes—gambling, usury, drugs, pornography, and prostitution."[9] As Blumberg notes, however, one of the major objectives of organized crime is similar to that of upperworld crime: "monopoly of a particular activity."[10] Distinguishing underworld from upperworld crimes and criminals may often be impossible, and sometimes there may even be cooperation between the two in larger criminal enterprises.

3. *Violent personal crime:* These are homicides, assaults, and forcible rapes. Blumberg does not indicate whether robbery belongs here.

4. *Public-order crime:* Blumberg states that this category covers offenses that seem to "impede the smooth functioning of a society" and includes the so-called victimless crimes of drug abuse, gambling, prostitution, and sexual deviations as well as disorderly conduct and vagrancy.[11] These may be seen as included in the *mala prohibita* category discussed earlier.

5. *Commonplace crime:* The "least honorific" and "least remunerative" of crimes, says Blumberg. This group includes most thefts, burglaries, and vandalism. Shoplifting, employee pilfering, kickbacks, and commercial bribes are also listed as belonging here.[12]

6. *Political crime:* This is a tough level to define. Blumberg states that three characteristics must be present: the crime is committed by those opposing the group in power, the power holders prosecute them as a warning to other opponents, and the trial is used to label the views of the opponents as dangerous.[13]

7. *Professional crime:* This is not so much a distinct category of crimes as it is a category of criminals. Professional crime is crime engaged in by persons who develop certain skills and commit themselves to crime as a way of life.[14]

As we have indicated, the preceding categories, or levels, are not without their problems of definition and distinction. Some obviously overlap others, and some concern the person committing the crimes as much or more than the acts they are committing. Nevertheless, several concepts covered, such as professional, organized, and white-collar crimes, are virtually household words these days, and no examination of crime as a major element in the criminal justice environment would be complete without some discussion of them. In fact, the very difficulty of identifying organized crime and the arguments raised by asserting that some crimes are victimless are definite factors in the environment affecting the behavior of the criminal justice system. These factors are just two among the many social and political issues that become input into the system, place constraints on the system's operation, and create feedback in response to the way the system copes, or fails to cope, with them.

Levels of Crime

Now that we have briefly described various classifications of crimes, let us return to the question of how much crime there is and whether the country is really in the midst of a crime explosion. Answers to these questions must depend largely on a rather limited number of data sources. Most data, in fact, are drawn from just one source, the FBI's "Uniform Crime Reports" originated in 1930. While other attempts have been made to secure additional crime data, none really furnishes us with actual crime rates or crime rate increases. Thus we must rely heavily on UCR data.

"Uniform Crime Reports" Data Regardless of the nature of the crime, UCR data show a steady, if not drastic, increase over the period from 1970 through 1975. Further, it is among the FBI's Index crimes—those that also attract the most public attention and concern—that we find some of the most alarming statistics. Murder, for example, rose from 7.8 per 100,000 people in 1970 to 9.6 in 1975, a 23.0 percent increase.[15] Other Index crimes saw similar rate increases during the 1970–75 period, with the largest being rape (43.7 percent) and burglary (42.9 percent). Lowest of the increasing rates was that of automobile thefts, which stood at 3.6 percent. See Table 2.1.

With homicide, rape, aggravated assaults, and robberies combined into the more general category of "crimes of violence" and burglary, larceny, and motor vehicle theft lumped together as "crimes against property," the FBI produces the charts in Figures 2.1 and 2.2. Figure 2.3 illustrates the trend for all Index crimes combined. All charts clearly show heavy increases in crime rates for the period of 1970–1975.

To some, their alarm over rising crime rates seems even more justified if the focus is extended back a few years before 1970. James Wilson has chosen 1963 as an appropriate year because he sees it serving as the beginning point for a drastic increase in crime rates. Wilson

TABLE 2.1   Rate Increases for FBI Index Crimes, 1970–1975

	1970 per 100,000	1975 per 100,000	Percentage Increase
Murder	7.8	9.6	23.0
Aggravated assault	162.4	227.4	40.0
Robbery	171.5	218.2	27.2
Rape	18.3	26.3	43.7
Burglary	1067.7	1525.9	42.9
Larceny-theft	2079.0	2804.8	34.1
Motor vehicle theft	453.0	469.4	3.6

Source: FBI, *Crime in the U.S., 1971* and *Crime in the U.S., 1976* (Washington, D.C.: Government Printing Office, 1972 and 1976).

states, "It all began in about 1963. That was the year, to overdramatize a bit, that a decade began to fall apart."[16] Furthermore, Wilson notes, "It [crime] did not just increase a little; it rose at a faster rate and to higher levels than at any time since the 1930's and, in some categories, to higher levels than any experienced in this century."[17] Perhaps Wilson is right, as Table 2.2 tends to show.

Victimization Surveys   While data on officially reported crime are the basis for the FBI's "Uniform Crime Reports," in recent years a new source of crime data has appeared: **victimization surveys.** Sponsored by the Law Enforcement Assistance Administration (LEAA) and conducted by the Bureau of the Census, these surveys attempt to measure

TABLE 2.2   Rate Increases for FBI Index Crimes, 1963–1975

	1963 per 100,000	1975 per 100,000	Percentage Increase
Murder	4.6	9.6	108.7
Aggravated assault	91.7	227.4	148.0
Robbery	61.6	218.2	254.2
Rape	9.3	26.3	182.8
Burglary	572.9	1525.9	166.3
Larceny-theft	1211.9	2804.8	131.4
Motor vehicle theft	215.9	469.4	117.4

Source: FBI, *Crime in the U.S., 1963* and *Crime in the U.S., 1975* (Washington, D.C.: Government Printing Office, 1964 and 1976).

FIGURE 2.1 Crimes of Violence 1970–1975, Percentage Change over 1970

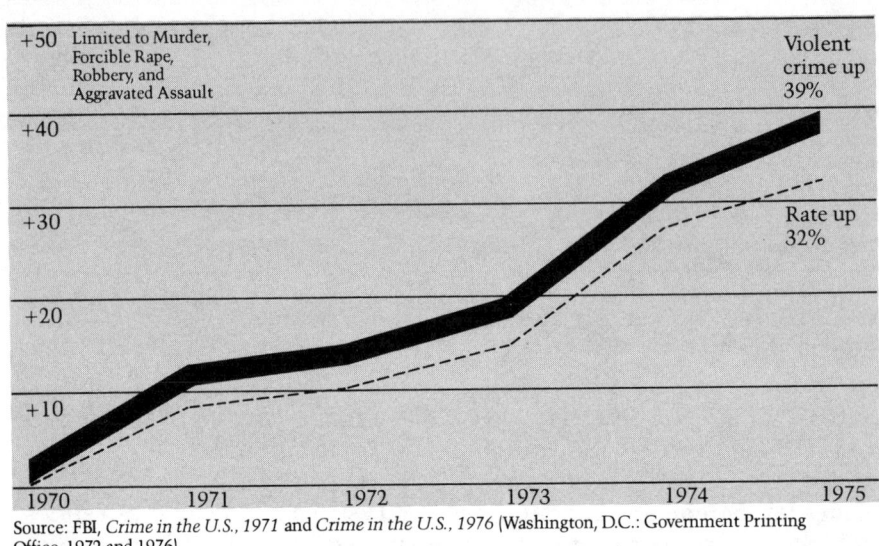

Source: FBI, *Crime in the U.S., 1971* and *Crime in the U.S., 1976* (Washington, D.C.: Government Printing Office, 1972 and 1976).

FIGURE 2.2 Crimes against Property 1970–1975, Percentage Change over 1970

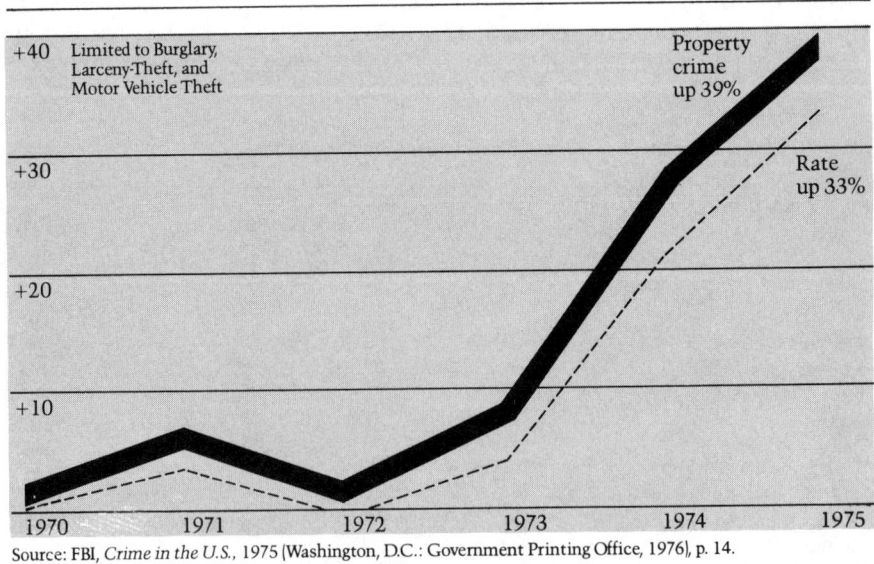

Source: FBI, *Crime in the U.S., 1975* (Washington, D.C.: Government Printing Office, 1976), p. 14.

FIGURE 2.3 Crime and Population 1970-1975, Percentage Change over 1970

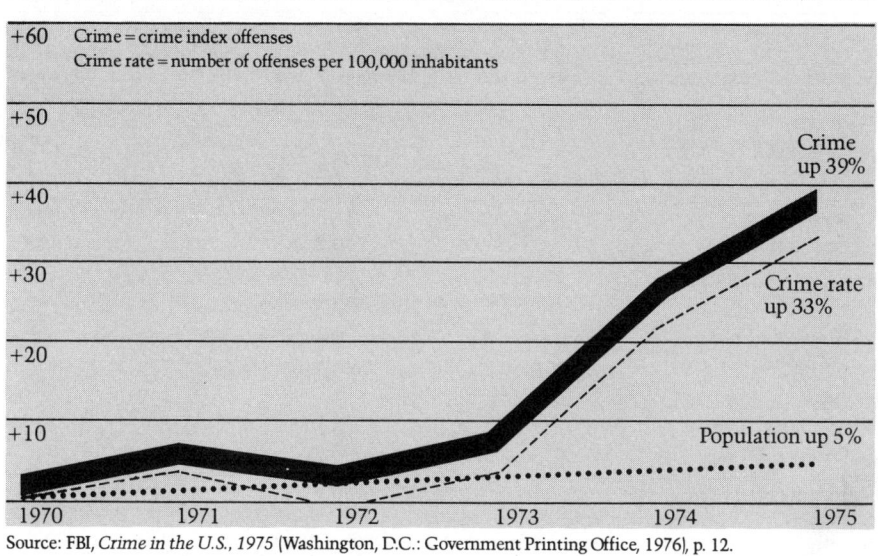

Source: FBI, *Crime in the U.S., 1975* (Washington, D.C.: Government Printing Office, 1976), p. 12.

not criminal incidents but the extent to which citizens are victimized by crimes. In addition to the fact that only selected types of crimes are studied, the methods are very different from those used by the police and the FBI.[18] The most fundamental difference is that the LEAA and Census Bureau search for victims through sampling and survey techniques, while the police report only the crimes they observe or are brought to their attention by citizen complaints. While isolated studies for years have indicated that there is a lot of unreported crime, the National Crime Panel Surveys (NCPS), as they are called, have begun to document and measure the gaps in certain categories of crime. Crimes involving small property losses were least well reported, high-loss crimes best reported, and violent crimes fell somewhere in between.[19]

As to the extent of criminal victimization found by the National Crime Panel Surveys for 1973, "selected crimes of violence and common theft, including attempts, accounted for approximately 37 million victimizations of persons age 12 and over, households, and businesses."[20] Table 2.3 provides the breakdown of these victimizations by type of crime.

One cannot directly compare NCPS figures with those in the UCR— only victims 12 years old and over were surveyed, and many criminal

TABLE 2.3 Percentage Distribution and Rates of Victimizations, by Type of Crime

	Percentage	Rate per 1000 Persons*
Crimes against persons	54.9	
Rape	0.4	1.0
Robbery	3.0	6.9
Assault	11.2	26.0
Personal larceny	40.3	93.5
Crimes against households	40.8	
Burglary	17.1	—
Household larceny	20.2	—
Motor vehicle theft	3.5	—
Crimes against businesses	4.4	
Burglary	3.7	—
Robbery	0.7	—
All crimes surveyed	100.1†	100.1†

Source: Law Enforcement Assistance Administration, *Criminal Victimization in the U.S.*, 1973 Advanced Report, vol. 1 (Washington, D.C.: Government Printing Office, 1975), p. 1.

*The rate is based upon the number of personal victimizations occurring among a national population of persons 12 years of age and above.

† Total is higher than 100 due to rounding of figures.

incidents have more than one victim. Nevertheless, it is interesting to note that the UCR for 1973 reported approximately 8.6 million Index crimes, including almost 20,000 homicides. The victimization survey turned up 37 million victimizations for Index crimes, excluding murder. It is highly unlikely that these crimes averaged four or more victims. It appears there is indeed a vast amount of crime not picked up by the UCR.

Let us sum up our discussion of crime with the following observation: crimes appear to victimize increasing numbers of citizens, but whatever the real crime rates for any given period and the real rates of increase from year to year, citizens perceive crime as an ever-growing menace. The fear of crime is increasing. This heightening of concern about and reaction to crime can be said to be as much a part of the environment for the criminal justice system as crime itself. In short, both crime and public perceptions about crime are key inputs into the system.

LAW

Earlier in this chapter we referred to crime as behavior prohibited by society and for which society may apply sanctions. The primary instrument through which society makes known what crime is and what sanctions may be applied to those who engage in it is law. As we have already noted, some scholars define crime as acts prohibited by laws providing sanctions, or as acts that violate criminal law. In their view there is no crime in the absence of law.

Nature of Law

Of course, not all law is criminal law, but in the beginning all law had its origin in a common purpose. Hazel Kerper identifies this purpose as "the need for social control which comes about whenever men begin to live together in groups." Means of social control introduce "order into society and the element of predictability into social relations."[21] Bloch and Geis similarly focus on social control, referring to means used in a society "to maintain itself as a coherent and functioning unit."[22] These writers refer to two methods of social control. One is attitudes and values—or morals, mores, and ethics. The other is established behavior patterns—or customs, traditions, habits, manners, fashions, and acquired inhibitions.

All authors agree that customs and values historically preceded the emergence of law. Turk comments that either social norms or cultural norms can be and have been translated into **legal norms** (law), which are norms backed by official sanctions.[23]

Bloch and Geis offer an excellent discussion of the distinct characteristics of law:

The law as distinct from customary controls over human behavior tends to be more specific about behavior defined as an offense and about the nature of the sanctions or punishments to be meted out. Second, the law is conceived as universal in its scope, within the confines of a given society. The law ... is meant to be applicable to all segments of the society and to impose the same degree of sanction regardless of group, class, ethnic, and sectional differences. The law is also a formal enactment. Unlike customary usages ... the law is deliberately contrived through some type of formal mechanism in which specially delegated personages and legislative bodies play significant roles.[24]

Thus it is the law's specificity in substance, its universality of applicability, and the formality of its enactment and enforcement that set it apart from other devices for social control. This leads us to our definition of **law:** that means of social control that is formally enacted or promulgated by the agency or agencies of government duly authorized in that society to make law and that is subject to interpretation by and application through the courts.

Forms of Law

The American system of law incorporates three distinct sources of law and legal principles. These may be referred to as **forms of law,** and they are common law, statutory law, and case law. Let us very briefly look at the differences among these forms.

Common Law **Common law** was the original case-made law of England in which the common law courts of the realm, later joined by the court of chancery, or equity courts, established the fundamental principles of English law by rendering decisions in specific cases. These decisions were customarily treated as precedent for future decisions. Thus judges made law that became binding—up to a point. The common law tradition was basic to the development of American law as well as the law of other English colonies.[25] Many principles of our law are still in the form of common law, though this form has been largely supplanted by statutory law.

Statutory Law **Statutory law** is legislated law—or law made by legislatures. This is the predominant form today, both here and in England. Of course, some common law principles have been incorporated, many with modifications, into statutes.

Case Law **Case law** is law made by American judges in cases decided in the appellate courts of our states and nation.[26] While the form is basically the same as common law, the term "case law" is used to distinguish the more recent and American law from its predecessor. The fiction that courts merely apply the law in cases before them has long been discarded. The only issue still argued is the extent to which appellate courts should engage in policymaking and lawmaking. We will have more to say on this shortly.

Types of Law

Now we will address the types of law. There are two basic categories: civil and criminal. Let us take them in that order.

Civil Law No precise definition of **civil law** seems possible, but Kerper tells us that civil law "has to do with such things as contracts, wills, inheritances, marriage, divorce, adoption and the like, and with private injuries which are called 'torts.' "[27]

Criminal Law Few writers provide any precise definitions of criminal law, but several describe its character or functions. Basically, **criminal law** is said to be that law which deals with crimes or criminal behavior. But crime is itself difficult to define except by referring back to criminal law. Most writers thus leave us caught in a vicious circle.

There are two sources to help us out, however. *Black's Law Dictionary* states that criminal law deals with "any act done in violation of those duties in which the law has provided that the offender shall make satisfaction to the public."[28] Joseph Goldstein comments as follows:

> The criminal law is one of many intertwined mechanisms for the social control of human behavior. It defines behavior which is deemed intolerably disturbing to our destruction of community values and prescribes sanctions which the state is authorized to impose upon persons convicted or suspected of engaging in prohibited conduct.[29]

There are two essential elements, it seems, that set criminal law apart from other law. In the first place, there is reference to threats to or destruction of community values and the individual's obligations to the community at large. The stress is thus on preservation of social order or the society itself as the major purpose or function of criminal law. This is in contrast to the civil law's concern with protection of individuals or private parties within society.

The second element is that of **sanctions,** referred to as "satisfactions to the public," which are imposed on the person by the state. The old cliché is that a person convicted "pays his debt to society." In other words, society or the community as a whole exacts its satisfaction from the violator. This contrasts with the civil law approach of requiring the violator to make restitution directly to the party who was injured.

So, simply put, criminal law can be defined as that law which has these characteristics: the specific purpose of protection and preservation of social order and community values, the provision that duly authorized government agencies will initiate the pursuit of legal action (i.e., file cases) against persons accused of violations, and the provision that sanctions will consist of punishment by or restitution to the state or community.

Criminal law thus creates corresponding demands and constraints upon the criminal justice system. This system is the apparatus of the state designed to enforce the law by arresting, prosecuting, and adjudicating those accused of violating it and by applying the proper sanctions to those found guilty.

JUSTICE

A topic obviously related to that of law and crime is **justice.** While crime and law are clearly environmental inputs into the criminal justice system, its outputs are supposed to be characterized as "just" or to be justice itself. But justice is largely an abstract and normative concept, and justice, like beauty, can be said to be in the eye of the beholder. Karl Popper has written that even to attempt to pin down the meaning of the term is to raise "an unimportant question to which no definitive answer can be given."[30]

Justice as a System Input

What is important about the term "justice" to our discussion is that people use various perceptions about what is "just" to evaluate the behavior and tangible outputs of the criminal justice system. People's evaluations of output result in feedback and, as we have already indicated, feedback is an important form of input from the environment to the system.

Not only the public but other officials use notions of justice in their dealings with the system. Legislators employ either their own sense of justice or that of constituents in the enactment of laws defining crimes and providing sanctions. It is equally obvious that judges on appellate courts decide criminal cases appealed to them in the light of their views about justice. At the same time, criminal justice officials and agents, including trial judges, employ some notions about justice in determining their own actions and in evaluating the behavior of others in the system. As an environmental factor, therefore, concepts of justice motivate and constrain the criminal justice system, from both without and within. Perceptions of justice are therefore as important a set of inputs to the system as are laws and crimes.

Justice Defined

We agree with Otto Bird "that the most famous and influential definition in the entire discussion of *justice* is the one the Roman lawyers enshrined in the Justinian Code: 'Justice is the constant and perpetual will of rendering to each his right.' "[31] To be just is to render to each what is his or her due. What is each person's "right" or "due" is, of course, the matter of unending discussion.

It is beyond the scope of this book to trace the development of theories and concepts of justice through history or even to survey current arguments on the matter. We must, however, attempt to clarify the important uses to which the term "justice" is put within the context of criminal justice.

Uses of Justice

Lon Fuller offers the first appropriate clarification. He writes that within the concept of justice there is "a hidden conflict or tension between opposing conceptions of the end sought by justice." He explains:

> On the one hand there is what has been called **legal** justice, a justice which demands that we stick by the announced rules and not make exceptions in favour of particular individuals, a justice which conceives that men should live under the same "rule of law" and be equally bound by its terms. On the other hand, there is the justice of **dispensation,** a justice ready to make exceptions when the established rules work unexpected hardship in particular cases, a justice ready to bend the letter of the law to accomplish a fair result. [Emphasis added.][32]

This is the conflict between the notions of equal justice and individualized justice and is particularly relevant to criminal justice. It is a matter for policy decisions. Exercises of discretion by police in law enforcement, by prosecutors in charging and plea bargaining, by judges in sentencing, and by parole boards in issuing paroles are among the focal points of the controversy.

Continuing with our discussion of the uses of justice, we must point out that criminal justice is said to have both substantive and procedural aspects. **Substantive aspects** are those concerned with what acts are defined as criminal and what sanctions are provided for violators. **Procedural aspects** are those concerning what is generally referred to in the United States as "due process of law," the rules governing the processes of apprehension, prosecution, adjudication, and sanctioning of those accused of crimes. Let us look at some issues that can be raised within each of these categories.

Substantive Justice Questions concerning the substantive aspect of criminal justice include the following:

What behavior is threatening enough to society or to the welfare of citizens to be prohibited and sanctioned? Should only acts that have direct victims be criminal? Or should criminal law encompass acts that victimize people indirectly or as members of classes? What about acts that may have no victims other than possibly the actor himself?

What sanctions are proper and appropriate for each type of criminal behavior? Should the purpose of the sanctions be retribution on behalf of the victims by the state, the incapacitation of the criminal for a period of time, the deterrence of crime through desire to avoid punishment (general deterrence) or of the criminal (specific deterrence), or the rehabilitation of the criminal?

Does the law as written deal effectively with the targeted behavior? Does it leave loopholes for those with criminal intent as an element in establishing a prosecutable violation of the law? Can the criminal justice system be reasonably expected to enforce the law?[33]

These issues are not merely academic. They are a matter of constant and unsettled controversy. Some years ago one observer surveyed criminal law for signs of a consensus on substantive justice as it relates to appropriate sanctions. He wrote:

Law seems to consider punishment, now as a threat to discourage other possible criminals, now as a ritual act of expiation on the part of the guilty man, now as a device for removing him from society and for protecting the latter from the danger of repeated misconduct, and now as an agency for the social and moral reform of the individual. These are four different tasks, to be accomplished by four different methods; and unless we know an accurate way of proportioning them, our whole attitude to the criminal will be at cross-purposes. At present, the criminal law speaks now in one language, and now in another. Until we in the community have made up our mind that what we really want is expiation, or removal, or reform, or the discouragement of potential criminals, we shall get none of these, but only a confusion in which crime breeds more crime. Any code which is made, one-fourth on the eighteenth-century British prejudice in favor of hanging, one-fourth on the removal of the criminal from society, one-fourth on a half-hearted policy of reform, and one-fourth on the policy of hanging up a dead crow to scare away the rest, is going to get us precisely nowhere.

Let us put it this way: the first duty of the law, whatever the second and third ones are, is to know what it wants.[34]

Procedural Justice The procedural aspects of justice include at least the three following sets of issues and questions:

What is the proper balance between methods of fact finding in any given case? What are the relative roles of administrative informal fact-finding processes, such as are involved in a case of a negotiated plea, and the full-blown adversary process of a criminal trial?

How is the burden of proof distributed in a case? Is the accused treated as innocent by police, prosecutor, and magistrate until proven guilty beyond and to the exclusion of every reasonable doubt? Is this rule reasonable and fair in light of the realities of crime and the burdens on the system, such as the numbers of professional criminals and recidivists?

What specific rights of the defendant are protected and how are they protected at each step of the criminal process? How are these rights counterbalanced with the rights of victims and law-abiding citizens of society as the steps are taken?

To conclude this review of the subtopics of justice, let us repeat in question form a matter fundamental to the entire legal system and to criminal justice in particular: Is every citizen afforded the equal protection of the law, and, at the same time, is the system being flexible enough to provide the proper degree of individualized justice?

THE CONSTITUTION

As you may have noted, we have been discussing law and justice without any specific reference to the Constitution of the United States. This has not been an oversight. We simply believe that you should think about principles or issues surrounding law and justice before being confronted with the Constitution and told, "Look. Here are *the* fundamental principles of law and justice, especially criminal procedure, as provided by our Founding Fathers in their infinite wisdom."

The Constitution is indeed the fundamental legal document of our American system of government and law. It is, in its own words, "the Supreme Law of the Land." It contains the basic principles that guide the development of law and legal systems in the United States. Consequently, no other document has had such an impact on the criminal justice system.

Provisions in the Original Text

In an examination of the Constitution and its impact, we must first note that the original text was very limited in its references to matters relevant to criminal justice. As we stated in Chapter 1, the police powers were left to the states. In fact, article I, section 9, of the Constitution provides limitations on the powers of Congress. These include the following:

1. no suspension of the writ of habeas corpus—a writ that protects citizens from imprisonment without trial on specified charges—except in cases of rebellion or invasion that threaten public safety
2. no bills of attainder—punishment of citizens by legislative act
3. no ex post facto laws—laws that create retroactive criminality and subject the citizens who committed then legal acts to possible sanctions

In article III there is also a constrictive provision as to the requirements faced by the United States government in making a case of treason. Finally, in article IV the only direct reference to criminal justice comes in section 2. It provides for extradition of persons who flee from one state to another to avoid prosecution or imprisonment for commission of a felony.

The Bill of Rights

It remained for the passage of the first ten amendments to the Constitution, commonly called the **Bill of Rights,** for the most familiar and pervasive protection of defendants to be spelled out. Having promised such a list of protections during the debates on the Constitution's ratification, James Madison managed to persuade a reluctant First Congress, occupied with "more important business," to put twelve of his sixteen proposals out for ratification by the states. Ten of them were ratified and became effective in 1791. But despite the importance attached to such guarantees of rights by most states, many persons were not impressed. A leading legal scholar in 1886 referred to the Bill of Rights as "a certain number of amendments on comparatively unimportant points."[35] It is true that the rights protected were guaranteed against federal action only, and that states could—and frequently did—ignore the principles so stated. This situation, however, has changed dramatically, especially over the past forty years. We will get to that story momentarily.

The Bill of Rights' provisions regarding criminal justice are as follows:

Amendment IV

1. "The right of people to be secure in their persons, houses, papers and effects, against unreasonable searches and seizures. . . ."
2. The requirement that search warrants shall
    a. be based on "probable cause,"
    b. be supported by "oath or affirmation,"

c. particularly describe the place to be searched and the persons or things to be seized.

Amendment V

3. The requirement that charges on "capital or other infamous crime" shall be by grand jury indictment.
4. The protection against "double jeopardy," or being tried twice for the same crime.
5. The right of persons to refuse to be witnesses against themselves, that is, the protection against self-incrimination.
6. The protection against being "deprived of life, liberty, or property, without due process of law...."

Amendment VI

7. The right to "a speedy and public trial...."
8. The right to be tried by "an impartial jury of the State and district wherein the crime shall have been committed...."
9. The right to "be informed of the nature and cause of the accusation...."
10. The right to "be confronted with the witnesses against him...."
11. The right to "have compulsory process for obtaining witnesses in his favor...."
12. The right to "have the assistance of counsel for his defense."

Amendment VIII

13. Protection against "excessive bail" and "excessive fines...."
14. Protection against "cruel and unusual punishment."

These rights and protections were of limited value in most criminal prosecutions in the United States except where they were duplicated in state constitutions, statutes, or rules of criminal procedure. Most states had no such sweeping provisions. It waited the ratification of the Fourteenth Amendment before even the potential of the Bill of Rights could be realized in most places. The key passage in that amendment provides that states shall not "deprive any person of life, liberty, or property, without due process of law...." This is a restatement of the protection against federal acts contained in the Fifth Amendment. What has occurred, however, is that the rights stated throughout the Bill of Rights have been incorporated within the meaning of the term "due process of law." This incorporation has been primarily the work of the Supreme Court of the United States, and it is to that agency we now turn.

THE SUPREME COURT AND CONSTITUTIONAL LAW

Professor E. S. Corwin once wrote:

As employed in this country, Constitutional law signifies a body of rules resulting from the interpretation by a high court of a written constitutional instrument in the course of disposing of cases in which the validity, in relation to the constitutional instrument, of some act of governmental power, State or National, has been challenged.[36]

In other words, **constitutional law** is a special variety of case- or judge-made law arising from appellate cases in which someone is seeking to have a statute or executive action nullified as unconstitutional.

States have high appellate courts that produce state constitutional law. The Supreme Court of the United States sits as the ultimate national court of appeals and the promulgator of federal constitutional law. Through the power of **judicial review**, the court may nullify the act of any other federal or state agency that it determines is in violation of terms set forth in the U.S. Constitution. In so doing the Court may either uphold or overturn the decision of any court inferior to itself, whether federal or state.

Obviously, among the acts of government subject to this scrutiny are those of the criminal justice system at both the state and federal levels. When dealing with a challenge to a federal prosecution, the Supreme Court measures the government's actions against the requirements set forth in the Constitution. When reviewing a state case, the Court usually asks itself if the state provided the defendant with due process of law as is required of all states by the Fourteenth Amendment.

APPLICATION OF THE BILL OF RIGHTS TO STATES

As we have indicated, the Bill of Rights had no real effect on the states until the adoption of the Fourteenth Amendment. And it was not until 1925 that the Supreme Court used the amendment to incorporate a specific right stated in the Bill of Rights within the meaning of the Fourteenth Amendment and declare it binding on states—in this case, the freedom of speech.[37] Not until 1937 did the Supreme Court even take up the issue of whether any of the procedural criminal rights could be invoked against the states. And in *Palko* v. *Connecticut* the Court ruled that it could insist that states provide only those rights "essential to a scheme of ordered liberty." The right against double jeopardy was not one of these, the Court said.[38] The Court continued

Police procedures have been profoundly affected by Supreme Court decisions: "You have the right to remain silent."

to refuse to apply specific Bill of Rights' procedural requirements to state actions until 1949. It did not insist on state compliance with specific federal standards until 1961.

The Warren Revolution The case that marked the turning point in the development of constitutional law as it relates to criminal justice was Mapp v. Ohio.[39] Evidence that had been illegally seized was used to convict Mrs. Mapp in her Ohio trial. As early as 1914 the Supreme Court had expanded on the meaning of the Fourth Amendment and established the rule that illegally seized evidence could not be used in federal trials—the "Weeks exclusionary rule."[40] The Court in 1949 agreed to apply the Fourth Amendment requirement of a search warrant to states in *Wolf* v. *Colorado*.[41] But the Court had heretofore refused to apply the exclusionary rule that made the requirement effective. In *Mapp* the Court reversed its earlier rulings and incorporated this procedural right with its exclusionary expansion into the meaning of the Fourteenth Amendment's due process clause. The Court, under Chief Justice Earl Warren, had begun a legal revolution — of sorts.

A leading scholar has written that there were

three principal developments in the Warren Court regarding the protection of personal rights: (1) acceptance of the preferred position theory; (2) extension of the trend of making Bill of Rights guarantees binding on the states; and (3) broadening of the substantive content of the rights themselves.[42]

The **preferred position theory** holds that personal rights are more important than property rights. The extension of Bill of Rights guarantees has occurred through a process known as **selective incorporation.** This means that specific rights are incorporated one by one within the due process clause of the Fourteenth Amendment. Rights that are incorporated must be abided and protected by the states. The broadening of substantive content, on the other hand, occurs as the court interprets and gives new — usually expanded — meanings to the actual language of the Bill of Rights. Examples include the finding that the Fourth Amendment protection against unreasonable searches and seizures included the right to have illegally seized evidence barred from use in trials and the finding that several specified rights imply or include a definite, though unmentioned, right to privacy. In no area of law was the impact of these three trends more intensely felt than in criminal justice.

Within ten years (1963–1972) the Supreme Court made each of the following rights binding on the states:

1. the right to counsel in all felony trials, including the requirement that states appoint one in cases of indigent defendants[43]
2. the right against double jeopardy[44]
3. the right against self-incrimination[45]
4. the right to a jury trial in all criminal cases[46]
5. the right to a "speedy trial"[47]
6. the right to confrontation of witnesses for the state[48]

The simultaneous expansion of the meaning of the rights themselves can best be seen in the decisions regarding the point at which counsel must be made available to suspects and the warning of a list of rights that police must give all persons who are treated as suspects.[49] The *Escobedo* and *Miranda* cases perhaps involved the most sweeping change in police procedure and had a great impact on public opinion — if not on the criminal justice system itself.

The Burger Court Consolidation After Earl Warren retired and was replaced as chief justice by Warren E. Burger, and President Nixon appointed three associate judges, some anticipated a counterrevolution, or a swinging back of the pendulum in favor of the state as opposed to defendants. But the period from 1969 through 1976 has rather been one of consolidation of the Warren era changes. Some rights have been clarified or—in the view of some—chipped away, but there have been no outright reversals of any decision. At the same time the Court has ventured into new areas. Some major changes include the following:

1. The right to court-appointed counsel was extended to misdemeanor cases.[50]
2. Wiretaps, even for national security reasons, require court orders.[51]
3. States may use juries of less than twelve members in noncapital cases.[52]
4. States need not require that juries be unanimous to convict defendants.[53]
5. Most importantly, all state capital punishment laws in 1972 were ruled in violation of the Eighth Amendment protection against "cruel and unusual punishment."[54] In 1976 the Court accepted some states' revised capital punishment laws.

The preceding discussion focuses on the Supreme Court and its role in matters of procedure. But the Court has not ignored the substantive content of criminal law in its work. It entered into matters of substantive justice when it attempted to define what is and is not punishable obscenity and pornography, when it nullified laws against drunkenness and birth control, and, most dramatically, when it struck down state laws making abortion a crime. In *Roe* v. *Wade* the Court ruled that such laws violated a right to personal liberty and privacy protected against state interference by the Fourteenth Amendment's due process clause.[55] This is another example of the Court broadening the meaning of constitutional rights.

The Supreme Court has thus become extremely active as a reviewer of criminal law and criminal justice processing of cases. This activism is unlikely to diminish, even if the Court tries to reverse outright some of the changes made over the past decade and a half.

Appellate Courts and the Criminal Justice System

It should be noted that state appellate courts have inevitably become much more active in the criminal justice arena. This has been largely due to pressures to clarify the meaning and impact of Supreme Court decisions and doctrines within their own systems, but it also reflects the rising concerns of all persons with criminal law and its process.

Some might argue that appellate courts have become as much a part of the criminal justice system as the trial courts. While we are not taking this position, we must state that they have permanently altered and become a participating part of what we have called the environment of the system. How they affect the operations of each component of the system will be dealt with in the chapters discussing the components. An understanding of them is important, since they contribute mightily to the concepts and the perceptions of justice that permeate the environment of and become major inputs into the entire criminal justice system.

We have looked at three environmental elements—crime, law, and concepts of justice—and have suggested that they form the *foundations* of the criminal justice system. We have said they are major inputs into the system. This does not, however, exhaust the subject of the environment of that system. The criminal justice system is part of a larger political system that includes other agencies of government. The criminal justice and political systems, in turn, belong within a larger physical and social environment. Each component of criminal justice (police, prosecutors, courts, and corrections) and each agency are subject to many different influences from their complex environment. We will look at some of these other influences later.

TEST YOURSELF

Define these key terms:
felony crimes
political crimes
clearance by exception
statutory law
sanctions
legal justice
judicial review
selective incorporation

Answer the following questions:

1. What are the "Uniform Crime Reports," and why don't they tell us everything we should know about crime in the United States?

2. List and define each of Blumberg's seven categories of crime.

3. Write down a definition of law. Now write a definition of criminal law. How are they different?

4. Explain the difference between "legal justice" and the "justice of dispensation."

5. What three questions can be asked concerning the *substantive* aspect of criminal justice?

6. Describe the change in relationship between constitutional protections and state criminal justice proceedings that resulted from the Warren Court revolution.

NOTES

1. Yong Hyo Cho, *Public Policy and Urban Crime* (Cambridge, Mass.: Ballinger, 1974), pp. 23-28 and 30-35.
2. George F. Cole, *The American System of Criminal Justice* (N. Scituate, Mass.: Duxbury Press, 1975), p. 77.
3. See John Kaplan, *Criminal Justice* (Mineola, N.Y.: Foundation Press, 1973), fn. p. 65; and Rollin M. Perkins, *Criminal Law and Procedure*, 4th ed. (Mineola, N.Y.: Foundation Press, 1972), pp. 4-6.
4. Federal Bureau of Investigation, *Crime in the U.S., 1975* (Washington, D.C.: Government Printing Office, 1976).
5. Ibid., p. 6. Definitions of some crimes have been omitted or edited for the sake of brevity.
6. Harry M. Shulman, "The Measurement of Crime in the United States," *Journal of Criminal Law* 57 (December 1966), pp. 483-92. See also Yong Hyo Cho, *Public Policy*.
7. Abraham S. Blumberg, *Law and Order: The Scales of Justice* (New Brunswick, N.J.: Transaction Books, 1973), pp. 11-18.
8. Edwin H. Sutherland, *White Collar Crime* (New York: Dryden Press, 1949). For a recent revision of traditional concepts of white-collar crime, see Herbert Edelhertz, *The Nature, Impact and Prosecution of White Collar Crime* (Washington, D.C.: Government Printing Office, 1970).
9. Blumberg, *Scales of Justice*, p. 13.
10. Ibid., p. 14. See also Donald Cressy, *Theft of the Nation* (New York: Harper & Row, 1969); and Frederick D. Homer, *Guns and Garlic* (W. Lafayette, Ind.: Purdue University Press, 1974). There are many books and articles on organized crime but these two constitute the best presentation of divergent views on the subject.
11. Blumberg, *Scales of Justice*, p. 15. The literature on victimless crimes is extensive, but among those who focus on it are the following: Edwin Schur, *Crimes Without Victims: Deviant Behavior and Public Policy* (Englewood Cliffs, N.J.: Prentice-Hall, 1965); and Gordon Hawkins and Norval Morris, *The Honest Politician's Guide to Crime Control* (Chicago: University of Chicago Press, 1970.)
12. Blumberg, *Scales of Justice*, pp. 16-17.
13. Ibid., p. 18. There is little scholarly treatment of this subject. For an exception see Stephen Schafer, *The Political Criminal: The Problem of Morality and Crime* (New York: Free Press, 1974).

14. Blumberg, *Scales of Justice*, p. 18. For a solid treatment of the history and types of professional crime, see James A. Inciardi, *Careers in Crime* (Chicago: Rand McNally, 1975).
15. UCR crime rates are figured on the following formula:

$$\text{rate} = \frac{\text{raw number of crimes}}{x} \times \frac{100{,}000 \text{ persons}}{\text{national population}}$$

In 1975, for example, 20,510 murders for a national population of 214,500,000 yields a murder rate of 9.6 per 100,000 persons.
16. James Q. Wilson, *Thinking About Crime* (New York: Basic Books, 1975), pp. 5-6.
17. Ibid., p. 4.
18. LEAA, *Criminal Victimization Surveys in Thirteen American Cities* (Washington, D.C.: Government Printing Office, 1975), pp. iii-v.
19. LEAA, *Crime in the Nation's Five Largest Cities* (Washington, D.C.: Government Printing Office, 1974), p. 4.
20. Law Enforcement Assistance Administration, *Criminal Victimization in the United States*, 1973 Advanced Report, vol. 1 (Washington, D.C.: Government Printing Office, 1975), p. 1.
21. Hazel Kerper, *Criminal Justice System* (St. Paul, Minn.: West Publishing, 1972), p. 3.
22. Herbert A. Bloch and Gilbert Geis, *Crime, Man and Society*, 2d ed. (New York: Random House, 1970), p. 36.
23. Austin Turk, *Criminality and the Legal Order* (Chicago: Rand McNally, 1969), pp. 34-39.
24. Bloch and Geis, *Crime, Man and Society*, p. 37.
25. For an excellent short summary of common law, see Lon L. Fuller, *Anatomy of the law* (New York: Praeger, 1968), pp. 84-85. Fuller treats common law as synonymous with case law and goes on to fully examine its nature and development on pp. 85-112.
26. Trial courts do not make judicial policy or law. Their decisions do not bind other courts—or even themselves—in future cases. See Herbert Jacobs, *Justice in America*, 2d ed. (Boston: Little, Brown, 1972), chaps. 2 and 3.
27. Kerper, *Criminal Justice*, p. 6.
28. *Black's Law Dictionary*, 4th ed. (St. Paul, Minn.: West Publishing, 1951), p. 445.
29. Joseph Goldstein, "Police Discretion Not to Invoke the Criminal Process: Low Visibility Decisions in the Administration of Justice," in George F. Cole, *Criminal Justice* (Belmont, Calif.: Wadsworth, 1972), pp. 59-60.
30. Karl Popper, *The Open Society and Its Enemies*, vol. 1 (New York: Harper & Row, 1945), p. 89.
31. Otto A. Bird, *The Idea of Justice* (New York: Praeger, 1967), pp. 122-23.
32. Fuller, *Anatomy of Law*, p. 38.
33. See, for example, Bernard Schwartz, *The Law in America* (New York: American Heritage, 1974), pp. 40-48.
34. Norbert Weisner, as quoted in Fuller, *Anatomy of Law*, pp. 26-27.
35. Sir Henry Maine, as quoted in Schwartz, *Law in America*, p. 47.
36. E. S. Corwin, as quoted in Rosco J. Tresolini and Martin Shapiro, *American Constitutional Law*, 3d ed. (New York: Macmillan, 1970), pp. 14-15.
37. *Gitlow* v. *New York*, 268 U.S. 652 (1925).
38. 302 U.S. 319 (1937).
39. 367 U.S. 643 (1961).
40. *Weeks v. United States.*, 232 U.S. 383 (1914).
41. 338 U.S. 25 (1949).
42. Schwartz, *Law in America*, pp. 285-86.
43. *Gideon v. Wainwright*, 372 U.S. 335 (1963).
44. *Benton v. Maryland*, 295 U.S. 784 (1969).
45. *Malloy v. Hogan*, 378 U.S. 1 (1965).
46. *Duncan v. Louisiana* 391 U.S. 145 (1968).

47. *Klopfer v. North Carolina*, 386 U.S. 213 (1967).
48. *Pointer v. Texas*, 380 U.S. 400 (1965).
49. *Escobedo v. Illinois*, 378 U.S. 478 (1964), and *Miranda v. Arizona*, 384 U.S. 436 (1966).
50. *Argersinger v. Hamlin*, 307 U.S. 25 (1972).
51. *U.S. v. U.S. District Court*, 407 U.S. 297 (1972).
52. *Williams v. Florida*, 399 U.S. 78 (1970).
53. *Johnson v. Louisiana*, 406 U.S. 356 (1972).
54. *Furman v. Georgia*, 408 U.S. 238 (1972).
55. 410 U.S. 113 (1973).

CHAPTER 3
An Overview of Criminal Justice: Functions, Structures, and Processes

OUTLINE

SYSTEM FUNCTIONS
- Perceptions of Criminal Justice Functions
- Criminal Justice Functions

SYSTEM STRUCTURES
- Law Enforcement
  - Types of Agencies
  - Law Enforcement by Level
- Prosecutors
- Courts
  - Types of Courts
  - Courts, by Level
- Corrections
  - Types of Institutions
  - Corrections, by Level

BASIC SYSTEM PROCESSES
- Stages of the Criminal Justice Process
  - Arrest Stage
  - Charging Stage
  - Adjudication Stage
  - Sentencing Stage
  - Corrections Stage
  - Appeals
- Juvenile Justice

OBJECTIVES

After reading this chapter the student should be able to:

Describe the relationships among various functions of the criminal justice system.

Give some reasons why there are differing views of what the system's functions are.

Explain why the concept of system functions is important.

Describe the basic structure of the criminal justice system by component and by level.

Name five types of criminal justice law enforcement agencies in terms of their function and give an example of each.

Give some examples of law enforcement agencies at each level of the system.

Name the office of prosecutor at the several levels of government.

Describe U.S. courts by type and by level.

Name four major types of corrections and give examples of each.

List the various corrections agencies at the different levels of government.

Describe the flow of cases through each of five stages in the criminal justice process.

Explain what may happen to an accused at each process stage.

Discuss the appeals process available to a defendant.

Describe some of the differences between the adult and juvenile processes of justice.

KEY TERMS

general police
limited-area police
specialized law enforcement
 agencies
administrative and regulatory
 agencies
private police
courts of original jurisdiction
courts of general jurisdiction
courts of limited or special
 jurisdiction
courts of nonrecord
incarceration facilities
community corrections facilities
parole
probation
juvenile corrections
booking
screening
information
true bill of indictment
no true bill
diversion
bail
initial appearance
release on own recognizance
 (ROR)
preliminary hearing
bind over
arraignment
nolo contendere
continuance
plea bargaining
nolle prosequi
court or bench trial
pre-sentence investigation
jury charge
points of law
points of fact
trial de novo
adjudicatory hearings

☐ In Chapter 1 we set forth the systems approach as a tool for understanding the field of criminal justice. Chapter 2 presented several important environmental elements that have an impact on the system. In this chapter we present an overview of the criminal justice system with three focal points: (1) system functions, (2) system structures, and (3) the process of criminal justice.

SYSTEM FUNCTIONS

While we have suggested that the functions of the system are fourfold—law enforcement, order maintenance, protection of rights, and crime prevention—we must make note that other authors have stated other functions, or at least used different terms to describe them. It is difficult to tell with some writers whether these differences are real—that is, the result of disagreement over what the criminal justice system should try to do—or basically a matter of semantics. Another source of confusion is the tendency of some authors to confuse the functions of the entire system with the more narrow functions or goals of specific components within. A brief survey of some leading statements regarding criminal justice functions will serve to at least illustrate the problem.

Perceptions of Criminal Justice Functions

One position taken is that the overall function is "enforcement of the laws that society has enacted for its self-protection and preservation." The proponent of this view notes that "the system is designed to remove a violator from his normal social setting, and, if possible at a later time, reintroduce him into society as a person who now understands his obligation as a law-abiding citizen." He concludes that another result "is supposed to flow" from this processing of violators: "deterrence of others from committing criminal acts."[1] Thus the overriding function is law enforcement defined in terms of processing criminals. A secondary function is crime deterrence.

Another view states that the criminal justice system "is directly involved in the maintenance of ordered liberty in a free society."[2] Its author makes no attempt to clarify these terms. "Ordered liberty" is an especially difficult concept to grasp. "Order" and "liberty" are frequently seen as opposing goals.

A third position is that "the goals of criminal justice are to control crime and to prevent or deter criminal behavior." The author of this statement notes that it can be argued that "prevention and control so overlap that they cannot be described as truly separate functions." He goes on to describe crime control in terms of the processing of offenders and to point out that deterrence as a goal has two aspects: deterring the offenders caught (special deterrence) and potential offenders (general deterrence).[3]

A fourth view describes the criminal justice system as "the instrument of society to enforce its standards of conduct necessary for the protection of the safety and freedom of individual citizens and for the maintenance of the order of the society." Thus the twin overriding goals of protection of citizens and order maintenance are served by the specific function of the enforcement of "standards of conduct." This author does add that the system's role is "palliative" or reactive in the sense that it deals with crimes already committed, and he states that the system "is, in fact, not meant to be preventive or curative of crime, for it is not designed to eliminate the causes of crime so that crime can be prevented from occurrence." There may be spotty deterrence by police presence denying specific opportunities for crime but no modification of "crime-inducive influences within the community."[4] Thus we have a direct disagreement with other writers. Or do we? It depends on what one means by "crime prevention." If we mean denial of opportunities, we agree that at least this much is expected. If we mean elimination of "crime-inducive influences" (or what some call "root causes" of crime), then it is doubtful anyone would claim this as a function of the criminal justice system. Many doubt whether any social agencies can change human motivations, behavior, and interactions enough to eliminate or even seriously reduce crime—at least not without resorting to some form of totalitarianism.[5]

Criminal Justice Functions

To return to our position about the functions of the criminal justice system—law enforcement, order maintenance, protection of rights, and crime prevention—we believe that the four we have stated are comprehensive, distinct from one another, yet complementary in their relationship. Let us look at each one.

By *law enforcement* we mean the detection and investigation of crimes and the arrest, charging, adjudication, sentencing, and application of sanctions to offenders. Thus this function is performed not only by police but by every component of the system. Prosecutors are often called law enforcement officials, and corrections officials obviously enforce law within residential institutions and in the supervision of probationers and parolees.

By *order maintenance* we refer to the prevention of disorder by the presence of police in situations of potential violence or crime and also the preservation of order within corrections facilities and courtrooms, and the more general notion that criminal justice agencies support the social system against radical change. We do not argue that the criminal justice system prevents or should prevent social change, only that the system has the function of limiting change, especially of keeping it within legal and socially tolerable channels.

The function of *protection of rights* has several aspects. In the first place, we mean the protection of all those citizens' rights that are legally recognized—that is, to life, liberty, and property. In a sense, then, this is similar to what we mean by law enforcement. In the second place, however, we mean the more specific protections of the rights of those citizens directly involved in the criminal justice process. In theory the emphasis, if not the sole concern, has been the rights of the accused or defendant. This theory was not always and everywhere honored in fact—at least not until the Supreme Court, especially the Warren Court, compelled states to follow more rigid procedures to guarantee protections of defendants' rights. There are those who argue that the assembly-line nature of most criminal justice processes still denies effective protection to many defendants, but there are many others who insist that the pendulum has swung too far in favor of defendants.

In addition to the rights of the accused as stipulated in the Constitution, we also include the rights of victims and other law-abiding citizens of the community. These rights are not stipulated in the Constitution, but they are said to be part of human rights—those "inalienable rights" spoken of in the Declaration of Independence. The efforts to give reality to these rights can be most clearly seen in the evolution of victim compensation programs and in the changes in laws relating to the crime of forcible rape. We will examine some of these developments later. For now it is necessary only to define this third goal, protection of rights, and to assert that it is a valid and operational function of the criminal justice system.

By *crime prevention* we mean two things: the denial of opportunities for persons to commit crimes and the deterrence of would-be offenders from criminal acts by presenting risks of capture and punishment. Paul Whisenand comments on the difficulty of "attempting to draw a definitive line around crime prevention so as to make it easily dis-

The criminal justice system cannot be expected to stop people from wanting to commit crimes, but it is expected to create a fear of the consequences.

cernible" from other system functions, but he notes that "a common understanding of what is meant by crime prevention seems necessary in order to provide at least a loose guideline for us to follow...." He continues: "In its broadest sense ... crime prevention is the reduction or elimination of the *desire* and/or *opportunity* to commit a crime."[6]

The elimination of the desire to commit crime refers here to deterrence and not to the elimination of the causes of crime. In other words, the criminal justice system cannot be expected to stop people from wanting to commit crimes or being driven to crime. But it is expected to create a fear of the consequences, which would cause some persons to consider the risk and be dissuaded from committing some crimes. Crime "suppression" might be a more accurate term than prevention, but the latter term is entrenched in the literature and common usage.

As for the distinctness of each of the four functions, we admit to some overlapping. But we believe that in many situations officials are called upon to choose one from among the four functions as the primary one to be served in an instance at hand and that taking action to accomplish one may in fact hinder the realization of one or all the remaining functions. In many situations involving crowds, for example, police must choose between making arrests (law enforcement) and clearing the streets (order maintenance). The frequent conflict between law enforcement and the protection of defendants' rights in the process is obvious. Such conflicts led Herbert Packer to develop two models of criminal justice: "crime control" and "due process." The first emphasizes law enforcement and order maintenance with a theme of efficiency in the processing of cases and defendants. The second emphasizes protection of defendants' rights and seeks effectiveness in separating the legally innocent from the legally guilty.[7]

Despite the distinctness, and even conflicting aspects, of the four functions, we assert that they are complementary. Often a course of action best serves all four goals. Citizens' rights—including those of defendants—cannot be protected without enforcement of law. The rule of law means little if it does not mean the protection of the rights of citizens and the maintenance of social order. The interest of order itself cannot be successfully served if it comes at the expense of law and the rights of citizens. This is behind the reaction of those who wish to add the tag "with justice" to the slogan "law and order."

Before leaving the subject of system functions, we should make clear that each component of this system—police, prosecution, courts, and corrections—has distinctive functions all its own in addition to and in support of the functions of the entire system. We will examine the specific functions of each component, and individual agencies within each component, in later chapters.

We should also note that what we have been describing as functions are the goals that the system is supposed to accomplish or toward which the system is supposed to move. We do not claim that the system performs up to anyone's standards in terms of these four functions. We know that laws are enforced, order is maintained, rights are protected, and crimes are prevented—at least much of the time. There is, in other words, at least partial realization of each of these functions, and performance can be measured with respect to at least certain aspects of each of them.

Having examined what we believe to be the functions of the criminal justice system, we move now to a consideration of the structure of that system in the United States.

SYSTEM STRUCTURES

Earlier we spoke of the fragmentation of the criminal justice system, and mentioned that this fragmentation of the system was both vertical (federal, state, and local) and horizontal (a wide variety of agencies). What we have in the United States can be described as a multilevel system incorporating four major components: law enforcement, prosecution, courts, and corrections.

Our purpose in this section is to indicate what types of agencies fit into each component at each level of the system. Unfortunately, at least from the perspective of trying to study the system, there are dozens of types of agencies that could be listed, especially those under police and corrections. We will take the components in order and see what units are present at the various levels.

Law Enforcement

Law enforcement agencies vary tremendously by type. Here we mean not only the distinction by level (federal, state, county, and local) but also the wide variety of agencies at the different levels.

Types of Agencies Our study suggests that there are at least three types. These types differ by assigned functions and by the appropriate authority and jurisdiction granted to them to perform their functions. They are general police, limited-area police, and specialized law enforcement agencies.

General police are given the functions of order maintenance, law enforcement and the provision of other services to broad geographic jurisdictions. These are the municipal police departments, most sheriffs' offices, and some state agencies.

With the same broad authority of general police, **limited-area police** are assigned to specific areas usually within the jurisdiction of a general police agency. Examples include federal and state parks, state university and college campuses, and, within cities, transit systems, public housing areas, and other public places.

Specialized law enforcement agencies have the function of enforcing specific laws. They are not usually given order maintenance or other service functions. These agencies include virtually all federal investigative agencies and state agencies assigned to such activities as alcohol and drug violations, horse racing and other legalized gambling, and tax evasion and fraud.

Some have stretched the concept of law enforcement beyond persons carrying badges and firearms and having specific powers of arrest. They would view as law enforcement agencies those various federal and state **administrative and regulatory agencies** whose primary responsibility is to administer and enforce laws and regulations regarding virtually all economic activities—for example, manufacturing, communications, agriculture, transportation, labor and trade practices.

A few people assert that another category of law enforcement agencies exists, that of **private police.** Included within this category are the vast numbers and wide variety of industrial security agencies, neighborhood security patrols, business guards, and watchmen. Private police personnel may wear uniforms, badges, and guns, but they are nonpublic in nature and their authority to arrest is usually no more than that of any other private citizen.

We intend to limit the term "law enforcement" to the first three of these categories of agencies. The difficulties presented by including the administrative agencies and the private security firms are several. However, the most important difference between them and other agencies is that they do not engage in the type of law enforcement that regularly creates input in the form of arrested persons and cases for the prosecutors and subsequent system components. Thus by "law enforcement" we mean public agencies which, in addition to maintaining order and detecting crime, routinely arrest violators and initiate the formal criminal justice process.

Law Enforcement by Level Agencies of law enforcement exist at each level of government in the United States. At the federal level there are law enforcement agencies in several cabinet-level departments. The Department of Justice includes the best known of these—the Federal Bureau of Investigation—and incorporates others as well. The departments of the Treasury, Interior, and Transportation also house federal law enforcement agencies.

At the state level there are state police departments or highway patrol agencies as well as specialized agencies. Counties boast sheriff's departments, and cities have police departments of every imaginable size and description. An overview of law enforcement agencies by level is shown in Table 3.1.

Prosecutors

The problem of identifying prosecutors is not as severe as that of law enforcement. There are no private offices of prosecution; they are all public tax-supported agencies. There are also not as many varieties of agencies as there are in police. This does not mean there are no varia-

TABLE 3.1 Law Enforcement Agencies, by Level

FEDERAL
Justice Department
  Federal Bureau of Investigation (FBI)
  Drug Enforcement Agency (DEA)
  Immigration and Naturalization Service (INS)
  U.S. Marshals
Treasury Department
  Secret Service
  Internal Revenue Service Intelligence Division (IRS Intelligence)
  Bureau of Customs
  Bureau of Alcohol, Tobacco, and Firearms
Interior Department
  National Park Service (Rangers)
  Bureau of Indian Affairs
Transportation Department
  U.S. Coast Guard
  Office of Civil Aviation Security

STATE
State Police or Highway Patrol (Texas and Arizona have their own Rangers)
Beverage or alcohol units
Bureau of Narcotics
Fish and Game Wardens
Intelligence or investigative divisions or departments (usually assigned to specific types of crime)

COUNTY
Sheriffs' departments

CITY
General Police Departments
Limited area, police (park, housing, transit, port authority, or other)

tions or problems, however. For example, the involvement of the state attorney general in criminal prosecution differs from state to state. At the local level many cities have clearly identified city prosecutors; others assign prosecutorial functions to the more generalized office of city attorney, and the extent to which the city attorneys are prosecutors varies.[8] In many states, counties, and cities there is also the problem of part-time prosecutors who are private attorneys or businesspeople as well as public prosecutors. Some chief prosecutors are part-timers, and many assistant prosecutors earn a good share of their incomes in private pursuits.

There is one additional fact about prosecutors that sets them apart from most other criminal justice personnel: the relative brevity of their terms in office. Many attorneys spend a period of time in prosecution as a means of developing experience for later private practice; some seek higher political office; and relatively few seem to approach prosecution as a career activity.[9] We will deal with matters of personnel later, however. For now we merely want to survey the agencies and offices of prosecution.

As with law enforcement, agencies or offices of prosecution are found at each level of government. At the federal level prosecutors all work for the Justice Department, though in varied capacities. States have attorney generals who may or may not have prosecutorial functions. In some states prosecution in local courts is handled by state prosecutors. The general pattern, however, is for prosecutors to be employed at the county or municipal levels. Table 3.2 provides an overview of prosecution by level.

Courts

Although we stated earlier that criminal trial courts are within the criminal justice system and appellate courts are active parts of the en-

TABLE 3.2 Prosecutors, by Level

FEDERAL
Justice Department
  Attorney General
  Chiefs of the divisions (such as criminal and antitrust)
  Office of Special Prosecutor (1974–1976) (the ad hoc office created by Congress to carry out Watergate prosecutions)
  U.S. attorneys (in each of the 94 federal court districts within the United States)

STATE
Attorney Generals (and their staffs)
Special prosecutors (for corruption or organized crime)
State or District Attorneys (SA, DA)

COUNTY
County prosecutors or solicitors (usually where SAs or DAs do not exist at the state level)

CITY
City prosecutors (where cities maintain their own courts)

vironment of the system, we will deal with the entire court structure here for the sake of clarity.

Types of Courts Trial courts—called courts of **original jurisdiction** because they are the first to deal with the case—are divided into at least two types: (1) **courts of general jurisdiction**—sometimes called "superior courts"—which process cases in both civil and criminal law without special limitations as to the parties who may come before them or the subject matters with which they may deal; and (2) **courts of limited or special jurisdiction**—sometimes referred to as "inferior courts"—which process cases that fall within narrow limits as to parties or subject matter. Examples of these latter courts are small claims, probate, family, magistrate, and, in a few states, juvenile courts. (The latter, incidentally, usually handle all sorts of matters in which juveniles are the focus of the activity, thus combining civil with criminal functions.) Among the inferior courts, many keep no transcript of their proceedings and are thus called **courts of nonrecord**.[10]

Courts, by Level Courts, of course, can be found at both the federal and state levels. Federal courts are organized into three tiers. The U.S. Supreme Court is the court of final appeal. The U.S. Court of Appeals exists in eleven districts and acts as an intermediate court of appeal. Federal trial courts are the U.S. district courts.

At the state level there is a wide disparity among court systems. Some states, notably California, Hawaii, and North Carolina, have consolidated or unified all courts under their state government. Many states have a bewildering variety of county and municiple courts—some of them traceable to colonial times—with virtually all matters triable at the local level and state courts handling only the most serious cases. Therefore, the attempt to develop a scheme that shows the types of courts related to levels of government becomes virtually impossible on a nationwide basis. The outline appearing in Table 3.3 is largely a presentation of the most common forms of courts.

Corrections

The picture in the corrections component is almost as complex as that of police. Again, it is not simply a matter of level but also one of types of corrections facilities and programs. Private and voluntary or charitable agencies and associations are involved in many states and localities. Some are direct and officially sanctioned participants; some act indirectly and on an unofficial basis.

TABLE 3.3 Courts, by Level

FEDERAL
U.S. Supreme Court (the ultimate court of appeal for the entire court system of the United States)
Federal district courts of appeal (the 11 intermediate appellate courts)
U.S. district courts (the 94 trial courts of general jurisdiction)
U.S. courts of special jurisdiction
    U.S. Tax Court
    U.S. Customs Court
    Court of Customs and Patent Appeals
    Court of Military Appeals (to process appeals from court-martials)
    U.S. Court of Claims

STATE
State court of last resort (State supreme court or court of appeals)
Intermediate courts of appeals (in 23 of the states)
Courts of general trial jurisdiction
    superior courts, courts of criminal record, courts of common pleas, or even (in New York) supreme courts)
Courts of limited or special jurisdiction (existing in 30 states)
    District courts
    Justice of the peace courts
    Courts of claims
    Juvenile courts
    Others

COUNTY
Courts of general trial jurisdiction
Limited or special jurisdiction courts
    Magistrate or justice of the peace courts
    Family or domestic relations courts
    Justice courts
    Any special jurisdiction courts not provided by the state

CITY
General courts of limited or special jurisdiction
    Traffic courts
    City misdemeanor courts, magistrates, mayors' or police courts
    Any other special purpose courts not furnished by the state or county or required because of the size or populations of the city

Types of Institutions We are able to distinguish at least four major types of corrections institutions and programs, each having various subcategories.

1. **Facilities for incarceration:** These facilities have a common function—to confine and isolate convicted persons from society at large. They include prisons and jails. Prisons have at least three subtypes, known as maximum, medium, and minimum security institutions.

2. **Community correction facilities:** Most of these facilities are found at the county or municipal level, and they include residential centers, halfway houses, and rehabilitation centers and programs. There are wide differences among states and among localities within states as to what is available, but in general their purpose is to prevent the separation of the offender from the community.

3. **Parole and probation programs:** Probation is used as an alternative to incarceration and allows convicted persons to remain at large under varying degrees of restriction and supervision. Parole follows a period of time in prison but allows a person to complete a sentence at large, subject to restrictions and supervision.

4. **Juvenile corrections:** These run the gamut from reform schools and other institutions of incarceration, through various community-based facilities, to forms of probation. Whatever the types of facilities or programs provided for juvenile offenders, they are usually distinct from all adult facilities and programs and are usually operated by juvenile authorities or divisions separated bureaucratically from those administering adult corrections.

We mentioned that private organizations are involved in corrections work in many places. They may be voluntary associations, such as Alcoholics Anonymous, or various service agencies linked with United Appeals. They may be hospitals or other rehabilitation or self-help agencies. Even profit-making businesses become involved when they make jobs available to convicts, thus enabling them to gain or remain on parole or probation or be diverted from formal corrections. However, we will not include these private entities in our designation of corrections since they are not publicly funded, and most do not have as a primary function the participation in corrections work and the processing of persons sentenced to them by courts. They do not, in other words, routinely receive input from the criminal process nor are they responsible for any regular output.

Corrections, by Level Attempting to describe corrections by level is as difficult as describing courts by level. The federal corrections system is organized under two agencies—the Federal Bureau of Prisons and the Federal Office of Parole and Probation—both housed within the Justice Department. The state systems and localities present a staggering array of arrangements. Table 3.4 attempts to present a generalized overview of corrections agencies by level.

This brief overview of the structure of the criminal justice system and its key components is by no means comprehensive. Any attempt to describe all agencies present in the nation, states, and localities would be impossible and unnecessary at this point. We will, of course, discuss agencies in more detail in later chapters. Here we intend only to give you an appreciation for the complexity of the system while, at the same time, showing that the components are identifiable and distinguishable.

To appreciate how the components fit into a system of criminal justice, we turn to a discussion of the process in which these components play essential and interrelated roles.

TABLE 3.4 Corrections, by Level

FEDERAL
Bureau of Prisons
  Prisons (maximum security)
  Adult correctional institutions
  Short-term institutions
  Juvenile centers
  Medical centers
  Behavioral research centers
  Metropolitan corrections centers
Federal Office of Probation and Parole

STATE
Division, bureau, or corrections agency or authority
  Prisons
  Correctional centers
Parole and probation (usually a separate agency)
Youth or juvenile division or authority
  Detention or residential facilities
  Training schools
  Camps or other facilities
  Probation programs

COUNTY AND CITY
Jails (and other detention facilities)
Halfway houses (or other community corrections facilities)
Local diversion programs

BASIC SYSTEM PROCESSES

Recall that in our diagram of the criminal justice system within the political and social environments, we spoke of inputs, processes, and outputs. Now we are going to present a step-by-step presentation of criminal justice *processes*, showing the general flow of persons and cases through the system and the roles played by each system component—law enforcement, prosecution, courts, and corrections.

Before describing the processes of justice, let us note two points for consideration:

1. As we have stated, there are several levels at which our discussion might be aimed—national, state, and local. Like most authors, our focus is basically on state and local criminal justice processes. Our reasons for this are derived from the importance of state and local systems to the total output of the overall criminal justice system and not from the unimportance of the criminal justice system at the national level. It does not take a lengthy look to see that most crimes are violations of state and local laws and that, consequently, state and local agencies bear most of the burden of performing the functions ascribed to the criminal justice system.

2. With the focus being on state and local criminal justice, we encounter some variation in the processing of persons and cases through the system. You should note that this is generally the case and seek information on specific systems in appropriate sources.

We must stress that at this point our remarks can only represent an oversimplification of what happens at any stage and for the process as a whole. For the moment we wish merely to present an overview of the criminal justice process. More flesh will be added to the skeleton in the chapters on each of the system's components.

Stages of the Criminal Justice Process

Basically, we may say that there are five stages in the criminal justice process: (1) arrest, (2) charging, (3) adjudication, (4) sentencing, and (5) corrections. Each of these stages begins with an action (input) that stimulates a process resulting in a crucial decision being made for the accused (output).

To assist in our description of the criminal justice process, we turn to the much-used flowchart created by the 1967 President's Commission on Law Enforcement and Administration of Justice. This rather imposing chart presents the most comprehensive view of the movement of cases through the criminal justice system yet devised. The chart has been modified only slightly to emphasize our suggestion of a five-stage process and certain steps within each stage (see Figure 3.1).

FIGURE 3.1 A General View of the Criminal Justice System

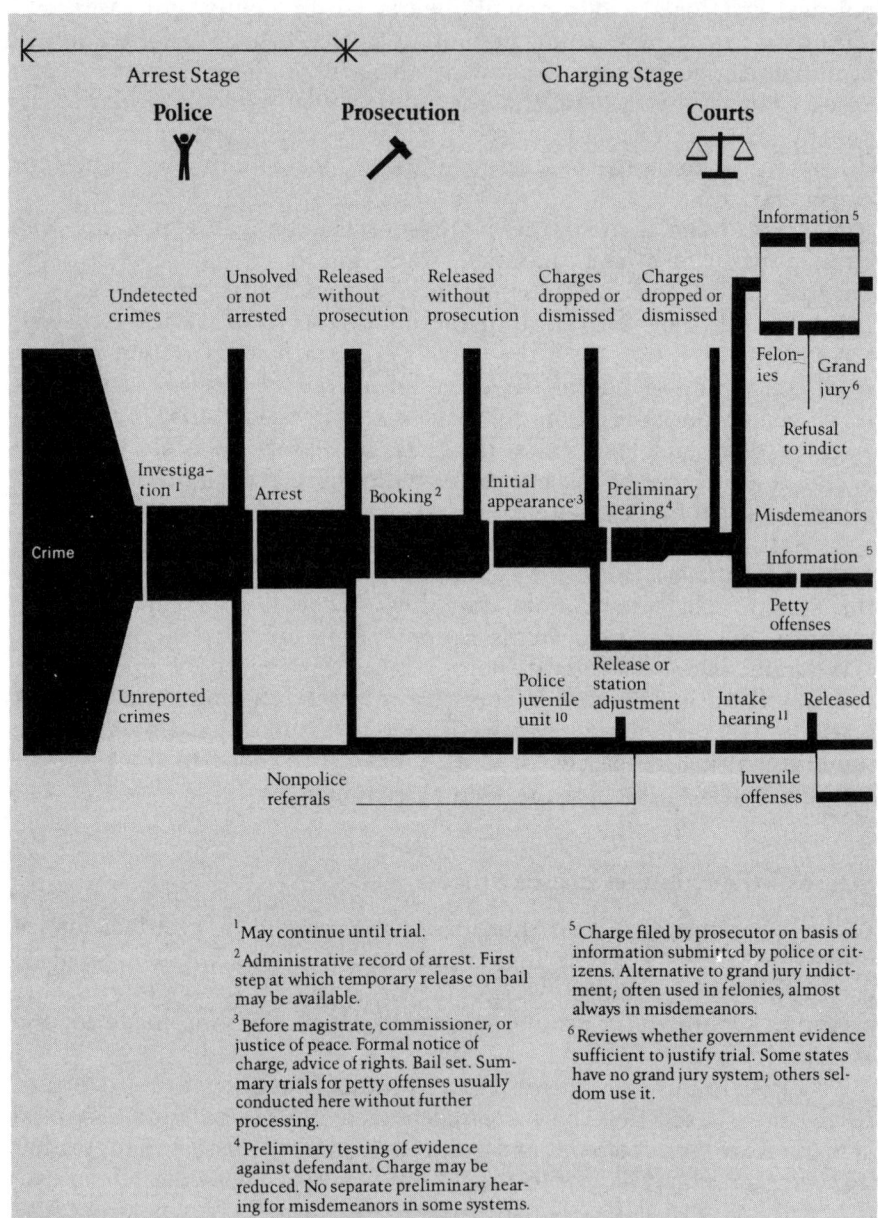

[1] May continue until trial.

[2] Administrative record of arrest. First step at which temporary release on bail may be available.

[3] Before magistrate, commissioner, or justice of peace. Formal notice of charge, advice of rights. Bail set. Summary trials for petty offenses usually conducted here without further processing.

[4] Preliminary testing of evidence against defendant. Charge may be reduced. No separate preliminary hearing for misdemeanors in some systems.

[5] Charge filed by prosecutor on basis of information submitted by police or citizens. Alternative to grand jury indictment; often used in felonies, almost always in misdemeanors.

[6] Reviews whether government evidence sufficient to justify trial. Some states have no grand jury system; others seldom use it.

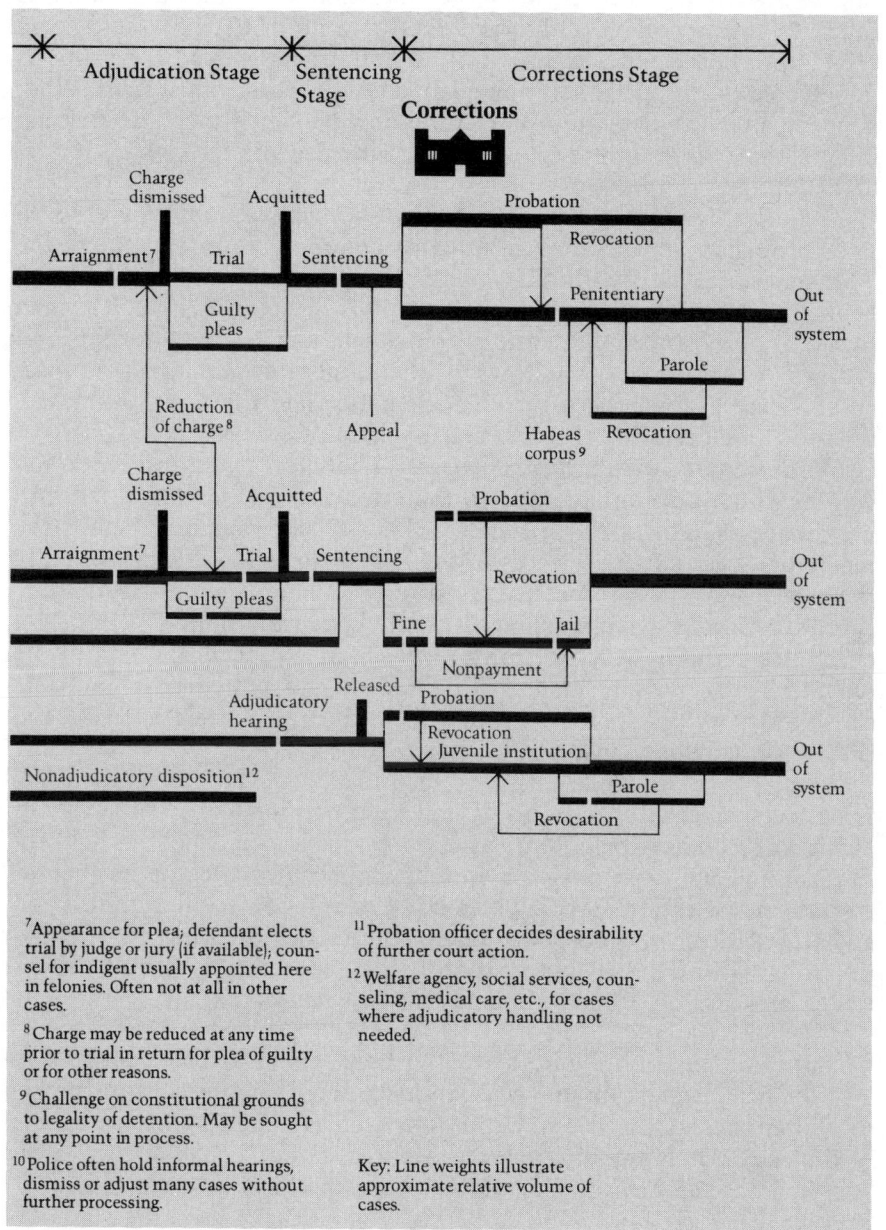

[7] Appearance for plea; defendant elects trial by judge or jury (if available); counsel for indigent usually appointed here in felonies. Often not at all in other cases.

[8] Charge may be reduced at any time prior to trial in return for plea of guilty or for other reasons.

[9] Challenge on constitutional grounds to legality of detention. May be sought at any point in process.

[10] Police often hold informal hearings, dismiss or adjust many cases without further processing.

[11] Probation officer decides desirability of further court action.

[12] Welfare agency, social services, counseling, medical care, etc., for cases where adjudicatory handling not needed.

Key: Line weights illustrate approximate relative volume of cases.

Source: President's Commission on Law Enforcement and Administration of Justice, *Task Force Report: Science and Technology* (Washington, D.C.: Government Printing Office, 1967), pp. 58-59.

Arrest Stage As the flowchart makes clear, the criminal justice process begins with the commission of a crime. Actually, it is more accurate to say that it begins with the *detection* of crime. Detection is taken to mean not only observed acts of crime but the results of a crime (e.g., homeowner returns to find home burglarized). If a crime is undetected or unreported, it obviously does not enter the system. What happens after the detection of a crime depends largely on the method of detection. We can note two distinct sequences of steps which follow detection:

1. *Police observation — arrest — booking — investigation:* When the police witness an actual crime in progress and are able to apprehend the offender, arrest is usually immediate. The suspect is then taken and **booked** into the city or county jail. This procedure involves such things as fingerprinting, identification check, and reading of rights and charges. An investigation follows for the purpose of developing a prosecutable case against the suspect. If the police feel that it is warranted, they pass the case into the next stage — charging.

2. *Complaint — investigation — arrest — booking:* The most common way in which crime is brought to the attention of those in the criminal justice system is by citizen complaint to the police. Whether the report of a crime is by witness or victim, an investigation is normally the next step. Unlike the investigation following police observation, this investigation is aimed more at the determination of whether a crime has actually been committed and, if so, the identification of the offender(s). If enough evidence is obtained and police have probable cause to believe a specific person is the culprit, an arrest is made and the person is booked into a jail.

To these two sequences of steps, we can add another in which there is police suspicion of a crime having been committed, in progress, or about to be committed. Through a variety of means, such as field interrogations and undercover operations, police may become suspicious and an investigation is conducted for evidence of crime commission and the identity of a suspect. Again, arrests and booking may follow investigation. One final observation: police sometimes consult the office of prosecution prior to the arresting of a suspect.

Charging Stage Police output in the form of an arrested or booked suspect becomes input into the charging stage. While specific procedures vary across the country, the first step is generally the **screening** of the case. At this point evidence is sifted, police behavior evaluated, law studied, and key officers and witnesses perhaps interviewed in order to assess the nature of the case and decide on one of these courses of action:

1. *Rejection of the case:* If this is the option decided on, and if the person has been booked and appeared before a judge, the prosecutor notifies the court that the case is formally dropped.

2. *Filing of a direct charge (or information) against the defendant:* An **information** is a document filed with the court formally charging the accused with specific crimes.

3. *Taking the case to a grand jury:* This means presenting the evidence to a grand jury and allowing that body of citizens to decide whether or not to charge the accused. If it decides to do so, it issues a **true bill of indictment**—a document by which a grand jury files charges with the court. In cases where the grand jury decides not to file charges, it issues a **no true bill** with the court.

4. *Diversion:* More will be said about this later, but diversion is basically a process that defers prosecution or adjudication of nonviolent crimes in exchange for an agreed-to period of supervised activity and good behavior on the part of the accused.[11] This option is becoming available in a growing number of jurisdictions.

Before leaving the second stage, attention should be paid to other activities concerning the defendant. A person booked into a jail may, in many jurisdictions, seek release by putting up **bail** immediately. Bail is a sum of money that is posted to assure the later appearance of the accused in court. If he cannot post bail, the accused appears before a judge within a very short and specified period of time, at which time he is informed as to his rights and the reason for his arrest. This is generally referred to as an **initial appearance.** At this time formal bail is also set. If bail requirements cannot be met, arrangements may be made in many places, and for certain nonviolent crimes, for the accused to be released in the recognizance of a relative or friend or even **released on his own recognizance** (ROR). This is done when the accused has community ties or responsibilities and is therefore unlikely to disappear.

Another step that may take place is a **preliminary hearing.** This usually is done prior to the filing of formal charges when persons are unable to secure release from jail or when defense counsel requests it. Its purpose is to determine whether or not there is enough merit in the state's case to continue to hold the defendant. Some evidence is presented, and witnesses may give brief testimony. The judge then decides from among three alternatives: (1) dismiss the charges and release the accused; (2) **bind over**—or hold—the accused on the police charges; or

(3) bind over the accused on lesser charges, even reducing them from felony to misdemeanor. While the judge may release the defendant or reduce the charges (and bail), his decision may not dictate what, if any, formal charges will later be filed by the prosecutor or what indictment might be handed down by a grand jury. The original charges could thus be reinstated, or new charges could be filed.

These parallel processes—one involving the preparation of a criminal case against the defendant and the ancillary process of dealing with the pretrial status of the accused—constitute the second phase of the criminal justice process. It is completed with the filing of charges, the dropping of the case, or the diversion of the defendant into noncriminal justice processing.

Adjudication Stage The input triggering this stage is the information or indictment. As noted, these are the instruments through which formal charges are filed against the accused. Each charge is read to the defendant at a proceeding known as an **arraignment.** In addition to the reading of charges, there are the determination that the defendant has an attorney and the taking of a plea. In most places a person may plead guilty, not guilty, or **nolo contendere** (no contest) to the charges. If a guilty or no contest plea is entered, the defendant awaits sentencing.

A not guilty plea at arraignment results in a trial date being set for a later date. Presumably, enough time will be allowed for the preparation of an adequate defense but not so much as to violate the need for a speedy trial. Some states and the federal courts are establishing definite time requirements covering the period from arrest to trial.

Between the arraignment and the opening of the trial, any number of things can happen. Among them are the following: (1) defense may request repeated **continuances** (delays of the trial); (2) **plea bargaining** may be conducted to seek a reduction in charges in return for a guilty plea; (3) prosecutor may issue a **nolle prosequi**—a document withdrawing charges; (4) the defendant may plead guilty to the original charges. Any guilty plea leads to sentencing procedures, though a judge can (and a few do) reject pleas to reduced charges. Plea bargaining is a crucial part of most criminal processes, but attitudes, requirements, and actual usages vary widely from place to place.

Assuming the trial date finally arrives and no change in the plea occurs, a trial will be conducted. Trial generally involves a number of identifiable steps: (1) selection of a trial jury, unless it is to be a **court** or **bench trial,** that is, before the judge alone; (2) attorneys' motions regarding evidence, witnesses, venue, and a multitude of matters; (3) opening statements for counsel for defense and the state; (4) presentation of prosecution's case, including the state's evidence and witnesses (both civilian and police); (5) defense motion for directed verdict of acquittal; (6) presentation of defense case; (7) presentation of defense and prosecution's concluding statements; (8) charging of the jury by the trial judge—that is, instructing members about the law they must apply to the facts and arguments presented during the trial—or taking the case under the judge's personal advisement; (9) rendering of a verdict by the judge or jury.

At two points the judge may dismiss the case during the trial, and at conclusion the judge in a jury trial may direct the jury to acquit the defendant or even (rarely) overrule a jury verdict of guilty. Only in a bench trial, however, may the judge render a verdict of guilty. In any case, the verdict, or the earlier guilty plea, is the final output of the adjudication stage.

Sentencing Stage A conviction becomes the input of the fourth stage: sentencing. In all cases except those involving a court or bench trial, the judge has played a very important, but secondary, role. With sentencing, the judge exercises full discretion since the law usually allows plenty of room for it and also places full responsibility for sentencing in the judge's hands.

In most jurisdictions the judge may order, or the defense may call for, **pre-sentence investigation** of the offender. This process may be conducted by law enforcement, court, or corrections agencies calling for information (input) from police officers, prosecutor, defense counsel, and others. The pre-sentence investigation usually results in a formal report to the sentencing judge and covers the defendant's background, character, home, occupation, and social environment. The judge may take this report into consideration in pronouncing sentence.

The sentence involves two aspects: type and severity. Type refers to the facility or program to which the defendant is assigned. Severity means the length of service or amount of fine imposed. The law prescribes certain limits within which the judge must choose. A misdemeanant, for example, usually cannot be sent to the state prison, and the length of any period of confinement is limited, usually to one year. Various classes of felonies carry appropriate maximum sentences, and mandatory minimums are becoming popular in some states for some crimes. In general, however, the legal parameters are very broad, and judges exercise considerable discretion in pronouncing sentence.

Sentencing alternatives available to the judge include a fine, probation, time in local corrections facilities such as jail, and time in a state prison or facility. The court may exercise another option—to suspend whatever sentence has been pronounced and release the person. This usually means that if the person is convicted of another crime, the original as well as any subsequent sentence may be imposed. The sentence becomes the input of the corrections stage except in the cases of fines or suspended sentences.

Corrections Stage The corrections stage involves, of course, the convicted person's serving of the sentence imposed. This stage is not, however, without its discretionary aspects. For example, state prisoners become eligible for parole after a prescribed period of time, but a parole board or authority must review each case and decide whether to grant parole. In some states even the decision about the facility to which the prisoner is assigned is left to corrections officials, and a transfer from one facility to another may be made within the term of sentence. Within any given facility, authorities make decisions regarding the prisoner's living space, work, or educational program. Prisons have their own internal disciplinary processes as well, but these are matters for the corrections portion of this text. Suffice it to say that various officials make decisions that alter the processing of individuals through the corrections stage in terms of both the character and the length of their service.

There is also the matter of dealing with persons who violate conditions of probation or parole and are subject to revocation proceedings. While there are differences between the revocation proceedings for probationers and parolees, the common effect is to incarcerate the individual for the duration of his or her sentence.

At some point the vast majority (over 90 percent) of individuals are released from corrections and reenter society. In some states there is an additional step at which full citizenship rights (the right to vote, to make contracts, and so on) are returned to ex-convicts, but it is the release from incarceration, parole, or probation that signals the final output from the criminal justice system itself.

Appeals During the corrections stage another process of importance may be going on—appeals of court rulings. Appeals of cases from a trial court to a court of appeal are made on **points of law** and not usually on the **points of fact** at issue in the original trial. Whether a piece of evidence was or was not the murder weapon or whether in fact the accused was guilty or innocent are not matters for review by a higher court. These are points of fact. What is subject to review is whether evidence was or was not legally seized and admitted, whether correct trial procedure was or was not followed, and, in short, whether the client received his or her full rights to due process of law. Of course, the distinction between points of fact and points of law is often fine or fuzzy, but this is the general guideline followed. An exception to this general rule is an appeal from an inferior court of nonrecord to a general trial court. The superior court's agreement to hear the case results in a **trial de novo**—a new trial.

The appeal usually goes to a court immediately superior to the court that handled the trial, from there to the next highest, and so on. Whether we are talking about the federal courts or those of a state, rarely do cases bypass a level of the structure, and then only under specific circumstances. Generally, appeals courts, especially state supreme courts and the U.S. Supreme Court, will not hear a case until all lower appeals channels have been exhausted.

Once the appellate courts have accepted a case for a hearing, the alternatives open to them are essentially two: denial or affirmation of the appeal. Denial of the appeal means that the lower court's judgment is upheld and the defendant continues toward the completion of the sentence. If the appeal is affirmed, it overturns the lower court's decision and generally leads to either complete dismissal of the case or retrial. In rare instances it may even result in the dismissal or retrial of an entire class of cases in which similar points of law are at issue. For example, after the *Gideon* v. *Wainwright* appeal decision, the state of Florida was ordered to retry every accused felon in a state prison who had not been represented by counsel at trial.[12]

Up to this point we have described the basic process of criminal justice by focusing on five different stages and the system components primarily involved at each one. The fact that we have proceeded in this fashion should not be taken to mean that each component operates only at one stage. It is common for each to have some responsibility at varying points in the total process. For example, while the police function primarily during the arrest stage, they play roles in both the prosecution and adjudication stages, such as giving testimony at grand jury hearings and at trials. The prosecutor is involved not only in the prosecution stage but in others as well; for example, the prosecutor tries cases for the state and may influence sentencing through plea bargaining.

Juvenile Justice

Any attempt to distinguish between the treatment accorded to adults accused of crime and the processing of juveniles is fraught with peril. Two generalizations seem appropriate: (1) the states' juvenile justice systems differ from each other to a greater extent than their adult criminal justice systems; and (2) even where the differences between a state's adult and juvenile systems appear to be greatest, these differences are frequently more symbolic than real—that is, structures and terminology may be different but behavior and outcomes are largely the same.

Nevertheless, there are several characteristics generally common to the juvenile justice process that set it apart from that provided for adults.[13] (Note the separate track across the five stages in Figure 3.1.)

While adults are accused of specific crimes or offenses, juveniles may, in addition, enter the system due to behavior or conditions never considered with regard to adults—for example, incorrigibility, truancy, or juvenile status offenses.

While adults must have complaints filed against them by citizens or be arrested by police, juveniles may be referred by neighbors, teachers, friends, or even their own parents.

Instead of being booked and possibly interrogated by police, juveniles are handled by juvenile intake officers who may interview or counsel the juvenile, thus acting partly as law enforcement officials and partly as defense attorneys.

Juveniles are usually filed upon by means of petition rather than being subject to indictment or information.

Instead of trials, juveniles are given **adjudicatory hearings** before a judge. Juries are never present. (In some states a juvenile may be tried in an adult court under certain conditions.)

Juveniles are not found or adjudicated guilty of an offense but are adjudicated "delinquents" by the court.

Juveniles are not sentenced but are made subjects of disposition.

Corrections are almost never designed merely to incarcerate or punish but are almost always measures of rehabilitation. Approaches may run the gamut from detention centers or shelters, work or training schools, group centers including halfway houses and foster homes, or probation back to the parents or home environment.

Throughout most of this process, juveniles are usually being handled by officials and agencies that are separate in various ways from those pertaining to adults. We will, of course, deal with all aspects of juvenile justice in the Juvenile Justice System on p. 386.

In this first part of our book, we have introduced the systems approach to the study of criminal justice, examined some of the most important elements in the system's environment, and provided a brief, but necessarily superficial, overview of the criminal justice system and processes. We turn now to a full examination of each of the major components of the system, their structures, roles, personnel, and behaviors.

TEST YOURSELF

Define these key terms:
general police
courts of original jurisdiction
booking
true bill of indictment
preliminary hearing
continuance
nolle prosequi
adjudicatory hearings

Answer the following questions:

1. What are two aspects of the criminal justice function of protection of rights?

2. Why might "crime suppression" be a more appropriate function of criminal justice than "crime prevention"?

3. Name three types of law enforcement agencies and give an example of each.

4. What are the four types of corrections institutions and programs?

5. Name the five stages of the criminal justice process, and indicate the output of each.

NOTES

1. George T. Felkenes, *The Criminal Justice System* (Englewood Cliffs, N.J.: Prentice-Hall, 1973), pp. 3–4.
2. Thomas F. Adams, *Introduction to the Administration of Justice* (Englewood Cliffs, N.J.: Prentice-Hall, 1975), p. ix.
3. George F. Cole, *The American System of Criminal Justice* (N. Scituate, Mass.: Duxbury Press, 1975), pp. 39–41.
4. Yong Hyo Cho, *Public Policy and Urban Crime* (Cambridge, Mass.: Ballinger, 1974), pp. 43–45.
5. Ibid.
6. Paul M. Whisenand, *Crime Prevention: A Practical Look at Deterrence of Crime* (Boston: Holbrook Press, 1977), p. 4.

7. Herbert L. Packer, *The Limits of the Criminal Sanction* (Stanford: Stanford University Press, 1968), pp. 1547-73.

8. Law Enforcement Assistance Administration, *Criminal Justice Agencies* (Washington, D.C.: Government Printing Office, 1975), p. 7.

9. See Herbert Jacobs, *Urban Justice: Law and Order in American Cities* (Englewood Cliffs, N.J.: Prentice-Hall, 1973), pp. 53-62.

10. For a discussion of the differences between courts of general, limited, and special jurisdiction, see Law Enforcement Assistant Administration, *National Survey of Court Organization* (Washington, D.C.: Government Printing Office, 1973), pp. 1-3.

11. See National Pretrial Intervention Center, *Descriptive Profiles on Selected Pretrial Criminal Justice Intervention Programs* (Washington, D.C.: American Bar Association, 1974).

12. 372 U.S. 335 (1963).

13. For a more thorough discussion of juvenile processing, see Hazel Kerper, *Criminal Justice* (St. Paul, Minn.: West Publishing, 1972) pp. 386-402.

PART II
Law Enforcement

CHAPTER 4
Law Enforcement Functions and Structures

OUTLINE

MUNICIPAL POLICE
    Historical Development
        English Origins
        American Development
    Municipal Police Functions
        Sources of Police Functions
        Major Police Functions
        Function-Related Issues
    Police Organization
        Organizational Principles
        Operations Bureau
        Administration Bureau
        Services Bureau
        Other Units
        Small Departments

THE OFFICE OF SHERIFF
    Historical Development
    Functions
    Organization

STATE LAW ENFORCEMENT AGENCIES
    Historical Development
    Functions
    Organization

FEDERAL LAW ENFORCEMENT
    Department of Justice
        Federal Bureau of Investigation
        Drug Enforcement Administration
        United States Marshals
        Immigration and Naturalization Service
    Department of the Treasury
        Bureau of Alcohol, Tobacco, and Firearms
        Secret Service
        Customs Service
        Internal Revenue Service Intelligence
            Division

OBJECTIVES

After reading this chapter the student should be able to:

Discuss the reasons for the importance of municipal police departments.

Explain the English developments that provided the foundation for municipal police departments.

Discuss the evolution of municipal police departments within the United States.

Explain the functions of municipal police.

Explain the principles of police department organization.

Discuss the major bureaus within a municipal department and the roles of each.

Explain the organization of police patrol.

Present a brief history of the development of the office of sheriff.

Discuss the unique functions of sheriffs.

Discuss the origins of state law enforcement agencies.

Explain the differences between state police departments and state highway patrols.

List the major federal law enforcement agencies and state their respective functions.

KEY TERMS

modus operandi
criminalistics
law enforcement
order maintenance
crime prevention
public service
division of labor
chain of command
unit of command
definition of responsibility
span of control
line and staff
patrol
beats, sectors, and precincts
platoons and shifts
standard patrol
aggressive patrol
reactive patrol
team policing
community relations unit
internal investigations unit
state highway patrols and state police

☐ In an examination of law enforcement in America, one may focus on several types of agencies at several different levels of government. Recognizing, however, that most law enforcement activities occur at the local level, we will devote the bulk of our attention to the generalist agencies of municipal police and county sheriffs. Other law enforcement agencies will be described but not in as much detail.

MUNICIPAL POLICE

There is little doubt that among the types of law enforcement agencies in the United States, the most pervasive is the municipal police department. In 1967 the President's Commission on Law Enforcement and Administration of Justice estimated that there were 40,000 law enforcement agencies in the United States and that approximately 36,700 of these were municipal police departments. The commission noted that most of these were spread around the country in relatively small boroughs, towns, and villages.[1] Recent Department of Justice research tends to confirm the commission's findings.[2]

Not only are municipal police departments the most pervasive of law enforcement agencies, they are the biggest consumers of system resources. Over two-thirds of all individuals working in American law enforcement and almost 40 percent of all criminal justice personnel are employed by city and town police departments. These departments spend over 56 percent of the funds allocated for law enforcement in the United States and over one-third of all criminal justice monies. Even this lion's share of system resources is often considered to be insufficient to perform the many tasks expected of police.[3]

Without question, municipal police have the highest public visibility of any element of the criminal justice system. For many citizens police officers are their only contact with the criminal justice system. Except for those persons who are either victims, witnesses, or perpetrators of crimes, most citizens have few, if any, dealings with prosecutors, judges, or corrections officials. Almost everyone, however, has some contact with municipal police, even if it is only through receiving traffic tickets, observing marked police vehicles on patrol, or observing security activity at sporting events and other crowd gatherings. Public visibility has generally been of such magnitude that citizens associate the term "law enforcement" almost exclusively with municipal police.

Associated with high public visibility is a rather broad and intense set of expectations placed on police by citizens and their representatives in government. Police are expected to enforce laws, investigate crimes, capture all culprits, resolve all sorts of special conflicts, and provide a vast array of services having little to do with law enforcement directly. Further, many people expect police to do all these things with a minimum of inconvenience to them personally.

We have stated that municipal police are the most pervasive of all law enforcement agencies in the United States, that they consume the most system resources, that they have the highest public visibility, and that they are expected to perform many functions. We may go a step further and note that they occupy a rather important position in the criminal justice system. Police personnel are the primary detectors and investigators of crimes, the apprehenders of suspects, and the initiators (in most cases) of the criminal justice process—that is, arrest, prosecution, adjudication, sentencing, and corrections. If municipal police were to stop performing their detection and apprehension activities, the rest of the system would have little to do. If, on the other hand, every person suspected of a criminal act was arrested and the criminal justice process initiated, the system would soon crack under the strain. This is not to deny the importance of the roles played by other law enforcement agencies, such as sheriffs, or by other criminal justice components (i.e., prosecutors, courts, corrections) but to suggest the vital contribution to the criminal justice system by municipal police.

Historical Development

It is important to understand that our law enforcement institutions and practices have evolved over a considerable period of time. We will look at the English origins and the American development of municipal police.

English Origins As is the case with many of our society's institutions, we may seek the origin of municipal police in English history.[4] In the thirteenth century Henry III initiated the long path to today's police by creating a night watch to guard city gates and arrest nighttime law violators. They were also given the task of spotting and fighting fires, a noncriminal function. While today's police do not fight fires, they continue to perform functions that are not criminal in nature. By the fourteenth century the night watch was joined by the day ward and a semblance of twenty-four-hour protection was provided.

In the sixteenth century businessmen added their own merchant patrols, who guarded business properties and attempted to recover goods stolen from their patrons. By now the Industrial Revolution was spawning the worst urban slum conditions and a huge class of desperate people whose very survival depended on thievery. To the merchant patrols were added church-supported parish police to protect members of their respective congregations and dock police to guard the goods passing through the ports. This highly fragmented, partially private police system was notorious in both its inefficiency and lack of discipline.

In 1748 novelist Henry Fielding and his brother John were instrumental in the development of the first detective force in London, called the "Bow Street Runners." Henry Fielding was magistrate for two sections within London, and this force was intended to enforce the orders of his court, which was located on Bow Street. The force did develop a certain ability, and John Fielding was later able to add such features as foot and horse patrols and programs to aid prostitutes and wayward children. Still, the authority of the force was limited, and by the nineteenth century, when the impact of industrialization was at its devastating peak, London was practically lawless.

By now almost every student of police history, and the police themselves, have heard of Sir Robert Peel, the man who is generally credited with the creation of the forerunner of modern urban police departments. As home secretary—the equivalent to our attorney general of the United States—Peel persuaded Parliament to pass the Metropolitan Police Act in 1829, thereby creating a whole new police force. The home secretary was determined to have as professional and disciplined a body of officers as the times permitted, and he personally screened all 12,000 candidates to select the 1,000 charter members of the department. He promulgated a dozen basic principles of police work, some of which were downright revolutionary for their time and many of which are still honored. Their continued relevance merits mentioning some of these principles: strictness of discipline to ensure high standards of behavior; a neat appearance in a distinctive uniform to command respect; training to produce efficiency; a perfect command of temper; selection based on merit; territorial distribution of the force; and provision of round-the-clock protection by means of established hours and shifts.

Peel's demands on his men were so great that in the first three years 11,000 men were either dismissed or resigned from the department. His efforts were rewarded as city dwellers' hostility gradually gave way to respect, and the term "bobbies," originally used derisively, became a term of affection used to this day.

The success of the London Metropolitan Police led Parliament in 1839 to create a separate force for the city of London—the smaller unit within the metropolitan area. By 1856 Parliament required all counties and boroughs in England to establish police departments similar to London's. By the end of the nineteenth century, the structure of the nation's entire police system and its financing were firmly established.

American Development The importance of developments in England cannot be overstated because of their impact on law enforcement in the United States. The early 1800s saw night watches established in Boston and New York. Philadelphia set up the first two-shift, round-the-clock force in 1833, and in that same year New York officials traveled to London to study its Metropolitan Police Department, then only four years old. At that time New York City boasted a patchwork of elected constables in the wards, marshals appointed by the mayor, a high constable with broad enforcement powers, and a night watch of several hundred persons. It was not until 1844, however, that the London model was adopted, and the New York City Police Department was created. By the close of the Civil War, formal police agencies had been established in a dozen other major cities throughout the north and in San Francisco. The metropolitan police department with military-style organization, uniforms, and rotating shifts covering twenty-four hours was entrenched as the dominant model for urban law enforcement throughout the country.

Other trends we should at least mention were the development of investigative or detective units, distinct from the uniformed troops, and an increasing reliance on technology. Detectives emerged as the investigators of unsolved crimes and the trackers of criminals. They introduced to police work the notion of **modus operandi** (modes of operation) of criminals, the use of informers, and the so-called third-degree interrogation.

Technological developments — including telephones, automobiles, radio (especially two-way radios), aircraft, and changes in weaponry — were quickly adapted to law enforcement uses. Improvements in communications enhanced commanders' supervision of officers in the field, in addition to whatever contribution they made to the ability to serve the public and fight crime. The application of scientific techniques, to the investigation of crimes created the discipline of **criminalistics.** Among the sciences incorporated within criminalistics are chemistry, physics, physiology, psychology, and pathology. Applications of these sciences include analysis of drugs and blood samples, ballistics, and handwriting comparisons. More recently, automated data processing has been added to the storage and retrieval of information by law enforcement agencies. This development, like those in communications, is as useful for management purposes as it is for improving service.

Municipal Police Functions

In reviewing the literature on police, we find a significant amount of disagreement among various authors, including some practitioners, on the subject of the functions of police departments. Some of these differences are largely a matter of how specific one wants to be in listing them and thus how many distinct functions one wants on the list. Lists of functions run from two to seventeen—from something as sweeping as "crime control" to one as specific as "maintaining a property and evidence storage facility."[5] There are differences, however, over whether or not police should be assigned this or that function. The best examples are the arguments over whether police should be expected to prevent crime and whether police should provide various general public services.

Before addressing these arguments, let us be clear that by "functions" we mean goals, objectives, and expectations—in other words, what it is that police should do. What police do in fact may or may not coincide with assigned functions. Logic requires that functions be stated as goals so that activities and performance can be measured against them. It is not uncommon for any agency or organization to lose sight of its reason for being and develop its own functions. Nor is it unknown for people to expect an agency that was created to serve some specified purpose to begin serving others.

Sources of Police Functions It is also important to note that there are a number of sources of police functions which are part of the environment of police. Richard Myren has written: "In addition to forces within the police agency itself, there are at least four kinds of external influences to be reckoned with: private citizens, both as individuals and as members of pressure groups; legislative bodies; and executive agencies."[6]

Myren explains that legislative bodies are the "most obvious source" since they enact statutes dealing with police organization and operation, pass criminal laws, and control the purse strings. As for executive influences, he states that "perhaps the most important ... is that of the prosecutor" through his discretion over filing charges in court. Prosecutorial charging policies "determine that the police play some roles and not others."[7] Other important executive influences include the allocation of fiscal resources, the setting of policies for police departments by mayors or city managers, the setting of policies by police commissioners, chiefs, and other administrators, and the decisions taken by the rank and file police personnel themselves.

For our purposes police functions are viewed as determined by forces outside the departments: citizens and other government bodies. It is largely these members of the police environment who decide what it is that the police should be doing.

Major Police Functions Having looked at how police functions are determined, we can examine what these functions are. Despite the disagreements, current literature suggests that there are four general functions of police agencies: law enforcement, order maintenance, crime prevention, and public service.

While the core function of the entire criminal justice system is **law enforcement,** there are aspects of this general function that are assigned primarily to agencies which are part of what we call the law enforcement component of that system. Law enforcement agencies are the initiators of the entire criminal justice process. Their special functions are the detection of crime, the investigation of those crimes to determine the culprit, the apprehension of suspect offenders, and the preparation of evidence and a case for consideration by the prosecutor.

Order maintenance, sometimes referred to as "peacekeeping," is the most difficult function to define, but it is widely regarded as a very important function performed by law enforcement agencies, especially local police. A study sponsored by the International Conference of City Managers refers to order maintenance as the "regulation of noncriminal acts."[8] It includes such specific matters as crowd control, traffic regulation, and riot prevention and control. In a broad sense it also includes the duty to protect and preserve the political order and social system against radical or subversive forces.

The **prevention of crime** is a function that has two aspects: the denial of opportunities for persons to commit crimes and the deterrence of crimes through the risk of being caught and the inability to profit from crime. Police seek to prevent crime by being present in places where crimes might be committed and by alerting citizens to refrain from practices that make them or their property vulnerable—this is opportunity denial. Police also participate in the deterrence of crime by increasing the risk that offenders will be subject to arrest, prosecution, conviction, and punishment. This aspect of crime prevention overlaps the function of law enforcement and involves police interaction with other criminal justice agencies.

While authorities sometimes argue over whether the law enforcement or order maintenance functions are the most important, studies reveal that providing **public services** is the most demanding function in terms of the time and resources of law enforcement agencies, especially municipal police. Most calls for service received by these agencies have little to do with crime or disorder, either real or threatened. They are calls for various emergency services and aid, assistance in locating lost persons or property, help in getting rid of dangerous animals, assistance in gaining entry to locked autos or residences, and help in getting the family cat down from the roof.

Function-Related Issues There is little disagreement in the literature and among law enforcement officials with the proposition that the functions described above are assigned to police departments. They constitute real expectations people have regarding the role of police in their communities. There are two issues, however, that arise from this list: Is it realistic to expect police to prevent crime and should police really be expected to perform all those general service functions?

We assert that crime prevention is a distinct function of police departments, though some observers—cited earlier—question this. Police officials themselves use terms such as "preventive patrol." The study of police work sponsored by the City Managers Association made a useful distinction, however, between "crime prevention," which is aimed at altering the intent of potential offenders, and "crime suppression," which means denying opportunities to commit or profit from crime. As indicated earlier, "suppression" would perhaps be a better term. It is one thing to argue that a police function is to minimize crime by denying targets of opportunity or increasing the risks to the offender of being caught. It is quite another to assert that police can be expected to alter the inclinations people have toward committing crimes—in other words, change the social conditions or the attitudes that breed criminal behavior.

It is true that many departments are involved in various social projects, especially programs aimed at young offenders or would-be offenders. But in most communities the primary responsibility for such projects is assigned to other nonpolice agencies of government or private and volunteer associations. It is true, on the other hand, that many police departments are running various prevention programs in which they teach people how to protect their properties against burglaries, how to defend themselves with guns, karate, or other means, and how to spot and report suspicious activities. As we said earlier, these efforts are attempts to deny opportunities for crimes—an aspect of crime prevention.

The other controversy surrounds the function of providing general services to the public. It was not until very recently that this function was elevated to a status relative to law enforcement and order maintenance, though some departments have performed such services for years.[9] Citizens certainly expect police to perform these general services. Every analysis of citizens' calls to police shows that most calls are requests for information or for general services having little or nothing to do with crime or disorder.[10] The argument, therefore, is not over whether police have been assigned the service function. It is over whether police departments should be stripped of this responsibility or have their capabilities enhanced so they can better perform these services. Richard Myren represents those who believe that demands for general services have weakened police departments' crime-fighting capacities. He cites several problems arising from police being assigned service functions: (1) inflation of police budgets and distortions of the apparent costs of crime control; (2) prevention of professionalism in crime fighting; (3) dilution of police attention to their primary assignment of combatting crimes; and (4) prevention of more satisfactory performance of service functions by an especially constituted agency. He strongly recommends that another agency or agencies assume the service functions currently burdening most police departments.[11]

Thomas Bercal speaks for the opposing point of view when he notes that "police performance is being judged on but one-fifth of their activity" (crime-related activity). He writes:

> [I]t is imperative that his [policeman's] current role in the community be identified and understood. In order to do this, the role of metropolitan police departments in "crime prevention and control" must be deemphasized and placed in a framework which recognizes this activity as being only one of many services with which it is concerned.[12]

He asserts that police have a unique ability to "determine the 'needs' of the community they serve" since "consumer demands for governmental service" come in as calls for assistance to police departments. In addition, then, to identifying community problems, the police can "stimulate and assist in the development of programs aimed at the solution of these problems," and "assist in the effective performance by other agencies."[13]

We cannot, of course, resolve this issue of whether police should be expected to perform general service functions. We merely note that the function has been assigned to them and that, despite some calls for change, is likely to remain with them for the forseeable future. It is also likely to remain as important and distinctive as their functions of law enforcement and order maintenance.

Police Organization

Virtually every police department in the land has adopted the military style of organization common to the Western world: the uniforms, the hierarchy of rank, and the principles of organization are greatly like those of the military. There is always a chief of police (similar in nature to a military general) at the top of the organization. The chief is followed in rank by deputy chiefs, assistant chiefs, captains, lieutenants, sergeants, and patrol personnel (like privates in the military). It must be noted that the size of a police department will generally determine whether such a hierarchy exists. Extremely small departments may only have a police chief and several patrol officers. Swaton and Morgan note:

> At one end of the ... spectrum is the one-man department in the smallest hamlet. He does everything and if he gets in over his head he calls on a county or state agency for help. At the other end of the spectrum is the super large municipal ... agency with a chief, a sprinkling of deputy chiefs, fifteen or twenty division commanders, inspectors, and specialists for everything from fingerprints to press relations.[14]

Organizational Principles Police departments, with modifications corresponding to size, are organized on the basis of certain concepts and principles.[15] These include the following:

1. **Division of labor:** Units within the agency are given authority over designated tasks of a common nature and other units are supposedly precluded from performing in that area.

2. **Chain of command:** Each order, request, or piece of information should flow up or down through each level in the organizational hierarchy and no level of supervision or command should be bypassed. Very closely related to this chain of command doctrine is an additional principle involving delegation of responsibility and authority. This means that supervisors in the chain of command have complete authority over their subordinates and, in turn, are fully responsible to their superiors for their actions.

3. **Unit of command:** Each employee has but one immediate supervisor to whom he must answer—at least at any one time.

4. **Definition of responsibility:** All personnel in the hierarchy are supposed to know what they are responsible for—what tasks they and their units are expected to accomplish.

5. **Span of control:** The number of subordinates each supervisor is responsible for should not exceed his or her capacity for control. In most organizations, including the police, the higher up in the chain of command, the smaller the number of subordinates directly reporting to a supervisor.

6. **Line and staff:** "Line" elements refer to those units within an organization that do the work directly related to the assigned functions of the agency. "Staff" units are those that back up the line elements with administrative support and specialized services.

We have suggested that police organization is militarylike in nature and influenced by the set of principles just discussed. This is particularly true of large urban police departments and often true of even the smaller ones. While smaller departments are less likely than large ones to employ principles like line and staff, they do not completely ignore them.

In 1967 the President's Commission on Law Enforcement presented a model of a well-organized police department.[16] Many of the principles above are reflected in this model, which represents not only the ideal in departmental organization but a general description of many existing police departments.

The general organizational structure presented by the commission can be viewed in the organization chart shown in Figure 4.1. It suggests a division into three bureaus: administration, operations, and services. The administration bureau performs staff functions such as planning, personnel, typing, and legal advice. The units within the operations bureau perform what we have earlier described as line functions. Included here are patrol, traffic, detective, juvenile, and vice personnel. Those units in the service bureau offer support to the line units in the nature of records and identification, data processing, communications, criminalistics, prisoner detention and care, and supply and maintenance.

Let us look a bit closer at the units within each of the bureaus. This will give us a good indication of how departments operate.

Operations Bureau There are generally five units or subdivisions within the operations bureau: patrol, traffic, detective, juvenile, and vice. We will consider each of these in turn.

Most observers agree that **patrol** is the most important unit in police service. Many refer to it as the backbone of the department. Patrol officers are on the streets performing a wide range of activities and services to the public: keeping watch to repress crime and disorder, controlling traffic and issuing traffic citations, rendering first aid to

FIGURE 4.1 Model Organization of a Modern Metropolitan Police Department

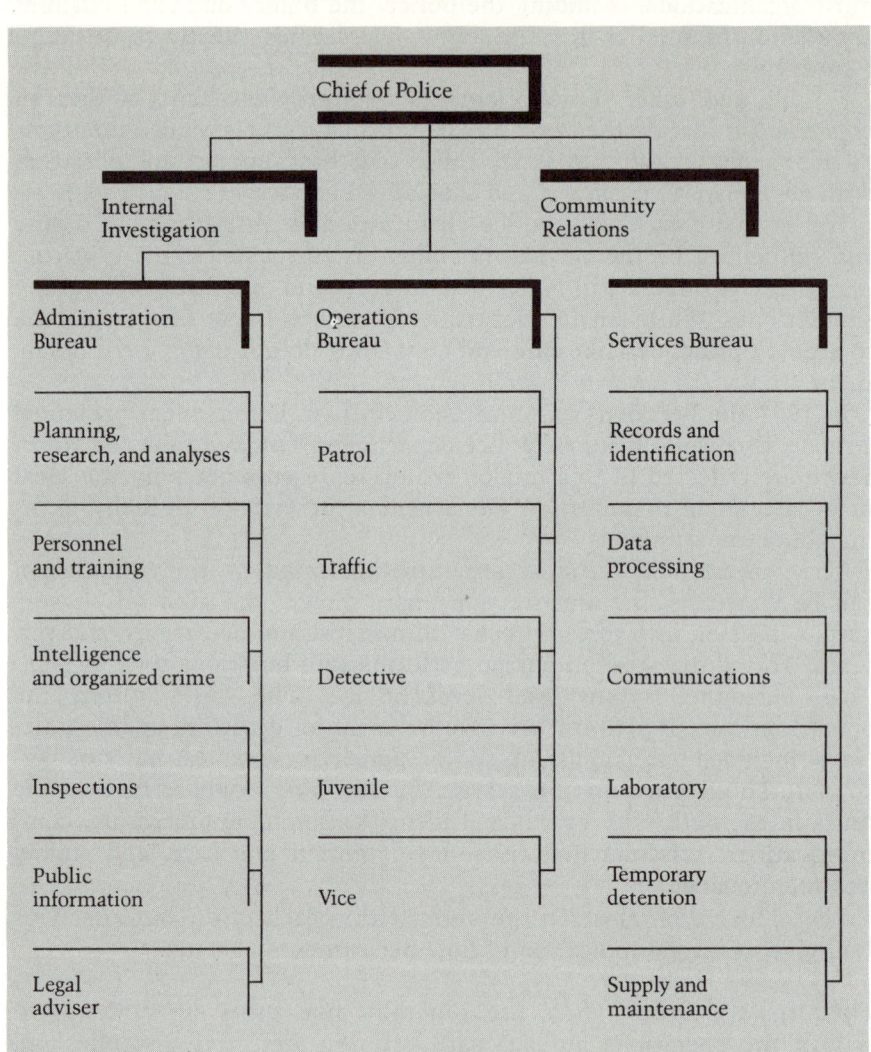

Source: President's Commission on Law Enforcement and Administration of Justice, *Task Force Report: The Police* (Washington, D.C.: Government Printing Office, 1967), p. 47.

victims of crimes or accidents, maintaining communications with citizens, gathering intelligence, searching for persons or property, investigating crimes, apprehending offenders, and processing evidence and reports.

Patrol was originally performed by men on foot, augmented in some places by a mounted patrol. Naturally as automobiles and other vehicles became available, they were utilized. Today a police department may employ aircraft, boats, motorcycles, or whatever other means are appropriate for the territory to be covered. Even observation of certain streets, plazas, parks, or other locations by closed-circuit television is a form of patrol.

Patrols are organized along two dimensions: geographic distribution and time.[17] The fundamental geographic unit is usually the **beat.** This is the area that one patrol officer or patrol unit is assigned to cover. Beats are constructed on the bases of area size, population density, area development (e.g., residential, business, industrial), and the area's potential for crime. Beats are generally organized into **sectors** for supervisory purposes, and, in the biggest cities, sectors are organized into **precincts.**

As for the dimension of time, the most common pattern involves **platoons** (bodies of officers) being assigned to each beat and each platoon covering a designated **shift** (time period). There are several ways of establishing shifts, and recent trends are toward overlapping coverage during periods of rush hour traffic and high rates of crime.

There are three styles of police patrol that may be employed. One is the **standard style** in which the patrollers cruise the area of their beat (to observe and be observed) and respond to calls for service. A second style used by some departments under some circumstances is the **aggressive patrol.** It involves concentrating a high number of officers and units within a beat or sector and utilizing field interrogation techniques. This means that persons are stopped, asked for their identification, and asked what they are doing in this place at this time. Suspicious persons are sometimes frisked—patted down for weapons or contraband. This style of patrol was used in San Francisco during the effort to apprehend the so-called zebra killers who had murdered persons on the streets for no apparent reasons. A third style involves no cruising at all, only responses to calls or alarms. It is called **reactive patrol.**

A recent study in Kansas City, Missouri, involved the selection of three areas of the city that were similar in most respects, including crime patterns. The three different patrol styles were applied in the different areas. The study found no significant difference between the three areas in crime trends.[18] The experiment, if repeated with similar results, could have very important implications for policing in the United States. Unfortunately, it has not been repeated in any other city.

It is generally agreed that whatever the patrol style, patrol officers spend little of their time and energy in crime-related activities. The duties of patrol officers regarding investigations of crime vary from department to department, but, in general, the patrol officer is said to engage in only "hot" investigations—that is, crimes that are occurring or have just occurred with the offender still in the vicinity. As a crime cools, and especially if identification of the offender is not immediately forthcoming, the patrol officer in most cities is generally expected to turn the matter over to investigators or detectives and return to the beat as soon as possible. In a few cities, though, patrol officers are also

Police may employ whatever means of patrol are appropriate for the territory to be covered.

investigators of some types of crime. In small cities and towns, for example, patrol officers must also do investigations because separate units are not available to do them.

Where *traffic units* exist, they have several specific functions to perform: expedition of traffic flow, enforcement of traffic laws, investigation of accidents, rendering of aid to accident victims and persons with automotive problems, and advisement of those persons and agencies responsible for traffic patterns and street planning. Activities in these areas consume a great deal of police time and resources, even though they are noncriminal in nature.

Backing up patrol and traffic officers in their enforcement functions is the *detective unit*. The men and women assigned to this unit are primarily concerned with the investigation of crimes, apprehension of suspects, and the preparation of cases for possible prosecution. Once an unsolved crime comes to their attention, detectives are generally expected to perform the tasks necessary to solve the crime. This involves examining evidence, interviewing victims, witnesses, and informants, comparing the modus operandi with those of other crimes, and contacting other agencies for information.

Recently a study of the investigative process, done by the California-based Rand Corporation, found that departments differed considerably in their division of the investigative function between officers assigned primarily to patrol and sworn personnel called detectives. The study also found that a number of big departments were trying out various innovations in the organization of their detectives. For example, some departments were assigning detective squads to each of the precincts or patrol sectors instead of keeping them all downtown. Some were using the **team-policing** concept in which patrol officers and detectives are assigned to work together within the same geographic units (for example, sectors, neighborhoods, or precincts). Others were allowing patrol officers to handle all investigations except the most serious or complex matters for which experts are required. And some were creating strike forces of patrol officers and detectives to work specific target crimes in selected areas.[19]

The men and women who work in the *juvenile units* with delinquents, or potential delinquents, spend most of their time trying to divert juveniles from a career in crime and its consequences — reform school or even prison. Counseling, sports activities, and other efforts are usually tried, but investigations leading to court hearings are performed where the crimes are serious or the juveniles are known repeaters.

The most controversial service in a police department is in the *vice unit*—the unit assigned to deal with such matters as prostitution, gambling, pornography, and sexual deviation. Vice units may also deal with drug abuse, or this particular function may be assigned to a narcotics and drug abuse unit. A considerable problem in this area is the presence of organized crime. It has not been uncommon for organized crime to attempt to corrupt police officers and deal harshly with those it could not sway. The difficulties of working vice and maintaining a normal life cause some departments to assign specially screened persons to this service for long periods and other departments to rotate officers through it as rapidly as possible.

Administration Bureau There are several units possible within the administration bureau of a police department. The planning, research and analysis unit, in the words of Felkenes, "conducts research of general policies and department operations, recommends improvements, prepares directives, updates rules and regulations, and prepares plans to carry out the objectives of the department."[20]

The personnel and training office recruits, tests, screens, and oversees the training of new personnel. It also evaluates the performance of all officers and employees. A training academy may be operated or supervised by this unit.

In the intelligence unit former detectives and other experts in information gathering and analysis obtain and sift through countless reports, files, and other pieces of information regarding the operations and behavior of persons and organizations thought or known to be connected with organized crime. There is rarely emphasis on producing large numbers of arrests or prosecutions. Instead the emphasis is on developing sizable and sophisticated cases against the most dangerous or important of organized crime figures.

The inspections unit may be called on to check the conditions of vehicles, arsenals, police stations, and the morale of officers. Depending on the department, inspections may include functions of evaluation and planning, communications, and crime reporting for the "Uniform Crime Reports."

The public information unit, the public relations arm of the department, gives out press releases, schedules news conferences, and generally tries to project a favorable image of the department.

An increasingly important person within the administrative department is the legal advisor, who participates in the training and briefings of officers, gives legal advice to the command structure, and sometimes guides the conduct of an especially important investigation.

Services Bureau In the services bureau there are also several units. The records and identification unit maintains case files and assists in the identification of persons or property. The data processing unit, with the aid of computers, stores and retrieves all sorts of information, both operational and administrative in nature.

The communications unit maintains communications among units and personnel within a department, between a department and other criminal justice agencies, and between a department and the public (from which come reports, complaints, and calls for service).

The laboratory or evidence technical unit analyzes physical evidence for purposes of solving a crime or developing a case for prosecution. The jail or detention unit houses and cares for persons awaiting disposition of their cases or those who may be serving short sentences for violations of city ordinances. The supply and maintenance unit provides a range of services, which include janitorial, mechanical (repair, etc.), and supply (paper, pencils, patrol cars, and other essential items).

Other Units Among the other units that exist in many departments are those engaged in **community relations** and **internal investigations.** The former has the function of seeking understanding, cooperation, and support from groups of citizens—especially minorities and juveniles who might be more hostile than other groups—and of running crime prevention and other service projects. The internal investigations unit investigates charges of police corruption, brutality, or other questionable practices. It may also stage routine investigations of all shootings or other uses of force that result in death or injury to citizens. It does so with a view of determining whether the behavior in question was justified or prosecutable. It may also forestall investigations of such behavior by outside, and potentially hostile, community groups. These two units may be located within a regular bureau or attached directly to the office of the chief.

Many innovative units are being developed by the larger departments across the United States. This would include fiscal or auditing units, special units such as SWAT (Special Weapons and Tactics), and investigative strike forces assigned to specific types of crime. The traditional pattern has been for new units to simply be added to the existing bureaucratic structure as the need for them becomes clear. More recently, however, administrators have begun to experiment with reorganization of bureaus and divisions.

Small Departments As most readers realize, the foregoing discussion relates generally to the larger police departments in the United States.

However, there are thousands of departments, perhaps over twenty thousand, which serve towns or villages with anywhere from one officer on up. The small departments cannot afford specialization on the part of their officers or much of anything other than patrol and routine investigative work. Most of these departments must rely on the cooperation and assistance of larger departments of nearby cities, on the office of the sheriff, or on state police agencies for communications, investigative, and other technical and administrative support functions. In many places today small departments are cooperating in joint ventures in communications, criminal investigation, and other specialized services. This cooperation is aimed at enabling small departments to maintain their separate identities (so important to many of them) and yet derive some benefit from modern technological and administrative improvements in police work.

The next decade may prove to be the most innovative in fifty years due to the combined influences of increasing crime rates, demands for planning and coordination among agencies, technological changes, and the increasing awareness of the whole systems approach to police work and criminal justice in general.

THE OFFICE OF SHERIFF

Few authors who write criminal justice texts discuss the office of sheriff in any detail, and many fail to mention it at all except in connection with the history of law enforcement. There is a tendency, therefore, to leave the impression that municipal police departments monopolize the law enforcement field at the local level. This is unfortunate, especially with respect to the southern and western regions of the United States. Throughout these regions, and in various other parts of the country, sheriff's offices provide the full range of law enforcement services. In many counties, small-town police departments depend on the sheriffs for investigative, technical, and administrative support. While there are states, especially in the Northeast, where the sheriff plays a relatively limited role in law enforcement and order maintenance, by and large the sheriff's department is a very important element of local police.

Historical Development

The office of sheriff is the oldest in the Anglo-American tradition of law enforcement.[21] In fact we must go back to the tenth century to find its origins. The Anglo-Saxons organized their communities into a hierarchy of interdependent units, with the largest ones known as "shires," entities roughly equivalent to our counties. To protect the king's interests and uphold the authority of the Crown, a royal officer called a "reeve" was sent to each shire. These "shire reeves" proved to be so valuable to the Crown that the Norman kings continued the office after their conquest of England. Under the Normans, shire reeves assumed broad powers over many matters in addition to criminal law enforcement. These included collection of taxes, seizures of property for tax nonpayment, and even some military affairs. From this height, however, the office was reduced in authority by subsequent regimes until it was eventually replaced by other law enforcement agencies.

In America the colonies adopted the English model of shire reeves. Virginia established county governments in 1634 and sheriffs became the primary law enforcement officers. The southern colonies, settled mostly by the English, followed Virginia's lead. Those colonies adopting the office of sheriff generally vested it with powers similar to those enjoyed by English sheriffs. These included the power to call able-bodied men into temporary service as deputies (power of *posse comitatus*—giving rise to the very familiar term "posse"), powers with respect to tax collection, such as seizure and auction of properties on which taxes were delinquent and mortgage foreclosures, and powers for the servicing of a broad range of legal papers.

After American independence was won, the sheriff became an elective official in virtually all counties in the United States. The powers of the office were not altered appreciably, but the sheriff became responsible to the voters of a county rather than to the governor or state legislature. It is very rare today for a sheriff to obtain that office other than through popular election by county residents.[22]

Today there are over three thousand sheriffs in the United States. Most are elected by their constituents to two- or four-year terms of office. In many states they are constitutional officers who, at least in theory, answer only to their constituents. The general rule, however, is that they are supervised to varying degrees by the attorney generals of their states. All sheriffs depend on other governmental bodies—usually a board of county commissioners or county council—for funds and facilities.[23]

Functions

It is very difficult to generalize about the functions of the sheriff's office in the United States since they vary widely from county to county and state to state.[24] In counties having large unincorporated areas—primarily those in the South and West—sheriffs are expected to perform all the police functions: law enforcement, order maintenance, crime prevention, and provision of general services. In New England, and some other states where towns and cities are contiguous, sheriffs' functions are generally limited.

Certain functions are common to virtually all sheriffs regardless of location. These functions are providing bailiff services to the courts in their counties and enforcing court orders, serving civil process on behalf of courts and other agencies, maintaining county jails, and providing custody, care, and transportation for county prisoners. These are the functions that even the smallest sheriffs' offices are expected to perform.

Depending on the state and county, the sheriff may be expected to act in any number of other capacities. Some of these additional roles may include acting as county coroner, collecting taxes, acting as public administrator, overseeing public highways and bridges, participating in civil defense planning, providing various rescue services, acting as county treasurer, certifying lists of prospective jurors, and selling confiscated and unclaimed property.

Organization

In general, the organization of the sheriff's office is like that of municipal police departments.[25] The military style of organization, with its hierarchy of rank, uniforms, and principles of organization, is prevalent. At the top of the hierarchy is the sheriff, followed in rank by an assistant sheriff (or under sheriff), chief deputy, captains, lieutenants, sergeants, and deputies. Some departments use other military titles such as major and corporal. Again, it must be noted that department size has much to do with the kind of organizational hierarchy that exists. Small departments may have only a sheriff and one or two deputies.

One major difference in organization between sheriffs' offices and municipal police departments stems from a greater emphasis by sheriffs on civil functions and operation of corrections facilities. There are often, for example, separate divisions or bureaus within sheriffs' departments for performing the civil function of process serving and for operating the county jail and caring for prisoners. Other than these, the units of sheriffs' departments are usually duplicates to those of like-sized police departments (patrol, traffic, investigative, juvenile, vice, evidence labs, communications, and administrative offices).

STATE LAW ENFORCEMENT AGENCIES

When we discussed law enforcement for the first time in Chapter 3, we made a distinction between generalist law enforcement agencies (e.g., police departments and sheriffs' offices), limited-area police (e.g., housing and transit police agencies), and specialist law enforcement agencies that limit their activities to specific crimes. At the state level we find agencies that fit into each of these three categories. Most states have a generalist police force known as **state police** or **highway patrol**; most states also have limited-area police to cover such specific areas as parks, university campuses, bridges, tunnels, and harbors. Almost all states have narcotics abuse and fish and game control agencies. Other activities important to the particular state—whether race tracks, food processing, mines, or lotteries—tend to result in the creation of departments to enforce the applicable laws. A few states also have equivalents to the Federal Bureau of Investigation. These agencies not only investigate crimes but offer skilled investigative services and technical support to other police departments in the state.

The importance of state law enforcement agencies, whether of the specialist or more generalist variety, is that they investigate crimes or suspected criminal activities, arrest people, and thus initiate the criminal justice process. In most states the cases developed by these agencies are handled by the same officials and through the same channels of prosecution and adjudication as are those cases produced by local law enforcement agencies and police departments.

Historical Development

As an aftermath of the revolt of Texans against Mexico, the provisional government of Texas formed the Texas Rangers, the forerunners of state police agencies (1835). In fact, the Rangers were a paramilitary organization sponsored by the new Republican government, and their original duties had more to do with defending the border and Texas cattle against Mexicans than with law enforcement in any general sense. However, the force evolved into a kind of state police following Texas's admission to the union and the Mexican War (1844–1845).

Arizona and New Mexico founded similar mounted-patrol organizations in 1901 and 1905, respectively. Pennsylvania created a state police in 1905, basically to defend mine owners' interests against strikers but also to provide the governor and local police agencies with general law enforcement support. Because organized labor saw state police as antilabor organizations, unions and others opposed the development of more state police agencies. Nevertheless, beginning with New Jersey in 1921, state after state formed agencies known variously as state police or state highway patrol. The highway patrols were, for the most part, primarily concerned with highway traffic and related crimes such as highjacking. Gradually, however, they have taken on broader law enforcement responsibilities and authority.[26]

Specialized law enforcement agencies at the state level also appeared in number, especially after World War I. Originally set up to enforce prohibition and other antivice laws, these agencies now cover a broad spectrum of activities: organized crime, corruption, fish and game conservation, and a variety of manufacturing, mining, agricultural, processing, and labor activities.

In recent years state police and patrol agencies have taken on increasing roles in direct law enforcement and in support of local police departments and sheriffs' offices. They provide assistance in such matters as criminalistics, criminal histories, data processing, specialized investigations, and other related matters.

Functions

As indicated, at the state level law enforcement agencies run the gamut from highly specialized bureaus and departments to generalist state police forces. The specialized agencies are assigned functions in keeping with the needs perceived by the state legislatures. Since the states vary so widely as to what specialized agencies they operate, the functions vary accordingly. In some states, for example, alcoholic beverage regulations are enforced by a single beverage-control agency. In other states a number of agencies may be involved. The regulation of alcohol distribution may be assigned to a division of the department of trade or commerce; tax stamp enforcement may be handled by a department of revenue; and the enforcement of criminal provisions regarding sale to minors and restrictions on alcohol consumption may be assigned to a police agency.

As for the more generalist state departments of law enforcement, they are designated either as a state police or as a state highway patrol. Norman Darwick has noted that "the factor which distinguishes state police from highway patrol organizations is their assigned responsibilities." While highway patrols are generally given functions related to motor vehicles, "state police responsibilities are broad, including activities in various fields of law enforcement."[27] In other words, while most highway patrols are partly specialist and partly generalist in nature, state police are more clearly generalist departments. Both types of agencies are expected to enforce the law, maintain order, and serve the public in numerous ways, but they differ as to the range of activities over which they have responsibilities.

Organization

Since the specialized law enforcement agencies of states vary considerably in their respective functions and sizes, and the states they serve differ greatly as to size and population, it is virtually impossible to generalize about their organizational patterns. One relatively consistent element seems to be the maintenance of branch offices throughout the states rather than the concentration of operations in one location. Most states are too large or have too many population centers to centralize everything in one office.

State police and highway patrols, as more generalist agencies, tend to favor decentralization not only of operations but of command as well. States are divided into troops, barracks, zones, posts, or regions, with each acting relatively independently of the other. This autonomy, of course, differs from state to state, but in most cases day-to-day operations appear to be conducted under decentralized supervision. In some states these regional commands are further divided into substations.[28]

A recent study of state police and highway patrols in the United States reveals that twenty-six states have highway patrol organizations while twenty three maintain state police. Hawaii is the only state with no statewide police department. In his study, Norman Darwick notes two organizational trends of recent years: "(1) State highway patrols are less often found as a subordinate agency within departments of motor vehicles or roads; (2) the practice of combining state police and highway patrol agencies under a superagency devoted to either public safety or transportation is growing."[29] He found that eleven of the twenty-six highway patrols were independent branches of the executive while the other fifteen were parts of larger departments of government.

A difference between the organizations of state police and highway patrols can be seen in the services each type of agency offers to local law enforcement agencies and the public. These are reflected in Table 4.1. It can be seen from this data that, in general, state police agencies are organized to provide more generalized services than are state highway patrols. The state police are involved in more phases of law enforcement and concerned with other than vehicle-related crimes.

TABLE 4.1 State Law Enforcement Agencies, by Services Offered

Service	State Police	Highway Patrols
Offender identification and or criminal histories	100	38
Detectives	95	15
Crime laboratory	91	42
Homicide and injury investigations	86	38
Felony investigations	95	46
Misdemeanor investigations	73	46
Expert testimony	95	65
Routine patrol	55	35

Source: Norman Darwick. "State Police and Highway Patrols," *The Book of the States, 1974–75* (Lexington, Ky. Council of State Governments, 1975), p. 421. Reprinted by permission.

FEDERAL LAW ENFORCEMENT

Law enforcement at the federal level is distinct from that of other levels in that it is almost exclusively specialized in nature. This means that most agencies have been created to enforce a variety of federal laws and play very limited roles in the more generalized functions of order maintenance and public service.

Recall that we have defined order maintenance in both specific terms (e.g., riot, traffic, and crowd control) and general terms (sustaining the social order against subversive elements). Only in the broadest sense is there federal involvement in order maintenance, and it is limited primarily to the Federal Bureau of Investigation. Order maintenance, from the more restricted view, has belonged, with few exceptions, to state and local agencies.

As for the function of providing services to the public, federal law enforcement agencies rarely engage in such activities. It is usually left to local police to rescue kitty from a tree and Johnny's finger from the sink and to rush expectant mommy to the hospital. Each federal law enforcement agency has been established for the purpose of enforcing specific laws related to a particular kind of activity. This is made clear by an examination of the most important of these agencies.

Department of Justice

The Department of Justice houses several of the most important law enforcement agencies at the federal level. They include the Federal Bureau of Investigation, the Drug Enforcement Administration, the United States Marshals, and the Immigration and Naturalization Service.

Federal Bureau of Investigation The biggest and best-known federal law enforcement agency in the United States is the Federal Bureau of Investigation. The Bureau, as it is called by its employees, has recently moved into its new headquarters in the J. Edgar Hoover Building, a $126 million edifice in Washington, D.C.[30] There are over nineteen thousand employees working for the FBI, of which over three thousand are special agents. There are fifty-nine district offices and hundreds of branch offices around the country, staffed by agents and support personnel. In 1975 the Bureau's budget was $450 million for salaries and expenses.[31]

The jurisdiction of the FBI covers a broad spectrum of federal crimes. Among the laws enforced by the Bureau are those concerning kidnapping, burglary and robbery of banks, violations of citizens' civil rights, assaults and killings of federal officers, espionage and sabotage by subversive elements, bribery of federal officials, and violations of antitrust and bankruptcy laws. The Bureau is also concerned with a wide range of interstate activities, such as shipments of illegal or stolen goods and vehicles, flights from justice, fraud by mail, and so-called white-slave traffic. The Bureau has broad law enforcement powers on Indian reservations and other federal properties, primary responsibility in the areas of organized crime, and also the protection of national security against subversive groups.[32]

In addition to enforcement duties, the FBI engages in a number of activities in support of local and state law enforcement. Among these support resources are a crime lab for analysis of evidence, the National Crime Information Center (with criminal histories of persons arrested throughout the United States) and the collection, collation, and publication of crime and arrest data, the "Uniform Crime Reports."[33]

The Bureau, despite some recent criticisms of certain questionable activities, is thought of by many as providing a model of professional law enforcement. This has been attributed largely to the efforts of its first and long-tenured director, J. Edgar Hoover. Director from 1924 to 1971, Hoover was undoubtedly one of the most powerful law enforcement officers in our history. Under Hoover the Bureau went from a very small organization to its current size and stature.

Despite the recognizable accomplishments of the Bureau under Hoover, recent times have seen the revelation of a number of questionable activities in which the agency has been engaged. These include attempts to subvert the power of the late Martin Luther King, a pattern of burglaries and other illegal acts against groups thought to be radical or subversive, and Hoover's practice of maintaining at his home highly sensitive dosiers on many prominent persons.[34] Congressional inquiries and news media investigations have kept the Bureau very much in the news and have tended to make it more controversial and less respected than at any time in its history. Whether its former prestige can be restored remains to be seen.

Drug Enforcement Administration The newest federal law enforcement agency is the Drug Enforcement Administration (DEA). The agency was created in 1973 through a merger of the old Bureau of Narcotics and Dangerous Drugs with other federal narcotics enforcement agencies.

The DEA has several functions. Its primary duties are to enforce federal laws related to illicit narcotic drugs and to cooperate with state and local agencies in the enforcement of state narcotics laws. There are some secondary functions performed by DEA: regulating the manufacture and flow of legal but controlled drugs; gathering intelligence on traffickers in illicit drugs; operating the National Training Institute for narcotics law enforcers from other agencies and countries, and running drug abuse prevention programs.[35]

A great deal of controversy has surrounded the agency. Most of it has resulted from the undercover nature of most of the enforcement efforts and the roughness of the raids made on dwellings of suspected drug traffickers. The raids are often performed by teams of DEA, FBI, local and state police agents. The agents are dressed in plain clothes and have been known to break doors and windows and roughly handle suspects found within the dwellings. This may often be a necessary approach when dealing with evidence as easily destroyed or disposed of as narcotics. In a few instances, however, the incorrect house was entered and innocent persons were subjected to a terrifying experience. Out of a few of these instances, considerable negative publicity and court suits have originated.

United States Marshals The oldest unit of federal law enforcement is that of the United States Marshal. Marshals were first appointed during the Washington administration after Congress created the positions in 1790. They have responsibility over all federal laws not specifically delegated to some other federal agency. Marshals execute the orders and directives of the federal courts and act as bailiffs for the courts. They are the process servers for the entire federal government, including congressional committees, and they are responsible for the

In addition to their other duties, U.S. Marshals serve as bailiffs for the federal courts.

custody, care, and transportation of federal prisoners and property under the courts' jurisdictions. Marshals are probably best known for their role during various federal-state confrontations over school integration and other civil rights matters.

The Executive Office for United States Marshals is headed by a chief marshal who supervises the various offices in each of the ninety-three federal court districts and coordinates the activities of the marshals with those of other agencies and other Justice Department divisions and bureaus. The chief marshal is directly responsible to the attorney general of the United States.[36]

Immigration and Naturalization Service Created in 1891, the Immigration and Naturalization Service (INS) has responsibility for all laws regarding smuggling and the admission, exclusion, deportation, and naturalization of aliens. The enforcement agents of this bureau make up the U.S. Border Patrol. In the area of smuggling, the Border Patrol agents work with those of the Bureau of Customs, a division of the Treasury Department. Border Patrol agents oversee all the ports and roads of entry into the United States and, as their name indicates, patrol the borders to prevent smuggling and illegal entries.

In addition to the enforcement bureaus listed above (FBI, DEA, INS) with their specialized fields, the Department of Justice has investigators assigned to special areas within the Criminal Division, including organized crime, fraud, and violations of federal regulatory acts.[37]

Department of the Treasury

A number of law enforcement functions are performed by bureaus within the Department of the Treasury. These include the Bureau of Alcohol, Tobacco, and Firearms, the Customs Service, the Secret Service, and the Internal Revenue Service (IRS).

Bureau of Alcohol, Tobacco, and Firearms The Bureau of Alcohol, Tobacco, and Firearms was created in 1972 with duties related to each of the commodities mentioned in its title. It also enforces laws regarding the sale, use, and shipment of explosives, and in 1974 it assumed responsibility for enforcement of the Federal Wagering Tax Law. The Bureau has divided its functions into criminal and administrative enforcement, with emphasis placed on the latter in the hopes of using the criminal approach as a last resort. This means that the bureau generally attempts to settle most disputes or complaints without resorting to criminal prosecution.[38]

Secret Service Probably the best known of the law enforcement agencies within the Department of Treasury is the Secret Service. Everyone knows the Secret Service protects the President of the United States and a number of other federal officials, presidential candidates, and persons designated by Congress. The original and primary purpose of the service, however, was—and is—the enforcement of federal laws related to counterfeiting of currency, securities, and coins.[39]

Customs Service Another agency within the Treasury Department is the Customs Service. It oversees the ports of entry into the United States to prevent smuggling and collects duties on goods being brought into the country. A primary area of concern for this agency is the illicit drug traffic into the United States. The service works closely with the Border Patrol of the Justice Department.[40]

Internal Revenue Service Intelligence Division Under the Commissioner of Internal Revenue is the IRS Intelligence Division. It enforces the federal tax and has the power to seize property and valuables of persons and businesses judged to be delinquent in tax payments or having committed fraud against the government. IRS Intelligence also cooperates closely with the FBI and other law enforcement agencies in investigations of criminal conspiracies of the white-collar and organized crime variety. Persons receiving payment or anything of value for illegal acts often fail to declare such illegal income and thus can be charged with tax evasion in addition to, or in lieu of, charges related to the criminal income-producing acts themselves.[41]

There are dozens of other federal agencies with various law enforcement powers and responsibilities located in several other cabinet-level departments and in the so-called independent regulatory agencies. But since the major functions of these other agencies are regulatory in nature rather than criminal, we will not go into them here. They fall outside our definition of law enforcement agencies.

It is obvious, however, that whether one includes these other agencies or not, there is a large and multifaceted federal law enforcement establishment operating out of Washington and from branch offices all over the country. The scope of authority and the role of these federal agencies in law enforcement continue to grow. While conflicts sometimes arise among the different levels of law enforcement, it is agreed that federal agencies generally complement police and law enforcement agencies of the states and local governments.

TEST YOURSELF

Define these key terms:
modus operandi
chain of command
line and staff
span of control
beat
reactive patrol

Answer the following questions:

1. Why are municipal police said to be the most "pervasive" of all law enforcement agencies?

2. What contribution is Robert Peel credited with making to law enforcement?

3. What are police departments expected to do beyond their strictly criminal-related functions? What are arguments for and against police having this additional function?

4. Write down at least three differences between most sheriffs' offices and municipal police departments.

5. Name two United States cabinet departments with law enforcement functions, and list three law enforcement bureaus or agencies within each.

NOTES

1. President's Commission on Law Enforcement and Administration of Justice, *Task Force Report: The Police* (Washington, D.C.: Government Printing Office, 1967), p. 7.
2. Department of Justice, *Criminal Justice Agencies in Region 1* (Washington, D.C.: Government Printing Office, 1974), p. 1. We have excluded coroners and medical examiners from these figures.
3. Department of Justice and Department of Commerce, *Expenditure and Employment Data for the Criminal Justice System, 1974* (Washington, D.C.: Government Printing Office, 1975), pp. 26 and 46.
4. This historical overview is based on several sources, including the President's Commission, *Task Force Report, Police,* pp. 3-7; The Royal Commission on the Police, *1962, Final Report* (London: Her Majesty's Stationery Office, 1968), pp. 9-20; Captain W. L. Melville Lee, *A History of Police in England, 1901* (Montclair, N.J.: Patterson Smith, 1971), esp. pp. 155-308; Patrick Pringle, *Hue and Cry, the Battle of the British Police* (London: Museum Press Limited, 1955); and Vern L. Folley, *American Law Enforcement* (Boston: Holbrook Press, 1973).
5. See George F. Cole, *The American System of Criminal Justice* (N. Scituate, Mass.: Duxbury Press, 1975), p. 165; Jerome H. Skolnick, *Justice Without Trial* (New York: Wiley, 1967), p. 6; and Thomas F. Adams, *Introduction to the Administration of Justice* (Englewood Cliffs, N.J.: Prentice-Hall, 1975), pp. 6-7.
6. Richard A. Myren, "The Role of the Police," in Harry W. More, ed., *Critical Issues in Law Enforcement* (Cincinnati, Ohio: Anderson, 1972), pp. 21-49.
7. Ibid.
8. George Eastman, ed., *Municipal Police Administration* (Washington, D.C.: International City Managers Association, 1969).
9. Jack E. Whitehouse, "Historical Perspectives on the Police Community Service Function," *Journal of Police Science and Administration* 1 (1973).
10. Thomas C. Bercal, "Calls for Police Assistance," in Harlan Hahn, ed., *Police in Urban Society* (Beverly Hills, Calif.: Sage, 1971), pp. 272-75; James Q. Wilson, *Varieties of Police Behavior* (Cambridge, Mass.: Harvard University Press, 1968), p. 18.
11. Myren, "Role of the Police," p. 31.
12. Bercal, "Calls for Police Assistance," pp. 274-75.
13. Ibid.
14. J. Norman Swaton and Loren Morgan, *Administration of Justice* (New York: Van Nostrand, 1975), p. 160.
15. See Jerry Wilson, *Police Report: A View of Law Enforcement* (Boston: Little, Brown, 1975), pp. 130-51; and O. W. Wilson and Ray C. McLaren, *Police Administration,* 3d ed. (New York: McGraw-Hill, 1972), pp. 59-72.
16. President's Commission, *Task Force Report: Police,* p. 47.
17. For a full discussion of patrol design, see Paul M. Whisenand and James L. Cline, *Patrol Operations* (Englewood Cliffs, N.J.: Prentice-Hall, 1971), pp. 10-17.

18. George L. Kelling and Tony Pate, *The Kansas City Patrol Experiment: Summary Report* (Washington, D.C.: Police Foundation, 1974).
19. Peter W. Greenwood and Joan Petersilia, *The Criminal Investigation Process*, vol. III, *Observations and Analysis* (Santa Monica, Calif.: Rand Corporation, 1975), pp. 19-25.
20. George T. Felkenes, *The Criminal Justice System* (Englewood Cliffs, N.J.: Prentice-Hall, 1973), p. 26.
21. For treatments of the origins and development of the office of sheriff, see Folley, *American Law Enforcement*, pp. 31-33 and 41-42; Lee, *Police in England*, pp. 1-8, 13-18, 34-43, and 43-46; Frank R. Prassel, *The Western Peace Officer, A Legacy of Law and Order* (Norman, Okla.: University of Oklahoma Press, 1972), pp. 94-125; and Bruce Smith, *The State Police (1925)* (Montclair, N.J.: Patterson Smith, 1969), pp. 15-19 and 26-27.
22. Department of Justice, *Criminal Justice Agencies in Regions 1 through 10*.
23. Felkenes, *Criminal Justice System*, p. 55.
24. Ibid., p. 56. See also Adams, *Administration of Justice*, p. 124; and A. C. Germann, F. Day, and Robert R. J. Gallati, *Introduction to Law Enforcement and Criminal Justice* (Springfield, Ill.: Thomas, 1968), p. 126.
25. Felkenes, *Criminal Justice System*, pp. 60-63.
26. Smith, *State Police*, esp. pp. 36-42 and 54-65.
27. Norman Darwick, "State Police and Highway Patrols," *The Book of the States: 1974-75* (Lexington, Ky.: Council of State Governments, 1975), p. 420.
28. Felkenes, *Criminal Justice System*, p. 42.
29. Darwick, "State Police and Highway Patrols," p. 419.
30. "126 Million Dollar Fortress," *U.S. News and World Report*, 6 October 1975, pp. 58-59.
31. Executive Office of the President, Office of Management and Budget, *The Budget of the United States Government: Fiscal Year 1977* (Washington, D.C.: Government Printing Office, 1976), app. p. 835.
32. General Services Administration, National Archives and Record Service, *U.S. Government Manual: 1975/76* (Washington, D.C.: Government Printing Office, 1975), p. 316.
33. Adams, *Administration of Justice*, p. 141.
34. See "The FBI's 'Black Bag Boys'," *Newsweek*, 28 July, 1975, p. 18; "FBI Tried to Kill Rev. King's Reputation," *New York Times*, 23 November, 1975, Section 4, p. 1.; "As Charges Mount Against the FBI," *U.S. News and World Report*, 5 April, 1976, p. 30; "FBI Sought Doom for Panther Party," *New York Times*, 9 May, 1976, pp. 1 and 20; and "The FBI Was Not as Advertised and Won't Ever Be the Same," *New York Times*, 1 August, 1976, Section 4, p. 4.
35. *Government Manual*, p. 321; and Neil Chamelin, Vernon Fox, and Paul Whisenand, *Introduction to Criminal Justice* (Englewood Cliffs, N.J.: Prentice-Hall, 1975), pp. 15 and 44-47.
36. *Government Manual*, p. 319.
37. Ibid., pp. 319-21.
38. Ibid., pp. 408-9.
39. Ibid., p. 407.
40. Ibid., pp. 398-400.
41. Ibid.

CHAPTER 5
Law Enforcement Processes

OUTLINE

POLICE AUTHORITY
- Arrest
- Search and Seizure

CRIME DETECTION
- Methods of Crime Detection and Crime Stages
  - Direct Observation by Patrol Officers
  - Calls, Complaints, or Alarms
  - Response Time
- Steps Taken by Patrol
  - Preliminary Investigations
  - Field Interrogation
- Proactive Crime Detection
  - Undercover Agents
  - Confidential Informants
  - Electronic Eavesdropping

CRIME INVESTIGATION
- Investigative Functions
- Preliminary Investigations
- Follow-up Investigations
  - Custodial Interrogation
  - Use of Physical Evidence
  - Use of Confidential Informants
- How Crimes Are Solved

CASE PREPARATION
- Crimes Cleared Versus Prosecutable Cases
- Investigative Thoroughness and Case Disposition
- New Emphasis on Case Preparation

THE ENVIRONMENT OF LAW ENFORCEMENT
- Organizational and Individual Behavior
  - Police Styles
  - Individual Behavior and Discretion
- Internal Influences on Departmental Behavior
- External Environmental Influences on Departmental Behavior
  - Physical Environment
  - Community Influences
  - Governmental Influences
  - Impact of Other Criminal Justice Agencies
- Environmental Influences on Individual Behavior

OBJECTIVES

After reading this chapter the student should be able to:

Describe police authority to arrest under various conditions.

Describe police authority to perform searches and seizures.

Discuss the various means of crime detection.

Outline and describe the steps taken by patrol units following a crime.

Discuss the controversies surrounding the uses of aggressive patrol, undercover agents, and confidential informants.

Describe the functions of crime investigation and the types of investigation.

State the major findings of the Rand Corporation, which sponsored the study of investigation and case preparation.

Discuss the different styles of police department behavior.

Explain how the behavior of individual officers can be seen as the making of police department policy.

Explain how the physical environment, the community, and the government each have an impact on police behavior.

List the various forms that governmental influences take and describe the areas of police concern upon which they have an impact.

Explain what is meant by "police culture" and how it affects individual police officers.

KEY TERMS

probable cause
arrest warrant
citation
summons
search warrant
frisk or pat down
proactive crime detection
 measures
response time
hot, warm, and cold searches
preliminary investigation
field interrogation
vice crimes
undercover agents
entrapment
confidential informants (CI)
electronic bug
in-custody investigations
follow-up investigations
custodial interrogation
fence
burning a CI
case preparation
police styles
watchman style
legalistic style
service style
counselor-enforcer model
police discretion
internal environmental influences
external environmental
 influences
formal environmental influences
informal environmental
 influences
working personality
police culture

☐ It would appear that the great variety of law enforcement agencies discussed in Chapter 4 would make it very difficult to generalize about law enforcement processes. If we were to lump together the generalist and specialist agencies at all levels, it might be an impossible task. It will be simplified to some extent by focusing on local police (including sheriffs' departments) since, as we have already indicated, they provide the vast majority of law enforcement services to the public. Despite huge disparities in size, these local departments have much in common in their generalist character.

In discussing the police process the focus will be on the steps related to the function of law enforcement, though it is clear that certain activities serve order maintenance or public service functions at the same time. Recall that there are four subfunctions related to the law enforcement function. They are crime detection, crime investigation, apprehension of suspects, and preparation of evidence and cases for prosecution.

POLICE AUTHORITY

To understand the activities of police, it is necessary to examine briefly the legal authority upon which they are based. Specifically, police have legal authority to arrest persons and place them in custody pending court action, to perform legal searches, and to seize evidence for use in court.

Police are required to have **probable cause** to exercise their authority to perform arrests or searches. J. Shane Creamer asserts that any "law enforcement officer who does not thoroughly understand the standard of probable cause is in the unenviable position of a man who doesn't know what he is doing." He then discusses the definitions of the term:

> *Probable cause for an arrest is defined as a combination of facts or apparent facts, viewed through the eyes of an experienced police officer, which would lead a man of reasonable caution to believe that a crime is being or has been committed. Probable cause for the issuance of a search warrant is defined as facts or apparent facts viewed through the eyes of an experienced police officer which would lead a man of reasonable caution to believe that there is something connected with a violation of law on the premises to be searched.*[1]

Arrest

The authority to arrest is the authority to seize a person and take him or her into custody of the law. Arrest authority is granted in laws which invariably make two sets of distinctions: between arrests performed with a warrant and those performed without and between arrests on felony charges and those on misdemeanor violations.

The power to perform an arrest without a warrant is related to the type of crime involved. Police may arrest without a warrant any person whom they have reasonable or probable cause to believe has committed a felony crime. In most places a warrantless arrest for a misdemeanor charge may occur only if the police believe it was committed in their presence. Where this is true, it means that police may not arrest someone for a misdemeanor simply on the complaint of a citizen; they must get an arrest warrant or have witnessed the offense themselves.

If police do not have sufficient probable cause to perform a lawful arrest on their own authority, they must get an **arrest warrant** from a magistrate or judge. The judge will review a complaint—perhaps even look at some evidence or listen to some testimony—and decide if there is sufficient probable cause to grant the warrant. Arrest warrants are used in some felony cases but are used more frequently in misdemeanor situations where police arrest authority is more limited.[2]

Brief mention should be made of the fact that persons may be brought to justice for misdemeanors without ever being arrested. In many instances of misdemeanor violations, police may issue a **citation** to the suspect, which calls upon the person to appear before a judge or waive appearance and pay a specified fine. This is done in the vast majority of traffic violations, for example. The person may thus avoid being detained or even making a court appearance. Another possibility is the issuance of a **summons** to appear. These are issued by judges or other magistrates for misdemeanor violations upon the complaint of citizens or police officers. They require a court appearance but no detention. Persons who fail to respond to citations or summons, however, may find themselves arrested under a warrant issued by the court.

Search and Seizure

Almost as important as the authority to arrest (seize persons) is the authority to perform searches and to seize evidence. Like arrests, searches may be performed with or without court-issued **search warrants.** Warrants, however, are advisable in all but a few situations where speed is of the essence.

To obtain a search warrant from a magistrate, law enforcement agencies must supply the address or description of the place or vehicle to be searched, the time of the search, the crime or activities being investigated, and the things to be seized. Search warrants are issued when the magistrate has probable cause to believe the evidence sought is related to criminal activity. Such warrants are required for any search of a residence, business property, or person when it is not performed in connection with a legal arrest; and for thorough searches of premises even when an arrest is being made at the same time, or with the express consent of the resident.

Warrantless searches are allowed following a lawful arrest of a person as long as they are limited to the person and the immediate vicinity. In other words, if someone is arrested in his or her home, even on an arrest warrant, the entire home may not legally be searched without a separate search warrant.

A gray area of the law relates to the **pat downs,** or **frisks,** of persons acting suspiciously or fitting the description of persons being sought by police. In general, a suspicious person may be stopped on the street. If the officers fear for their safety or believe a crime is in the offing, they may detain, question, and frisk but not thoroughly search. More will be said about this shortly.

Appellate courts have been struggling with cases involving search and seizure for years, but police practices at the local and state level were generally unaffected by federal rulings until 1961. In *Mapp* v. *Ohio*, decided that year, the Supreme Court ruled that evidence seized illegally—without warrants or not following lawful arrest—must be excluded from any trial of the persons involved.[3] Since then numerous decisions have dealt with whether specific searches were legal or not and whether specific questionable evidence could be used for purposes other than as admissible trial evidence. In 1975, for example, the Supreme Court ruled that grand juries may consider illegally seized evidence in deciding whether or not to indict.[4] Thus the so-called exclusionary rule has not rendered all dubious searches entirely useless to police.

Some observers point out that police sometimes stretch their authority by arresting persons or performing searches they know will not result in prosecutable cases. Some police have been known to seize weapons, drugs, or other contraband for the purpose of denying persons the use of these things. Persons have also been taken into custody for the purpose of keeping them out of circulation and thus eliminating the offenses they commit. The most common examples of these questionable arrests are the arrests of drunks, prostitutes, petty gamblers, sexual deviates, and others who are considered public nuisances.[5] On the other hand, police may refrain from making legally supportable arrests or searches if they believe the public or their superiors frown on the full enforcement of certain laws. Ironically, prostitutes, drunks, and gamblers may be the beneficiaries of underenforcement in these instances. Police enjoy considerable discretion in the exercise of their authority, which may be stretched — or even abused — by some officers.

CRIME DETECTION

In discussing the law enforcement process, we will refer to several aspects: methods of crime detection, the stage a crime is in when it is observed by police, the steps taken by patrol officers at a crime scene, and the steps taken by investigators or detectives.

Methods of Crime Detection and Crime Stages

There are several ways in which crimes come to the attention of police:

1. receipt of citizen complaints or calls for assistance, whether by telephone, visits to police headquarters, or the approaching of officers in the field
2. receipt of signals from alarm devices, whether a loud racket heard by patrol officers or a silent alarm whose transmitted signal is received in the communications unit of the department
3. observations by officers on patrol of suspicious behavior, a crime in progress, or the aftermath of a crime, such as a ransacked store or the body of a homicide victim
4. observation of the planning or execution of crimes by **proactive measures** — measures through which police seek to detect crimes, or attempt to be present when they are committed, through the use of such means as undercover agents, electronic devices for wiretapping or bugging, or stakeouts

The first three of these methods involve the patrol officers. The proactive measures usually involve other sworn personnel such as vice agents or detectives but can involve patrol officers in special roles. An example of the use of patrol officers in this manner is the stakeout of a store or other location likely to be the scene of a crime.

Direct Observation by Patrol Officers It is obvious that the most effective means of crime detection is that of direct observation of the crime by patrol officers. When police happen upon a crime in preparation or progress, they have the best opportunity to capture the offend-

Direct observation of crime by patrol officers offers the best opportunities for capture, prosecution, and conviction of suspects.

ers red-handed. Direct observation also establishes the most favorable situation for prosecution and conviction of culprits in subsequent stages of the criminal process. Unfortunately, such occurrences are relatively rare.

When police discover the effects or aftermath of a crime—a body, a ransacked business, a stolen vehicle stripped and abandoned in an alley—the likelihood of solving the crime and capturing suspects declines sharply, especially if there are not witnesses immediately available at the crime scene. The steps taken by patrol officers in this situation are similar to those taken following a response to citizens' calls or alarms, and arrival at the scene of a crime following its occurrence.

Calls, Complaints, or Alarms By far the most common means by which crimes come to police attention is by citizens' calls or complaints. Calls may occur while a crime is in progress, immediately after, or long after the completion of a crime. Operators receiving citizens' calls must screen them to determine the nature of the crime (if any), the stage it is in, and the address or site of the crime. A judgment must be made as to whether immediate response is required and what level the response should be (e.g., how many units should be sent in).

A completed property crime (burglary, larceny, fraud, and so on) does not usually require or receive an emergency type of response. A violent crime will, however, receive prompt action, and so will any crime that appears to be still in progress.

When an alarm is received by the communications center, or when a bell or siren alarm is heard by patrol officers, it may mean a crime is in progress, and police respond as rapidly as possible. There are false alarms, of course, and there are skillful criminals who can prevent alarms from being triggered.

Response Time When dealing with crimes detected by calls or alarms, a key element in whether the crime will be solved and the culprit caught may be the time that elapses between receipt of the call or alarm and the arrival of patrol units at the crime scene. This is known as **response time,** and the shorter it is, the better.

A study performed in Los Angeles found that the average response time for incidents resulting in arrests of suspects was 4.1 minutes, while the average for incidents in which no arrest was made was 6.3 minutes.[6] The National Advisory Commission on Criminal Justice Standards and Goals notes that FBI studies found a definite relationship between response time and clearance rates: the longer the time, the fewer the clearances. (Recall that crimes cleared are crimes for which persons are arrested or the culprit known but not arrested for the crime in question.) The FBI reported that two-thirds of crimes involving response time of 2 minutes or less are solved, while a response time of 5 minutes or longer reduces the rate to one out of five.[7]

Steps Taken by Patrol

If the response time of police is short enough and the culprit is still at or near the scene, then the arrival at the scene or a **hot search** of the immediate vicinity may result in apprehension. If this is not the situation, warm or cold searches may be necessary. **Warm searches** are those in the general vicinity of the crime—an area ranging from the neighborhood to the entire city, depending on the nature of the crime and the mode of transportation being used by the suspected culprits. If this warm search turns up a suspect, the need for a cold search is bypassed. The **cold search** is one in which investigators other than the patrol officers—usually detectives—are called in. If the crime is serious enough—homicide, armed robbery with injuries, a bank robbery—the patrol officers will secure that scene and locate as many witnesses as possible until the detectives arrive.[8]

Preliminary Investigations The duties of patrol officers at a crime scene have been described as involving both direct action and investigative functions. The Chicago Police Department created an anagram to help depict the steps to be taken during a **preliminary investigation,** at the crime scene, with allowances, of course, for the type of crime and other circumstances:

P   Proceed to the scene with safety and dispatch
R   Render assistance to the injured
E   Effect the arrest of the perpetrator
L   Locate and identify witnesses
I   Interview complainant and witnesses
M Maintain **the scene and protect evidence**
I   Interrogate suspects
N   Note all conditions, events, and remarks
A   Arrange for collection of evidence
R   Report the incident fully and accurately
Y   Yield responsibility to detectives[9]

Whether suspects are apprehended or not, the actions taken by patrol officers and their preliminary investigation and report are crucial since the crime conditions will never be completely re-created. Many departments emphasize the use and development of investigative skills by patrol officers for reasons of efficiency, as well as for detective training. Some departments have patrol officers conduct all investigative steps in all but the most serious or complicated cases.

It should be pointed out that even when detectives are assigned to cases, this does not mean that patrol officers no longer have any responsibility regarding the crime in question. In motor vehicle thefts, for example, police routinely check license plates or other descriptive material regarding suspicious vehicles or vehicles stopped for routine traffic violations. If the check results in a "hit" (matches information in a master file of stolen vehicles), the driver or person in possession of the vehicle is also checked out. An arrest will likely follow if police have probable cause to believe he or she is the thief.

Field Interrogation Before leaving the roles of patrol officers in detecting, responding to, and investigating crimes, some discussion should be given to the subject of **field interrogation.** In this process suspicious persons are stopped and asked to identify themselves. Under certain circumstances they may be asked questions relating to their current residence, occupation, and reasons for being in the area at the time of the contact. Such an interrogation may then lead to a frisking or patting down of the individual if the officer has good reason to believe he is in danger or a crime is about to be committed. If such a rudimentary and limited search does turn up incriminating evidence of past or potential criminal activities, probable cause then exists for the person to be arrested and thoroughly searched. This procedure was given legal approval by the Supreme Court in 1968. The Court said that in order to conduct the frisk, the police officer must have reason to "conclude in the light of his experience that criminal activity may be afoot," that the person may be "armed and presently dangerous," and that this "reasonable fear" remains after the officer identifies himself and makes "reasonable inquiries."[10] In a 1973 case the Court provided a different avenue of approach: If police have initial probable cause to believe they are confronting a criminal suspect, they may arrest first then conduct a full search of the person arrested (not just a frisk) as a follow-up to the arrest.[11]

Under some conditions police are ordered to conduct field interrogations of broad numbers of persons in an area, especially after a very serious crime or a series of serious crimes. This is usually done in association with the aggressive patrol, the concentration in an area of an unusually high number of patrol units. In San Francisco, Mayor Allioto ordered police to combine these tactics in parts of the city following a series of apparently random killing of whites by a gang of militant blacks (so-called zebra killings). The police were ordered to stop and interrogate all young black males who generally fit descriptions of the killers. Since many young men were being repeatedly questioned and the effort was confined to black neighborhoods, a judge ordered it stopped. Suspects were later arrested following more routine investigation.[12]

A major objection to field interrogations and occasional frisks has been that they are forms of harassment that police direct primarily at minorities and young persons. It is also frequently suggested that widespread use of such tactics does not create good police-community relations. Police argue, on the other hand, that such tactics are effective in suppressing crime and in solving crimes already committed that have grown cold. Some studies have been conducted to determine whether field interrogations are an effective crime-fighting technique. In Oakland, California, it was determined that the tactic was rarely used for investigative purposes and that it was of little value in solving crimes.[13] A study by the American Bar Foundation discovered that of 8400 such field contacts made by the Milwaukee police, only one person was arrested.[14] While these studies question the real value of field interrogations, many departments nevertheless make a practice of using the tactic regularly.

Proactive Crime Detection

There are tactics used by police that are often as controversial as field interrogations but are of a somewhat different character than other efforts to detect crime and apprehend offenders. These tactics include the use of undercover agents, confidential informers (known as "CIs"), and various electronic techniques for overhearing and recording conversations of suspects. Not only are these tactics different from the others, they are most commonly used on crimes of **vice.** These are the crimes of gambling, prostitution, pornography, drug trafficking, and abuse—the so-called victimless crimes. Such tactics are also used to try to uncover criminal conspiracies of various types: those engaged in by organized crime, those involving embezzlements, frauds, and other white-collar crimes, and those in the realm of violence-prone political activism.

A factor that all these criminal activities have in common is the relative lack of victims who are conscious of their victimization or who can identify the perpetrators. In the absence of citizens' calls, alarms, or the ability of street police to see the crimes, police have been forced to resort to various means to get inside the criminal operation so they can witness a crime or gather evidence. Undercover agents and CIs have been two such means.

Undercover Agents **Undercover agents** are, of course, police officers who take on the appearance and demeanor of the people they are trying to bust. They try to win the confidence of the suspects so that they can be present when the criminal activity occurs.[15] If it involves drugs, they want to be there when the deal goes through. To assure their presence and their ability to arrest offenders at the time of the crime, agents often arrange for the deal to be made at a time and place convenient to the police department. In such situations agents may provide the materials to be sold (drugs, weapons, or contraband), do the buying themselves, or a combination of both.

This practice gives rise to situations in which **entrapment** can be charged to police. Entrapment is illegal and results when police cause the crime to be committed rather than simply arrange for their presence when it occurs. In a recent case the Supreme Court ruled that it was not entrapment for an agent to supply drugs to a suspected dealer and then for another agent to act as buyer when there was reason to believe the suspect was "predisposed" (inclined) to commit the crime anyway.[16] This ruling was met with cheers from police—and jeers from civil libertarians, who wondered how courts could determine whether suspects had been inclined to criminality prior to such busts.

Confidential Informants Related to the use of undercover agents is the use of **confidential informants (CI).** These are citizens who provide information to police in return for some favors. CIs not only provide information regarding the activities of all sorts of suspects, they are sometimes recruited as amateur undercover agents when it is convenient to police or when department agents cannot penetrate the group under suspicion.

The problems with CIs are said to be several. For one thing, they are often lawbreakers themselves—prostitutes, drug abusers, and the like—whom the police allow to remain on the street in return for their help. For another thing, the information provided by the CIs is not always reliable. To stay out of trouble, they have been known to inform on persons who are less criminal or certainly no worse than themselves. The result may be that some who should be prosecuted are given a sort of license to commit further small crimes.

Police argue that the use of CIs, and even tolerance of their crimes, is a necessary price to pay for being able to get at the big criminal—the drug wholesaler, the prostitute's pimp, or the leader of a gang of thieves. Many critics, however, contend that the big criminals usually manage to avoid capture, prosecution, or conviction anyway.[17]

Electronic Eavesdropping Electronic eavesdropping is used less often than other techniques and is usually conducted with search warrants issued by courts. As an evidence-gathering device, the eavesdropping method has been ruled to constitute searches subject to Fourth Amendment rules. Warrants must be obtained using the process we discussed earlier. It is not unusual, however, for police to bug or tap a suspected premise for the purpose of developing leads to other evidence or to gain knowledge of the identities of suspects so that they can be investigated by other means. If the use of such tactics is discovered, any evidence thus developed is barred from use in trials.

Often used in electronic surveillance is a combination of an undercover agent or CI with a **bug.** The agent or informant wears a radio or recording device, and any conversation incriminating the other party is acceptable in court. This is because the suspect is talking willingly to a party who is aware the conversation is overheard.[18]

What we have called proactive tactics of detection are quite often controversial, but police use them to detect crimes they would otherwise not know about and to apprehend offenders they would otherwise not be able to arrest. In the view of most police officials, these are reasons enough for using them, whether certain segments of the community like them or not.

CRIME INVESTIGATION

We have indicated that the law enforcement process includes four steps: detection, apprehension of suspects, investigation, and case preparation. While detection and apprehension occur at specific points in time, investigation and case preparation are steps that consist of several tasks and occur over a period of time. Investigations can be very simple, as in the case of a burglar caught red-handed with stolen goods, or they can be exceedingly complex, as in the case of developing evidence that will prove that a particular person gave the orders for a string of gangland-style executions.

Investigative Functions

Whatever the ease or complexity of investigations of crimes, police officials cite three purposes or functions that they serve:

1. the identification and apprehension of suspects
2. the conviction of defendants
3. the satisfaction of the victim's demand for police attention[19]

While the first two goals seem obvious enough, the third requires some clarification. A study of investigative processes sponsored by the Rand Corporation found that the function of public satisfaction was very important to police departments and that some tasks—especially the search for fingerprints at a crime scene—are performed as much for reasons of appearance as for their likely contribution to crime solving.[20]

As public agencies dependent on the positive support of cititzens, police departments not only engage in activities unrelated to crime (or disorder) but also select certain types of crimes for investigative attention and perform investigative tasks that are questionable from the standpoint of crime-solving effectiveness. Kalmanoff cites studies that show that police use considerable discretion in determining which crimes deserve time and effort, and that this discretion is as often based on social and political considerations as it is on the solvability of the crimes. He notes, for example, that "crimes considered 'typical' of lower class or ethnic communities" are less likely to get attention than those committed against "established" citizens.[21]

The National Advisory Commission on Criminal Justice Standards and Goals urges police departments to establish "a priority of investigations" but acknowledges that each agency "should consider community problems and attitudes as well as its own resources" in deciding which crimes will receive each level of attention.[22] The commission urges, however, that the priorities be stated as public policy rather than being kept as internal secrets. Obviously discriminatory priorities would not be acceptable to the community. Some police officials wonder whether any method of defining priorities would work since taxpayers tend to demand attention to even the most trivial offenses.

Before continuing with a discussion of criminal investigations, let us recall that there are essentially two types: in-custody investigations and investigations of unsolved crimes. **In-custody investigations** follow the apprehension of suspects. Their purpose is to determine whether the suspect actually committed a crime and whether he or she can assist police in solving crimes that may have been committed by others known to the suspect. Investigations of unsolved crimes are, of course, for the purpose of identifying and capturing suspects.

Apart from types of investigations, there is the breakdown of the investigative process into its two stages: the preliminary investigation and the follow-up investigation.

Preliminary Investigations

We have already mentioned the role of patrol officers in the conduct of the preliminary investigation and the importance of that role. We have also pointed out that in some crimes evidence technicians and even detectives are called to the scene. A study of criminal investigative processes by the Rand Corporation has found that a few departments routinely dispatch detectives with patrol units, while most follow the traditional pattern of assigning detectives to a case only after the patrol unit has filed its report.

Assuming that a suspect has not been caught, the Rand report notes, the initial-incident report filed by patrol officers "usually contains the basic facts of the crime, the identity of the victim, a description of the suspect, and the identity and location of any potential witnesses, as well as a description of the crime scene and any pertinent statements by witnesses or the victim."[23] The only variation an apprehension would make in the list above would be the identity and address of the suspect.

The study points out that patrol units are generally "under considerable pressure to cut short their investigation and get back on patrol." Depending on departmental policy regarding the investigative role of patrol units and the training of patrol officers in the performance of investigative tasks, the incident report "will be something between a cryptic incident report providing only the essential facts of the case and a complete preliminary report of all pertinent information available at the time the patrolman responded, with most departments tending toward the former."[24] Even if a suspect is in custody, overly cryptic reports damage the effectiveness of the department, since case preparation depends on completeness of information about the crime.

The National Advisory Commission on Criminal Justice Standards and Goals has urged that patrol officers receive "adequate training as criminal investigators." It also has suggested that patrol units should remain at the scene of a crime until further expenditure of time "seems unlikely to produce additional benefits." The commission has emphasized the importance of investigative specialists to proper preliminary investigations of very serious or complex crimes. In these cases, the commission states, "the uniformed officers should protect the scene from contamination and request a specialist at once."[25]

Follow-up Investigations

Follow-up investigations are those conducted by detectives or other investigative specialists after the initial investigation is complete. Investigators may be called to the scene of the crime or receive the incident report the first working morning following the crime. The Rand study found that apart from in-custody situations, cases assigned to an investigator tend to fall into three categories: (1) those in which the next steps are obvious because a suspect's name, address, or license plate number are provided or because witnesses are named who were not interviewed by the patrol officers; (2) those involving serious or notorious crimes or influential victims; and (3) those that appear to be unsolvable because of a lack of leads and the routineness of the crime committed. Detectives tend to take new cases in just this order of priority.[26]

According to some observers, detectives subscribe to certain myths about their roles as crime solvers. Some of these myths persist from earlier times when they constituted an elite force operating with fewer constrictions. Some myths are generated and sustained by popular media images of crafty and persistent trackers of criminals.[27] The fact is that most detective work consists of routine, uninspiring clerical tasks and that very few crimes are solved by the sorts of activities Kojak, McGarrett, or Baretta engage in week after week. Let us look at some of the tasks performed by investigators and detectives.

Custodial Interrogation Detectives place a good deal of importance on the task of interrogating suspects in custody—that is, **custodial interrogation.** They have been generally critical of the Supreme Court for restricting the use of interrogations and for requiring the *Miranda* warning to be given to all suspects.[28] We have heard officers describe examples of how some cases were solved through interrogation of suspects held in custody and have heard discussions of some tactics employed in interrogation. A common tactic is the "Mutt and Jeff" routine in which one officer acts as though he is about to tear the suspect apart in his righteous anger and the other officer alternately holds him off and pleads with the suspect to talk so he will not get hurt. Another tactic has been labeled the "God bit." This involves suddenly dropping into the conversation a discussion of whether the suspect believes in God, followed by the officer's plea with the suspect to pray with him for a solution to the crime and redemption for the offender.

Some studies suggest police may have an inflated notion of the importance of interrogation as an investigative tool, although no thorough nationwide analysis has been done and the matter was not touched on by the Rand study. One California city's police case files were examined for data on pre-*Miranda* and post-*Miranda* interrogations and their relative importance. The observer concluded that while interrogation was an essential tactic in solving about a quarter of the cases, the *Miranda* restrictions had little impact on clearances of crimes or convictions of suspects. There were measurable declines in such matters as implicating accomplices, recovery of stolen property, and helping suspects clear themselves. The results did not show that police interrogation is unnecessary—only that the *Miranda* restrictions had not affected its effectiveness very much.[29]

Use of Physical Evidence The collection and processing of physical evidence is an important investigative tool. According to the Rand study:

> Police departments across the United States are emphasizing more efficient collection and processing efforts by allocating more personnel to them, establishing crime scene search units, purchasing sophisticated equipment, and processing a larger percentage of crime scenes for physical evidence.[30]

But the study concluded that no clear relationship exists between the amount of physical evidence retrieved and the number of suspects identified. The Rand team even claims that vast fingerprint files may, in fact, be counterproductive because they tend to discourage file searches.

Rather than the collection of evidence, it is the processing of evidence that counts. It is not the taking of more fingerprints that produces better results but a more thorough means of searching present fingerprint files and matching prints from the scene of a crime with those of known offenders. The Rand study concludes that "the relatively investigation is not likely to increase significantly under current procedures,"[31] though improved processing could result in more suspect identifications. But reorganizing fingerprint or mug shot files, or improving the means of searching them, is relatively invisible to a public that demands more police on the street or even to officers whose pay has utterly failed to keep pace with inflation.

Use of Confidential Informants We have mentioned the use of confidential informants in crime detection. Now we want to discuss their use in investigations of unsolved crimes. Police officials generally assert that many crimes are solved on the basis of information given by CIs. The value of CIs is based on the fact that almost all crimes and criminals are known by others. Robbers often brag of their feats, and burglars must sell the things they steal to persons who act as **fences**— those who knowingly receive stolen merchandise for resale. Police purchase information from persons who know about these activities. The price of this information may be cash or an agreement to overlook or limit police reaction to crimes committed by the informant.

Criticisms of the use of CIs tend to fall into four categories: (1) an ethical argument that it is wrong to allow some law violators to escape justice in return for their informing on others; (2) a related ethical argument that police often blackmail some violators of minor or vice laws in order to develop a stable of CIs; (3) a practical, as well as ethical, argument that informers sometimes give false information to protect themselves, thus not only hampering effective law enforcement but endangering the rights of others they accuse; (4) a moral argument that any accused has a right to confront his or her accuser and that this is violated in spirit (though not in law) by the practice of keeping CIs' identities secret and not using them as witnesses in trials of persons they accuse. Among the counterarguments are the following: while CIs may not be admirable people, they contribute a vital service to law enforcement; CIs who give false information will be found out and given their full measure of justice; and when CIs' testimonies in court are needed they are **burned.** This means their identity is revealed and their usefulness to law enforcement ended.[32]

The effectiveness of CIs has never been documented, nor can it be, given the secretive nature of the matter. Individual police officers and investigators often keep the identities of CIs hidden from their own superiors. Thus there is no record from which to determine the value of their contribution to criminal justice. And even when informers are "burned" and used as witnesses, the price paid in terms of crimes overlooked is not recorded. There is no doubt that crimes are solved based on information gained from CIs. The question that remains unanswered is how many crimes are solved by this means and at what cost.

How Crimes Are Solved

Knowledgable observers agree that most crimes are solved by relatively routine steps. The Rand Corporation scholars studied cleared cases in a number of specialized investigative units. The team attempted to discover what portion of cases required little or no investigation, what portion required routine steps, and what portion fell into what is called "special action" cases—that is, cases that required careful analysis and physical evidence and other intensive steps. The report concluded:

> In more than half of the cleared cases, the identification of the offender was available at the time of the initial report because (1) the offender was arrested at the scene; (2) the victim or witnesses identified the suspect by name and address; or (3) some evidence available at the crime scene, such as a license plate or employee badge number, uniquely determined the identity of the suspect.
> Most of the remaining cases that were eventually cleared were done so through simple routine administrative actions: fingerprint search, informant tips, reviewing of mug shots, or arrests in connection with the recovery of stolen property. In only three crime categories were any special action cases observed. These were commercial burglary, robbery, and homicide; in each of these categories special action cases accounted for about 10 percent of the solved cases.[33]

The report further claimed that with the possible exception of homicide, "if investigators performed only the obvious and routine tasks needed to clear the 'easy' cases, they would solve the vast majority (97 percent) of crimes that now get cleared. All their efforts in relation to other cases have a very marginal effect on the number of crimes cleared."[34] Many police officials have disagreed with this assertion.

Most crimes are solved by relatively routine steps.

The actual work investigators do is largely clerical in nature: calling victims or witnesses to see if they can provide any additional information, checking mug shot and modus operandi files, and checking with CIs. The Rand study looked at Kansas City in some detail, since it has computer-readable case assignment and activity files, and found that less than half of reported crimes receive "any serious attention by an investigator."[35] Yet given the number of investigators and the volume of cases, this probably should not be surprising.

CASE PREPARATION

In a crime that is solved by an arrest, investigation evolves into **case preparation.** This is the process of putting all the information on the crime, suspect, victims, and witnesses into a case management file, which a prosecutor reviews to decide what, if any, charges will be brought to court. It is one thing to clear crimes by establishing the identity of suspects; it is quite another thing to persuade prosecutors to file formal charges.

Crimes Cleared Versus Prosecutable Cases

Recall from Chapter 2 that a crime may be cleared by an arrest or by what is called "exception." In other words, a crime is considered cleared when the identity of a suspect is established, whether that suspect is in custody or not. Clearances are the traditional means of evaluating the output of investigators, and departments' practices vary considerably on their criteria for listing a crime as cleared. In some places a crime is considered cleared when an informer says, "I happen to know Joe Smith did it," or a suspect says, "Yeah, I did the two gas stations and the three liquor stores, too." Other departments require a prosecutor to accept a case for prosecution before they pronounce it cleared. The disparity makes clearance statistics unreliable. More importantly for this discussion, it means that in many police departments no premium is placed on working on cases until they are suitable for prosecution. In these departments arrest and clearance of the crime is the end of police work, and further work on the case is considered the responsibility of the prosecutor. This does not yield effective law enforcement. Most prosecutors will not accept a case that is not ready for a decision, though offices differ on what they consider "ready." Thus an impasse tends to develop in some places.

A case ready for prosecutorial decision is a case in which all witnesses have been interviewed, all physical evidence analyzed, identifications of suspects clearly established by victims or other witnesses, and full reports on all these factors placed in the file. Some police departments make this thoroughness a matter of policy, but many do not.

Investigative Thoroughness and Case Disposition

The effect of investigative thoroughness on case disposition was studied by the Rand Corporation. It compared two California cities, one having strict prosecutorial requirements for case preparation, which the police worked hard to meet, the other having lower standards and more routine investigative procedures. The study found widely differing levels of information in the files of the two police departments and, more importantly, found that the dispositions of cases varied considerably. In the first city, among the cases selected for study, there were no dismissals, or refusals to prosecute, and 60 percent of the defendants pled guilty to original charges. On the other hand, the study noted that more severe allegations were often considered by the second prosecutor in his filing decisions, thus opening the way for more plea bargaining and reductions of charges in that city. It is also of interest that the Rand observers found no clear pattern of differences in severity of sentences.[36] Thus the thoroughness in case preparation may have had an impact on the number of defendants charged by prosecutors and the severity of charges filed, but its effect on eventual disposition of cases was not measurable.

New Emphasis on Case Preparation

Whether or not it makes much difference in eventual disposition of most criminal defendants, more police departments are placing emphasis on case preparation by investigators. Some agencies are trying various types of investigative strike forces to deal with the more serious crimes or career criminals. These forces, often run in cooperation with prosecutors' offices, place a premium on the thoroughness of investigation and on substantiating the highest or most severe charges that can be filed.

Other agencies are establishing more formal liaison with prosecutors' offices so that mutual exchanges of information can result in better case preparation. Some prosecutors regularly participate in police academies and in-service training of investigators. Regular conferences with arresting and investigating officers are held in which problems are discussed. In some cities those prosecutors or their assistants who screen cases do so with the responsible officer present so that the best case can be made or the weaknesses in the case made immediately apparent. In the police departments trying these approaches, it is obvious that case preparation as a final step in the law enforcement process is being taken more seriously. In the long run this can only result in improved law enforcement effectiveness, especially in a time of intensified judicial requirements and constraints on police behavior.

The various steps and tasks involved in the process of enforcing the law have been examined. We have looked at crime detection, apprehension, investigation, and case preparation, the roles played by police officers in each step, and the criticisms of and problems with police performance. We next turn to an examination of the environment within which police operate.

THE ENVIRONMENT OF LAW ENFORCEMENT

On a number of occasions we have mentioned the concept of an "environment" within which the criminal justice system and the system components operate. No organization or individual functions in a vacuum. All of us have our behavior influenced by the surrounding environment. From our environment comes a variety of inputs into the determination of thoughts and behavior. Law enforcement agencies and personnel are no exception. Output from this criminal justice component is influenced by a variety of forces, and in this chapter we will explore a few of the more important ones. Though many of our remarks may be applied to law enforcement agencies in general, we will continue our previous practice of concentrating largely on the local level—police and sheriffs' departments.

Organizational and Individual Behavior

In discussing environmental influences on law enforcement output, one may focus on two different levels: output of organizations and behavior of individuals. It is obvious that neither agencies nor individuals act with complete uniformity. To the contrary, variations in behavior have long been recognized by scholars and practitioners alike. One scholar has noted that "as organization and as individuals, they [police] differ among themselves in philosophies of policing." He goes on to define "philosophies of policing" as "viewpoints and opinions about how they should enforce the laws and preserve the peace." Some police departments, for example, "spend a lot of time on juvenile delinquency programs; others concentrate on patrol and the investigation of crimes, and deal with juveniles only when they arrest them for specific offenses. Some departments have large, separate traffic divisions; others let the patrol division handle traffic along with its other duties."[37]

Police Styles To characterize the variations in behavior of law enforcement agencies—most commonly police departments—several scholars have developed what we may call **styles** of operation. Probably the best known of these attempts has been made by James Q. Wilson. Focusing on eight police departments of varying sizes and locations, Wilson identified three basic styles of police operation: watchman, legalistic, and service.[38] Each of these styles revolved around the way in which police tended to handle the functions of order maintenance, law enforcement, and public service.

Wilson noted that three of the eight cities studied had what could be labeled the **watchman style** of conduct. In these cities emphasis was on the performance of order maintenance. Law enforcement, while not completely ignored, took a back seat. Police, unless the offense was a major one, tended toward a hands-off policy or some action short of arrest. This was especially true if the potential offender was someone important in the community or a juvenile. If a juvenile, he or she was likely to be let off with a warning or some relatively light sanction was applied. One scholar has characterized this style of policing as "sloppy and discriminatory."[39] Not unexpectedly, in this category police were found to be poorly paid, short of staff personnel, and lacking in written rules, education, training, and departmental specialization.

In another three cities could be found **legalistic styles** of operation. While other functions were performed, emphasis was on the enforcement of laws, and the individual police officer was encouraged to view most situations in legal terms. This tended to produce a high rate of arrests in the areas of traffic, juvenile offenders, misdemeanors, and vigorous activity against any illegal enterprise. In contrast to the watchman style, the legalistic style viewed the law as applying equally to all persons. Also, professionalization in the form of rigorous training, educational standards, and adherence to written policies was very much evident in these departments.

The third style of police operations, labeled by Wilson as **service,** was noted in two of eight cities. This style can be viewed as somewhat of a cross between the other two styles. It is like the legalistic style in that it takes every situation seriously and does not fail to intervene where necessary and against any person. It approaches the watchman style in its nonemphasis of arrests and the use of informal sanctions.[40] Departments which were in this category also placed a heavy emphasis on community relations and services and tended to be professionalized.

Let us mention one other model of police styles. Authors of this model, called the **counselor-enforcer model,** suggest four basic styles of operation as police attempt to control crimes and maintain public order. Each of several methods used by police to accomplish their tasks is classified as being "enforcer" or "counselor." If the community sees a method (e.g., education of the public about home protection, diversion of an offender out of the criminal justice system) as helping to solve crime and disorder problems, it will be labeled "positive" in nature and placed into the counselor category. If a particular method, such as apprehension (catching of offenders) is seen unfavorably by the community, it is listed as "negative" and categorized as enforcer. Each of the four styles within the model, as Table 5.1 indicates, reflects the extent to which police act essentially as enforcers or counselors.[41]

While the preceding model is just that and not a study of specific de-

TABLE 5.1 Police Styles

Degree of Emphasis	Policing Style
Low counselor, low enforcer	Passive
Low counselor, high enforcer	Punitive
High counselor, low enforcer	Personalized
High counselor, high enforcer	Integrated

Source: Harry W. More, *Principles and Procedures in the Administration of Justice* (New York: Wiley, 1975), p. 124. Reprinted by permission.

partments such as conducted by Wilson, it serves to point out the general recognition by numerous observers of police operations that behavior can vary greatly from department to department.[42] In fact, the variation may be even greater. It has been suggested that "one organization can have several styles. These styles can follow shift lines (such as days or evenings), specialty (such as traffic or investigations), or neighborhoods in the community."[43]

Individual Behavior and Discretion Variation in the behavior of police departments and other law enforcement agencies is more than matched by that of individual officers. While operating under the constraints of departmental policy and the requirements of law, officers nevertheless exercise a great amount of personal **discretion.** The President's Commission on Law Enforcement and Administration of Justice went so far as to characterize this discretion as the making of law enforcement policy. The commission noted:

At the beginning of the process ... something happens that is scarcely discussed in lawbooks and is seldom recognized by the public: law enforcement policy is made by the policeman. For policemen cannot and do not arrest all the offenders they encounter. It is doubtful that they arrest most of them. A criminal code, in practice, is not a set of specific instructions to policemen but a more or less rough map of the territory in which policemen work. How an individual policeman moves around that territory depends largely on his personal discretion.[44]

The exercise of discretion, observed the commission, makes the individual police officer an interpreter of the law. It is the officer who takes legislative creations of law and introduces it to reality. He or she decides, "How much noise or profanity makes conduct 'disorderly' within the meaning of the law? When must a quarrel be treated as a criminal assault? . . . How suspicious must conduct be before there is 'probable cause,' the constitutional basis for an arrest?'"[45]

Bent and Rossum point out that the police officer's use of discretion exists not only in the realm of law enforcement but in the more frequently performed functions of order maintenance and public service. They suggest that discretion is especially pervasive in these areas, for they occupy most of an officer's time and subject him or her to the least control.[46]

Internal Influences on Departmental Behavior

We have spoken of police department styles and the behavior of individual police officers. As with any organization or person, there are a variety of forces influencing behavior and variations in behavior from department to department and officer to officer. Let us look at some of the more important ones.

We may begin by separating all influences into two categories: **internal** and **external.** The former refers to those things within a department having an impact on its output and may include such items as leadership at all levels of command and departmental organization, policies, and procedures. The latter term pertains to a variety of forces located outside the departments within its environment (we will look at these factors in the next section). It is the external forces that furnish input into the decision-making arena of the police system (department).

While there are many things internal to a department that may affect its mode of operations, one of the more important factors is that of leadership. It is common, for example, for police commissioners or chiefs to hold and implement their own conceptions of department goals and functions. Decisions from leadership may result in policies of selective enforcement, organizational change, or specifications for operating procedures. They may drastically affect police officer morale and job satisfaction, which, in turn, would help shape the direction and quality of department output. More than one study has noted this impact of leadership on police behavior.[47]

In addition to leadership, the operations of a department will naturally be determined in part by its internal organization, policies, and procedures. Even in the complete absence of any outside influences (an obvious impossibility), a department's behavior would nevertheless be given direction by these things: the lines along which a department is organized—for example, functional (traffic, patrol) versus geographical (district, sectors)—its leadership structure, and policies setting forth guidelines for individual behavior and operating procedures.

External Environmental Influences on Departmental Behavior

Were police able to determine entirely for themselves their functions and how to perform them, it is unquestionable that many things would be different than they presently are. Such is far from the way it is. Influences or determinants of police behavior are many and they are strong. We have placed these various influences into specific categories, as indicated in Figure 5.1.

Physical Environment It is clear that elements of the physical environment directly affect police departments. First there are the geographic boundaries of the department's jurisdiction, which establish the size and shape of the area. Then there is the topography of that

FIGURE 5.1 Effects of the Environment on Police Behavior

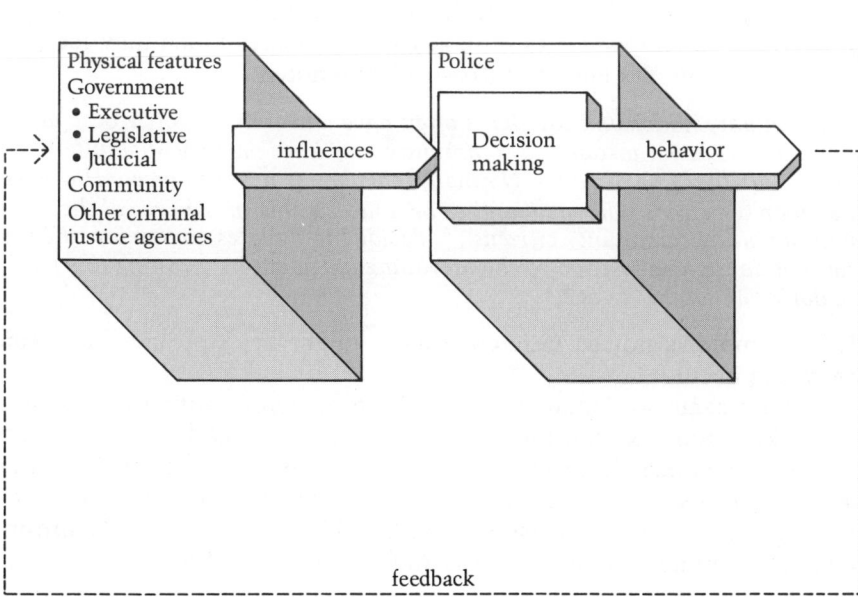

area: Is it flat or hilly? Is it a port city, divided by rivers, or partially covered by large lakes? Next there are the demographic factors of population size, characteristics, and density. Is the area highly urbanized or relatively rural with sparse population? What is the nature of the people? Finally, there are human-made environmental features such as the presence of super highways, tall buildings, industrial areas, commercial districts, and parks and playgrounds. These physical features help determine the levels of crimes and other social problems, the amount of demands for service of all kinds, and the ability of police to respond to crime and community needs.

Community Influences A prime source of influence on police behavior is the communities in which they operate. This influence may range from community norms and standards to specific expectations about selective law enforcement; from demands for public service of infinite variety to pressures for changes in operating procedures; from the seeking of laws to the clamor for better community relations. The vehicles for this great variety of influential forces are both individuals and groups, and the paths of influence are both direct and indirect. Figure 5.2 isolates and illustrates the real and potential influences flowing from community to police.

Looking at Figure 5.2, we see that community norms and standards play a role in police behavior. Influence from this source may take the form of law or simply act as general guidelines that police may feel obligated to follow. As Bent and Rossum have noted:

Community norms and standards often have a bearing on police occupational behavior. For instance, a community may have an ancient statute that forbids kite-flying on Sundays. Normally, this law is never enforced. However, if a group of persons who are found to be unacceptable in the eyes of the majority of the community citizens ... decided to fly kites on Sunday, then the community can respond to the prevailing judgment by arresting this particular group of kite-flyers.[48]

This example is not as farfetched as it might appear. Such has been known to occur.

Looking again at Figure 5.2, we see that community expectations may take a more explicit form than norms and standards. Citizens who live in the police department's community often have some rather strong ideas about police behavior and they usually try to find ways of making them known and listened to. The National Advisory Commission on Criminal Justice Standards and Goals has observed:

The specific goals and priorities which the police establish within the limits of their legislatively granted authority are determined to a large extent by

FIGURE 5.2 Effects of the Community on Police Behavior

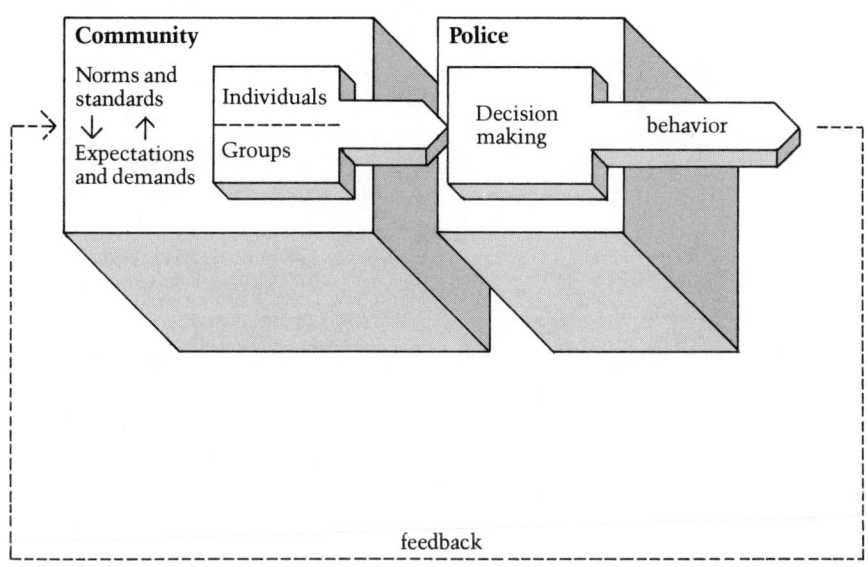

community desires. . . . *For example, elements of the community might urge increased patrols around schools, stricter enforcement of parking regulations in congested areas, or reduced enforcement activities against violators of certain crimes. The priorities established by police agencies in such cases are often influenced more by the wishes of those policed than by any other consideration* [emphasis added].[49]

Finally, let us comment about how community influences are channeled to police. Such influences may be transmitted through individuals or groups. They may also be direct or indirect. By this we mean that persons and groups in the community may exert direct pressure and have direct impact on the police department itself, or the path of influence may be indirect, through other government institutions instrumental in determining the limits of police functions and behavior.[50] Thus if citizens do not get what they want from police, there might be attempts to influence the passage of a law or the securing of a court ruling to achieve the desired result.

Governmental Influences It takes little effort by anyone to look around and see the extent of governmental influence in their lives. In fact, one would be hard pressed to list any activities that are not touched in some way by government. The components of the criminal justice system, government institutions themselves, are no exception. Government has had and continues to have an impact on the output of every criminal justice component and agency. Let us look at the nature of this impact of government on police agencies, as outlined in Figure 5.3 below.

The first thing to note is that there are several branches (legislative, executive, and judicial) and levels (federal, state, and local) of govern-

FIGURE 5.3 The Effects of Governmental Influences on Police Behavior

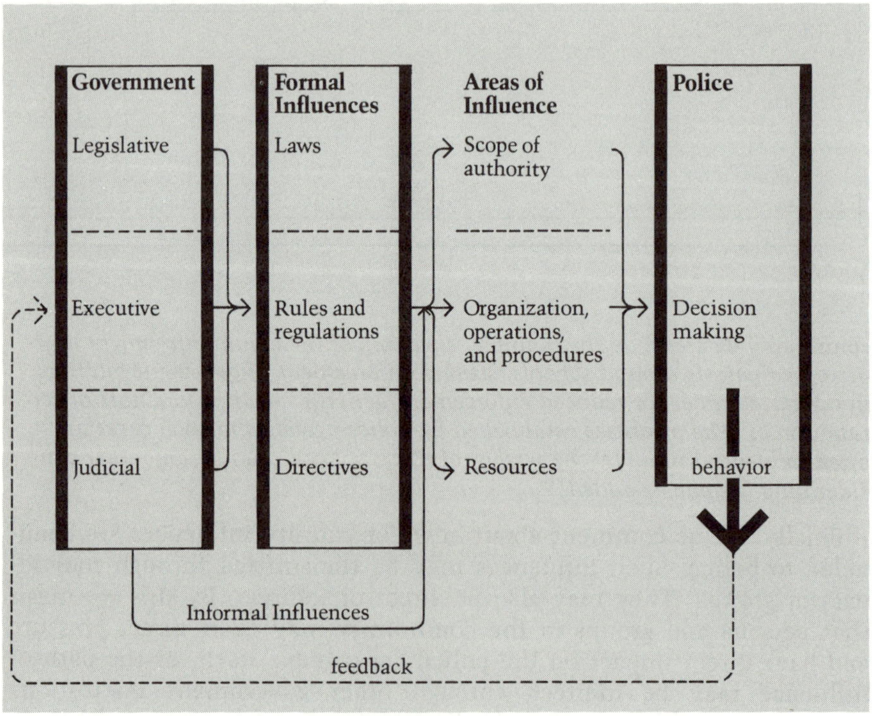

Government	Formal Influences	Areas of Influence	Police
Legislative	Laws	Scope of authority	
Executive	Rules and regulations	Organization, operations, and procedures	Decision making
Judicial	Directives	Resources	behavior

Informal Influences

feedback

ment that influence police behavior. From each branch comes some output that affects what police will do and how they will do it. This is multiplied at the different levels of government. Ruchelman, in a study of police and politics, notes that "state government has always played a role in local law enforcement," and that there are numerous units of the federal government—courts, Congress, administrative agencies— that "are capable of intervening in the law enforcement affairs of local governments."[51] Local mayors, city and county managers, councils, and courts have an even more direct impact.

As you can see from Figure 5.3, we have indicated that the governmental influences are both formal and informal in nature. The **formal influences** include laws passed by legislatures with executive cooperation (statutes) or enunciated in appellate court decisions (case law). Another source of formal influence is the promulgation of rules and regulations by executive departments and agencies, which establish or clarify policies. Even directives from executives that deal with specific problems or cases are formal, especially if they are written.

Informal influences operate through the person-to-person, largely verbal contacts between politicians and police officials. Some police assert that these informal influences, which include requests about specific cases or issues, can often affect their behavior more than the requirements of law, rules, or directives.

There are frequent conflicts between the messages police receive through formal channels and the messages they receive informally from government leaders. When these conflicts occur, police officials must choose which of the messages their departments should heed. For example, with the sudden energy shortage crisis of several years ago came a rash of new state laws lowering the maximum speed limit on all highways to 55 miles per hour. If enforced, this formal action of the government would propel police much more into one form of behavior (traffic regulation) than ever before. In at least one state, though, a legislative committee overseeing this matter passed along informally to police leaders the word that a leeway of from 8 to 10 miles per hour should be granted to motorists. While this was through informal means and not in the form of law, administrative rules, or directives, it had the same impact and likely presented some police with conflicting situations.

Whether the influence of government takes place through formal or informal channels, it affects three basic areas of police department behavior: the scope of law enforcement authority, police operations, and police resources.

Recall that police agencies came into existence initially because of crime and situations of public disorder. It was government that created police and government that determined the scope of police authority by defining what constituted crime. It has been a never-ending process, with both state and local governments turning out uncounted numbers of laws and ordinances. While few expect enforcement of every one of these, laws do make clear to the police the areas into which they may enter. As Ruchelman puts it, laws "set much of the agenda for what police are expected to do—i.e., enforcement of . . . laws which regulate the health, welfare, safety, and morals of the people."[52]

In any discussion of this nature, we must recognize the impact of the courts. They also contribute to the police agenda through the process of judicial review. The appellate courts of both the state and federal levels interpret the laws and rule on their constitutionality. Such action may either expand or contract the scope of law enforcement authority. As an example, until 1973 abortions for reasons other than protecting the life of the mother were against the law in most states. At that time the Supreme Court ruled such laws unconstitutional and placed severe restrictions on the jurisdiction of state and local law enforcement agencies.[53]

Governmental influence on police departments does not stop with the defining of law enforcement authority. It extends, much to the chagrin of many police personnel and others, to departmental organization and the procedures used to enforce laws and bring to justice those accused of crime.

The most obvious source of government's impact is the constraint on law enforcement procedures levied by appellate courts on both the federal and state levels. Recall that in Chapter 2 we discussed the special role of the Supreme Court and constitutional law in the system of criminal justice. We noted that they contribute to concepts of justice and provide specific guidelines for and limits on law enforcement procedures. State courts play an equal, if not more important, role in these matters. They not only enforce the provisions of state constitutions and federal constitutional principles but in some states the Supreme Court is the primary source of the rules of criminal procedure applicable to all criminal justice components.

Courts are just part of the many government institutions that have some impact on police organization and procedures. Executive and policymaking bodies at both state and local levels also exert some influence. State legislatures, for example, have not only been the sources of basic arrest powers of police but have often involved themselves in such important matters as recruitment standards, working conditions (e.g., hours of work), and work benefits (pay, pensions, and other fringe benefits). Of both state and municipal influence, Myren has written:

> Direct control of police organization and operation may take the form of enactment of individual city charters, each of which contains a section on the police department of the city. It may also take the form of general statutes governing the organization and operation of classes of cities, each of which will again contain a section on the police department. In addition, individual statutes may be passed dealing with specific problems in organization or operation of the police agency.[54]

Undoubtedly as important as any of the environmental influences that we have discussed thus far are the resources given to the police to do their job. Without adequate budget support from appropriate policy-making institutions, such as state legislatures, police operations would obviously be affected. Carried to the extreme, the lack of resources would be destructive to the entire police system. While this is not likely to happen, police do often have to fight hard for what they believe to be adequate levels of funding.

Most departments draw some financial support from federal programs in addition to their primary source of funding—the county or city. This can lead to certain conflicts affecting police policies and procedures, such as the recruitment of minorities (federal goal) versus the recruitment of persons who meet traditional standard qualifications (local goal). These conflicts can result in modifications if not wholesale changes in police practices.

Impact of Other Criminal Justice Agencies In addition to the influence that citizens and government have on law enforcement, there is the influence of other components of the criminal justice system itself: prosecution, trial courts, and corrections. Apart from the fact that most city departments and sheriffs' offices operate jails, and are thus organizationally involved in a limited way in another component, law enforcement responds to influences, pressures, demands, and other forms of feedback from the other components.

At this point we do not wish to examine this matter in any detail since we have barely touched on what the other components do. For now it is only necessary to point out the major ways in which law enforcement is dependent on their activities.

Law enforcement agencies are dependent on prosecutors to receive and make a charging decision on most of their cases. The pattern of acceptance or rejection of police cases in prosecutors' offices is a primary form of feedback to the agencies. Ideally, prosecutors' actions on cases should be a form of quality control, that is, their actions should result in rejection of poor cases or cases poorly investigated and prepared. Whether prosecutors can be said to perform quality control or not, it is clear that their policies and actions have an impact on police departments and other law enforcement agencies.

The trial courts also provide feedback to law enforcement in terms of decisions regarding issuance of warrants, suppression of evidence, dismissal of cases, and verdicts, as well as in their treatment of officers as witnesses and colleagues. Corrections have an impact on police in terms of both the treatment of offenders and the effects of corrections measures on crime itself.

Environmental Influences on Individual Behavior

While it is not within the scope of this book to examine at length the behavior of individual police officers, we do want to note briefly that their behavior on the job is influenced by a variety of factors. These include not only all those things that affect the department as a whole and departmental norms and policies but the police officer's own personal orientations and working environment.

Entering into any job, a person will bring along attitudes and predispositions that have been shaped by a host of factors such as age, sex, race, socioeconomic status (income, education, occupation), and family environment. In short, each person brings to a job his or her own personality. The police officer is no exception. Whether or not most of those who choose police work have personalities with particular traits—such as authoritarianism, as some have claimed—each new officer brings his or her own personality to the job.

In addition to the nature of the person entering police work, many scholars have suggested that police officers develop a **working personality**—a particular way of perceiving and responding to their working world. Contributing heavily to the molding of this personality is a police officer's occupational culture, often called **police culture.** Cole has noted that "policemen share a set of expectations about human behavior that they carry into professional contacts because they are policemen and are members of the police community."[55] Whatever individuals bring with them on entry into the police world, they become, through training and the influence of departmental goals, behavioral standards, peer group influence, and working conditions, a police officer.[56]

Perhaps the best illustration of the impact that police work and police culture can have on an individual is the work of Dr. George F. Kirkham, assistant professor of criminology at Florida State University, who became a full-time policeman with the Duval County Sheriff's

Department in Jacksonville, Florida. The transformation of Dr. Kirkham's views, attitudes, and personality have been documented in his perceptive articles. In the most widely read of these, he points out that he came to see the offender as the "real menace," the victim as the person deserving compassion and rights, the courts as a plea-bargaining source of frustration, and the cops as humane and compassionate. What had been police "paranoia" became "that chronic suspiciousness" that "a good cop cultivates in the interest of going home to his family each evening." He became proud to be a cop.[57]

It should be clear from the discussion in this chapter that police are greatly influenced by a multitude of forces within their environment. Whatever the source of influence or whatever its form, it exists and it shapes the police behavior of today. We will return to the subject of environmental influences as we focus on other criminal justice components.

TEST YOURSELF

Define these key terms:

probable cause
citation
proactive crime detection
cold search
entrapment
confidential informants
fence
police culture

Answer the following questions:

1. How do crimes come to the attention of police?

2. What do police officers do during preliminary investigations? What sorts of crimes receive intensive follow-up investigations?

3. What are the criticisms of police use of confidential informants?

4. What is the difference between "clearing" a crime and preparing a case for prosecution?

5. What are some of the ways in which other government agencies influence law enforcement?

NOTES

1. J. Shane Creamer, *The Law of Arrest, Search and Seizure* (Philadelphia: Saunders, 1975), p. 11.
2. Ibid., pp. 10-11 and 48-52.
3. 367 U.S. 643 (1961).
4. *U.S.* v. *Calandra*, 42 LW 4104 (1974). See also Creamer, *Arrest, Search and Seizure*, pp. 313-25.
5. Wayne R. Lafave, *Arrest: The Decision to Take A Suspect into Custody* (Boston: Little, Brown, 1965, pp. 437-489.
6. Alan G. Kalmanoff, *Criminal Justice: Enforcement and Administration* (Boston: Little, Brown, 1976), p. 50.
7. National Advisory Commission on Criminal Justice Standards and Goals, *Police* (Washington, D.C.: Government Printing Office, 1973), p. 193.
8. Ibid., pp. 58-59.
9. O. G. Wilson and Roy C. McLaren, *Police Administration*, 3d ed. (New York: McGraw-Hill, 1972), p. 353.
10. *Terry* v. *Ohio*, 392 U.S. 1 (1968).
11. *United States* v. *Robinson*, 414 U.S. 218 (1973).
12. See *New York Times*, April 19, 21, and 27, 1974.
13. Mark O. Morris, *Field Contact Report* (Oakland, Calif.: Oakland Police Department, 1974), p. 47.
14. Lawrence P. Tiffany et al., "Detection of Crime," in *The American Bar Foundation Survey of the Administration of Criminal Justice in the United States* (Boston: Little, Brown, 1967), p. 74.
15. See Creamer, *Arrest, Search and Seizure*, pp. 41-42; International Association of Chiefs of Police, *Criminal Investigation*, 2d ed. (Gaithersburg, Md.: IACP, 1971), pp. 255-57; and Robert Daley, *Target Blue* (New York: Delacorte Press, 1971), pp. 446-72, for a view of the use of agents by the New York City Police Department.
16. *Hampton* v. *U.S.*, 48 L Ed 113, 96 S Ct (1976). See also *U.S.* v. *Russell*, 414 U.S. 218 (1973).
17. Kalmanoff, *Criminal Justice*, pp. 81-83 and 94-95. For a discussion of how informants should be used, see IACP, *Criminal Investigation*, pp. 71-77. For legal and other issues concerning CIs, see Creamer, *Arrest, Search and Seizure*, pp. 27-28, 46, 101, and 143.
18. For discussion of legal aspects of eavesdropping, see Creamer, *Arrest, Search and Seizure*, pp. 42-44; and the cases of *Burger* v. *New York*, 338 U.S. 41 (1967); *Katz* v. *United States*, 389 U.S. 347 (1967); and *U.S.* v. *White*, 401 U.S. 745 (1971).
19. Peter W. Greenwood and Joan Petersilia, *The Criminal Investigation Process*, vol. I (Santa Monica, Calif.: Rand Corporation, 1975), p. 12.
20. Ibid., p. 5.
21. Kalmanoff, *Criminal Justice*, p. 83.
22. NACCJSG, *Police*, p. 235.
23. Greenwood and Petersilia, *Criminal Investigation Process*, p. 8.
24. Ibid.
25. NACCJSG, *Police*, p. 234.
26. Greenwood and Petersilia, *Criminal Investigation*, p. 8.
27. Ibid., pp. 5-6; and Kalmanoff, *Criminal Justice*, p. 77.
28. See IACP, *Criminal Investigation*, pp. 48-53, for guidelines for interrogation.
29. James W. Witt, "Non-Coercive Interrogation and the Administration of Criminal Justice: The Impact of *Miranda* on Police Effectuality," *Journal of Criminal Law and Criminology* 64 (1973), pp. 320-32.
30. Greenwood and Petersilia, *Criminal Investigation*, p. 15.
31. Ibid., p. 18.
32. See Kalmanoff, *Criminal Justice*, pp. 81-83 and 94-95; and "The Informers," *Miami Herald*, 12 January 1975, A1 and A24.
33. Greenwood and Petersilia, *Criminal Investigation*, p. 14.

34. Ibid.
35. Ibid., p. 19.
36. Ibid., pp. 21-22.
37. Robert E. Blanchard, *Introduction to the Administration of Justice* (New York: Wiley, 1975), p. 171.
38. James Q. Wilson, *Varieties of Police Behavior* (Cambridge, Mass.: Harvard University Press, 1968), pp. 85-89.
39. Herbert L. Packer, "The Police and the Community," *Stanford Law Review* 22 (1969), 1314-17.
40. Wilson, *Varieties*, pp. 85-89.
41. Blanchard, *Administration of Justice*, pp. 180-88; and Harry W. More, ed., *Principles and Procedures in the Administration of Justice* (New York: Wiley, 1975), pp. 120-27.
42. For other discussions of police styles, see E. Jerome Hopkins, *Our Lawless Police* (New York: Viking Press, 1931); William A. Westley, *The Police: A Sociological Study of Law, Custom, and Morality*, (Cambridge, Mass.: M.I.T. Press, 1970); Michael Banton, *The Policeman in the Community* (New York: Basic Books, 1964); and Jerome H. Skolnick, *Justice without Trial* (New York: Wiley, 1967).
43. More, *Principles and Procedures*, p. 127.
44. President's Commission on Law Enforcement and Administration of Justice, *The Challenge of Crime in a Free Society* (Washington, D.C.: Government Printing Office, 1967), p. 10.
45. Ibid.
46. Alan E. Bent and Ralph A. Rossum, *Police, Criminal Justice, and the Community* (New York: Harper & Row, 1976), p. 67.
47. See Robert D. Pursley, "Leadership and Community Identification Attitudes Among Two Categories of Police Chiefs," *Journal of Police Science and Administration* 2 (1974), pp. 414-22; and Martin Reiser, "Some Organizational Stresses on Policemen," *Journal of Police Science and Administration* 2 (1974), pp. 157-67.
48. Bent and Rossum, *Police*, p. 72.
49. NACCJSG, *Police*, pp. 9-10.
50. Richard A. Myren, "The Role of the Police," in Harry W. More, ed., *Critical Issues in Law Enforcement* (Cincinnati, Ohio: Anderson, 1972), pp. 22-23; and Leonard Ruchelman, ed., *Who Rules the Police* (New York: New York University Press, 1973), pp. 7-8.
51. Leonard Ruchelman, *Police Politics* (Cambridge, Mass.: Ballinger, 1974), pp. 23-24.
52. Ibid., p. 23; see also Ruchelman, *Who Rules the Police*, pp. 4-7.
53. *Roe v. Wade*, 410 U.S. 113, 93 Sup. Ct. 705 (1973).
54. Myren, "Role of the Police," p. 23.
55. George F. Cole, *The American System of Criminal Justice* (N. Scituate, Mass.: Duxbury Press, 1975), pp. 177-90.
56. The question of factors influencing the behavior of police officers has been the topic for many studies. For some of these see Larry L. Tifft, "The 'Cop Personality' Reconsidered," *Journal of Police Science and Administration* 2 (1974), pp. 266-78; C. E. Teasley, III, and Leonard Wright, "The Effects of Training on Police Recruit Attitudes," *Journal of Police Science and Administration* 1 (1973), pp. 241-48; William H. Kroes, Bruce L. Margolis, and Joseph J. Hurrell, Jr., "Job Stress in Policemen," *Journal of Police Science and Administration* 2 (1974), pp. 145-55; Reiser, "Organizational Stresses," pp. 156-59; James G. Fisk, *The Police Officer's Exercise of Discretion in the Decision to Arrest: Relationship to Organizational Goals and Societal Values*, (Los Angeles: Institute of Government and Public Affairs, 1974); and Skolnick, *Justice Without Trial*.
57. George F. Kirkham, "A Professor's 'Street Lessons'," *FBI Law Enforcement Bulletin* (March 1974).

PART III
Prosecution

CHAPTER 6
Prosecution Functions and Structures

OUTLINE

IMPORTANCE OF PROSECUTION
    Wide Discretion in Prosecution Decisions
    Scope of the Office
    Consumer of System Resources

HISTORY OF PROSECUTION

FUNCTIONS OF THE PROSECUTOR
    Charging
    Trial Advocacy
    Civil Responsibilities
    Other Functions

STRUCTURE AND ORGANIZATION
    Federal Level
    State Level
    Local Prosecutors
      Internal Organization
      Personnel in the Prosecutor's Office

OBJECTIVES

After reading this chapter the student should be able to:

Explain why the prosecutor often is labeled the "most important" of criminal justice officials, and explain how resources spent by prosecutors seem to belie this importance.

Discuss the historical development of public prosecution.

Describe the functions of prosecutors.

Outline the organization of prosecution on the federal level.

Describe the disparities among states on the role of attorney generals in criminal prosecution.

List the varieties of titles and jurisdictions of local offices of prosecution.

Discuss those factors affecting the internal organization of a prosecutor's office.

State the problems that interfere with having qualified, experienced personnel in prosecution.

KEY TERMS

torts
charging
trial advocacy
civil functions
habeas corpus
extradition
superseding of local prosecutor

☐ It is traditional to view the criminal justice system as having three components: law enforcement, courts, and corrections. However, as we pointed out earlier, in recent years observers and participants in the field have come to recognize that a fourth and quite distinct component exists—that of prosecution. Prosecutors have traditionally been treated as belonging to the court component. Prosecutors are indeed "officers of the court," but their functions are more administrative than judicial, and the role they play in the criminal process is both unique and crucial.

IMPORTANCE OF PROSECUTION

No official in the criminal justice system is more important than the prosecutor. Various authors have said that the prosecutor is "the country's most powerful and influential law official,"[1] "probably the most important actor" in the court-centered stage of the criminal process,[2] and simply "the most important official in the criminal justice system."[3] One writer has stated that in legal theory "the discretionary power vested in the prosecutor's office is almost unlimited and basically unreviewable," and he adds that his actions "are felt strongly throughout the justice system."[4]

Wide Discretion in Prosecution Decisions

The discretion enjoyed by prosecutors in the United States has been the subject of much comment and controversy, especially over the past few years. The decision as to what charges, if any, will be filed against an individual in court is almost entirely that of the prosecutors. They may file, drop, or amend charges with virtually no judicial review or other formal checks on the exercise of their prosecutorial authority. Prosecutors may enter into negotiations with defendants and their attorneys in which the prosecutors' powers to drop or amend charges may be used as a device to obtain pleas of guilty to some charges that will at least serve to convict the defendants. In the absence of pleas, prosecutors can command the resources of their offices, of law enforcement agencies, and of citizen witnesses in the attempt to gain convictions in court. How much effort must be made to obtain convictions is almost entirely up to the discretion of the prosecutor. After a conviction the prosecutors may also play a vital role in the determination of the sentence of the defendant by providing information or recommendations to the trial judge. Each of these matters will be examined in turn, but the point to be made here is that prosecutors exercise considerable discretion at various stages of the criminal process and, in the charging act alone, can determine the entire future of defendants.

Scope of the Office

As is surely clear from the previous discussion, the activities of prosecutors involve them in all aspects of the criminal justice system. In one of the most perceptive of recent treatments of the system in operation, David Neubauer writes:

> *The importance of the prosecutor flows directly from his central position, for his duties encompass the entire range of criminal justice. While other law appliers specialize in one area (police in arrests, for example), the prosecutor must be concerned with all stages of a case. He is the only official who works with all the other law appliers. The prosecutor is dependent upon police for input into his office. The processing of these cases requires contacts with judges, defense attorneys and probation officers.*[5]

Neubauer goes on to note that the "centrality" of the position of the prosecutor is unique, and adds: "Few political actors have the complex and varied strategic environment of the prosecutor."[6]

Prosecutors receive initial input from the police and other law enforcement agencies for most of the cases they process, and the relations between the prosecution office and these agencies are very important. Prosecutors also have the grand jury at their disposal, and this body of citizens—whose functions will be examined later in this chapter—generally rely on the prosecuting attorneys for information and evidence as well as advice on what actions they can take. The importance of contacts between prosecutors, defense attorneys, and trial court judges is obvious within the context of judicial action on criminal cases. Officials who conduct pre-sentence investigations of convicted persons usually take some of their information from prosecutors in preparing their reports on the offenders' backgrounds. At sentencing prosecuting attorneys may make comments or even offer recommendations to the trial judge. Parole boards often listen to the arguments of prosecutors in deciding whether to parole convicts. Probation and parole revocation actions also involve prosecutorial input and action. Prosecutors' offices are also becoming increasingly involved in various pretrial diversion and alternative rehabilitation programs throughout the country. In most of these programs, successful completion of a period of supervised activity results in the dropping of charges by the prosecutor.

This survey of the scope of prosecutorial involvement in the criminal process and with other agencies does not even include the many civil functions which offices of prosecution perform in association with other agencies of government. Each of these activities will be covered later. The broadness of the scope of prosecutorial actions and relations should, however, be clear by now. Indeed, it is appropriate to state that if one wants to observe the operations of the entire criminal justice system from a single vantage point within it, the prosecutor's office is the only place to be.

Consumer of System Resources

The relative importance of offices of prosecution seems belied by the resources they consume relative to the other components of the criminal justice system. There are federal prosecutors' offices in each of the ninety-two U.S. judicial districts, fifty state attorney generals offices, and about twenty-seven hundred local offices of prosecution within the states. All these offices spend less than 5 percent of criminal justice appropriations and employ about 5 percent of all criminal justice personnel.[7] Of the resources devoted to criminal justice, 5 percent going into prosecutors' offices seems out of line with the responsibilities and authority assigned them. It is true that many prosecutorial activities are supported indirectly by law enforcement, the courts, and other government agencies. Nevertheless, the power of prosecutors in terms of the criminal justice process is clearly not matched by their power to command resources from legislative bodies.

HISTORY OF PROSECUTION

The American office of prosecution is, like so many other legal and political institutions, both a derivation from and a reaction to the English tradition.[8] In the Middle Ages kings used special attorneys to prosecute selected criminal cases, and it was up to citizens to retain their own attorneys to prosecute persons who had injured them in any way. There was no distinction between crimes and other **torts** (injuries against citizens that are not offenses against the state). Prosecutions were private legal actions in all but a handful of cases. Eventually the Crown declared that offenders against the "king's peace" would be punished by the government, and justices of the peace became agents of prosecution and judgment. In the fifteenth century Henry V began the distinction between felonies (murder, arson, treason, and counterfeiting) and misdemeanors and ruled that crimes were offenses against society as a whole. This opened the way for publicly funded police, criminal trials, punishment, and prosecutions of felonies. Later in that century the first attorney general was appointed by Edward IV. Henry

VIII further developed prosecutions by establishing a system of sergeants who would be police prosecutors but who could nevertheless maintain private businesses and law practices. No office of full-time public prosecutor appeared, however, and it remained for Americans to create the post.

In 1704 the British attorney general appointed the first public prosecutor in the American colonies in Connecticut.[9] The office was beyond colonists' control, however. It was largely in reaction to royally appointed prosecutors that the Americans chose to create locally elected prosecutors as the means of bringing criminal offenders to justice. States that retained attorney generals made them either elected officials or subject to the appointment of elected governors and legislatures. Some states avoided having an attorney general until late in the nineteenth century.

The overwhelming choice of the citizens was to elect locally accountable prosecutors who would be independent of both federal and state governments and who would shoulder almost the entire burden of criminal prosecution. This is not to say that local prosecutors were full-time professionals. Until recently most were not. They were, however, lawyers who received public funds rather than fees for prosecuting cases. They were also officials who were not formally part of the police or other executive departments of government.

At the federal level the Judiciary Act of 1789 (which established federal courts below that of the Supreme Court and created U.S. Marshalls) created the office of U.S. attorney general. But it was not until 1870 that the Department of Justice was established and with it the offices of U.S. attorney in each of the federal judicial districts.[10] Thus came about the peculiarly American phenomenon of prosecutors on at least three levels of government.

FUNCTIONS OF THE PROSECUTOR

We have discussed the power and discretion of the prosecutor and outlined some of the major activities in which his or her authority is exercised. Let us look more closely at the specific functions prosecutors are expected to perform throughout the United States.

Charging

It is generally agreed that the most important single function assigned to prosecutors—and the one that is the key to their authority throughout the criminal justice process—is **charging:** deciding whether individuals should be brought before the bar of justice and to what criminal charge or charges they should answer.

We have said that there is little in the way of formal checks on the discretion of the prosecutor in the exercise of the charging function. There are, however, definite factors prosecutors must take into consideration in choosing among alternatives, and these factors go beyond the prosecutor's own sense of what is just or right. After all, judges can dismiss and juries or judges can acquit persons of unsupportable charges. Charges must have a basis in both the law and the provable facts of the case. It is even possible for the public to become incensed at a pattern of failure to bring proper charges and subsequently vote to remove an ineffectual prosecutor from office.

The process of charging may involve several steps: reviewing a case file, deciding on charges (or presenting the case to the grand jury), testing charges in a preliminary hearing, negotiating with the defense on

One of the functions of a prosecutor is to advocate the case for the state in court.

the possibility of reducing charges, and deciding whether to withdraw or reduce charges at various stages of the process.

Trial Advocacy

The second most vital function of the prosecutor is **trial advocacy,** that is, to represent the state in criminal trials and to present the case for the state to the judge or jury. Prosecutors are expected to prepare their cases well enough to win the majority of cases they take to the trial court. They are also expected to present their evidence, witnesses, and arguments in a fair and effective manner in the courtroom.

Civil Responsibilities

Depending on the jurisdiction, prosecutors are assigned certain **civil functions.** Most offices of prosecution are called upon to represent the government at their level—federal, state, county, or municipality—in any civil action to which that government is a party. The types of cases and legal matters they can become involved in are many and varied, but some are directly linked to the criminal process. A few examples will illustrate the point: The **habeas corpus** process is a civil one involving a claim of illegal custody of an accused person. **Extradition** proceedings are important in obtaining custody of those fleeing or absent from the state where they are to be prosecuted. In many cases involving child support, consumer fraud, or other white-collar offenses, there is a mix of civil and criminal processes available, with the latter resorted to when necessary.

Other Functions

There remains a variety of additional functions that most prosecutors are expected to perform. These include such things as providing legal advice to governmental bodies (especially law enforcement agencies), providing training for police in criminal law and processes, preparing drafts of search warrants and wiretapping applications, participating in decisions regarding court administration, and engaging in a wide variety of public information and community relations programs. The chief prosecutor must also administer his own office and engage in the political activities essential to remain in office.

These functions are appropriate for almost all offices of prosecution in the United States. They are usually complementary rather than competitive. Choices made by prosecutors are not generally over which of their functions to emphasize at the expense of others but rather over what style or approach to adopt with regard to each function.

STRUCTURE AND ORGANIZATION

Offices of prosecution appear at various levels of government and manifest various styles of organization depending on the area they serve. Chief prosecutors also carry varying titles.

Federal Level

At the federal level, prosecutors all work for the Department of Justice. The attorney general of the United States is the chief prosecutor for the government. As a practical matter, however, the attorney general is an administrator of a huge federal department with cabinet-level status. It encompasses bureaus of law enforcement (FBI, DEA, etc.) and corrections as well as divisions of prosecution. The top officer in terms of actual work in the federal courts is the solicitor general, but his function is primarily to argue cases before the Supreme Court, and he exercises no authority over other federal prosecutors. Under the attorney general is a deputy attorney general to whom nine assistant attorney generals report. Six of these assistants head divisions that engage in preparation and trial of cases, but only one of these—the Criminal Division—routinely and consistently engages in criminal prosecution. Two others—the Antitrust and Tax Divisions—mix criminal and civil practice depending on the cases they develop.

Attorneys from the criminal and other trial divisions of the department focus most of their activity in Washington. Prosecution of most violaters of federal laws is the responsibility of the U.S. district attorneys in each of the ninety-four federal court districts. These districts cover every state and territory of the United States. The U.S. attorneys in these districts have authority to command the resources of all federal law enforcement agencies within their jurisdictions and, in turn, are responsible to the U.S. attorney general through the Criminal Division and the deputy attorney general. Harry More has pointed out that this system provides "far more opportunity and authority for coordination of activities in the federal system than is available at the state or local level."[11]

Policy for all offices is made in Washington. In recent years the possibilities inherent in the structure of the Justice Department were realized in the creation of several Organized Crime Strike Forces in the largest cities. Not only could U.S. attorneys be directed to establish such forces and to assign certain office resources to them, but law enforcement investigators from the FBI and DEA could be assigned to them. Their counterparts from the Treasury Department's Bureau of Internal Revenue and Bureau of Customs were also directed to participate to overcome the usual jurisdictional divisions. U.S. attorneys and their own assistant U.S. attorneys were backed up by specially assigned assistant U.S. attorney generals in the preparation and trial of specific criminal cases generated by the strike forces. These efforts were very successful in some areas, especially where they also won loyal cooperation from state and local law enforcement agents and prosecutors.

U.S. attorneys are appointed by the president, as is their boss, the attorney general. Their terms of office coincide with that of their appointer. Assistant U.S. attorneys are in turn appointed by the U.S. attorneys. The work of the offices includes all the activities normally associated with criminal prosecution. The charging function, however, largely belongs to federal grand juries since all felony cases in federal criminal courts must originate with an indictment—a process to be more fully explained in the next chapter. The U.S. attorney, on the other hand, screens the fruits of federal investigations, decides what charges are proper, files any misdemeanor charges, and usually obtains the indictment of the accused on the felony charges he would have filed directly if permitted to do so.

U.S. attorneys' offices also perform the other functions associated with prosecutors in general: civil actions (including securing compliance with the Civil Rights Act, condemnation of land for federal public works projects, and defense of the government against claims of negligence); legal advice and training for federal law enforcement agents; participation in the administration of the entire criminal justice apparatus in the district; and public relations.

Though U.S. attorneys are not elected, their appointment is clearly a political process, and the turnover that results in the staffs of the ninety-four offices at the change of administrations in Washington weakens the professionalism of many offices.

State Level

At the level of state government there are the offices of attorney general. In most states the post is an elected one, but in thirteen it is appointive. All attorney generals have civil responsibilities and authority to represent the state in appellate cases. Their roles in criminal cases, however, vary greatly from state to state.

In three states (Alaska, Delaware, and Rhode Island) the state attorney general is the chief prosecutor for the state, and all criminal prosecutions are conducted by assistant attorney generals.[12] In other states the task of prosecution is left to local prosecutors and the variations among the states concern the extent to which attorney generals supervise or intervene in various aspects of prosecution.

Criminal cases before appellate courts are the direct responsibility of the attorney generals in forty-three states. In seven states the argument of appeals is handled by the attorney general on an occasional basis. And in four states the attorney general's role is limited even on the appellate level, with local prosecutors carrying their own cases forward.[13] As for prosecutions at the trial level, attorney generals may intervene on their own initiative in twenty states; at the request of others— including the local prosecutor—in thirteen states; and may not intervene at all in thirteen.[14] In practice, however, intervention by the attorney general in a local case is extremely rare. Thirteen states also allow the attorney general to **supersede the local prosecutor** (displace him for the duration of a particular case) on his own initiative. In a handful of states, supersession is not allowed or is severely restricted, and most states are unclear on the matter. In practice, however, acts of superseding local prosecutors are few and far between, even where it is authorized.[15]

Apart from the matter of the role of the attorney generals in criminal cases, there is the matter of their role as administrators in the supervision or coordination of local prosecutors. Here, too, the states vary. In some states quarterly or annual reports to the state office are required from prosecutors; in most others they are required occasionally or simply requested. Attorney generals may also make a habit of calling prosecutors together for meetings on common problems, may issue newsletters on criminal matters of interest, and operate or participate in training programs and seminars for prosecutors.

The most common pattern appears to be one in which the attorney general's office plays a primary role in criminal cases on appeal, little more than an advisory role in the daily activities of prosecutors on the local level, and a minimal role in the coordination of prosecution functions on a state wide basis. Some studies have advocated a more active role by attorney generals in the administration of prosecution functions, but surveys indicate a resistance by local prosecutors to any increase in the powers of attorney generals.[16]

Local Prosecutors

With the exception of the three states in which attorney generals are the chief prosecutors, the bulk of criminal prosecution is conducted from 2700 offices at the local level. In only three states are the local chief prosecutors appointed, the rest are elected by their constituents. The most common jurisdictional entity is the county, but fifteen states use judicial districts or circuits. The most common title given prosecutors is district attorney, followed in order of frequency by county attorney, state attorney, prosecuting attorney, solicitor, and commonwealth attorney. The number of units within each state varies from 313 in Texas to 4 in Hawaii.[17]

In addition to the county- or district-level prosecutors, many states also have city prosecutors or city attorneys who devote part of their work load to prosecuting offenses against municipal codes and ordinances. We will not, however, be especially concerned with them as a distinct entity. Insofar as their organizations and activities parallel those of the other prosecutors, they may be considered in the discussion.

In most states the prosecutors practice in civil as well as criminal matters, but a handful of states restrict district attorneys to criminal cases. A few divide the criminal case load into felonies and misdemeanors, assigning the higher crimes to district attorneys and misdemeanors to county or city prosecutors.[18]

The local offices of prosecution also vary tremendously in size and complexity. It is to their internal organization we now turn.

Internal Organization Local offices of prosecution vary in size from a single part-time attorney to the gigantic complex presided over by the district attorney of Los Angeles County. The latter has over four hundred deputy district attorneys serving an area of over 7 million inhabitants and forty arresting agencies.[19]

The internal organization of a district attorney's office begins with the same line-staff dichotomy that characterizes all organizations. Line personnel are the attorneys and the investigators who assist them. The staff or support personnel include administrators, secretaries, clerks, and specialists in such matters as research, statistics, auditing, and media relations.

How a particular office is organized depends on a number of additional factors, including the civil as well as criminal responsibilities assigned under the law, the number of law enforcement agencies reporting to the office, the number of and distance between court locations where business must be transacted and trials conducted, and the desires of the chief prosecutor in terms of managerial style and procedures. The Los Angeles County district attorney's office has an organizational structure that reflects divisions along both functional and geographic lines (see Figure 6.1). By contrast, relatively simple functional patterns of organizational structure are illustrated by the King

FIGURE 6.1 Organizational Chart of the Office of the District Attorney of Los Angeles County

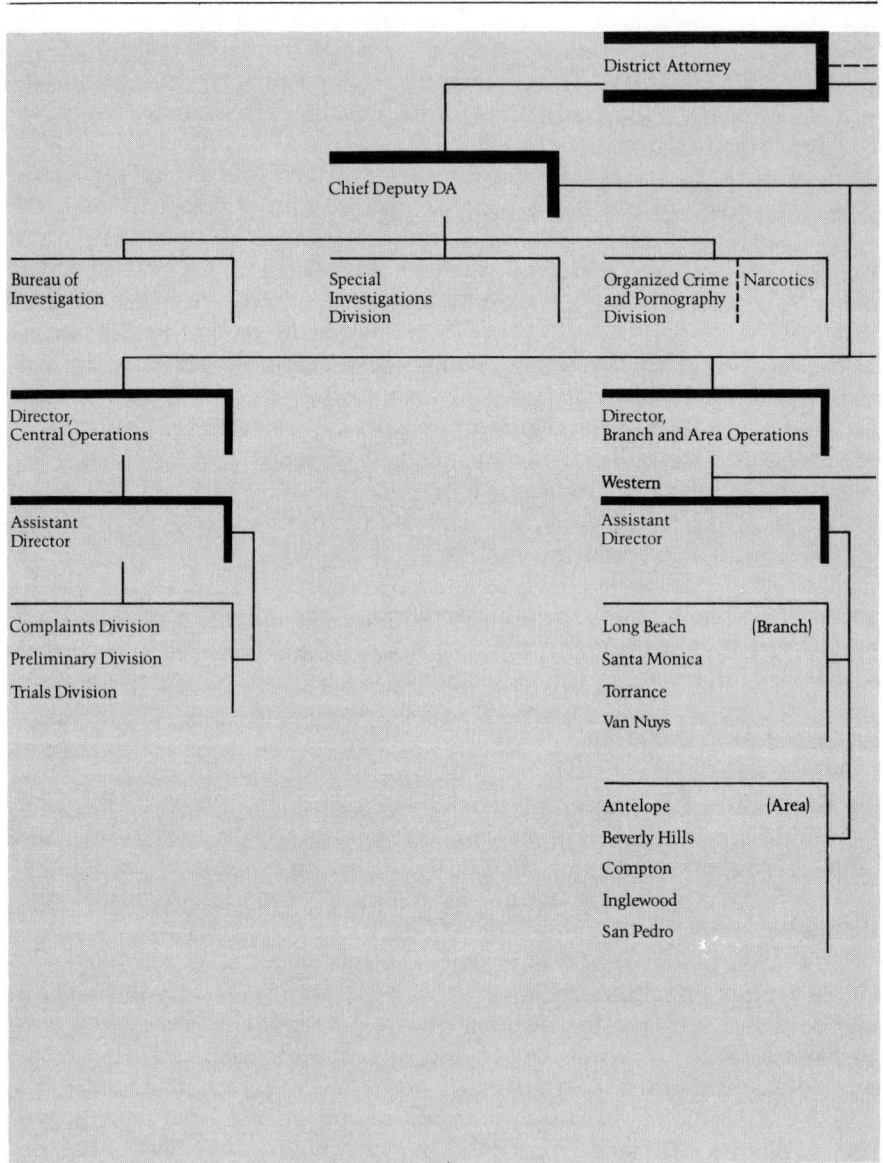

Source: Peter W. Greenwood, et al. *Prosecution of Adult Felony Defendants in Los Angeles County: A Policy Perspective* (Washington, D.C.: Government Printing Office, 1973). p. 9.

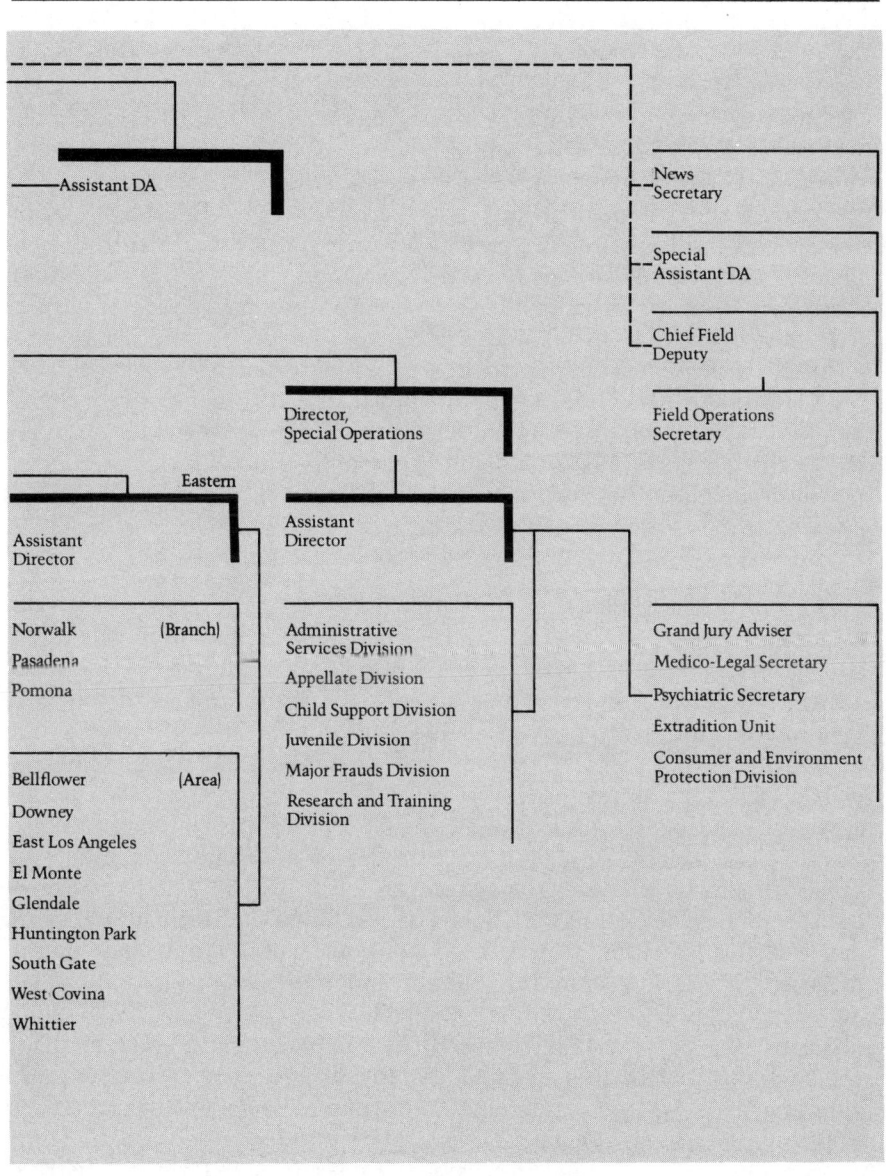

County district attorney's office in Seattle, Washington (see Figure 6.2).

Certain organizational issues seem to arise in jurisdictions of any appreciable size, and there is no single best answer to these issues. For example, should the intake and screening functions be performed by attorneys, investigators, or paralegals? Should attorneys specialize in specific stages of the criminal process, or should they be responsible for all aspects of a case from intake through post trial actions? How should liaison with the law enforcement agencies be handled—by investigators on police staffs assigned to the prosecutor's office or vice versa? In general, these issues boil down to the related issues of specialization versus generalization on the part of attorneys and the degree to which nonattorneys can be assigned certain functions within the organization. A prosecutor's responses to these issues are influenced, and sometimes determined, by the desires and the dictates of judges who decide procedural matters and by the wishes of police officials. The prosecutor may be the most powerful single official in the criminal justice system, but he is also the most responsible for maintaining cooperation among the police agencies, his office, and the courts of his district or county. How he organizes his own office and assigns responsibilities within it are among the keys to achieving the desired level of cooperation.

Personnel in the Prosecutor's Office We have mentioned issues concerning organization, relations with other agencies, including the attorney general, and functions assigned to prosecutors. But to perform the assigned functions under any organizational structure and within any given pattern of interagency relations, the prosecutor's office needs the people to do the job. It is often said that good, talented, dedicated people can make almost any system work and that, conversely, the absence of good people will prevent the best-designed system from performing effectively. The plain fact is, however, that most offices of prosecution do not attract the best attorneys in the field and have difficulty retaining attorneys who demonstrate talent and skill. Prosecution has traditionally been viewed as a temporary occupation that comes between graduation from law school and more lucrative and prestigious private practice.

Beginning with the chief prosecutors themselves, the vast majority of prosecutors are still part-time employees expected to conduct private and civil practice or conduct other business to supplement their salaries. One nationwide survey, taken a few years ago, found that only 35 percent were full-time professional prosecutors.[20] Only in districts containing populations of sixty thousand or more did the number of

FIGURE 6.2 Organizational Chart of the Office of the District Attorney of King County, Washington

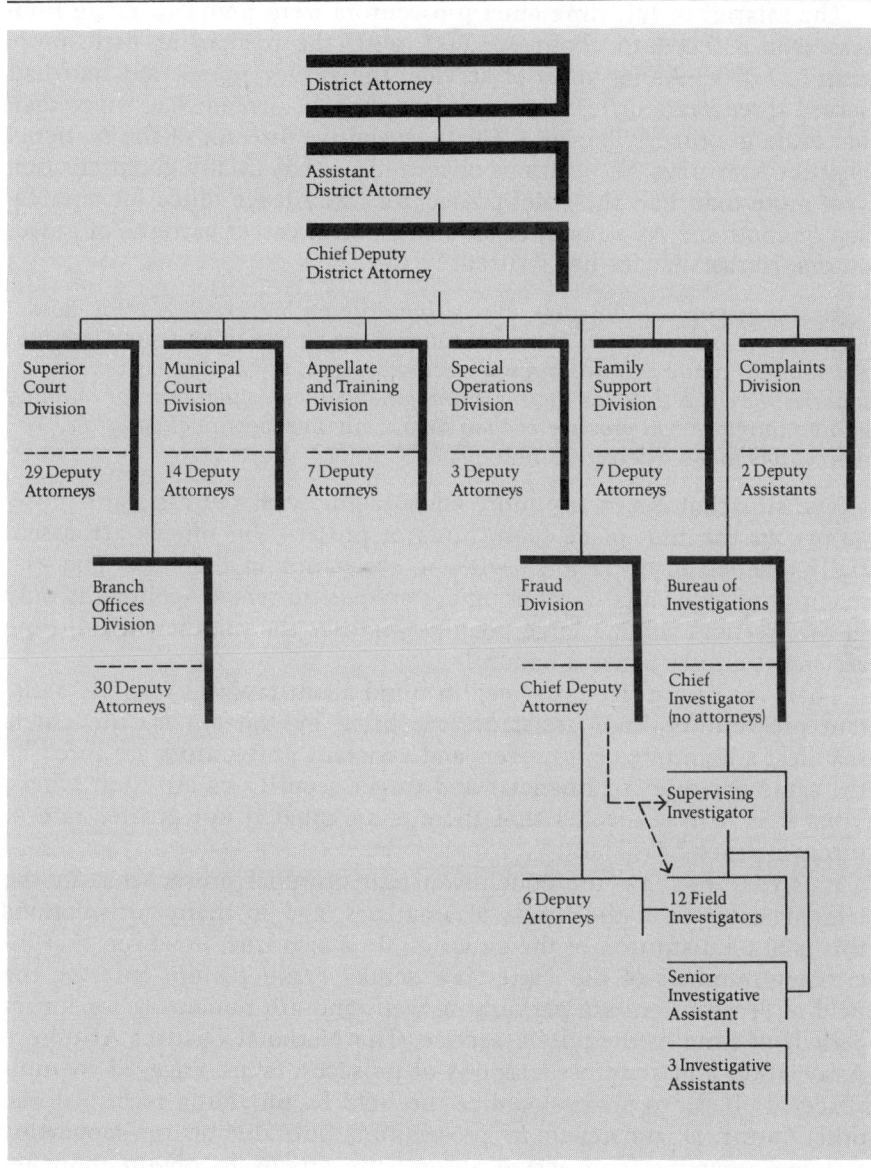

Source: Peter Finn and Alan R. Hoffman, *Exemplary Projects: Prosecution of Economic Crime* (Washington, D.C.: Government Printing Office, 1976). p. 31.

full-time prosecutors outnumber the part-timers, and only in the very largest districts of over a half million people did the portion of full-time prosecutors rise to about 75 percent.[21]

The salaries of full-time chief prosecutors were found to range from less than $10,000 to about $45,000, with the median at little more than $22,000.[22] As for years of service, the survey found that half had served three years or less and that less than 17 percent had more than ten years in office.[23] Patrick J. Healy, executive director of the National District Attorneys Association, once told us that in any given election year more than half the chief prosecutors may leave office for one reason or another.[24] As a result of studies made of career patterns of prosecutors, Herbert Jacobs has written:

> *Most prosecutors leave their office voluntarily for higher office or for more lucrative private practices. Many prosecutors are promoted by their parties to judgeships. Private practice lures prosecutors, especially in the less urban counties, because they see their position principally as a platform for building a more thriving legal practice of their own. Only in exceptional cases do prosecutors make a career of their office.*[25]

The situation is not any more encouraging with the assistant prosecutors. In the first place, two-thirds of prosecution offices are essentially one-person operations, with no assistants on the staff. The vast majority of assistants in other offices are part-timers.[26] Again, it is only in the districts serving large populations that the number of full-time assistants climbs above a handful.

There are certain facts to keep in mind about lawyers who are assistant prosecutors. Staff assistants are hired by the chiefs; the chiefs manifest a high rate of turnover; and assistant prosecutors are lured by the same promises of financial and career security as are their chiefs. Thus it is to be expected that there is an equal if not greater rate of turnover among assistants.

It is easy to draw the conclusion that criminal prosecution in the United States is in the hands of amateurs, and in many jurisdictions this is not a distortion of the situation. It is also true, however, that increasing numbers of the better law school graduates are entering the field of prosecution, are performing well, and are remaining for longer periods of time in the public service. The National District Attorneys Association and state associations of prosecutors are engaged in multifaceted efforts to professionalize the field by providing technical and other forms of assistance to prosecutors, introducing or supporting training programs, and acting as pressure groups to obtain more resources from legislative bodies for offices of prosecution.

We will examine more closely some of the improvements and innovations associated with attempts to develop a prosecutorial profession in the United States in our final chapter.

TEST YOURSELF

Define these key terms:

charging
extradition
superseding of local prosecutors

Answer the following questions:

1. What are the specific functions of most prosecutors?

2. How is prosecution organized at the federal level, and how are federal prosecutors selected?

3. Describe the general role of state attorney generals in criminal prosecution within states. What exception exists in three states?

4. What is the career pattern of most attorneys who become prosecutors?

NOTES

1. George T. Felkenes, *The Criminal Justice System* (Englewood Cliffs, N.J.: Prentice-Hall, 1973), p. 146.
2. Donald J. Newman, *Introduction to Criminal Justice* (Philadelphia: Lippincott, 1975), p. 188.
3. David W. Neubauer, *Criminal Justice in Middle America* (Morristown, N.J.: General Learning Press, 1974), p. 42.
4. Alan G. Kalmanoff, *Criminal Justice: Enforcement and Administration* (Boston: Little, Brown, 1976), p. 176.
5. Neubauer, *Criminal Justice*, p. 42.
6. Ibid.
7. Department of Justice and Department of Commerce, *Expenditure and Employment Data for the Criminal Justice System, 1974* (Washington, D.C.: Government Printing Office, 1975), pp. 27 and 47.
8. See Allen Harding, *Social History of the English Law* (Baltimore: Penguin Books, 1966).
9. Kalmanoff, *Criminal Justice*, p. 204.
10. *U.S. Government Manual: 1975/76* (Washington, D.C.: Government Printing Office, 1975), pp. 306-14.
11. Harry W. More, ed., *Principles and Procedures in the Administration of Justice* (New York: Wiley, 1975), pp. 134-35.
12. Advisory Commission on Intergovernmental Relations, *State-Local Relations in the Criminal Justice System* (Washington, D.C.: Government Printing Office, 1971), p. 112.
13. Committee on the Office of Attorney General, *Survey of Local Prosecutors* (Raleigh, N.C.: National Association of Attorneys General, 1973), p. 75.

14. ACIR, *State-Local Relations*, p. 116.
15. More, *Principles and Procedures*, p. 136.
16. COAG, *Survey*, p. 78.
17. Ibid., pp. 2-3.
18. ACIR, *State-Local Relations*, pp. 113-14.
19. Peter W. Greenwood et al., *Prosecution of Adult Felony Defendants in Los Angeles County: A Policy Perspective* (Washington, D.C.: Government Printing Office, 1973), pp. 6 and 7.
20. COAG, *Survey*, p. 35.
21. Ibid., p. 36.
22. Ibid., p. 33.
23. Ibid., p. 24.
24. Interview with Patrick J. Healy in NDAA offices in Chicago, Illinois, 13 June 1974.
25. Herbert Jacobs, *Urban Justice: Law and Order in American Cities* (Englewood Cliffs, N.J.: Prentice-Hall, 1973), p. 59.
26. COAG, *Survey*, p. 41.

CHAPTER 7
The Prosecution Process

OUTLINE

THE CHARGING STAGE
    Case Intake
    Case Screening
    Charging Decision
        Proper Charging Criteria
        Improper Charging Criteria
        Charging Criteria Often Used
        Prosecutorial Discretion
        Patterns of Charging
    The Grand Jury
    Precharge Hearings

THE ADJUDICATION STAGE
    Arraignment
    Pretrial Activities
        Trial Preparation
        Pretrial Motions
        Pretrial Negotiations
    Trial Activities
    Standards of Trial Practice

THE SENTENCING STAGE

POSTSENTENCING ACTIVITIES

ENVIRONMENTAL IMPACT ON PROSECUTORS' BEHAVIOR
    The Impact of Government
    The Impact of Community
    The Impact of Interagency Relations
        Relations with Police
        Relations with Judges and Defense Attorneys

OBJECTIVES

After reading this chapter the student should be able to:

Give a general description of the charging stage of prosecution.

Describe several factors contributing to the basic parameters within which the prosecutor works during the charging stage.

Describe case intake and screening.

List and describe the choices a prosecutor may make after screening cases.

Describe the criteria that the ABA and others suggest prosecutors should and should not use to make their charging decisions, and some of the criteria that prosecutors do use.

Define the concept of prosecutorial discretion and discuss criticisms of its use.

Describe four patterns of charging or prosecution styles suggested by Jacoby.

Discuss the grand jury in terms of functions and criticisms.

Describe the nature of initial appearances, preliminary hearings, and arraignments and discuss the prosecutor's role in each.

Discuss the kinds of activities engaged in by the prosecutor during trial preparation.

List and define several pretrial motions that might demand attention by the prosecutor.

Discuss the concept of plea bargaining (plea negotiations) in terms of its definition, the reasons for it, and criticisms against it.

Describe the different areas of concern and activity for a prosecutor during a trial.

Discuss the prosecutor's role in sentencing.

Discuss the post trial role of a prosecutor.

Describe some of the ways in which government, community, and other criminal justice agencies affect the behavior of prosecutors.

KEY TERMS

case screening
charging
docket entry
in-custody and at-large cases
affidavit
rap sheet
information
indictment
charging patterns
legal sufficiency pattern
system efficiency pattern
defendant rehabilitation pattern
trial sufficiency pattern
grand jury
presentment
immunity
contempt of court
use immunity
unindicted coconspirator
initial appearance
preliminary hearing
discovery of evidence
arraignment
nolo contendere
depositions
motion to dismiss
motion for change of venue
motion to suppress evidence
motion for pretrial discovery
motion for continuance
motion for bond reduction
plea bargaining
nolle prosequi
witness management
jury selection
voir dire
challenges for cause
peremptory challenge
opening statement
presentation of case
cross-examination
closing argument
substantive criminal law
procedural law

☐ We have pointed out that the criminal justice process consists of five stages: arrest, charging, adjudication, sentencing, and corrections. While the scope of prosecutorial activity encompasses the entire process, the prosecutor's role is not equally direct or important in all of the several stages. In certain situations there is some involvement in the arrest stage and a minor part may be played in the area of corrections. It is in the charging, adjudication, and sentencing stages, however, that prosecutors perform most of their activities. In one of these stages—charging—the prosecutor's role is clearly dominant. In another—adjudication—it is crucial, but the prosecutor shares the stage with others. In the sentencing stage the prosecutor's role is advisory but can be important in many jurisdictions. In this chapter we will focus primarily on these three stages.

THE CHARGING STAGE

The most important area of involvement for the prosecutor is in the charging stage. This stage begins with the initial intake of a case and concludes with the bringing of formal charges against a defendant. It may be viewed as consisting of two phases, **case screening** and the **charging** decision. In the first instance activity centers around the evaluation of case materials in order to understand the exact nature of the case and determine whether charges should be filed. The second phase concentrates more on what charges to file and filing alternatives.

Before looking at each of these phases, let us note briefly several factors contributing to the basic limits within which the office operates during the charging stage.

The first of these factors is the amount and type of law enforcement input into the office. Prosecutors have little control over this, if any. Joan Jacoby writes:

> State laws and local ordinances define crime, and what crimes are to be referred to his jurisdiction. The volume of crime in the community directly determines the volume of work in the prosecutor's office. Additionally, the quality of law enforcement activity directly affects the charging process in particular, and the prosecutive function in general.[1]

A second factor involves certain legal distinctions made between the prosecutor's screening and charging of misdemeanors on the one hand and felony cases on the other. In some jurisdictions the two classes of crime are processed by different offices: misdemeanors by city or county prosecutors and felonies by state or district attorneys. In other jurisdictions some misdemeanors are filed in court by means of a

docket entry—a direct filing from a police report. This means the police issue the formal charging instrument and no prosecutorial screening takes place at all. (Most places handle traffic offenses this way.) Some states require that grand juries process all felony cases. On the other hand, other states require grand jury action only in capital felonies (felonies that may carry the death sentence). The most common pattern is for prosecutors to screen all felonies and most misdemeanors with little direct interference from other agencies.

Case Intake

Cases come to the prosecutor's attention from either law enforcement officers or citizens. Most originate from municipal police and sheriffs but walk-ins (citizens coming to the office) are not uncommon. If the initial intake is directly from a citizen, the matter will receive whatever investigation it warrants and charges may or may not result. Cases from law enforcement come in essentially two forms, depending on whether the suspects have been arrested prior to the matter being brought to the prosecutor—**in-custody cases**—or remain at large until the prosecutor makes a decision—**at-large cases.**

For the in-custody cases, the accused is arrested and booked into a jail, where he or she will remain unless able to post bail. As soon as possible after an arrest, the arresting agency will deliver to the prosecutor's office a case investigative file on the accused. Substantial variations in the elapsed time between arrest and delivery of the case file exist from office to office, with the range of from one to sixty days.[2]

At-large cases result when the police are not able to make arrests in a crime. Thus they must take their case to the prosecutor while suspects are still at large. The case is evaluated and police are informed as to whether there is sufficient probable cause to make arrests. If a good case exists, the office may file charges and cause arrest warrants or court orders for arrest to be issued for those involved. Many prosecutors prefer this approach whenever circumstances permit, since it allows them more time to screen a case and seek correction of any weaknesses before the suspect is arrested.

Case Screening

However a case comes to the attention of the prosecutor, it must be thoroughly screened in order to reach a charging decision. The primary source for the prosecutor's evaluation is the case file. It generally contains such items as a full sworn statement (**affidavit**) by arresting or investigating officers as to the events of the crime and the role of the accused, affidavits by any witnesses to the crime, reports from any technicians, laboratories, or medical examiners contributing to case evidence, and **rap sheets** (sheets listing previous arrests) or other records of the defendant's criminal history. During this screening phase the prosecutor may seek other information felt necessary to reach a charging decision. In most states, law or rules of procedures regarding in-custody cases require that a charging decision be rendered within a given period of time from the arrest of the accused.

Charging Decision

Once the screening process is completed, the prosecutor may choose one of several paths: drop the case, divert the accused out of the criminal process and into some diversionary program, bring formal charges against the accused, or refer the matter to a grand jury for a charging decision. If the case is dropped, the state is withdrawing its accusations (all charges) against the accused. If the defendant is formally diverted out of the criminal process, he or she moves out of the prosecutor's immediate scope of concern and will remain so unless unable to abide by the terms of the diversionary program. (Diversion will be discussed later.) If charges come directly from the prosecutor's office, they will be in the form of an **information** (a document setting forth all state charges). Grand jury charges are issued in **indictments.** Figure 7.1 illustrates the flow of cases through the prosecutor's office.

Proper Charging Criteria In deciding which of the paths to take, the prosecutor usually considers many factors. First among these is the guilt or innocence of the accused. If there is proof that a crime took place and that the accused committed it, and if there is sufficient evidence to support a verdict of guilty, the prosecutor should ordinarily prosecute.[3] Even the assurance of guilt, however, does not necessarily mean that an accused should be prosecuted and to the fullest extent possible. As the American Bar Association (ABA) has noted:

> *The prosecutor is not obliged to present all charges which the evidence might support. The prosecutor may in some circumstances and for good cause consistent with the public interest decline to prosecute, notwithstanding that evidence exists which would support a conviction.*[4]

Some of the factors that a prosecutor might properly consider in the charging decision are outlined in the following paragraphs.

The prosecutor should consider whether the crime in question

FIGURE 7.1 Flow of Cases Through the Prosecutor's Office

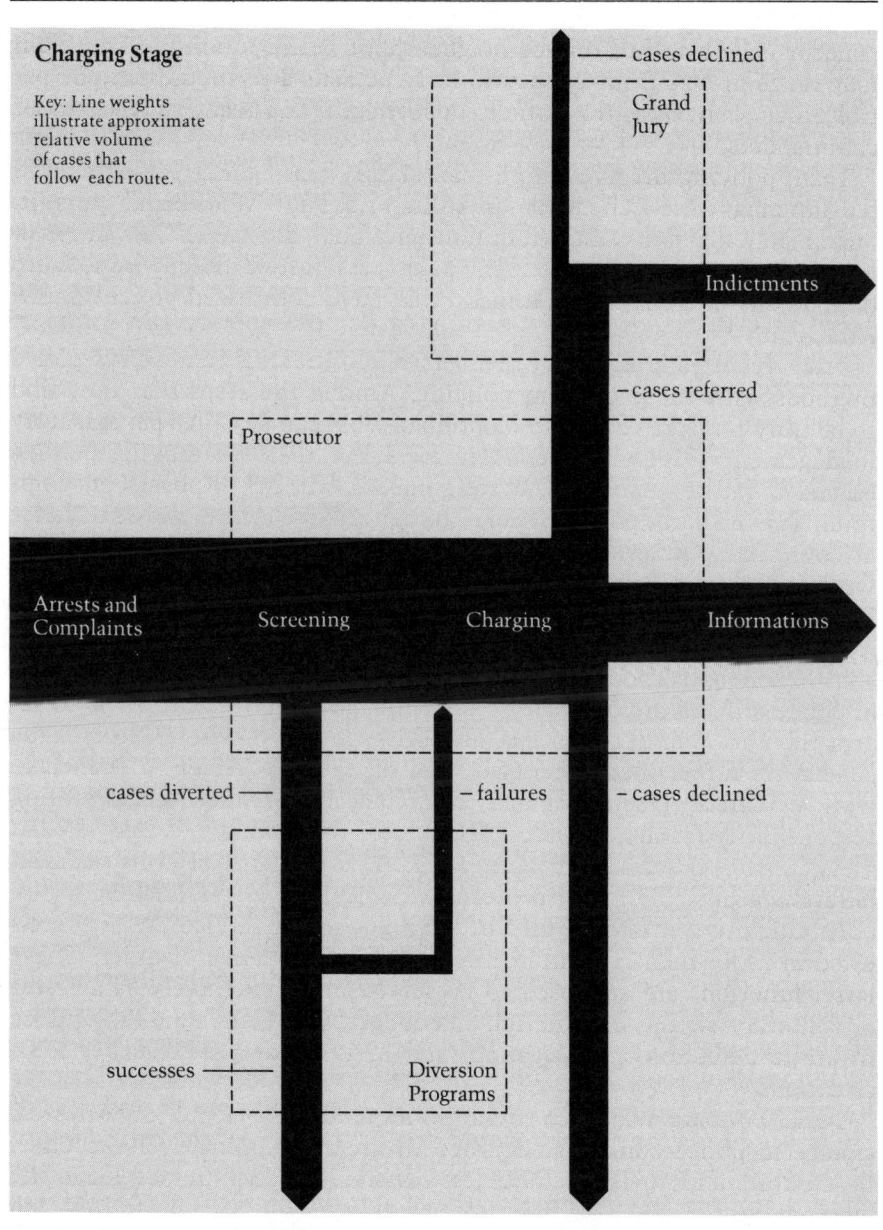

belongs to an area of criminal activity that poses "a threat to the security and order of the community."[5] Such crimes should draw the greatest concern from a prosecutor.

Prosecutors should weigh the extent of the harm to persons or property caused by the offense. They should also consider the motives of those seeking charges. "If the prosecution is sought by a private party out of malice or to exert coercion on the defendant, as is sometimes the case in matters involving sexual offenses or debt collection, for example, the prosecutor may properly decline to prosecute."[6]

Prosecutors should determine if the case in question falls under an obsolete law. The ABA points out that some laws are not generally enforced and that members of a community may be lulled into the belief that an activity is not prohibited (for example certain forms of gambling, such as bingo). Under these circumstances prosecution is not warranted.

The prosecutor should consider the likelihood of prosecution in another jurisdiction. If the defendant faces equal or more serious charges elsewhere, the prosecutor may defer to that jurisdiction.

In some cases the prosecutor may take into consideration certain factors related to the accused. These include his or her ability and willingness to provide information and evidence vital to the apprehension and conviction of other (perhaps more serious) criminals, general background, prior record, age, character, and motives or pressures causing or contributing to the committing of the offense. These factors are quite common to the prosecutorial decision.[7]

The prosecutor may consider the availability of alternatives to criminal prosecution. The ABA has recommended that the prosecutor "explore the availability of noncriminal disposition, including programs of rehabilitation, formal or informal, in deciding whether to press criminal charges." If the prosecutor decides that other factors do not demand prosecution and that the offender can best be dealt with outside the criminal justice system, the prosecutor should defer charges and allow the accused to enter some diversionary program.[8]

Finally, the prosecutor may wish to consider the probability of conviction. Sufficiency of evidence does not always result in the bringing of charges against an accused person. The prosecutor must also consider the likelihood of obtaining a conviction. The National District Attorneys Association (NDAA) has noted that *"the limited resources of the criminal justice system should not be diluted by the introduction of cases with a limited probability of conviction."*[9] This does not mean that a case should hinge simply upon the prosecutor's fear of not winning a conviction. It does mean, however, that the prosecutor may properly consider such factors as the reluctance or willingness of victims and witnesses to testify and supply evidence, the relationship of the victim to the accused, and the probability that victims or witnesses will change their attitudes and testimony between the time of charging and termination of the case (domestic fights often fall into this latter category).[10]

Improper Charging Criteria   In contrast to the criteria above, there are some criteria that the ABA suggests should definitely *not* be used by *any* prosecutor. The prosecutor should not consider the "personal or political advantages or disadvantages which might be involved or . . . a desire to enhance his record of convictions."[11] Some prosecutors have been known to seek a high conviction rate as a springboard to another term of office or election to another position.

In cases involving a serious threat to the community, the prosecutor should not consider "the fact that in his jurisdiction juries have tended to acquit persons accused of the particular type of criminal act in question."[12] Simply stated, if the case is serious enough, it should be filed on regardless of what the jury might do. This is a rule prosecutors have sometimes failed to follow.

The prosecutor should not "bring or seek charges greater in number or degree than he can reasonably support with evidence at trial.[13] The prosecutor should, in other words, file only those charges that the evidence supports. A persistent criticism by defense attorneys is that prosecutors file on more and higher charges than is warranted in a move to force a defendant to plead guilty to lesser or more appropriate charges.

Charging Criteria Often Used   All the preceding criteria are standards set to guide the prosecutor in the charging decision. While prosecutors undoubtedly take these into consideration, they may be resorting to others as well. In an NDAA list of "factors *often used* [emphasis added] to determine whether or not to bring charges," these are included: "Will the time and effort which will have to be spent on this case be justified if a conviction is obtained? Is there pressure from another agency or division of government? Will a conviction make it appear that the prosecutor is being heartless? Is the prospective defendant someone well known in the community so that the resulting publicity would impose a more severe penalty than justified? Would the resulting sentence be too severe for the crime committed? Would it be better to wait until he commits another offense with a stronger set of facts for the prosecution? Will the trial judge hearing this case be favorable? Even though the possibility of a conviction is slim, should it be undertaken because the defendant appears to be guilty of other offenses for which he was not charged? What are the prosecutor's personal feelings?"

As the NDAA notes, "Many other factors present themselves readily but this list should suffice as a brief rundown of typical questions that determine whether or not a charge is brought."[14]

Prosecutorial Discretion One area of criticism leveled at prosecutors has been the extent of the discretion they exercise during the charging stage. Critics point out that this has frequently led to charging inconsistencies from office to office and even within the same office. It has led to different charging decisions for essentially identical cases. Such inconsistencies do not best serve the interests of justice and, it is argued, they should be eliminated. Few argue that prosecutorial discretion be completely abolished. Most recognize its necessity but suggest that there be efforts to reduce its arbitrary exercise and assure that it is used honestly and openly.[15]

To achieve these goals the ABA, NDAA, and others have called for the establishment of office policy on charging procedures and standards that is made known to both those who prosecute and the general public. Such policy should be preserved in an office manual and "maintained in light of changes in rules, statutes, and judicial decisions and in light of day-to-day experience."[16]

In some places efforts have been made to follow the calls for establishment of charging standards in each prosecutor's office. Thus California has adopted a manual of statewide standards for prosecutors that sets forth specific items for evaluation. These include sufficiency of the evidence, selection of the charge, and alternatives to prosecution. Both the District of Columbia and the Bronx, New York, offices have such standards but have added the element of quantification. Each office assigns *weights* (numerical values) to a variety of case elements and the charging decision is related to the score obtained. Figure 7.2 illustrates the Bronx evaluation form. It is used during initial screening of cases to determine which are serious enough to be turned over to the office's major offense bureau. Use of such a form not only helps set priorities for prosecution, but tends to promote uniformity in charging decisions.[17]

Many prosecutors naturally reject the notion that all factors important to a charging decision can be assigned numerical values. Kalmanoff probably voices their thoughts when he states: "It is questionable . . . whether depersonalized systems will ever be able to evaluate personal factors and community values that may be relevant to particular cases."[18] Some prosecutors have been willing to use a scoring system as one tool in the making of a charging decision, but few would rely on it alone to determine their decision.

FIGURE 7.2 Case Evaluation Form

BRONX CASE EVALUATION

DOCKET NO._____ INDICTMENT NO._____

PEOPLE v._____ CHARGE_____ DATE_____

Please record those points which apply to your case. Where there are multiple defendants, compute a base on the defendant with the most serious offense(s).

A. NATURE OF CASE	check if applicable	pts.
VICTIM one or more persons	☐	2.0
VICTIM INJURY		
received minor injury	☐	2.4
treated and released	☐	3.0
hospitalized	☐	4.2
INTIMIDATION one or more persons	☐	1.3
WEAPON		
defendant armed	☐	7.4
defendant fired shot or carried gun or carried explosives	☐	15.7
STOLEN PROPERTY any value	☐	7.5
PRIOR RELATIONSHIP victim and defendant—same family	☐	−2.8
ARREST		
at scene	☐	4.5
within 24 hours	☐	2.9
EVIDENCE		
admission or statement	☐	1.4
additional witnesses	☐	3.1
IDENTIFICATION line-up	☐	3.3
TOTAL CASE SCORE		____

B. NATURE OF DEFENDANT		
FELONY CONVICTIONS		
one	☐	9.7
more than one	☐	18.7
MISDEMEANOR CONVICTIONS		
one	☐	3.6
more than one	☐	8.3
PRIOR ARREST—SAME CHARGE		
one	☐	4.5
more than	☐	7.2
PRIOR ARRESTS		
one	☐	2.2
more than one	☐	4.2
PRIOR ARREST—WEAPONS TOP CHARGE more than one	☐	6.4
STATUS WHEN ARRESTED		
state parole	☐	7.1
wanted	☐	4.2
TOTAL DEFENDANT SCORE		____

C. REFER TO M.O.B. IF ANY OF THE FOLLOWING CONDITIONS APPLY:
(check those applicable offense is most serious charge)

☐ FORCIBLE SEXUAL OFFENSES BETWEEN UNRELATED PARTIES
☐ ARSON WITH SUBSTANTIAL DAMAGE OR HIGH POTENTIAL FOR INJURY
☐ CHILD ABUSE, CHILD SEVEN OR UNDER
☐ MULTIPLE ROBBERIES OR BURGLARIES

D. SUMMARY INFORMATION

NO. OF VICTIMS_____
☐ received minor injury
☐ treated and hospitalized
☐ hospitalized and/or permanent injury
☐ law officer
☐ attempted murder of officer

WEAPON
☐ gun
☐ knife
☐ bomb or explosive
☐ other_____

BURGLARY
☐ night-time
☐ evidence of forcible entry
☐ Church, School, Public Bldg.
☐ no. of premises burglarized

VALUE OF STOLEN PROPERTY   recovered   not
☐ under $250   ☐   ☐
☐ $250 to $1499   ☐   ☐
☐ $1500 to $25,000   ☐   ☐
☐ over $25,000   ☐   ☐

PRIOR RELATIONSHIP
☐ other family
☐ neighbor
☐ friend
☐ acquaintance
☐ other

IDENTIFICATION
☐ photograph
☐ on or nearby scene
☐ other
☐ no. of persons making I.D._____
☐ time delay of I.D._____

SUPPORTING EVIDENCE
☐ crime observed by police officer
☐ fingerprints recovered

E. DISTRICT ATTORNEY'S EVALUATION_____
TOTAL SCORE_____
RANKING CLERK_____
A.D.A. NOTICED   yes ☐   no ☐
ACTION BY A.D.A.:
☐ accepted   ☐ furthered
☐ rejected   ☐ referred to M.O.B.
reasons:_____

Source: David McGillis, *The Major Offense Bureau:* Bronx County District Attorney's Office (Washington, D.C.: Government Printing Office, 1977), p. 112.

Patterns of Charging Despite the charging inconsistencies from office to office, some observers have seen evidence of **charging patterns,** which suggest the existence of certain prosecutorial styles. Kalmanoff, for example, points out that the normal pattern of charging usually means "primary emphasis on felonies, then on misdemeanors, and major traffic cases, and finally, on public nuisance cases."[19] While this is probably an accurate characterization of many office priorities, Jacoby suggests some more specific patterns or styles of charging:[20]

1. The legal sufficiency pattern: In this pattern prosecutors charge all cases in which the necessary elements of the case are present—enough evidence to establish probable cause—and drop only those cases in which there are legal defects, such as illegal searches. Jacoby believes this pattern, based on a sort of open-door charging policy, is most prevalent in the lower misdemeanor courts.

2. The system efficiency pattern: This pattern is aimed at the "speedy and early disposition of cases by any means possible." Here heavy emphasis is placed on careful screening of a case in order to bargain it to an early disposition, find a noncriminal channel into which to divert it, or find a lower court, or other jurisdiction, to process the defendant. It is a pattern that seeks to prevent or clear up court backlogs of cases.

3. The defendant rehabilitation pattern: This pattern seeks diversion of as many people as possible into noncriminal programs but not as a means of disposing of cases. Here the prosecutor believes that alternative rehabilitative efforts are more just and productive than prosecution of many accused persons. The cases that cannot be diverted, however, are charged with the most serious crimes that can be supported by the evidence.

4. The trial efficiency pattern: In this pattern the only charges filed are those the prosecutor believes will stand the test of court trial and result in convictions. Such a pattern depends on good police work to support and justify any charges filed.

Jacoby asserts that using these models of charging policy, one can determine the style of any given prosecutor's office and measure the effectiveness of that office in terms of expected disposition of cases associated with each style.

The Grand Jury

As one avenue of bringing charges against an accused, a prosecutor may—and sometimes must—take the matter before a **grand jury.** This is a body of citizens drawn from the voting population of the jurisdiction it serves. Composed of varying numbers of persons, it plays both an accusatory and investigatory role in the criminal justice system.

Grand juries initiate all federal felony charges and some state felony cases. The most common situation is for the grand jury to have matters placed before them by a prosecutor. Its function is then to determine if the evidence yields sufficient probable cause to bind an accused over for trial. If probable cause exists, the grand jury hands down an indictment—a formal charge against the accused. Grand juries are also empowered to bring charges against persons they have investigated on their own. The charging instrument in this case is called a **presentment**.[21]

In recent years the trend has been for states to decrease reliance on the grand jury as a charging source and to increase its use as an investigative tool. Grand juries have often proven of great value in cases involving organized crime and political corruption, and they have investigated crime committed by officials in the administration of justice. Some, notes Kalmanoff, have "even investigated such problems as court congestion and court administration and have recommended solutions to these problems."[22]

The grand jury's power, and hence its usefulness, in the investigative area is from statutes under which persons may be commanded to appear, given **immunity** from prosecution (a formal promise not to prosecute), and then jailed for **contempt of court** (refusal to obey a court directive) if they refuse to testify. Such persons could choose to forgo the grant of immunity and use the Fifth Amendment protection against self-incrimination, but they then run the risk of prosecution for their role in the matter under investigation. Former Attorney General John Mitchell, of Watergate fame, obtained passage of a federal statute that created the principle of **use immunity** for those testifying before a grand jury.[23] Under this statute immunity can be limited to the *use* of testimony and *not* to prosecution itself for crimes talked about while before the jury. This does not guarantee to persons testifying full immunity from prosecution of crimes they may talk about. It only promises that nothing they tell the jury will be used in any prosecution of them. This may actually encourage witnesses who are potential defendants to provide as much evidence and testimony as possible so that less is left to use against them in court.

Over the years there have been many criticisms of the grand jury system. A great number of them have focused on the weakness of the grand jury as a check on the powers of the prosecutor. The Supreme Court has said that a major function of the grand jury is "to stand between the accuser and the accused to determine whether a charge is founded upon research or was dictated by an intimidating power, or by malice and personal ill will."[24] It is clear that in most cases the grand jury has not performed this function. Citing the large percentage of cases in which the jury returned indictments in matters placed before it by the prosecutor—80 percent and above—some have applied to the grand jury the label of "rubber stamp" and even recommended its abolition.[25]

Another area of criticism is the secrecy of grand jury proceedings and the limited rights of those appearing before it. The jury always operates in secret, and, barring leaks, only its final product is made public. Defendants or potential defendants and their attorneys are rarely present and do not have the right to cross-examine other witnesses.

One other criticism, which has surfaced more since the recent Watergate period, is the grand jury's ability to damage people's reputations through the issuance of critical reports and through the naming of **unindicted coconspirators.** The latter amounts to the jury taking the position that a person was involved in some fashion in a conspiracy to commit a crime but is not indictable. These named but uncharged persons are not subjected to the criminal justice process and thus are not afforded the opportunity to establish their complete innocence in court.

Precharge Hearings

In the time between arrest and the bringing of formal charges against an accused, at least two court appearances may be demanded of the prosecutor. These are the initial appearance and the preliminary hearing. Whether the prosecutor actually has to be present at any one of them will vary from place to place depending on law, rules of procedure, office policy, and even the trial judge.

The **initial appearance** brings the accused before some judicial officer (for example, a magistrate or judge) where booking charges are explained, probable cause is established, the defendant's rights are read, formal bail—if any—is set, and counsel is provided if the charge and the defendant's financial condition warrants it. For petty or minor offenses requiring payment of a fine, the initial appearance may serve as a trial and the defendant's case disposed of.[26] In fact, "a typical misdemeanor concludes when the accused appears for his initial appearance, waives rights to counsel, pleads guilty, and receives his sentence." Such cases may require only a matter of a few minutes and normally take place within twenty-four hours of arrest.[27] Little, then, is required of the prosecutor except the presence of a representative from the office.

For those cases involving police felony charges, the next step may be the **preliminary hearing.** Its primary purpose is to determine if there is sufficient probable cause to bind an accused person over for possible prosecution and to prevent any unjustified restraints on pretrial liberty. Where such hearings are utilized, they are primarily for those situations in which an accused is held for an extended period of time without being formally charged in an indictment or information. Federal and state practices have generally limited preliminary hearings to felony rather than misdemeanor cases. Further, the right to such a hearing has been recognized to be mooted (voided) by the issuance of a grand jury indictment.[28] In these cases it is considered that the grand jury provides the necessary judicial oversight for the establishment of probable cause.

Where a preliminary hearing is held, the prosecutor's role is to argue that sufficient probable cause exists to bind over the accused for further action. The prosecutor usually does this within an adversary process in which witnesses are called to testify and some evidence is introduced.[29] An attempt is made to present only as much of the state's case as is needed to show probable cause. If the hearing is adversary in nature—and most are—defense counsel argues for dismissal of the charges against the client. Also, where a state has no law or rule (or a very weak one) requiring that all evidence and a list of state witnesses be given to defense prior to trial (known as **discovery**), the preliminary hearing becomes a handy way to see some of the evidence and question witnesses. While discovery is not sanctioned as a legitimate function for the preliminary hearing, it undoubtedly is a motivating factor in the defense's desire for holding one. Such use of the preliminary hearing may be avoided in those states having strong discovery rules.[30]

Should the preliminary hearing produce a dismissal of charges, the prosecutor may generally bring the case back to life by taking the matter before a grand jury (if one is available), directly filing an information (where permissible), or refiling "the complaint and attempting to obtain a bindover at a subsequent preliminary hearing (hopefully before a different magistrate)."[31] There are few, if any, jurisdictions in which a dismissal at a preliminary hearing means absolutely that. More will be said in Chapter 10 about the preliminary hearing when we discuss the role of the court during the early stages of the criminal justice process.

THE ADJUDICATION STAGE

Following the filing of an information or indictment with the trial court, the defendant is arraigned on the charges. The **arraignment** marks the beginning of the adjudication stage, which ends with the disposition of the case by a guilty plea, a dismissal or diversion from the criminal process, or a trial.

Arraignment

The purpose of arraignment is to read charges to the defendant and have the defendant enter a plea. If a plea of guilty or **nolo contendere** (no contest) is entered, sentencing is normally set for a later date and the prosecutor's role shifts to the provision of sentencing information and recommendations to the court. If the defendant pleads not guilty, a date is set for trial and the prosecutor enters into what we may call the "trial preparation" phase. In most places prosecutors play no role in the arraignment itself.

For most felony defendants the criminal process gets no further than arraignment. Depending on the place, from two-thirds to nine-tenths of them plead guilty during arraignment. Most of these are a result of plea negotiations between prosecutor and defense attorney. Some of those who do not plead guilty here will do so at some point before the adjudication process is over.

Pretrial Activities

The events involving prosecutors that unfold over the weeks following arraignment fall into three categories: trial preparation, responses to defense motions, and pretrial plea negotiations.

Trial Preparation Preparation for trial is often a continuation of work done in the initial investigation and charging of the case. It often involves follow-up investigations to tie up loose ends and make sure the case is as solid as possible. During this phase of the process, interviews may be conducted with witnesses, **depositions** taken (sworn statements from victims, witnesses, and perhaps the defendant), physical evidence ordered and evaluated, and tab kept on witnesses who might disappear or change their minds prior to trial. Prosecutors may be assisted in any investigation by detectives from the arresting department and investigators from their own office.

In addition to all these things, the prosecutor may spend some time preparing a strategy for presenting the case to the trial judge or jury. The extent and intensity of the efforts to prepare for a trial will normally depend on such things as the seriousness of the case, the number of defendants and counts filed against them, and the complexity of the case. The vast majority of cases, even felonies, are so simple and straightforward that no elaborate preparation is necessary. There are those occasional cases, however, that tend to devour the resources of the prosecutor's office for an extended period.

Pretrial Motions Some of the prosecutor's time on cases that proceed any distance along the criminal justice process is spent reacting to various motions made by defense attorneys on behalf of their clients. Aside from the value that each motion has to offer, if granted, the defense often makes them to delay the opening of the trial. The hope may be to use the time for plea negotiations or to stall until the state's case falls apart. As Waldron and his colleagues note, "The more time that elapses between the occurrence of the crime and the trial, the more likely there is to be a dismissal or acquittal because witnesses and evidence have failed or disappeared."[32]

Whatever the reason, a number of motions may be made that require responses from the prosecutor. Some of the more important ones include the following: A **motion to dismiss** is a request that the case be dismissed for some stated reason, such as a defective information or a violation of the statute of limitations. A **motion for change of venue** is a request that trial be changed to another place where people are less likely to know or have strong feelings about the case or defendant. A **motion to suppress evidence** seeks to suppress evidence—material or testimony—that the defense claims was improperly obtained. A **motion for pretrial discovery** is a request by one side to "inspect, review, and copy certain materials held by the opposition which are anticipated to be introduced as evidence during the trial." Most states granting the right of pretrial discovery do so only for the defendant and not the state.[33] A **motion for continuance** is a request that the trial be postponed. Such a motion can come before or during a trial and can be sought by defense or prosecution or ordered by the trial judge. A **motion for bond reduction** is a request that bond for the defendant be lowered or even eliminated.[34] If the prosecutor feels that the defendant will flee justice or threaten the safety of state witnesses and others, he will argue against the motion.

While it is within their power to do so, prosecutors do not generally make many of these motions. It is the defense that has the most at stake and thus takes every opportunity to seek rulings favorable to its position. However, because unfavorable rulings on these and other motions can make the prosecutor's job of convicting the defendant more difficult or even impossible, he will spend the time and effort needed to see that any motion is denied that would weaken the case.

Pretrial Negotiations The vast majority of cases are settled without trial. In major metropolitan areas, up to 95 percent of all cases result in pleas of guilty to one or more charges. In most of these cases, the plea is to charges less serious or fewer in number than were originally brought against the defendant. It is by now commonplace to refer to the process by which this result is achieved as **plea bargaining** (or plea negotiations). While the defense attorney and judge are also participants in the process, it is usually the prosecutor, more than anyone else, who controls the final result.

The prosecutor's authority to engage in plea bargaining is based on his or her ability to dismiss charges against a defendant at any point short of trial completion. The most common means through which this is done is the **nolle prosequi,** an instrument signifying no further intent to prosecute.

The basis upon which a decision is made to drop charges may have little or nothing to do with plea bargaining. In many cases some or all charges may be dropped because they rightfully should be. New evidence may exonerate the defendant. A witness or victim may change his testimony or disappear. The prosecutor may simply reappraise the case and the defendant. Plea bargaining refers to the process whereby charges are amended in order to obtain a guilty plea to lesser charges or a lesser number of charges.

Why do prosecutors engage in negotiations for pleas? Some have suggested that three things are sought: (1) the maximization of convictions through a process that avoids the uncertainties and procedural obstacles of a full trial; (2) the enhancement of the deterrence objectives of law enforcement by obtaining guilty pleas to some charge rather than risking possible acquittals; and (3) the movement of cases through the clogged criminal court system.[35]

Preventing the clogging of the court system is the reason most commonly cited whenever proposals to abolish plea bargaining are discussed. Preston Trimble, past president of the NDAA, spoke for many of his colleagues when asked, "Could the criminal system work without plea bargaining?" He stated:

> *Of course not, under the current setup . . . [there are] not enough people. You know, the crime rate is increasing substantially, and even if you established enough courts and prosecutors and assistants and secretaries for today . . . tomorrow with the rising crime rate, you're going to have to do it again. And the public is not willing to pay that price.*[36]

The 1967 report of the President's Crime Commission said flatly: "As a practical matter, many courts could not sustain the burden of having to try all cases coming before them."[37]

Some observers of plea bargaining have pointed to more humane or justice-oriented reasons for its use. While recognizing that it maximizes the disposal of cases and prevents overburdening of the court system, the President's Commission noted:

It imparts a degree of certainty and flexibility into a rigid yet frequently erratic system. The guilty plea is used to mitigate the harshness of mandatory sentencing provisions and to fix a punishment that more accurately reflects the specific circumstances of the case than otherwise would be possible under inadequate penal codes.[38]

Donald Newman and Edgar NeMoyer add their endorsement to this view:

Perhaps it can be demonstrated that the negotiation system is in many ways more equitable and more just than its maximum implementation counterpart.... Legislatures deal with offense and offender categories and not individual violators, [prosecutors deal] with individual people and with single cases, all with a myriad of aggravating and mitigating circumstances.[39]

In short, plea bargaining enables the prosecutor to play a key role in individualizing justice.

The objections to plea bargaining are many, but the most common are that criminals are allowed to obtain "cheap" convictions—that is, ones in which they do not pay for the real crimes they committed—that it is moving criminal justice into an administrative process rather than an adversary one, and that it is generating cynicism about criminal justice among the accused, the system's practitioners, and the public at large. There are prosecutors who agree with some of these. One of them has said:

The fact is that it's terrible the way guilty guys get bargain rates on crime: two for one, five for one, and stuff like that. That's the evil of it. The real evil is that it lessens the respect for the system.[40]

Arthur Rosett and Donald Cressey, authors of a recent book on plea bargaining, assert that courthouse workers, including prosecutors, "develop a group sense of justice," which differs with attitudes generally held in the community and which generally is more humane and pragmatic than that of the public. They argue that prosecutors use case loads as their public excuse for bargaining but rarely consider that in deciding whether to deal on specific cases before them. The real reasons for dealing out most cases, they argue, turn out to be weaknesses in cases that could result in acquittals, the desire to adjust the charges to more reasonable levels in terms of the facts and the character of the defendant, and the desire to comply with the courthouse consensus on concepts of fairness and justice.[41] They also point to a recent study in which the majority of defendants surveyed indicated it was their own attorneys who both initiated negotiations and urged settlement by pleas. Only a small minority of defendants identified the prosecutor as the initiator.[42]

What prosecutors actually do in the process of bargaining differs greatly from state to state and office to office. In a few cases negotiations may begin prior to filing the original charges. This is especially true when it is the police who come forward and suggest they want to obtain a deal for the accused because he is—or will be—a valuable source of information about other crimes or criminals. The usual pattern is for the bargaining to occur between arraignment and trial and for the defense attorney to make the first suggestion of a settlement. Whether a prosecutor bargains or not will depend largely on the strength of the case. If the prosecutor has a strong case, bargaining may not take place at all. If it is a case of some doubtful strength, the prosecutor may enter into negotiations with the defense attorney.

Following the entry of the plea, and assuming its acceptance by the trial judge, only sentencing remains to terminate the case. If part of the deal was that the prosecutor would recommend, or at least not object to, a certain acceptable penalty, the prosecutor must fulfill his part of that bargain. Thus the prosecutor has a direct role in the vast majority of criminal cases.

Trial Activities

Despite the vast number and importance of cases settled by plea, many cases in which the facts are closely contested or the applicability of the law to the facts is not clear or cases in which the defendant has nothing to lose wind up going to trial. The prosecutor has a major role to play in this phase of the process. Among the areas of the prosecutor's concern are witness management, jury selection, his opening statement, presentation of the state's case, cross-examination of defense witnesses, and his closing argument.

The prosecutor is responsible for **witness management,** that is, for seeing to it that the witnesses are present and ready to testify. This task requires that the prosecutor and staff stay on top of the court calendar and keep tabs on the witnesses. It is the prosecutor's responsibility to see to it that subpoenas to testify are issued and served on witnesses for the day and time of the trial and that any delays in opening the trial or using their testimony are communicated to them quickly and effectively. The tasks involved in witness management are among the most difficult and often costly ones for the state. An effec-

The prosecutor should be prepared to try those cases in which defendants maintain their plea of not guilty.

tive case cannot be presented with angry—much less absent—witnesses.

If the trial is to be conducted before a jury, there is a **jury selection.** The prosecutor must screen the prospective jurors who comprise the jury panel. The members of the panel are questioned by both prosecutor and defense in what is called the **voir dire** (speak the truth) of the panel. Juries are supposed to be objective, fair-minded, and unprejudiced evaluators of the evidence, but prosecutors—as well as defense attorneys—want to be certain that jurors are not biased against *their* case. They do this by exercising their rights to two methods of dismissing prospective jurors: **challenges for cause,** in which the judge dismisses a juror on the grounds of his or her obvious bias, and **peremptory challenges,** in which each attorney dismisses an allotted number of jurors on his or her own without explanation. The number of challenges for cause allowed is theoretically unlimited. The number of peremptory challenges allowed depends not only on the number and gravity of the charges but on the criminal rules of procedure in each state.

Once the jury is seated and sworn in, each attorney gives an **opening statement.** The prosecutor, of course, explains why the jury—or judge—will find the defendant guilty.

In the **presentation of the case,** the prosecutor presents witnesses and evidence that point to the guilt of the accused. The prosecutor listens carefully to the cross-examination of prosecution witnesses by counsel for the defense and objects to any improper questions asked of them. The prosecutor argues against any defense motions for suppression of physical evidence gathered, analyzed, and presented by the police. When the last witness and evidence have been presented for the prosecution, prosecution rests its case.

The prosecutor **cross examines** any witnesses for the defense during the presentation of the case for the defendant. After the defense rests its case, both attorneys give **closing arguments** as to why the testimony and the evidence clearly show that the accused is guilty, according to the prosecutor, or that the accused is innocent, according to the defense attorney.

Depending on the jurisdiction the prosecutor may play a role along with the defense attorney in assisting the judge in the preparation of jury instructions.

Standards of Trial Practice

The ABA and state bar associations have clear standards relating to each step in the adversary process of a trial.[43] Codes of ethics forbid the deliverate use or encouragement of falsified testimony or inadmissible evidence. They also stipulate what is allowed in terms of remarks to the jury and the demeanor to be exhibited to opposing counsel and the accused. Many states' rules of criminal procedure also speak to these matters, and the judge is supposed to keep counsel in line with these requirements. A good prosecutor, though, knows that a judge or jury will generally reject attempts to harass or intimidate opposing witnesses, the uttering of unnecessarily harsh or disparaging comments about the character of the defendant, and other obvious tricks. If the prosecutor wishes to win cases, and to remain in the good graces of judges, defense attorneys, and the voters, the prosecutor will abide by the rules. Apparent fairness, a professional demeanor, and careful understatement of the obvious are generally far more effective than bluster and harshness.

THE SENTENCING STAGE

The role played by prosecutors in sentencing varies greatly from state to state. It ranges from direct recommendations to the judge to no role at all. Generally prosecutors contribute information they have regarding the defendant's character and background to those conducting the pre-sentence investigation. If the sentence is part of a plea-bargained settlement, prosecutors do what they can to assure that the defendant is treated in the manner indicated or presumed during the negotiations. Prosecutors do *not* sentence, however, and many authorities warn against making explicit promises of certain sentences. Such promises are forbidden in most jurisdictions, and judges are required to inquire of pleading defendants whether unlawful promises or threats regarding the sentence were made by the prosecutor. The accused must assure the judge they were not, or the judge is required to refuse to accept the plea.[44]

POSTSENTENCING ACTIVITIES

After sentencing the only process that may directly involve the prosecutor in the case again is a probation revocation hearing. This would arise if the accused was sentenced to a period of probation, violated the terms of that probation, and was brought before the court for a revocation hearing. The prosecutor does not generally file the charges in such a matter but becomes counsel for the state in the hearing itself.

Other than these probation revocation hearings, then, the role of the prosecutor in the future developments concerning the case are very indirect. Even appeals of the case by defense usually do not involve an active role for the prosecutor, except perhaps the preparation of briefs for use by attorneys from the office of attorney general who will argue the case for the state. The participation of trial prosecutors in oral argument before appellate courts is the practice in only a few states and only an occasional event in others.

ENVIRONMENTAL IMPACT ON PROSECUTORS' BEHAVIOR

Earlier we discussed the impact of environmental factors on police departments and diagrammed some of the more important influences coming from the government and the community at large. Many of the same comments can be made with regard to the impact of the environment on offices of prosecution. The first matter we should make clear, however, is that there is a substantial difference between influences on the one hand and formal authority, control, or power on the other. Police departments, especially state and city departments whose chiefs are appointees, are more subject to outside authority from other agencies of government than are most prosecutors. (Perhaps elected sheriffs are on a par with prosecutors in this regard.) As the most visible and pervasive of criminal justice agencies, police departments are also handier targets for community pressures than are prosecutors. Prosecutors perform in the public arena some of the time, but day-to-day decision making takes place in offices and other places largely away from public view.

But while the prosecutors are relatively independent of direct environmental influences from other levels of government and the community, they are subject to influences nevertheless. The impact of relations with other criminal justice agencies, especially police and the courts, is substantial.

The Impact of Government

Each branch of government has some voice in the manner in which the prosecutor operates. The purse strings are in the hands of others, of course, and prosecutors cannot do more than their funds will allow. The resources—assistant prosecutors, supporting staff, office space, equipment and supplies—must be kept within budgetary limits. On the other hand, prosecutors are generally much freer than police chiefs in determining how to spend their funds—for example, how many assistants to have and what to pay them.

Substantive criminal law, that enacted by legislatures and interpreted by courts, obviously affects prosecutors as much as it does police. **Procedural law,** as set down in both the rules of criminal procedure and the rulings of appellate courts, also affects the way in which prosecutors do their jobs. Prosecutors make policies and perform with a good deal of discretion, as we have pointed out. They do so, however, within the limits of the law of which they are the sworn servants and chief enforcement officials.

A politician as well as a law officer, the prosecutor who wants to succeed in the job (or advance to a judgeship or higher office) will usually seek to maintain excellent informal relations with legislators, councilors, the governor's office, and any other possible source of support. We say "usually" because there are some situations in which a prosecutor's success and political future may depend on how well he or she investigates and prosecutes other government officials.

In summary, prosecutors are not often subject to the direct authority of anyone else and are generally freer of outside governmental interference with their behavior than are police. But the impact of government, especially through budget making and lawmaking, is very real.

The Impact of the Community

The community, of which a prosecutor is part, is also influential. In the first place, citizens as voters determine who the prosecutor is in almost all places. The electoral process is often cited as a means of keeping the prosecutor responsive to community norms and standards, even in the absence of more direct demands and expectations. Preston Trimble, a former president of the NDAA, phrased it quite bluntly:

The prosecutor is responsible to his constituents and if they don't like what he's doing ... they'll boot him out. You don't vote for police; you don't vote for courts as a practical matter; but you sure enough vote on prosecutors.[45]

There is a real question, however, whether very many elections for prosecutor are characterized by competition between an incumbent whose record is known by a large segment of the public and challengers who stake out positions opposing that of the current prosecutor. In few contests can the contestants argue about anything more than who will do a better job. The voters are not usually presented with a clear choice between alternative approaches to the task of criminal prosecution. Thus community standards and norms are only indirectly brought to bear on prosecutors through the electoral process.

The fact that prosecutors are politicians who require votes to obtain or stay in office usually means they also need money to run political campaigns. Some prosecutors are careful to cultivate, or at least not antagonize, persons who are, or could be, financial backers. The costs of campaigns for offices of prosecution, however, are usually considerably less than those of other offices, even at the same level of government.

There is another way in which community standards and norms make themselves felt—the jury system. Though only a small portion of criminal cases are brought before a jury of citizens, the fact that any case might be submitted to them for judgment may affect the way prosecutors work. We noted earlier that prosecutors are warned by the ABA and others not to allow the likelihood of acquittal to persuade them from prosecuting any persons believed to be guilty of crimes. Any good prosecutor, however, develops a feel for the kinds of cases that can be won and the kinds of defendants who are convictable, and this cannot but help to adjust or shape his or her charging behavior.

A prosecutor once commented on the impact of community and politics by saying that in the more sensitive or politically oriented offices, there is

> ... an intimate awareness of the problems and concerns of society which translates into greater effectiveness in the courtroom, where testimony often needs interpretation and a grasp of different social contexts and meanings.... Being attuned to the people and the community also contributes to a better use of discretion in meting out justice. Such knowledge is built into a political office where assistant prosecutors are expected to keep their fingers on the pulse of community attitudes and needs.[46]

The Impact of Interagency Relations

Because of their central positions in the criminal justice process, prosecutors are subject to certain cross-pressures from other criminal justice agencies. Their success depends on their ability to deal effectively with police, defense attorneys, and trial court judges. The relations between their offices and each of these other participants in the process are crucial.

Relations with Police Police departments provide the input of cases on which prosecutors take action. All but a few criminal matters are presented to their offices by officers who have investigated the crimes and apprehended the accused. Direct complaints from citizens and other sources provide a very small portion of the case load. Prosecutors have no direct control over the quantity or the quality of the cases presented by police. They are, of course, vested with full authority to reject police-prepared cases they believe are unfit for prosecution. They may also exercise their own judgment in substituting charges for the ones listed on the booking report and may file an information or seek a grand jury indictment on charges quite different from the ones used to arrest the suspect. Finally, the prosecutor may alter or drop charges as the process continues and may accept pleas to lesser charges, all without the approval of the police.

That prosecutors and police do not always see eye to eye is an understatement. Police are frequently unhappy with the charging practices of prosecutors and are especially frustrated and angry about the plea bargaining and cop-outs they believe are involved in the disposal of most cases. For their part, prosecutors often tend to be impatient with what they perceive as the sloppy work of many police, especially the failure of police to follow fundamental legal requirements in the performance of arrests and searches and the failure of investigators to put all relevant case facts into a logical order in their reports.[47]

David Neubauer has noted the existence of three "potentials for conflict" between police and prosecutors: (1) they "usually come from different social backgrounds" and have differing views about the nature and permanence of their role in law enforcement; (2) they develop "markedly different perspectives on the law," with police having little use for what they see as procedural restrictions on their ability to enforce the substance of law; and (3) the "work environments of the police and the prosecutor produce different perspectives." On this last point, not only are the goals different (capture versus conviction), but the places of action are in sharp contrast. "For the police the most relevant area is the scene of the crime; for the prosecutor the arena is the courtroom."[48] We have heard police remark that they would like to videotape crime scenes so they could bring some of the flavor of the actual events and behavior of crime participants into the sterile atmosphere of the prosecutor's office and the courtroom.

There is little doubt that both the police and the prosecutor believe there is little chance that the other will truly appreciate the realities of *his* situation. Nevertheless some understanding of the perspectives of the other official is absolutely necessary to the work of both. The good will and support of police can make the task of prosecution more rewarding than it otherwise would be. If police believe prosecutors are doing their best to win their cases, they will accept criticism and try to improve their own investigations and case preparations. Police will also be more willing to put up with the demands made upon them as witnesses. A truly effective prosecutor, then, is one who seeks to cultivate productive and mutually rewarding relationships with the police departments within the jurisdictions.

There are specific ways in which the prosecutor can develop good relationships with the police. One is by communicating charging and disposition decisions back to police and even involving them in those activities as far as possible. This helps overcome the common police complaint that they never know what happens to the people they arrest until they see them back on the street. Another means that prosecutors may employ is to act as legal advisors to police departments. Still another is to participate regularly in the training programs of the departments, at both the academy and in-service levels. Finally there are such administrative techniques as operating witness management programs, which prevent police from wasting time in the courthouse when not needed and from missing scheduled appointments. The fact that the NDAA and other organizations are pushing these efforts indicates the increasing value prosecutors and police administrators are placing on the development of solid police-prosecutor relations.

Relations with Judges and Defense Attorneys Prosecutors cannot cultivate excellent ties with police at the expense of their relations with the courts. They must be concerned especially with judges but also with defense attorneys. Rosett and Cressey have stated that they are all part of a subculture, the courthouse gang, which develops a group sense of justice with which they process the cases and defendants before them.[49]

Defense attorneys have the capacity to make life difficult for prosecutors through their ability to raise procedural objections at every step of the process. Judges can contribute to the success or failure of prosecutors through their decisions on both procedural and substantive issues: judges may release defendants or grant low bail; they can grant defense motions suppressing evidence or confessions; and finally they can dismiss charges and grant directed verdicts of acquittal when they find the state's case too weak to present to a jury. While the prosecutor has full authority to charge defendants, and while judges cannot interfere with these decisions, judges do have the authority to reject specific charges or cases they find unwarranted or supported by illegally seized evidence or other questionable means. In short, prosecutors do not operate in a vacuum. Their effectiveness depends largely on how they balance action based on their own convictions with response to pressures from their environment.

TEST YOURSELF

Define these key terms:
affidavit
indictment
legal sufficiency pattern
trial sufficiency pattern
use immunity
motion to suppress evidence
voir dire
peremptory challenge

Answer the following questions:

1. What are the two ways a formal charge can be filed with a trial court other than by an information from a prosecutor?

2. List at least five proper criteria for a charging decision and give an example of an improper reason for making a decision.

3. What is the difference between the legal sufficiency pattern and the trial sufficiency pattern of charging decisions?

4. What are the major functions of grand juries? What are some criticisms of their operations?

5. Give three reasons why prosecutors engage in plea negotiations.

6. In what two ways can citizens directly influence prosecutors and their operations?

NOTES

1. Joan E. Jacoby, *Pretrial Screening in Perspective*, National Evaluation Program Phase I Report (Washington, D.C.: Government Printing Office, 1976), p. 2.
2. Ibid., p. 78.
3. American Bar Association, *Standards Relating to the Prosecution and the Defense Function* (New York: Institute of Judicial Administration, 1971), p. 93.
4. Ibid., p. 92.
5. Ibid., p. 93.
6. Ibid.
7. Ibid., pp. 94-95.
8. Ibid., pp. 90-91. See also James Garber, "Screening of Criminal Cases and Recommendations" in National District Attorneys Association, *Screening of Criminal Cases* (Chicago: NDAA, 1973), pp. 70-72.
9. Garber, "Screening," p. 72.
10. Ibid., pp. 71-72. See also ABA, *Standards*, pp. 92-96.
11. ABA *Standards*, p. 92.
12. Ibid., p. 93.
13. Ibid.
14. Robert F. Leonard and Joel B. Saxe, "Alternatives to the Criminal Warrant Process: The Prosecutor's Discretionary Decision to Charge," in NDAA, *Screening*, p. 2.
15. Roscoe Pound, "Discretion, Dispensation and Mitigation: The Problem of the Individual Special Case," *New York University Law Review*, 35 (1960), pp. 925-927; Charles Breitel, "Controls in Criminal Law Enforcement," *University of Chicago Law Review*, 27 (1960), p. 427.
16. ABA, *Standards*, pp. 64-66.
17. Daniel McGillis, *Major Offense Bureau: Bronx County District Attorney's Office* (Washington, D.C.: Government Printing Office, 1977), pp. 24-32.
18. Alan G. Kalmanoff, *Criminal Justice: Enforcement and Administration* (Boston: Little, Brown, 1976), p. 214.
19. Ibid., p. 212.
20. Jacoby, *Pretrial Screening*, pp. 10-16.
21. Kalmanoff, *Criminal Justice*, p. 274.
22. Ibid.
23. Title 18, part V, section 6002. See also *Kastigar* v. *United States*, 406 U.S. 441 (1972).
24. *Wood* v. *Georgia*, 370 U.S. 375, 390 (1962).
25. Ronald J. Waldron et al., *The Criminal Justice System* (Boston: Houghton Mifflin, 1976), p. 157.

26. George T. Felkenes, *The Criminal Justice System* (Englewood Cliffs, N.J.: Prentice-Hall, 1973), p. 6; Robert E. Blanchard, *Introduction to the Administration of Justice* (New York: Wiley, 1975), pp. 9-10; Waldron et al., *Criminal Justice System*, p. 45; NDAA, *Screening*, p. 54.
27. Frank R. Prassel, *Introduction to American Criminal Justice*, (New York: Harper & Row, 1975), pp. 148-49.
28. Only in two states are there postindictment preliminary hearings. In these states the magistrate can, if he feels probable cause has not been established, dismiss the indictments. See Yale Kamisar, Wayne R. LaFave, and Jerold H. Israel, *Cases on Modern Criminal Procedure*, 4th ed., (St. Paul, Minn.: West Publishing Co., 1974), pp. 975-76.
29. Kamisar, *Criminal Procedure*, p. 996. See also Newman, pp. 199-200.
30. Kamisar, *Criminal Procedure*, pp. 960-61.
31. Ibid., pp. 991-92.
32. Waldron et al., *Criminal Justice System*, p. 207.
33. Gilbert B. Stuckey, *Procedures in the Justice System*, (Columbus, Ohio: Merrill, 1976), p. 121.
34. Ibid., p. 122.
35. Kalmanoff, *Criminal Justice*, p. 228.
36. As quoted in Kalmanoff, *Criminal Justice*.
37. President's Commission on Law Enforcement and Administration of Justice, *The Challenge of Crime in a Free Society* (Washington, D.C.: Government Printing Office, 1967), p. 135.
38. Ibid.
39. Donald J. Newman and Edgar C. NeMoyer, "Issues of Propriety in Negotiated Justice," *Denver Law Journal*, vol. 47, no. 367 (1970), pp. 374-76.
40. Kalmanoff, *Criminal Justice*, p. 229.
41. Arthur Rosett and Donald R. Cressey, *Justice by Consent: Plea Bargains in the American Courthouse* (Philadelphia: Lippincott, 1976), pp. 85-97.
42. Ibid., pp. 108-9.
43. ABA, *Standards*, pp. 117-30.
44. *Boykin v. Alabama*, 395 U.S. 298 (1969).
45. As quoted in Kalmanoff, *Criminal Justice*, p. 229.
46. John J. Meglio, "Comparative Study of the District Attorneys' Offices in Los Angeles and Brooklyn," *Prosecutor* 5 (1969), p. 238.
47. Frequent references to these matters were made at the NDAA Conference on Police-Prosecutor Relations, Chicago, Illinois, 10-13 June 1974.
48. David W. Neubauer, *Criminal Justice in Middle America* (Morristown, N.J.: General Learning Press, 1974), pp. 55-56.
49. Rosett and Cressey, *Justice by Consent*, pp. 91-94.

PART IV
The Courts

CHAPTER 8
Criminal Court Functions and Structures

OUTLINE

HISTORICAL DEVELOPMENT
    English Origins
        Criminal Justice in Medieval England
        English Development After 1066
    American Development

FUNCTIONS OF CRIMINAL TRIAL COURTS
    Provision of Justice
    Adjudication of Defendants
    Sentencing of Those Adjudicated Guilty
    Principles of Justice
        Presumption of Innocence
        Due Process of Law

STRUCTURE OF THE COURT SYSTEM
    Key Concepts and Principles
        Jurisdiction
        Venue
    State Court Systems
        Courts of Limited Jurisdiction
        Courts of General Trial Jurisdiction
        State Appellate Courts
    Federal Court System
        Federal District Courts
        U.S. Courts of Appeal
        U.S. Supreme Court

OBJECTIVES

After reading this chapter the student should be able to:

Explain why the criminal court is important to the achievement of justice for the individual and society.

Discuss the origins of the American court system.

Describe from a historical perspective the progress made in humanizing the process of determining the guilt or innocence of those accused of committing crimes.

Discuss the origin of grand and petit juries.

Explain why the United States developed a dual system of courts.

Discuss the concept of judicial review.

Describe the functions of criminal trial courts as well as certain underlying principles of justice.

Describe the due process rights contained in each of the amendments discussed.

Discuss the concepts of court jurisdiction and venue.

Outline and describe the structure of both federal and state court systems.

KEY TERMS

outlawry
blood feud
atonement
trial by ordeal
trial by battle
trial by compurgation
petit jury
dual court system
legal justice
justice of dispensation
presumption of innocence
due process
selective incorporation
self-incrimination
double jeopardy
change of venue
compulsory process
cruel and unusual punishment
court jurisdiction
limited and special jurisdiction
general jurisdiction
appellate jurisdiction
concurrent jurisdiction
exclusive jurisdiction
venue
lower or inferior courts
general trial court
superior courts
trial de novo
court of last resort
intermediate appellate courts
superintending control
writ of mandamus
writ of prohibition
writ of habeas corpus

☐ Prominent within the criminal justice process is the criminal court. It not only provides a forum for the disposition of cases but furnishes one of the primary participants in the criminal justice system—the judge. Though its primary activities occur in the adjudication and sentencing stages, it is involved in some way throughout the entire criminal process. It is a very important institution for it is a public arena where one may defend himself against criminal charges and have one institution of the state—the court—sworn to assure that another state institution—prosecution—prove guilt beyond every reasonable doubt. The criminal court is a highly visible structure—the court as an institition of justice and the judge as the embodiment of law and the protector of a defendant's due process rights. The court is all these things, but it is also a point in the criminal justice process where failure to adequately and speedily process cases often results in backlogs that clog the system and hinder the achievement of justice. It is a place where failure to assure that legal rules of fairness are observed may result in a miscarriage of justice for both defendant and society.

HISTORICAL DEVELOPMENT

Perhaps the importance of today's criminal court in the achievement of societal and individual justice might be better appreciated if we understood something of its origin and development. Despite current criticisms of slow, inadequate, and even nonexistent justice in our courts, few would deny that we have come a long way from the time when a person's guilt or innocence was determined primarily by "calls upon the supernatural or for signs from God."[1] Picture two scenes. In the first we see

> ... a comfortable courtroom with a judge sitting behind a desk on a raised platform and presiding over the trial proceedings in a dignified and formal manner ... the jury sitting in the jury box listening to the testimony of witnesses who have some knowledge about the facts of the case, and the prosecuting attorney presenting evidence in an effort to prove the defendant guilty beyond a reasonable doubt ... the defendant ... conferring with the attorney throughout the trial ... the jury deliberating on the evidence that has been presented, and their returning a verdict of guilt or innocence. This scene is substantially what takes place in jury trial.[2]

The second scene takes us back to medieval times in England where we see the accused lying on the ground with stones on his chest. More and more stones are added until he confesses (guilty) or until he dies (innocent). Punishment would follow confession while exoneration might follow death.[3] For these two cases the difference in degrees of justice for the accused is easily as great as the distance in time that separates them.

English Origins

While the origin of courts stretches far back into history and may include mention of such things as the Code of Hammurabi (ca. 2000 B.C.), the tribunals of Nineveh handing down sentences for murder and other crimes, and the courts of ancient Egypt (ca. 1500 B.C.), the ancestry of American criminal courts is more directly traceable to England.

Americans are fortunate that by the time the colonists had left England and settled in the new world, England's system of courts and justice had evolved into something worth adopting. The turning point in English judicial development seems to have been A.D. 1066 and the Norman Conquest. Prior to that point, determination of an accused person's guilt or innocence was usually of a nature that would bring cries of appreciation for our current system from anyone facing the necessity of utilizing it.

Criminal Justice in Medieval England Stuckey has noted that "from the time of the invasion of England by the Romans until the Norman Conquest, one who was accused of breaking the law could be handled in one of four ways":[4] outlawry, blood feud, atonement, or trial by ordeal, battle, or compurgation.

Outlawry was one of the earliest methods used. It involved the community waging war on the offender. Waging war meant killing the offender, burning his house, ravaging his land, and taking his possessions.

In the **blood feud** the offender was left to the revenge of those he had offended. The victim, or perhaps relatives, exacted punishment suitable to the crime committed, up to and including death.

In the method of **atonement** the offender was allowed to offer an atonement for the crime he had committed. The price varied according to the crime involved but virtually any crime, including murder, could be atoned. If an offender could not afford the price demanded, he might end up in bondage or be subjected to some other form of punishment. Today's practice of levying fines for certain crimes (sum of money) stems from the concept of atonement.

Trials by ordeal, battle, or compurgation were three methods of trial that relied on the intervention by God to determine guilt or innocence.

In each instance it was assumed that God would be on the side of the innocent person and would intervene in his behalf. Failure to win his case often left the offender dead (from the trial) or alive and subject to a rather severe penalty—death by hanging, beheading, stoning, burning, or drowning; cutting off of ears, nose, upper lip, tongue, hands, or feet; castration; flogging; tarring and feathering; banishment from the land; or selling into slavery.

One of the most prevalent forms of trial was trial by ordeal. To establish his innocence the accused person was required to successfully complete some physical act that most often was truly an ordeal. Probably the most common ordeal involved the holding of a red-hot iron and after three days returning to a priest to see if the hand had healed. If it had, the accused was judged innocent. If not, he was judged guilty and subject to the appropriate punishment for that crime. Other kinds of ordeals included removing a large rock from a pot of boiling water, walking barefoot and blindfolded over red-hot plowshares, and being thrown into water with thumbs tied to toes (sinking indicated innocence).

Trial by battle was just that. The accused and the accuser fought to the death with some weapon such as the battle-ax. The winner was innocent and the loser guilty. Prassal notes that from this trial method—where combatants could get someone to represent them— "developed the present system of attorneys for the state and the accused, fighting with rhetoric and legal rules."[5]

Trial by compurgation produced a judgment of innocence if the accused could get enough people to swear that he did not commit the crime. Such persons (oath helpers) swore to God that their testimony was the truth. It was thought that this would produce the truth because of a fear of jeopardizing one's immortal soul by swearing to a lie.[6]

English Development After 1066 After the invasion of England by the Normans in 1066, all the methods described above of handling accused persons gradually gave way to institutions and processes more closely resembling our court system of today. Over the next several centuries, there developed the concept of judicial districts (emphasizing the importance of localism in legal administration), the grand jury to aid in the process of levying accusations, the petit jury to render judgments of guilt or innocence, trial by jury for all, rules of evidence, due process of law, and appellate courts.

Development of these vital elements of the court system was neither speedy nor systematic. A prime example of this is the jury system.

Brought to England in 1066 by William the Conqueror, the jury was first used only as an accusatory body. King Henry II (1154–1189), for example, utilized a group of citizens (mostly noblemen) to hear accusations and determine if the accused should go to trial (by one of the methods described above). This group was the forerunner of our present grand jury.

As time passed, the use of the jury was extended to the rendering of verdicts, and the right to trial by jury for freemen (barons) was made a part of the Magna Charta in 1215. In 1275 the Statute of Westminster established jury trial rights for all common men. Before the end of the century, it was seen that accusations and trial verdicts should not be rendered by the same body, and so there developed the trial or **petit jury.** It took some two hundred years before the next major advancement—the impartial jury. Up until the sixteenth century, jurors were chosen on the basis of their familiarity with case facts and the parties involved. This was changed to selection of those with no knowledge of the case or participants. The jury system was brought to this country with the first group of English settlers, became an important symbol during the American Revolution and remains an important institution in the criminal justice system.[7]

American Development

During the colonial period of our country, the courts were essentially transplants from England. They were, in fact, "viewed as an extension of the British trial court system," and "all courtroom personnel, including trial judges, originally were appointed by the British crown."[8] After the American Revolution, British rule was cast off but its court system remained with us as a model for our own.

American courts were shaped by a number of factors, including the existence of states with their own governments and court systems, the need to have courts within a reasonable distance of everyone throughout an enormous land, and the American impulse to democratize every institution of government. The results included a **dual system** of courts with independent court systems at both the federal and state levels, the appearance of minor or inferior courts in every county or town of any size, and the replacement of judicial appointment with election in most jurisdictions. There grew an enormously complicated array of courts, which hardly constituted systems at all, even within each level of government.

At the federal level the Supreme Court was the only judicial body created by the Constitution, but the Judiciary Act of 1789 established the basis for the current federal court system by creating districts with trial courts and establishing their jurisdictions. The first Congress rejected the argument that cases should come to federal courts only after passing through state courts, and instead gave federal courts areas of trial jurisdiction. This decision was crucial to the development of American judicial institutions and processes. It allowed each level to develop its own areas of authority, while necessarily also leaving some matters to fall into an area of overlapping jurisdiction.

FUNCTIONS OF CRIMINAL TRIAL COURTS

Trial courts can be said to have three functions. The overriding one is to provide justice. Within this, however, there are the more specific functions of adjudicating defendants and sentencing those convicted.

Provision of Justice

The courts of the United States are the institutions through which most Americans expect to obtain justice. Recall that justice is an abstract concept, and that while it can have many—largely subjective—meanings, it can be defined broadly as rendering to each person his or her due. Recall that there are two different, and inherently contradictory, approaches as to how best to provide justice. One is **legal justice,** which emphasizes the standardization of rules, the binding of all persons to them, and the equal punishment of all those who disobey them. Legal justice is thus equivalent to the notion of equal justice under the law. The other approach is referred to as the **justice of dispensation.** Under this approach exceptions to the enforcement of laws are made where warranted to avoid unnecessary hardships. Thus this approach can be characterized as one of tempering justice with mercy, or individualizing justice. Legislatures, in making "just" laws, standardize rules and provide standard punishments for those who break them. Courts, on the other hand, are expected to strike a balance between the demands of equal justice and the individualization of justice to fit the case.

It is in criminal law that the conflict between equal justice for all law violators and the individualization of justice to fit the circumstances of the case becomes most acute. We have already discussed the importance of discretion used by both police and prosecutors in exercising their respective authority to arrest and to formally charge criminal defendants. Police and prosecutors are expected to be concerned about and to serve the interests of justice. It is the criminal trial courts, however, to which we turn when looking for justice to be assured. The overriding function of these courts is to take the cases from police and prosecutors and see to it that justice is done. Within this very broad function, the criminal trial courts are expected to perform two others: adjudicate the defendants and sentence those convicted.

Adjudication of Defendants

Providing justice is the overriding function of trial courts, and this function is served within the context of more specific tasks. One of these is the adjudication of defendants charged with criminal offenses. This function consists of two phases: providing a fair hearing for the prosecution and defense, and rendering a verdict and an adjudication of the defendant in accordance with the facts and the law. It has been pointed out that the adjudication of defendants in court amounts to a labeling process in which those found guilty are labeled as "criminals."[9]

The adjudication of defendants occurs by one of two means. One is by a plea of guilty, the other is by a full-scale trial. Jacobs comments: "The adversary [trial] process is the model that has been accepted as legitimate." He points out that it "operates under the simplifying assumption that conflicts are two-sided or can be presented in the framework of a two-sided dispute."[10] As everyone now knows, however, the adversary process is the exception. Cole refers to the cases that go to trial as "deviant."[11] The vast majority — perhaps 90 percent nationally — of criminal cases are disposed of by an administrative process resulting from a plea of guilty by the defendant. Many observers assert that the prevalence of pleas and the negotiations that result in most of these pleas are the antithesis of the adversary process. They go on to say that the settlement of criminal cases effectively negates the defendants' rights to due process of law and the various procedural rights discussed above. This may or may not be true. It is the court's function to see to it that these rights have been protected even in the absence of a trial. The judge should make certain that any guilty pleas entered by defendants are voluntary and given with full knowledge of the consequences, both in terms of the possible sentence and the development of a criminal record.

Sentencing of Those Adjudicated Guilty

The final and, to those convicted, the most important function of trial court judges is to pronounce sentence. While a few states provide alternatives to sentencing by judges, in the vast majority of situations the decision is left to the judge who accepted the plea or presided over the trial.

There are basically three alternatives open to judges at this point: *incarceration* in a prison, jail, or other corrections facility; *probation* within the jurisdiction of the court and with conditions that the person sentenced is expected to obey in order to remain at large; or a *fine* to be paid. Statutory law stipulates maximums to which persons can be sentenced and usually provides some minimums. There are, however, very broad areas of discretion allowed to sentencing judges. While such discretion has led many to write about the lack of consistency from court to court and from case to case, most judges view their role in sentencing as one of individualizing justice.

Principles of Justice

In attempting to provide justice while processing criminal cases and defendants, trial courts are expected to adhere to two fundamental principles: the presumption of the defendant's innocence and the right of the defendant to full due process of law.

Presumption of Innocence The **presumption of innocence** doctrine states that any defendant is innocent until proven guilty in a court of law. It is the most fundamental and well-known principle of Anglo-American criminal procedure. Rooted in English common law, this principle is the basis for the rule that the court—whether through the judge or jury—shall not convict a defendant unless and until he or she is proven guilty beyond a reasonable doubt. This means that the entire burden of proof rests with the state or prosecution; the defendant need prove nothing. In other words, the defendant can decline to take the stand and testify in his own behalf. In addition, the defense does not even have to put on a case if it believes sufficient reasonable doubts have been raised during the presentation of the state's case. The judge must instruct juries carefully as to how to apply this standard when considering their verdicts.

Due Process of Law The Fifth Amendment of the Constitution provides the basis for **due process**; it states that no person shall "be deprived of life, liberty or property without due process of law." Other amendments that make up the Bill of Rights contain other more specific protections of rights of defendants in federal criminal proceedings. The Fourteenth Amendment, adopted after the Civil War, repeated the due process clause of the Fifth Amendment in prohibiting denial of citizens' rights by state governments. Over the years the Supreme Court has used the due process clause of the Fourteenth Amendment to "nationalize" the Bill of Rights—that is, to bring states into conformity with national standards regarding the specific rights contained in the first ten amendments. This prohibits states from interfering with or denying such rights. The court has done this case by case and right by right, using a process called **selective incorporation.** This means that the Court has incorporated or included each specific right within the meaning of the due process clause of the Fourteenth Amendment. Thus in 1919 the Court ruled that states cannot deny freedom of speech. In 1931 freedom of the press was included, and in subsequent years the Court has added various other rights to the list of those incorporated and thus protected against state action.

The full list of constitutional provisions regarding defendants' rights in criminal proceedings was presented in Chapter 2, and mention was made of the date when each was applied to the states by the Supreme Court. Of course, criminal processes differ from state to state even today, and how each state handles the specific protections is still largely a matter of state concern. Nevertheless, the nationalization of the basic rights themselves has reached the point where it is possible to make a general statement about each one. This will be done for amendments four, five, six, and eight in the following paragraphs.

The Fourth Amendment protects persons and their houses, papers, and effects from "unreasonable searches and seizures." It outlines the requirements for warrants to perform arrests and searches. The authority of police to arrest persons both with and without warrants has been discussed, as has their authority to conduct searches with and without search warrants. Needless to say, the law of arrest and of search and seizure is the most complex and continuously contested area of criminal law. It is beyond our purpose to present a discussion of the developments or current state of the law on this subject. Suffice it to say that in many of the cases that come before them, trial courts are expected to rule on the legality of arrests and searches, and the admissibility of evidence seized either with or without warrants.

The Fifth Amendment's major contribution—other than its provision for due process—is its protection of defendants from being required to become witnesses against themselves. This is the protection against **self-incrimination.** It is important not only because it means a defendant need not testify in a trial but also because it relates to the matter of confessions and their admissibility as evidence. A confession that a judge rules is not entirely voluntary may be suppressed in the same manner as evidence the court rules is illegally seized.

Another provision of the Fifth Amendment prohibits a defendant from being "twice put in jeopardy of life or limb" for the same offense. This is the protection against **double jeopardy.** It prohibits the filing of the same charge against a person for which he or she was once acquitted. It does not, however, prevent prosecution on different charges arising out of the same criminal incident nor does it bar prosecution in both state and federal courts on similar charges. A thief who transports his stolen goods across state lines can be charged with interstate shipment of stolen goods in federal court and with the theft in a state court. Acquittal in one court will not prohibit prosecution in the other.

There are a number of procedural rights guaranteed in the Sixth Amendment, and they include the right to a "speedy and public trial." No national standard has as yet been adopted for what period of time must elapse between arrest and trial before the right to a speedy trial is violated, but the Supreme Court has said that unreasonable delays that prejudice the right of defendants to fair trials are unconstitutional.[12] Federal law requires that U.S. district courts begin trials within one hundred days of arrest, and some states have adopted rules or laws providing for definite speedy trial periods.

The Sixth Amendment also provides for "an impartial jury of the State and district wherein the crime shall have been committed." Two principles are involved here. One is that the system by which jury panels are selected shall not be prejudiced against specific elements of the community. The other is that if an impartial jury cannot be selected from within the district, circuit, or county where the crime occurred, defense or prosecution may secure the removal of the trial to another locale within the state; this is called **change of venue.**

Another right of the defendant provided by the Sixth Amendment is to be informed of the "nature and cause of the accusation"; that is, the information or indictment must be very specific in describing the statute violated and the time, place, and nature of the violation. Another is the right to "be confronted by the witnesses against him." This is the right to see witnesses for the prosecution in court and have an opportunity to cross-examine them. Still another right is "to have **compulsory process** for obtaining witnesses in his favor," that is, the state's power of subpoena to bring in defense witnesses.

The last, but certainly not least important, right in the Sixth Amendment is "that of assistance of Counsel for one's defense." Not only must the courts allow the appearance of defense counsel, now the courts must provide defendants with attorneys whenever they request them following their arrest on any charge—even a misdemeanor—that might result in a jail or prison sentence.[13]

The Eighth Amendment is the next that concerns the criminal process. It contains three protections for defendants: one against "excessive bail," one against "excessive fines," and one against "cruel and unusual punishment." No specific limits have been prescribed for bails or fines. The Supreme Court has ruled, however, that there is no right to bail and that denial of bail is proper in cases involving crimes serious enough to warrant a life sentence or death penalty.[14] In the matter of fines, the Court has held that no one can be imprisoned for inability to pay a fine. Thus while fines were not outlawed or subject to specific limits, the ability of states to punish persons for not paying them was restricted.[15]

As for **cruel and unusual punishment,** the infliction of tortures, beatings, and injuries were abandoned long ago. Recently two subjects have arisen in connection with this protection: conditions in prisons and the death penalty. Federal courts have begun to order limits on prison populations and specific changes in prison systems where they have found that the conditions amount to cruel and unusual punishment. The Supreme Court has also dealt with the death penalty: in 1972 the Court declared that all then-existing sentencing procedures were unconstitutional; in 1976 the Court accepted certain states' revised death penalty laws and rejected others. Capital punishment itself, however, has never been ruled cruel and unusual punishment.[16]

STRUCTURE OF THE COURT SYSTEM

It is no easy task to describe the structures of courts in the United States. Like the components of the criminal justice system already discussed—law enforcement and prosecution—courts have developed haphazardly and are very fragmented. Jackson has written:

The American court system is a bewildering maze of parallel, perpendicular, crisscrossing, and overlapping lines. Our history of dividing legal authority among the federal government, states, counties, and municipalities has created a residue of courts and jurisdictions which is incomprehensible to all but the best-traveled lawyers. No two states have precisely the same hierarchical court structure; courts with the same name (circuit court, say, or district court) may have totally different responsibilities in neighboring states; courts may be burdened with archaic names (chancery, surrogate's, common pleas) that have no relation to their function. And coursing alongside (or above, or around) the grand quagmire of state and local courts is the federal system, sometimes sharing jurisdiction with state courts, other times holding its own exclusive mandate, and in still other instances empowered to snatch a case from the grasp of state courts. A chart maker would collapse in despair.[17]

Some states have retained courts established a century or more ago, but others have reorganized their courts with a view to their unification and simplification into a conscious system of courts. Despite the variety and complexity of court systems, some features are common and some generalizations are possible. This is so because there are certain principles that provide a foundation for American courts.

Key Concepts and Principles

The principles that lie behind virtually all court systems include the distinction between lower or inferior courts and higher or superior courts. This distinction is difficult to explain, however, without reference to the matters of court jurisdiction and venue.

Jurisdiction **Jurisdiction** is defined as "the *authority* of courts or judicial officers over a particular *class of cases*" [emphasis added].[18] A court's jurisdiction is not only defined by geographic boundaries but also by grants of authority under the law to hear and decide certain types of cases. There are generally three types of jurisdiction granted to various courts: limited and special jurisdiction, general jurisdiction, and appellate jurisdiction.[19]

Limited and special jurisdiction describes the limits placed on courts either by the level of seriousness of the cases they are permitted to handle or by the subject matter with which they are authorized to deal. Examples of courts that are limited by the seriousness of their cases are those criminal courts that hear only misdemeanors or infractions for which very limited punishments are authorized (such as $1000 or less, or less than one year in jail). Limited civil courts include those in which the plaintiff (the person filing the suit) may ask for only a small amount (usually $1000 or less) from the defendant. Examples of specialized courts are those permitted to hear only domestic relations cases (divorces, child custody), probate matters (cases related to decedents' estates), or, in some states, those criminal cases dealing with juveniles.

General jurisdiction is authority given a trial court to hear all cases not restricted to courts of limited or special jurisdiction. These courts may hear either civil or criminal cases, or they may be organized into sections or divisions that hear different types of cases.

The authority to hear cases on appeal from lower trial courts is granted to courts that may have trial authority and to courts that are strictly appellate in nature. **Appellate jurisdiction** means, of course, the authority to review and overturn rulings of the lower courts from which the cases are brought. It includes the authority to reverse the previous ruling or to order a retrial in keeping with the ruling made by the appellate court.

There is one other topic involving the matter of jurisdiction. Courts at different levels—such as federal and state courts or county and city courts—may have authority over some of the same cases or matters. **Concurrent jurisdiction** results where a case may be brought to either of two different courts for trial or disposition. On the other hand, a court has **exclusive jurisdiction** over those matters upon which no other court may act. Federal and state criminal trial courts, for example, have concurrent jurisdiction over crimes covered by or prosecutable under either federal or state law, such as bank robberies and illicit drug trafficking. State courts, on the other hand, have exclusive jurisdiction over most homicides, and only U.S. district courts may hear charges of counterfeiting federal currency.

Venue Recall that **venue** refers to the geographic area in which a case may be heard. A crime committed within a specific judicial district is normally heard within that venue or district. If a case must be moved to another district to assure a fair trial, a change of venue occurs but not a change of jurisdiction. Generally the court with trial jurisdiction moves itself to the new location outside its venue, and the judge and prosecutor who would have presided in the original venue do so in the new one.

State Court Systems

The courts existing within any given state are the product of that state's history and the provisions of its constitution and statutory law. As noted earlier, some states have reorganized their courts to create more unified and integrated systems of courts. In the three years between 1971 and January 1975, eight states completely overhauled their courts with a view to streamlining their judicial systems, primarily by eliminating courts of limited or special jurisdiction.[20]

Though only trial courts are part of the criminal justice system, and appellate courts are said to be in the environment of that system, this discussion will include both in order to provide a complete picture of the structure of court systems.

Courts of Limited Jurisdiction Courts of limited jurisdiction are generally called **lower or inferior courts.** About three-quarters of all courts in the United States belong in this category, and they total over 13,700 in number. There are over 1,500 inferior courts in the state of New York alone, and Texas contains 1,151 as of the 1971 survey of court systems.[21]

Inferior courts are those with which most people have contact. They include traffic courts, municipal courts, most county courts, small claims courts, probate courts, magistrate's courts, courts presided over by justices of the peace, and many of the nation's juvenile courts. The criminal courts in this category handle minor offenses of the misdemeanor caliber. Of the almost eleven thousand nontraffic criminal courts, 90 percent may levy a maximum fine of $1000, 75 percent may sentence persons to only twelve months or less of incarceration, and 11 percent have no authority to issue any incarceration sentences.[22] Yet these limited courts hear up to 90 percent of all criminal cases.[23]

There are two characteristics of many of these inferior courts that should be noted. One is that most of them are courts of nonrecord—that is, no transcripts are kept of their proceedings. It thus is difficult for any review to be made of their actions. The other feature is that many are financed by costs assessed the losers in civil and criminal cases and by fees charged to those who obtain such services as licenses, marriages, and citizen-sworn warrants.

Many have pointed out that these "inferior courts" often deserve this label in more ways than one. Many of the judges who preside in these courts, and especially the justices of the peace, have neither the training nor the inclination to dispense a reasonable facsimile of justice. State after state is acting to improve or abolish their inferior courts. Within the past five years, two states abolished these courts entirely, four states abolished existing inferior courts while creating more centralized inferior court systems to replace them, and two states mixed partial abolition with mergings of such courts.

These changes are in keeping with recommendations made by the two national commissions that studied the criminal justice system. The President's Crime Commission urged a massive overhaul of the lower courts in 1967 and suggested that a partial solution would be to integrate them with the trial courts at the next level.[24] The Standards and Goals Commission said that at least the justice of the peace courts and the big city municipal courts should be replaced with county or district trial courts.[25]

Courts of General Trial Jurisdiction Every state has courts of general trial jurisdiction. There are 1558 general trial court systems in the United States, with courts in more than 3600 locations.[26] These courts are **general trial courts,** but are usually called county courts, district

STRUCTURE OF THE COURT SYSTEM

courts, circuit courts, courts of record, or courts of common pleas. As a group they may be referred to as **superior courts.** These are the courts with trial jurisdiction over serious criminal cases, including all felonies and, in some states, high misdemeanors. In most states there is an overlap in the jurisdictions between inferior and general trial courts. Three-quarters of the trial courts also hear appeals from inferior court decisions. If the lower court kept a record, the appeal may result in a hearing of the legal issues such as in any appeal. If the appeal is from a nonrecorded trial, then there is a **trial de novo,** that is, a completely new trial. But appellate matters take up only about 10 percent of the time of courts of general jurisdictions; 90 percent of their time is devoted to civil or criminal trials.

Not only are trial courts "courts of record," they generally boast more qualified judges than inferior courts. Virtually all their judges have law degrees and have had judicial experience before being placed on the bench. In the criminal area these courts have the authority to

Appellate courts are a very important part of the environment of trial courts and of the entire criminal justice system.

sentence persons convicted of capital crimes to life imprisonment or, in some states, to death.

About 10 percent of trial courts at this level are restricted to either criminal or civil cases; the rest process both. The larger general trial courts may be divided into sections or divisions that specialize in criminal, civil, probate, or juvenile cases. In many states, judges rotate assignments in the various divisions of the court.

State Appellate Courts All states have courts of appellate jurisdiction. Twenty-six states have only one such court—a **court of last resort,** within the state. The term "court of last resort" is somewhat misleading when discussing the highest state appellate courts since they are only last within the state judicial structure and litigants may appeal beyond them to the U.S. Supreme Court.[27] Twenty-four states have **intermediate appellate courts** in addition to the court of last resort. In these states there are 152 intermediate appellate courts serving seventy appellate districts or circuits.

While appellate courts may conduct trials in some matters, the bulk of their activities, depending upon state constitutions or laws, is the hearing of appeals from the trial courts below. In most states, litigants have no right to a review of their case by an appellate court. Appellate courts generally have the authority to accept or decline cases for review. An exception is a capital criminal case that results in a sentence of death. An appeal of a death sentence must be heard.

Appellate courts may have what is known as **superintending control** over trial courts. This means they have the authority to issue writs that order the trial courts to do something—**writ of mandamus**—or to refrain from doing something—**writ of prohibition**—or to justify its holding of a person in custody—**writ of habeas corpus.**[28] In addition to this superintendency authority, appellate courts also provide administrative guidance in some states, with the presiding judge on the appellate bench sitting as chief administrative officer for the entire state or for the courts within the appellate district. In some states the highest court is also the source of the rules of procedure for all courts in the state. Therefore, the influence of appellate courts as elements of the environment of the criminal justice system often goes beyond their formal authority to review criminal cases on appeal. They may shape the procedures of trial courts, become involved in cases still undisposed at the trial court level, and through their administrative rulings affect the ability of trial courts to dispose of their cases.

Federal Court System

The federal government's third branch is its system of courts. It is a three-tiered system, with courts of general trial jurisdiction, intermediate courts of appeals, and the U.S. Supreme Court as the court of last resort. There are some courts of special jurisdiction (e.g., the U.S. Tax Court), but they do not concern us since they handle no criminal matters.

Federal District Courts The trial courts at the federal level are the district courts in each of the ninety-four federal districts throughout the United States and its territories. The federal district court in the District of Columbia is that city's only court of general trial jurisdiction. These courts have jurisdiction in all criminal cases that arise from violations of the federal code and that are charged by U.S. grand juries. The judges who occupy the benches of these courts are appointed for life, as are all federal judges and justices.

U.S. Courts of Appeals The intermediate courts of appeals were created in 1891 to relieve the Supreme Court of having to review every case on appeal from the U.S. district courts. There are eleven of these appellate courts in as many circuits. Cases may be heard by anywhere from three to nine judges, but the vast majority are heard by three.

U.S. Supreme Court The U.S. Supreme Court is, of course, the pinnacle of judicial power and authority in the nation. It is often simply referred to as "the Court." Nine justices sit on the Court, with the chief justice presiding as a kind of "first among equals" with the eight associate justices. Terms of the Court begin each October and run into the spring or summer of the following year, depending on the case load.

The Supreme Court serves as the court of last resort not only for the federal court system but for the state court systems as well. Though the power of judicial review over decisions of other federal courts was granted in the Constitution, the extension of that authority to decisions of state courts was established by decisions of the Court itself. This review authority was ultimately legitimized by its general acceptance as the only logical way to prevent legal and constitutional deadlocks. Thus the dual system is linked at the top.

The Supreme Court has limited types of trial jurisdiction, but 99 percent of its case load is appellate. Similar to many of their counterparts at the state level, the Court has administrative and rule-making authority over the lower federal courts. Rules of federal criminal procedure are made by the Supreme Court to fill in whatever gaps that might exist within the federal code itself.

The importance and impact of Supreme Court decisions in criminal cases, especially over the past fifteen years, has already been discussed. The major thrust in recent case law has been to bring state systems into some conformity with basic rules of due process and to cause state criminal justice officials to seek common means of meeting the standards set by the Supreme Court. Thus it is not too much to say that the Supreme Court has become a driving force behind efforts to systematize criminal justice.

TEST YOURSELF

Define these key terms:

atonement
trial by compurgation
petit jury
compulsory process
concurrent jurisdiction
venue
trial de novo
writ of habeas corpus

Answer the following questions:

1. What were the origins of grand (accusatory) and petit (trial) juries?

2. Explain the two major principles of American criminal justice that judges are expected to adhere to.

3. What does "jurisdiction" mean? What types of jurisdiction are *trial* courts given?

4. Other than judicial review, what type of control might appellate courts be given over trial courts?

NOTES

1. Gilbert B. Stuckey, *Procedures in the Justice System* (Columbus, Ohio: Merrill, 1976), p. 77.
2. Ibid.
3. Ronald J. Waldron et al., *The Criminal Justice System* (Boston: Houghton Mifflin, 1976), p. 166.
4. Stuckey, *Procedures*, pp. 79-82.
5. Frank R. Prassal, *Introduction to American Criminal Justice* (New York: Harper & Row, 1975), p. 122.
6. Stuckey, *Procedures*, pp. 81-82.
7. Samuel McCart, *Trial by Jury: A Complete Guide to the Jury System* (Philadelphia: Chilton, 1964); Robert Von Moschzisker, *Trial by Jury* (Philadelphia: Bisel, 1930); Harry Kalven and Hans Ziesel, *The American Jury* (Boston: Little, Brown, 1966); H. C. Warner, "Development of Trial by Jury," *Tennessee Law Review* 26 (Summer 1959), pp. 459-67; Theodore M. Kravitz, "The Grand Jury: Past, Present, the Future," *Missouri Law Review*

XXIV (1959), p. 318; and Alan G. Kalmanoff, *Criminal Justice: Enforcement and Administration* (Boston: Little, Brown, 1976), pp. 245–49.
8. Kalmanoff, *Criminal Justice*, p. 248.
9. George F. Cole, *The American System of Criminal Justice* (N. Scituate, Mass.: Duxbury Press, 1975), p. 332.
10. Herbert Jacobs, *Urban Justice: Law and Order in American Cities* (Englewood Cliffs, N.J.: Prentice-Hall, 1973), p. 99.
11. Cole, *American System*, p. 334.
12. See *Klopfer* v. *North Carolina*, 386 U.S. 312 (1967), and *Barker* v. *Wingo*, 407 U.S. 514 (1972).
13. See *Gideon* v. *Wainwright*, 372 U.S. 335 (1963); *Escobedo* v. *Illinois*, 378 U.S. 478 (1964); *Miranda* v. *Arizona*, 384 U.S. 438 (1965); and *Argersinger* v. *Hamlin*, 407 U.S. 25 (1972).
14. *Carlson* v. *Landon*, 342 U.S. 524 (1952).
15. *Williams* v. *Illinois*, 399 U.S. 35 (1970).
16. *Furman* v. *Georgia*, 408 U.S. 238 (1972).
17. Donald D. Jackson, *Judges* (New York: Atheneum, 1974), pp. 10 and 11.
18. Law Enforcement Assistance Adminstration, *National Survey of Court Organization* (Washington, D.C.: Government Printing Office, 1973), p. 10.
19. Ibid., pp. 1–3.
20. Law Enforcement Assistance Administration, *National Survey of Court Organization, 1975 Supplement to State Judicial Systems*, (Washington, D.C.: Government Printing Office, 1976). p. 1. (Hereinafter referred to as *NSCO 1975*.)
21. Ibid., pp. 4–5, and Department of Justice, *Criminal Justice Agencies in Region 1*, (Washington, D.C.: Government Printing Office, 1974), p. 1.
22. Department of Justice, *Agencies*, p. 1.
23. President's Commission on Law Enforcement and Administration of Justice, *Task Force Report: The Courts* (Washington, D.C.: Government Printing Office, 1967), p. 29.
24. Ibid.
25. National Advisory Commission on Criminal Justice Standards and Goals, *Courts* (Washington, D.C.: Government Printing Office, 1973), p. 162.
26. *NSCO 1975*, p. 6.
27. Harry W. More, ed., *Principles and Procedures in the Administration of Justice* (New York: Wiley, 1975), p. 189.
28. Alvin W. Cohn, *Crime and Justice Administration* (Philadelphia: Lippincott, 1976), p. 245.

CHAPTER 9
Court Participants

OUTLINE

JUDGES
    Judicial Recruitment and Selection
        Election of Judges
        Political Appointment of Judges
        Merit Selection of Judges
    Quality of Judges
        Judicial Training
        Judicial Discipline and Removal

DEFENSE ATTORNEYS
    The Right to Counsel
    Defense Attorney Functions
    Selection of Defense Counsel
        Private Bar and Criminal Practice
        Office of Public Defender

CITIZENS AS JURORS
    Knowledge About Juries
    Selection of Jurors
    Conditions in Jury Service

WITNESSES

COURT SUPPORT PERSONNEL

OBJECTIVES

After reading this chapter the student should be able to:

Discuss the importance of and expectations placed on judges.

Explain the various means by which judges are selected for the bench and the pros and cons of each method.

Discuss the problem of providing training for judges.

Explain the four means by which judges may be disciplined.

Discuss the impact of Supreme Court decisions on the role of the defense attorney in the criminal process.

Describe the three roles played by defense attorneys and explain how these can conflict with each other.

Discuss the problems involved in selecting or assigning counsel for defense.

Discuss the advantages and drawbacks of the office of public defender.

Discuss the importance of juries.

Explain why we know so little about jury behavior.

Describe the various steps in jury selection.

Describe the role of prosecution and defense in jury selection.

Discuss the treatment accorded jurors and witnesses in most courts.

Describe the duties of the court support personnel: clerks of the court, bailiffs, court reporters, and court administrators.

KEY TERMS

partisan and non-partisan election of judges
merit selection of judges (Missouri Plan)
plebiscite
impeachment
recall
defense attorney as advocate
defense attorney as intermediary
defense attorney as counselor
public defender
venire
voir dire
challenges for cause
peremptory challenge
expert witness
clerk of the court
bailiff
court reporter
court administrator

☐ In discussing law enforcement it is possible to focus on law enforcement officers as the line personnel within that component. Prosecution involves prosecutors, including assistant prosecutors, as the key personnel. The criminal courts, on the other hand, involve not only judges but others who are absolutely essential to the courts' operations. Judges are dominant, to be sure. The difference, however, is that courts, unlike police departments and offices of prosecution, are largely arenas or forums within which many persons work, play certain roles, and conduct their business. The workings of criminal courts depend on more than judges and some staff support personnel. They depend on the participation of attorneys (both prosecution and defense), on the sometimes separate office of clerk of the court, on support personnel with specific tasks and skills (court reporters, bailiffs, court administrators), and on citizens as witnesses and jurors.

JUDGES

In the *National Survey of Court Organization* the Law Enforcement Assistance Administration reported that as of January 1972 there were 23,073 judgeships authorized for state and local courts. Of these 17,417 (75 percent) were for courts of limited and special jurisdiction, 4,929 (21 percent) were for general trial courts, and 727 (3 percent) were for positions on appellate courts. How many of these authorized judgeships were vacant is not known.[1]

The same source indicates that as of May 1973 the federal courts employed 396 judges in the ninety-two district trial courts (each bench ranging from one to twenty-seven judges), ninety-seven at the courts of appeal (between three and fifteen sit on each bench), and nine justices of the Supreme Court, for a total of 495. This excludes the courts of special jurisdiction at the federal level, none of which deal with criminal matters.[2]

The importance of judges, not only within the courts as a component of the criminal justice system but to justice as a whole, cannot be overemphasized. Maurice Rosenberg has observed that "there is no guarantee of justice except the personality of the judge," and "the quality of our judges is the quality of our justice."[3]

Yale law professor Geoffrey Hazard has noted that people expect a great deal of judges:

Scratch the average person's idea of what a judge should be and it's basically Solomon. If you had a benign father, that's probably whom you envision. We demand more from them, we look for miracles from them and spit on them when they don't produce them. It's romantic, emotional, unexamined, unadmitted, and almost undiscussable.[4]

Donald Jackson observes that we spin fantasies about judges being honest, wise, patient, tolerant, compassionate, strong, decisive, articulate, and courageous. A good judge is seen as "something beyond the normal attainment of man, something one feels almost a pathetic urge to venerate." He continues: "And so the corollary: a bad judge is worse than a bad anything else. A bad judge enters another dimension of evil, another circle of hell. The bad judge has betrayed our innocent trust, and such betrayal permits no forgiveness."[5] Furthermore, Jackson states:

> *A flaw in a judge's character is painfully visible, magnified by his power. The weaknesses of judges span the human landscape, from greed and bigotry to laziness and stupidity, from indisputable venality of a corrupt judge to the subtle misdirection of an intolerant judge.*[6]

Jackson examines the subjective nature of the criteria by which judges are judged, and observes that while the specific virtues are difficult to state, much less measure, the "failings are more easily identified."

Of course, most judges are neither paragons of virtue nor incarnations of evil. We have an unreasonable desire to elevate judges to the status of Solomon. This causes intense contempt for judges who fail to meet our standards. This may be due to a combination of the unusual status and power of judges with the realities of their recruitment, training, and consequent behavior on the bench—especially the criminal bench.

Judicial Recruitment and Selection

There are five means by which judges are selected for positions on the bench: partisan elections, nonpartisan elections, appointment by the chief executive, appointment by the legislative branch, and the so-called merit selection system. Much could be said about each of these: how each is supposed to work, how each actually works, how many states use each system and for which of its courts; and the benefits and disadvantages of each in terms of the quality of judges and justice produced. Volumes have been and are being written on these subjects. We must, however, make do with a few comments about the impact of selection methods, and three categories will be utilized: elections of judges, political appointments of judges, and merit selection of judges.

Election of Judges Except for parts of Switzerland, the United States is the only democracy in the world in which one finds judges being elected to the bench.[7] Popular election of judges was the natural product of Jacksonian democracy in which it was held that no public office—including judgeships—required special qualifications or should be placed beyond the control of the people. It was carried forward into the twentieth century by the populists and progressive reformers.[8]

Election of judges is no longer as popular as it once was. The defects of this method of selecting those most responsible for dispensing justice in our system have been catalogued and repeated by many observers. The National Advisory Commission on Criminal Justice Standards and Goals summarized the three most common complaints: it fails to encourage qualified attorneys to become candidates for the office; it provides an incentive for judges to render decisions which are popular instead of correct; and it fails in its stated function of selecting judges in accordance with the will of the people because most people are very poorly informed about the merits of judicial candidates—especially within the context of long ballots and scores of candidates running for dozens of offices.[9]

The above criticisms apply whether one is discussing **partisan elections**—those in which candidates are listed with party affiliations identified or under party columns—or the so-called **non-partisan elections** in which party identifications are not provided nor nominations of candidates by party organizations permitted. Distinctions, however, can be made between these two electoral processes. The President's Crime Commission, for example, points out that in the partisan model the nominations are dispensed on the basis of party considerations such as how loyal a party worker each candidate is and how the overall ticket of candidates for all offices should be "balanced." Under the theory of ticket balancing, there should be candidates representing the various ethnic, religious, and geographic characteristics of the electoral district. "Scant attention is given to the abilities of the proposed candidates."[10]

The nonpartisan election was adopted in many states during the reformist or progressive period of the early 1900s. The President's Commission comments that it probably substituted "other substantive evils" for the ones mentioned above. It nullified party responsibility for candidates and introduced equally irrelevant criteria into the process of judical selection—such as the wealth a candidate has to spend on election and the image he or she projects in the media and advertising. The commission notes that the American Judicature Society has labeled the nonpartisan election "the worst of the five traditional judicial selection methods." Popular interest and participation in selection are even reduced, the commission asserts.[11]

Political Appointment of Judges The process of appointing judges by the chief executive or the legislature is said to produce better qualified judges than do elections, but the success of the appointment process depends on the manner in which candidates are nominated. Where the governor (or legislature) is required to choose a candidate already selected by party officials or the legislative representative of the district in which the opening is located, the end result is not much different than that of partisan election because loyal party service is often a primary prerequisite for office. Jacobs has pointed out that most state judges who are appointed have been state legislators rather than full-time practicing attorneys.[12]

It should be noted that even in states with elective processes for choosing judges, the vast majority obtain their positions by appointment, and most often by executive appointment. Judges have a habit of resigning or retiring between elections, necessitating appointments to fill the vacancies. Since the above practice is followed in every state that elects judges (except Illinois), appointment generally is the rule in forty-nine states. This is pointed out by Glenn Winters in an article in which he states that most legislatures play no role in approving appointments to interim vacancies. "Thus a substantial percentage of all the state judges are the products of *one-man judicial selection.*"[13] When one couples the above facts with the recognition that "judges once appointed to office are almost invariably retained in office at the next election," one is forced to conclude that governors have more influence over who sits on the benches of most state courts than state constitutions and laws originally anticipated. Winters comments on this fact: "What is wrong with one-man judicial selection? Don't the governors appoint good judges? Fortunately, very often they do. Sometimes they do not. But in any event, a completely unrestricted appointing power is too much power to give to any individual."[14]

Federal judges and justices are, of course, appointed by the president with the "advice and consent" of the United States Senate. There are two differences, however, between the federal process and the appointive systems in most states: federal judges are appointed for life or good behavior rather than for terms of years; and the screening of nominees involves a number of parties. The parties engaged in the screening of candidates for federal bench positions include the American Bar Association, the deputy attorney general, the attorney general, the senators, special-interest groups who make their wishes known, and the press. Presidents Eisenhower, Kennedy, and Johnson relied heavily on the ABAs Committee on Judical Selection and its ratings of judicial candidates. President Nixon decided to pay less attention to the Bar when it failed to support his nomination of G. Harold Carswell to the Supreme Court. The Senate rarely rejects a presidential appointment to the courts of appeals or Supreme Court, but refused consent to two Nixon nominees, Clement F. Haynesworth, Jr., and G. Harold Carswell.

Appointments to the federal judgeships are subject to what is known as "senatorial courtesy." What this amounts to is the refusal of senators to support any nominee for any appointive federal office, including a judgeship, if the senators from the nominee's state oppose him. Thus it is very difficult for any president to appoint judges of his own party to a district court vacancy within a state if the state senators are of the other party. Deadlocks sometimes develop that keep seats unfilled and severely affect these trial courts for months or years. Nevertheless, the federal system is among the best appointive systems, and Donald Jackson credits its "genius" to "its pluralism." He comments that the interaction of executive, legislative, bar, interest group, and press provides "what solution there is: maximize, don't minimize, the participants in the selection process."[15]

Merit Selection of Judges The final selection process is variously called **merit selection** or the **Missouri Plan,** after the state which initiated it in 1940. Basically this approach involves the creation of a commission consisting of attorneys and laypeople who put together a short list of nominees for each position. The governor then appoints from this list, and the judge holds the seat for one year or until the next election. That election becomes a **plebiscite;** that is, an item on the ballot that asks voters to answer yes or no to the question of whether that judge shall remain in office. If retained, the judge sits until rejected by the electorate or leaves by the normal processes of resigning, retiring, or dying.

Incumbency becomes as strong a factor—if not stronger—in this process of selection as when the method is election. The growth of this approach, however, is due to several factors: the direct and formal role it gives the bar because of its selection of the lawyer-members of the commission; the involvement of representatives of interest groups and the public; and the maintenance of public involvement through the plebiscite.

Objections to the process when it was first proposed in Missouri were twofold. These have been repeated in other states where the plan has been considered. One objection is that such a formal lawyer-influenced nominating process would result in selection of blue bloods. This means attorneys with upper- or upper-middle-class backgrounds who went to the best law schools and whose experience is in the big firms representing the "haves" of society (banks, insurance companies, industries) rather than the "have-nots." This objection has been best expressed in the following song lyrics:

O, the Old Missouri Plan
O, the Old Missouri Plan
When Wall Street lawyers all judicial candidates will scan
If you're not from Fair Old Harvard
They will toss you in the can . . .
O, the Old Missouri Plan
It won't be served with sauerkraut nor sauce Italian
And spaghetti they will ban
There'll be no such dish
As gefilte fish
On the Old Missouri Plan.[16]

The other objection has been that this is an elitist process that removes selection from popular control—a continuation of the populist

The importance of the judge to the court and to justice as a whole cannot be overemphasized.

argument in favor of election of judges. The rebuttal to this argument is that elections have rarely provided effective popular control in the first place. The rebuttal to the "blue-blood" argument is now based on experience with the plan's operation. Richard Watson and Randal Downing of the University of Missouri studied a quarter of a century of merit selection in that state, and, as Donald Jackson puts it, "Their discoveries confounded both defenders and critics." Their findings were threefold: (1) the nominating process was as political as ever—bar politics replaced party politics and governors wound up appointing political allies who turned up on the approved lists; (2) locally born and bred judges were *not* replaced by blue bloods from the prestigious schools but legal mavericks were screened out; and (3) practicing lawyers overwhelmingly agreed on the increase in the quality of judges compared to those previously elected, since truly incompetent judges were eliminated. Jackson concludes: "The fools were apparently gone with the mavericks."[17]

In reviewing claims and counterclaims for the merit selection and election methods, Jackson asserts that "Neither system can guarantee good judges, especially when one identifies the chief ingredient of a good judge as his humility, his human perception and compassion." He continues: "It may be that merit judges, on the whole, are an improvement over elective judges. . . . But it is clear that merit judges are blessed with no greater resistance to the temptations of office, notably tyranny and corruption, than their elective brethren."[18]

There appears to be no clearly superior method of selecting judges, and this is due in large part to the absence of clearly objective criteria by which to evaluate judges or candidates. But if it is very difficult to distinguish between fair, good, and excellent prospective judges, it may be easier to pick out the bad judges already on the bench.

Quality of Judges

A decade ago reporter Howard James traveled throughout the country studying trial courts and the behavior of judges. He said that if the judges he observed were a fair sample, "perhaps half the trial judges are, for one reason or another, unfit to sit on the bench." Of the inferior court magistrates and justices of the peace he concluded that "probably not more than one in ten . . . is, in most states, really qualified to dispense justice today."[19]

Jackson surveyed trial judges during 1972 and 1973 and writes:

My impression is that between 30 and 40 percent of state trial-court judges are unfit to sit. On the federal trial bench, I would estimate the figure to be about 10 percent. At the magistrate's level, perhaps two thirds are unqualified for the responsibilities they hold. Their failures include intellectual inadequacy, corruption, bigotry, tyranny, temperamental instability, and physical or mental disabilities.[20]

Despite the seeming harshness of these words, Jackson is nevertheless more generous in his characterization of judges than was James:

> I believe that judges, as a class, are no more or less honest, industrious, or moral than any other group of comparably educated professional American men—dentists, say, or engineers, or corporate vice-presidents.[21]

Whether or not the quality of judges is significantly different than the quality of members in any other profession, both their virtues and their faults tend to be magnified by the sensitivity and power of their positions.

Judicial Training Judges are no better or worse than the systems by which they are selected, trained, and evaluated in the performance of their duties. Perhaps selection is a key element in determining the quality of judges, perhaps not. The absence of formal training is probably a greater factor. Most judges, like prosecutors, are thrown into their positions with little or no preparation for what their jobs require. They receive on-the-job training, at best. While prosecutors and other trial attorneys receive lessons from their colleagues, opposing counsel, and presiding judges, judges benefit from nothing similar since they have no one equal or superior to them working in the courtroom. Some have observed that support personnel—clerks, bailiffs, and secretaries—guide new judges into a pattern of how things are done, but this is a questionable practice, at best.

Recently efforts have been made to provide training programs for trial judges. The best known is the National College of the State Judiciary in Reno, Nevada. Founded in 1964, it provides four-week seminars for about a hundred judges at a time. Various states have established similar programs, most using federal grants to get started. At the federal level new district court judges attend seminars and sentencing institutes. These activities are helpful, but they are a sort of stopgap measure. Furthermore, judges are not required to attend training programs and many who want to cannot afford the expense since most states do not subsidize their attendance.

Judicial Discipline and Removal Perhaps as important as judicial selection is the matter of how states and the federal government deal with judges who are charged with corruption, ignorance, bias, and sheer incompetence on the bench. There are basically four methods available, with only the first applicable to federal judges: (1) **impeachment** which requires a trial and conviction of the judge before the judge can be removed; (2) removal by the governor after a concurrent resolution by both houses of the legislature; (3) **recall,** in which the people vote to remove a judge before a term is finished; (4) the imposition of sanctions—from reprimand to removal—by the supreme court of a state following an investigation and recommendation from a judicial qualifications commission.

Since none of the first three methods have been used in more than a handful of cases, the fourth method is a recent response to increased demands that something be developed that would be more effective. California, the state of so many innovations, established a Judicial Qualifications Commission in 1960 that has been duplicated or imitated by at least twenty-nine states.[22] Generally, the commission system provides a permanent body with a staff. This staff reviews complaints from attorneys and other citizens, investigates those with any validity, and refers substantial cases to the commission. The commission corresponds with the accused judge and schedules hearings on the cases it considers serious. These hearings can result in a recommendation to the state supreme court for removal or involuntary retirement. The entire process is secret and confidential until the recommendation is filed with the court.

As with most new ideas and programs, this one has its supporters and its critics. Chief among the arguments of supporters is the contention that the commission approach has provided sanctions for actual misdeeds and has been a deterrent to misbehavior. As Jackson notes, "In practice the greatest asset . . . has been what former California chief justice Roger Traynor calls its 'prophylactic value.'" In California, for example, only two removals have been recommended by the commission during the entire history (something the critics jump on). However, fifty-six judges have resigned or retired under investigation. Further, as the commission's executive officer points out, "in many other instances . . . the shock of finding themselves under scrutiny inspired erring judges to improve their conduct."[23]

Critics have been able to point to the low number of removal recommendations and the fact that most judges under investigation receive only a letter from the commission. Most cases go no further because a case generally has to be of a massive nature before being taken before the state supreme court. A related grounds for criticism is that judicial incompetence has not been within the scope of the commission, largely due to the inability to define or measure such behavior. This has left many judges on the bench who probably deserve to be removed.

Speaking in terms of the pros and cons of these commissions, Jackson concludes that "the arrival of discipline commissions has clearly been felicitous for the cause of justice, but it is not the millennium. There is still a double standard of judgment, one for judges and another for lawyers and the rest of us."[24]

DEFENSE ATTORNEYS

In addition to judges and prosecutors, attorneys for the defense are crucial to the criminal justice process in the courts.

The Right to Counsel

Recent Supreme Court decisions have increased the scope of the role defense attorneys play in the criminal justice process. In 1963 the Supreme Court ruled that the Sixth Amendment to the Constitution had been violated by the state of Florida when it failed to provide Clarence Gideon with counsel for his defense in a trial on a felony charge.[25] From this date forward, not only defendants who could afford them had a right to an attorney, all defendants had a right to counsel in felony trials, and the state would have to provide them to indigent defendants.

As important as this departure from tradition was, it was soon backed up with other equally vital decisions in which the right to counsel was extended backwards in the criminal process to the point where the subject of an investigation became a suspect who was arrested or otherwise underwent interrogation.[26] The *Miranda* decision even required police to notify suspects of their right to counsel and the right to have counsel appointed if they could not afford to retain one.[27] More recently, in another case from Florida, the Court ruled that the right to counsel extended to any misdemeanor that could result in jail time for the accused.[28] The role of the defense attorney was thus broadened again, and today only in cases involving minor offenses for which fines are the standard sanction is there no right to counsel. It is not possible to overemphasize the impact these Supreme Court decisions have had on the criminal justice system.

Defense Attorney Functions

While the role of defense attorneys is most often couched in the rather broad terms of "defending a client," there are several more specific functions or roles that are generally performed. Probably the most familiar one of these is **advocate** for the client. As Cohn puts it, "The primary function of defense counsel is to act as champion for his client, ensuring that due process is adhered to, and to take those procedural steps and to recommend those courses of action which the client, were he an experienced advocate himself, would fairly and properly take for himself."[29] In simple terms, this means taking all possible steps within legal and ethical bounds to achieve a victory for the client.

The advocacy role is joined by the defense attorney's responsibility to protect the rights of the client at each step of the criminal justice process. Often this can best be done by acting as an **intermediary** between client and the law, working through negotiation and compromise to secure the best possible benefits from the system. Cohn notes, for example, that where a client has violated the law, the defense attorney may work "with the prosecution in plea bargaining to provide for his client 'the best possible deal.' "[30]

A third role for defense counsel has been described as that of **counselor.** It is the responsibility of defense to give advice to the client as to what to expect and what appears to be in the client's best interest. The American Bar Association has stated:

The defendant needs counsel not only to evaluate the risks and advantages of alternative courses of action, such as trial or plea, but also to provide a broad and comprehensive approach to his predicament which will take the most advantage of the protections and benefits which the law affords him.[31]

While almost everyone would agree that a defense attorney ought to perform the above functions, it is frequently suggested that they fail to do so. Blumberg, for example, has set forth some harsh but not uncommon criticisms. He contends:

The real key to understanding the role of defense counsel in a criminal case is the fixing and collection of his fee. It is a problem which influences to a significant degree the criminal court process itself, not just the relationship of the lawyer and his client. In essence, a lawyer-client "confidence game" is played.[32]

Blumberg charges that the defense attorney makes sure that the clients know that "there is a firm connection between fee payment and the zealous exercise of professional expertise, secret knowledge, and organizational 'connections' in their behalf." Blumberg goes so far as to suggest that defense attorneys manipulate their clients and stage-manage cases to at least offer the appearance of services. He refers to the criminal lawyer as a "double agent" who has a major relationship with the court:

> *Criminal law is a unique form of private law practice. It simply* appears *to be private practice. Actually, it is bureaucratic practice, because of the lawyer's role in the authority, discipline, and perspectives of the court organization. Private practice, in a professional sense, supposedly involves the maintenance of an organized, disciplined body of knowledge and learning; the lawyer is imbued with a spirit of autonomy and service, the earning of a livelihood being incidental. But the lawyer in the criminal court is a double agent, serving higher organizational rather than professional ends.*[33]

Such criticisms as this last one by Blumberg have been especially applied by some to public defenders because of their status as employees of the same state that provides prosecution and adjudication of their clients.

Selection of Defense Counsel

There are generally four means of providing counsel for the defense: (1) clients can retain their own private counsel; (2) the court can appoint counsel from a list of bar members or a list of attorneys who are willing to provide their services on a part-time basis; (3) lawyers from offices of legal aid services (financed by the government or private grant) can be called upon; (4) where they exist, counsel may be provided by the office of public defender. The method of selection utilized will depend largely on the ability of defendants to provide counsel for themselves. When they are unable to do so, the court will see to it that counsel is provided through one of the other three means.

Private Bar and Criminal Practice While the typical lawyer is often viewed as the defender of those charged with crimes, the image is far from reality. Most attorneys either do not get involved in criminal defense at all or do so on a small scale. Various studies of the legal profession in the United States have pointed out its stratification into classes of attorneys.

Ladinsky sees the metropolitan bar as being structured into three rings or circles. The inner circle is made up of attorneys who work in the large firms or who are employed as house counsel in the big business firms. These are the graduates from the most prestigious law schools and the persons whose own backgrounds tend to be middle or upper middle class. The next circle consists of those attorneys who work in smaller firms or partnerships and who tend to represent the plaintiffs in suits against businesses represented by the inner circle. The outer circle is made up largely of individual practitioners whose backgrounds are more humble than the others and who are found "haunting the courts in hopes of picking up crumbs from the judicial table."[34]

Blumberg agrees with Ladinsky and suggests that the impact of such a situation affects the quality of criminal defense:

Published studies conclude that the minority group member, the ethnic, the individual educated in a part-time law school, the son of a laboring father, and the Jew or Catholic are likely to be engaged in individual practice and "end up doing the 'dirty work' of the bar: personal injury, divorce, criminal work, collections, title searching, etc." Further, since approximately 90 percent of those who appear in a criminal court are persons in the lower class, their limited resources will furnish them with the least qualified lawyers for their defense.[35]

Neubauer has found that medium-sized communities have a less stratified bar. In Prairie City, Illinois, the city he studied, most attorneys engage in general practice, "and the bar is fairly homogeneous."

This homogeneity is reflected in the distribution of poor clients among members of the bar.... This dispersion of poor clients ... is reflected in the large number of lawyers who do some criminal work. Whereas few New York City lawyers handled criminal matters, a fairly high proportion of lawyers in Prairie City did. Although criminal work was not an important source of employment for most lawyers, thirty-six out of seventy-five lawyers surveyed did some criminal work. Thus roughly a third of the lawyers have at least minimal contact with the criminal courts.[36]

Some have noted that many lawyers are kept away from criminal practice, and many of those in it made unhappy, by various environmental factors. These include the emotional and psychological strains from dealing with defendants and their distraught families, the general unpleasantness of the physical surroundings (for example, jails, overcrowded courthouses), the need to secure fees in advance of court disposition or possibly end up with none, the sheer case load, the hostility of a public that links attorneys with the criminality of their clients, and their treatment by other attorneys as virtual "outsiders."[37]

Whatever the reason, the extent to which the better class of attorney stays away from criminal practice will be the extent to which defendants have to rely on those who are ill equipped to do much else. This situation, however much it occurs today, is tragic for criminal justice and for the lives and fortunes of defendants and victims alike.

Office of Public Defender An idea whose time has come is that of **public defenders.** Public defenders are salaried government employees who take on the cases of most of the indigent defendants within their communities. There are several advantages to this system over others: It removes most of the worry over fees; attorneys working in the public defender office gain the expertise and contacts enjoyed by private attorneys; and it provides a framework within which consistency in defense work from case to case can be developed. If prosecution teams can develop policies, so can public defenders and their assistants, and incompetent attorneys can be released from the public service.

There are drawbacks to this idea, however. As public employees and members of the courthouse crowd, public defenders may lose their independence and ability to fight for their clients with all the tools at their disposal. After all, as has already been noted, public defenders serve two masters: their clients and the court organization of which they are a part. Rosett and Cressey assert that public defenders are generally viewed with some hostility by both and that they lead an occupational existence of isolation from each. Defendants assigned public defenders are generally uncooperative or hostile and often see the pub-

It is the responsibility of defense attorneys to advise their clients of what to expect and what appears to be in their best interests.

lic defender as a government agent rather than their lawyer.[38] Other criminal justice agencies and practitioners often tend to view the public defender as counterproductive to prosecution efforts and the goals of the criminal justice system. Rosett and Cressey have characterized the court system as consisting of a "productive bureau of prosecution, a counterproductive bureau of defense, both of which are mediated by a bureau of adjudication."[39] Since the public defender's office is seen in terms of being counterproductive, it is placed under a stress quite different from that placed on prosecutors.

Public defenders tend to be very conscious of the conflict built into their role. Many may feel that the approval of practitioners and associates in other agencies is more important to their function and chances of advancement than is the satisfaction or praise of clients with whom they have only transient contact. Besides, as Rosett and Cressey point out:

Through experience the public defender learns to view most of his clients as wrongdoers who should be convicted of some crime and punished, rather than as presumably innocent men who should be defended. In the selective process occurring soon after arrest, the cases of obviously innocent men are dismissed by the prosecutor, as are the men whose arrests were obviously illegal. The public defender's job, then, becomes more a matter of arranging pleas for the remaining guilty than of defending the innocent.[40]

Neubauer points out that in the small town he studied, the relationship between the prosecutors and the public defenders "is cordial and, in some cases, amiable." He notes that in other places they may view each other with suspicion and even hostility, but this is not the situation in Prairie City. Nor, he points out, does it have to be. Conflict may be real, yet confined to channels that make it manageable.

[I]f prosecution and defense are on good terms, this does not mean that the adversary process has broken down. It may be only a reflection of the normal rules of conduct expected of lawyers. The "cooperation" of defense and prosecution is a product of such general expectations about how lawyers should conduct themselves. We should not equate effective advocacy with hostility.[41]

This is a good point to keep in mind. Professional conduct does not require that opponents undermine each other's positions and respect, and effective advocacy for defendants does not require that public defenders seek to bring the criminal justice process to a halt. On the other hand, professional conduct does require public defenders to be effective counselors to their clients and effective advocates of their clients' cause when they insist they are innocent.

Let us conclude this examination of criminal defense attorneys by saying that the appearance of public defenders' offices has not solved the problems of providing adequate defense to accused persons. In addition to the role conflicts, there are related problems. For one thing, public defenders are generally paid significantly less than prosecutors, and the turnover problem is severe. For another thing, resources provided to public defenders for investigative and other support functions are generally meager, and this is especially important in areas that do not have tough discovery rules. Finally, public defenders are not yet established in a majority of states or localities. Cole has noted that of 3100 counties in the United States, 2750 still rely on court-appointed counsel for defense of indigent persons.[42]

It may be that until public defender offices are firmly established throughout the country (and a text such as this can treat them as a distinct fifth component of the nation's criminal justice system), the provision of an adequate defense to all defendants will remain a dream of scholars, theoreticians, and criminal justice planners.

CITIZENS AS JURORS

It has been repeatedly pointed our that the vast majority of criminal cases are disposed of without a formal trial. It is also true that the majority of trials are conducted without a jury. Though juries render verdicts in less than 10 percent of all criminal cases, they are considered essential to the operation of criminal courts and the administration of justice in the United States. Historically, the jury trial brought criminal justice out of the dark ages. The right to trial by jury is one of the fundamental rights of the Anglo-American legal tradition. It is guaranteed every criminal defendant through the Sixth Amendment to the Constitution. Today, though juries act on a small portion of the case load, their presence impacts on the entire criminal justice system and process. Police officers and prosecutors must be mindful of what juries might do with a case they are working. To some prosecutors the charging decision is based on what is referred to as the "trial sufficiency" standard—that is, "Will a jury convict this person of this crime?" Certainly the course and output of the plea-bargaining process is heavily influenced by what both prosecution and defense feel a jury is likely to do. Kalven and Zeisel emphasize the total impact of juries this way:

Thus the jury is not controlling merely the immediate case before it, but the host of cases not before it which are destined to be disposed of by the pretrial process. The jury thus controls not only the formal resolution of con-

troversies in the criminal case, but also the informal resolution of cases that never reach the trial stage. In a sense the jury, like the visible cap of an iceberg, exposes but a fraction of its true volume.[43]

Knowledge About Juries

Of all the participants in the criminal process, it is juries about which we probably know the least. This is due to two circumstances surrounding their role. One is that juries are made up of citizens called into temporary service, assembled as working groups for single cases, then dispersed when the cases are disposed. Each jury decides only a single case. Thus there is a lack of continuity over time and cases. The second circumstance is that the process by which a jury performs its task — the rendering of a verdict — is strictly secret. While the verdicts themselves are a matter of public record, the behavior of individual jurors and their interactions during the decision-making process cannot be observed or studied.

Social scientists and other scholars have attempted to overcome these obstacles by various means. Some have correlated the verdicts of juries with various demographic characteristics (age, sex, race) of jurors and defendants and with attitudes expressed by jurors on a wide variety of social and moral issues. It has been found, for example, that place of residency and national origin are influential in determining verdicts in criminal cases, and that jurors who have so-called authoritarian values tend to be more severe in rendering decisions (on both the guilt or innocence of the accused and sentencing of those convicted). But Stephan concludes that "with few exceptions, there are too little data employing these variables to draw firm conclusions about their effects."[44]

Another research device used has been the mock or simulated trial in which the deliberations of jurors can be directly studied. Various psychological, sociological, and political science methods have been employed in these endeavors, but Kessler notes two major weaknesses in the research so far conducted: the lack of consistency in the research methods (e.g., some used civil cases, others criminal cases), and the reliance on *mock* trials. She writes that since "no researchers have analyzed *real* juries deliberating ... the realism of the analyzed deliberations may be in question."[45]

While social scientists attempt to subject jury behavior to systematic analysis, practitioners have developed their own views about them. Some attorneys and legal scholars assert that juries cannot usually comprehend the complicated issues in many cases and are susceptible to plays on their emotions or baser instincts. These observers would limit the role of jurors and even eliminate juries in civil cases. Others assert that, to the contrary, juries generally do get the facts and the case straight.[46]

Another point of difference about jury behavior is whether or not verdicts are usually predictable based on juror characteristics. Some attorneys develop the skill of screening prospective jurors to eliminate those likely to oppose their position and seat those predisposed to support their side. Some manuals for prosecutors have carried instructions to new assistants on how to evaluate prospective jurors on the basis of race, sex, age, manner of dress and demeanor. These judgments are based on long experience with jurors in the particular district and are not consistently substantiated by more scientific means. Frequently such methods work, frequently they do not. Many practitioners, including some of the most experienced ones, believe that juries are generally unpredictable, and some who value the jury system hope that they continue to be so.

Selection of Jurors

There are three steps involved in the determination of who actually sits on the trial jury: (1) the placement of names on a master list of prospective jurors; (2) the drawing of the names from this list and the summoning of these persons to the courthouse to constitute a jury panel; and (3) the selection from the panel of persons to sit on trial juries.

Not every citizen can be placed on jury master lists. The qualifications vary from place to place, but one basic requirement is virtually universal: that eligible persons be registered voters. In several states there are taxpaying or property-owning requirements. Many courts will not use persons over a certain age, usually sixty-five to seventy. Many areas also require that persons be determined to possess good moral character. Felkenes points out that any of several other factors may disqualify persons from jury service; physical and mental disabilities, failure to express loyalty to the government, deafness, lack of education or literacy, lack of command of the English language.[47]

There can be arguments over some of these requirements but there can be none over the fact that the Supreme Court has forbidden exclusion from juries of any particular class of persons. It has said that "there is a constitutional right to a jury drawn from a group which represents a cross-section of the community—persons with varying degrees of training and intelligence and with varying economic and social positions."[48] In other words, jury master lists must contain representatives of various ethnic, social, and economic groups, and persons cannot be excluded from such lists on these bases. As a result, the most common list now in use is a list of registered voters in the area.

Each jurisdiction establishes its own procedure for drawing names from its master list, but the federal system and most local systems require that the selection process result in random choices—that all persons have an equal chance of being chosen. The persons whose names are drawn are then summoned to appear at the courthouse. At this point other screening devices are brought into play. Attorneys are exempted from jury service, and various jurisdictions excuse other occupational groups such as police, teachers, self-employed persons, and mothers with preschoolchildren. Persons who fit the categories of automatic exemption are excused, and the court—whether in the person of the judge, jury commissioner, or court clerk—takes under consideration any requests for being excused presented by others who are summoned. Persons not excused are then sworn in and constitute a **venire** or jury panel. One jury commissioner in a large city drew 300,000 names from the master list in order to create a panel of 15,000 persons for possible use during a given year.[49] In smaller communities, of course, the need for jurors and the number of names drawn are more modest.

When a criminal trial is scheduled to begin, a group of persons from the jury panel is brought into the courtroom and a **voir dire** examination is conducted. Voir dire means, literally, "to tell the truth," and in this instance it refers to the process in which both prosecuting and defense attorneys question the members of the panel, collectively and individually, about their backgrounds, their knowledge of the case to be tried, and their general attitudes toward criminal justice and other social issues. Vetter and Simonsen have observed that this procedure can be time-consuming:

> When an offense is involved that has acquired great notoriety, such as the case of Charles Manson and members of his "family" in California, the time required to impanel a jury may stretch into months and the number of prospective jurors examined may reach a total of hundreds or even thousands.[50]

It is during the voir dire period that attorneys apply the knowledge, hunches, or prejudices they have acquired in order to obtain a jury who will give their case a sympathetic hearing. They have two devices to use in screening out the prospective jurors who displease them. One is **challenges for cause.** The attorney moves that the judge dismiss certain persons on the grounds that these individuals are prejudiced against his case. Defense attorneys may even challenge an entire panel on the grounds that it does not represent a cross section of the community or contain any persons who are peers of their client. The trial judge grants or denies such motions, and the voir dire continues unless the entire panel is dismissed. There is no limit to the number of these challenges that may be granted.

The second device attorneys may use is **peremptory challenges.** Each attorney is allowed to challenge a certain number of potential jurors who then *must* be dismissed. The number allowed each attorney varies from state to state and also varies with the seriousness of the charges against the defendant, but a common number is ten per attorney per felony count. Thus each attorney gets a chance to eliminate persons the judge would not dismiss for cause. Those who survive both forms of challenge are, if needed, sworn in and become part of the trial jury.

It is only natural that this screening process sometimes results in the elimination of certain types and classes of persons from actual jury service. But while the Constitution and the Supreme Court decisions have eliminated racial and other forms of overt prejudice from the system by which jury panels are comprised, they cannot do so with respect to the seating of actual juries without overturning the equally important rights of the attorneys to seat a jury they believe will give their case a fair hearing.

Before leaving the subject of jury selection, it should be noted that there is increasing use of juries of less than twelve persons. Florida led in the adoption of a rule whereby six jurors plus one alternate hear all criminal trials except those involving capital felonies. The Supreme Court agreed to permit this reduction of jury size in 1970.[51] Some view this as a chipping away of the right to trial by jury, but others view it as a means of making jury trials less expensive and time-consuming.

Conditions in Jury Service

The conditions under which jurors serve are generally deplorable and are generally deplored. Courthouse facilities are very poor in most localities. The fees paid jurors do not approach what one can earn on the job, and many would-be jurors seek dismissal from service because they simply cannot afford it financially. Those who are summoned often spend their time waiting to be selected for service on a trial. Those placed on a trial jury are often kept waiting long periods of time while negotiations or legal arguments continue, and they are rarely informed about what is happening. When a case is pled out or taken out of the jury's hands by a judge, the jurors are often left puzzled as to what happened. In short, jury duty is expensive and frustrating for most citizens who serve. The President's Crime Commission concluded that the "waste of time, compounded by inadequate compensation, cannot be justified."[52]

It is probably not too much to say that the usual treatment of jurors is a much more serious threat to the jury system than selection processes or reduction in jury sizes. Even the most responsible citizen has sought ways of avoiding service, and juries have been without the citizens who would serve best. There have been several instances of citizens removing their names from voter registration lists rather than risk enduring the experience a second time.

Some jurisdictions are making attempts to correct the situation. The most common technique being employed is placing members of jury panels and even some jurors on call and telephoning them to appear when they are actually needed. This is the least expensive means of improving conditions and may even save courts money in unnecessary jury fees and transportation expenses.

WITNESSES

Among the direct participants in any criminal case are witnesses. The presence or absence of reliable witnesses is often a determining factor in decisions to arrest, charge, negotiate, plea, or go to trial. In court the function of witnesses is to give testimony under oath, and their importance lies in the extent to which their testimony persuades the court as to the guilt or innocence of the defendant.

Obtaining witnesses and assuring their testimony is a major aspect of the criminal justice process, and both prosecution and defense are guaranteed compulsory process to secure witnesses for their case. This means that the court will issue subpoenas to which witnesses must respond or they may be held in contempt of court by the judge.

Witnesses usually include the arresting or investigating law enforcement officers, any evidence technicians who processed physical evidence, and citizens with knowledge pertinent to the case. The latter are called because they either saw the crime committed or can testify as to relevant conditions at the time of the crime or to the character of the defendant.

The treatment of witnesses is generally just as poor as that given jurors. They, too, receive less than adequate fees and travel expenses and are often kept waiting in corridors while events transpire that negate the necessity of their being present. **Expert witnesses** — medical examiners, psychiatrists, and others whose knowledge about certain subjects make them valuable — are paid much higher fees and usually treated better than police and ordinary citizens. But they, too, often complain of the time they must waste in court and the harm done to their professional pursuits. Some jurisdictions are developing witness management programs similar to the program discussed in terms of jurors.

COURT SUPPORT PERSONNEL

There are many people performing various staff support functions to the courts. Among the more important are the clerk of the court, the bailiffs, the court reporters, and the court administrators.[53]

The **clerk of the court** heads an agency or office that is the keeper of official records of court proceedings. They are elected officials in most counties in the United States and often have a certain independence from the judges and the court itself. Among the specific duties of the clerk's office in criminal matters are the keeping of all indictments and informations, pleadings, motions, court orders, jury instructions, verdicts, and sentences; the issuance of warrants and subpoenas; the maintenance of a secure chain of custody on evidence; the collection of all fines and court costs; and the dispersement of witness and juror fees. In most jurisdictions the clerks also swear in witnesses, handle the calendaring and docketing of court events in cases, and keep statistics on court proceedings and case dispositions.

The court's **bailiffs** are its security guards. They may be employees of the court or of the sheriff's office. Their functions include the maintenance of order in the courtroom and its immediate vicinity, custody of defendants on trial, the summoning of witnesses to the stand, and the care and custody of jury members.

Court reporters record proceedings and testimony in the courtroom and often produce typed transcripts for use in subsequent court actions (appeal). Since the transcript becomes the basis for decisions by appellate courts, accuracy is absolutely essential and this requires a great deal of skill by the reporter. The work is considered highly demanding but this is usually offset by the attractiveness of the pay.

There have been several methods of recording events and testimony: stenotype machine, manual shorthand, and tape recorder. The latter may be in the form of multiple microphones feeding directly into a recorder system or the stenomask, whereby the court reporter repeats all testimony into a mask containing a microphone. Despite some increase in the use of tape recorders, stenomasks, and even experimentation in videotaping, the most common method used by court reporters has been the stenotype (stenograph) machine. For the time being there seems to be no real threat to this approach.

A relatively new profession is that of **court administrator.** It is difficult to describe the functions of such persons since it is by no means settled just what it is that such persons should and can do. The areas of responsibility, however, generally include court budget planning, supervision of expenditures, management of courthouse space (including the courtrooms), and any other duties assigned by the presiding judge in the court system. It has long been recognized that the courts of this country, at all levels of government, desperately require the introduction of the processes and techniques of modern management or public administration.[54] The increasing use of court administrators, and the development of educational and training programs to produce persons qualified to perform the functions of such offices, is one of the most encouraging developments we see today in the criminal justice system. This subject receives more detailed attention in Chapter 15.

TEST YOURSELF

Define these key terms:
Missouri Plan
impeachment
venire
expert witnesses

Answer the following questions:

1. What are the two ways judges can be *elected* to the bench? Why was the second method devised?

2. Where they exist, what is the role of judicial qualification commissions?

3. What are the various ways defense attorneys come to represent those accused of crimes?

4. Who may be exempted or excluded from jury duty?

5. By what two means may attorneys exclude persons they don't want from serving on a jury?

NOTES

1. Law Enforcement Assistance Administration, *National Survey of Court Organization, 1975 Supplement to State Judicial Systems* (Washington, D.C.: Government Printing Office, 1975), p. 6.

2. Ibid., pp. 79-81.
3. Maurice Rosenberg, "The Qualities of Justice—Are They Strainable?" in Glenn R. Winters, ed., *Judicial Selection and Tenure*, rev. ed. (Chicago: American Judicature Society, 1973), p. 1.
4. Geoffrey C. Hazard, Jr., as quoted in Donald D. Jackson, *Judges* (New York: Atheneum, 1974), p. 7.
5. Ibid., pp. 7-8.
6. Ibid., p. 10.
7. President's Commission on Law Enforcement and Administration of Justice, *Task Force Report: The Courts* (Washington, D.C.: Government Printing Office, 1967), p. 66.
8. National Advisory Commission on Criminal Justice Standards and Goals, *Courts* (Washington, D.C.: Government Printing Office, 1973), p. 145.
9. Ibid., p. 146.
10. President's Commission, *Task Force Report: Courts*, p. 66.
11. Ibid., p. 67.
12. Herbert Jacobs, *Justice in America*, 2d ed. (Boston: Little, Brown, 1972), p. 107.
13. Glenn R. Winters, "One-Man Judicial Selection," in Winters, ed., *Judicial Selection and Tenure*, (Chicago: American Judicature Society, 1967), p. 86.
14. Ibid.
15. Jackson, *Judges*, p. 388.
16. Malcolm R. Wilkey, "Judicial Background and Decision Making," in Winters, *Judicial Selection*, fn. p. 179.
17. Jackson, *Judges*, pp. 385-86.
18. Ibid.
19. Howard James, *Crisis in the Courts*, rev. ed. (New York: McKay, 1971), p. 4.
20. Jackson, *Judges*, p. 379.
21. Ibid.
22. President's Commission, *Task Force Report: Courts*, p. 71.
23. Jackson, *Judges*, p. 393.
24. Ibid., pp. 393-95.
25. *Gideon* v. *Wainwright*, 372 U.S. 335 (1963).
26. *Escobedo* v. *Illinois*, 378 U.S. 478 (1964).
27. *Miranda* v. *Arizona*, 384 U.S. 436 (1965).
28. *Argersinger* v. *Hamlin*, 307 U.S. 25 (1972).
29. Alvin W. Cohn, *Crime and Justice Administration* (Philadelphia: Lippincott, 1976), p. 261.
30. Ibid.
31. American Bar Association, *The Administration of Justice: ABA Standards* (Chicago: American Bar Association, 1974), p. 112.
32. Abraham S. Blumberg, *Criminal Justice* (Chicago: Quadrangle Books, 1967), p. 110.
33. Ibid., p. 114.
34. Jack Ladinsky, "The Impact of Social Backgrounds of Lawyers on Law Practice and the Law," *Journal of Legal Education* 16 (1965), p. 128.
35. Blumberg, *Criminal Justice*, p. 103.
36. David W. Neubauer, *Criminal Justice in Middle America* (Morristown, N.J.: General Learning Press, 1974), p. 69.
37. George F. Cole, *Politics and the Administration of Justice* (Beverly Hills, Calif.: Sage, 1973), pp. 165-68.
38. Arthur Rosett and Donald R. Cressey, *Justice by Consent: Plea Bargains in the American Courthouse* (Philadelphia: Lippincott, 1976), pp. 122-23.
39. Ibid., p. 125.
40. Ibid., p. 126.
41. Neubauer, *Criminal Justice*, pp. 77-78.
42. Cole, *Politics*, p. 169.
43. Harry Kalven and Hans Zeisel, *The American Jury* (Boston: Little, Brown, 1966), pp. 31-32.

44. Cookie Stephan, "Selective Characteristics of Jurors and Litigants," in Rita Simon, ed., *The Jury System in America* (Beverly Hills, Calif.: Sage, 1975), pp. 114-15.
45. Joan B. Kessler, "The Social Psychology of Jury Deliberations," in Simon, *Jury System*, p. 86.
46. Philip H. Corboy, "From the Bar," in Simon, *Jury System*, pp. 185-87.
47. George T. Felkenes, *The Criminal Justice System* (Englewood Cliffs, N.J.: Prentice-Hall, 1973), p. 225.
48. *Fay* v. *New York*, 322 U.S. 261 (1947).
49. Gilbert B. Stuckey, *Procedures in the Justice System* (Columbus, Ohio: Merrill, 1976), p. 155.
50. Harold J. Vetter and Clifford E. Simonsen, *Criminal Justice in America:* The System, the Process, the People, (Philadelphia: Saunders, 1976), p. 213.
51. *Williams* v. *Florida*, 399 U.S. 78 (1970).
52. President's Commission, *Task Force Report: Courts*, p. 90.
53. Vetter and Simonsen, *Criminal Justice*, pp. 178-80; and Hazel Kerper, *Criminal Justice System* (St. Paul, Minn.: West Publishing Co., 1972), pp. 457-60.
54. NACCJSG, *Courts*, chap. 9.

CHAPTER 10
Courts: Pretrial Activity and Process

OUTLINE

ARREST AND CHARGING STAGES
    Determining Probable Cause
      Issuing Warrants
      Initial Appearance
      Preliminary Hearing
    Assuring Appearances by the Defendant
      Bail
      Some Effects of Bail
      Preventive Detention
      Pretrial Release Programs

ADJUDICATION: PRETRIAL ACTIVITIES
    Arraignment
    Hearings on Motions
      Motion for Discovery
      Motion for Change of Venue
      Motion for Suppression
      Motion for Severance of Defendants
      Motion for Severance of Charges
      Motion for Continuance
      Motion to Determine Sanity
      Motion for Reduction of Bail
      Motion for Dismissal
    Pretrial Conferences
    The Court and Negotiated Pleas
      Participation by Judges in
        Plea Negotiations
      Judicial Review of Negotiated Pleas
      Impact of Sentencing on Plea Negotiations

OBJECTIVES

After reading this chapter the student should be able to:

Describe the three basic tasks performed by criminal courts during the arrest and charging stages.

Discuss the court's role in the issuing of arrest and search warrants.

Discuss the nature of initial appearances and preliminary hearings.

Describe some of the variations around the nation in the nature and use of the preliminary hearing.

Name and describe each of the three basic methods of assuring the appearance of a defendant during the adjudication stage.

List the criteria used for setting bail, discuss the criticisms of certain criteria, and describe some effects of bail.

Discuss the criticisms of the concept of preventive detention.

Describe several pretrial release programs.

Outline the process of arraignment for a defendant.

Describe each of several motions commonly made by defense counsel on which the court must rule.

Give the reasons for pretrial conferences between opposing attorneys and the court.

Discuss the role of the court in the negotiation of guilty pleas.

Discuss various criticisms of judicial intervention in the process of plea negotiations.

Explain how judges determine whether a plea of guilty has been made voluntarily, with knowledge of consequences, and to the correct charges.

Discuss the impact of sentencing patterns on plea negotiations.

KEY TERMS

initial appearance
bail
bond
bail bondsman
preventive detention
release on recognizance (ROR)
pro forma decision
field citation
station house citation
summons
standing mute
not guilty by reason of insanity
once in jeopardy
former judgment
discovery
depose
reciprocal discovery
suppression of evidence
severance of defendants
severance of charges
trial continuance
pretrial conference

☐ Like offices of prosecution, the criminal trial courts are involved in more than one stage of the criminal justice process. The courts are the center of activity during the adjudication and sentencing of defendants. In fact, formal adjudication and sentencing are performed solely within the confines of the court. One cannot overlook, however, the roles performed by judges and the involvement of courts as institutions during the earlier stages of arrest and charging. Courts are also involved in the corrections stage through their control of probation. It is not too much to say that courts are direct participants in every stage of the criminal justice process.

ARREST AND CHARGING STAGES

The activities of judges and the courts in the arrest and charging stages will be considered together since in some felonies charging precedes arrest and in some minor misdemeanor offenses a police citation serves as the charging instrument. There are three basic tasks performed by the court during these stages: (1) determining whether there is sufficient probable cause to perform searches and arrests and to bind a defendant over for possible prosecution; (2) determining the most appropriate means to assure appearances by the accused at court hearings and trial; and (3) making certain that the accused is represented by counsel. In all these tasks the court is expected not only to assure that the rights of accused persons are adequately protected but to balance the rights of the accused with the interests of society in avoiding possible future crimes by the accused. We will look at how the courts perform these tasks as specific steps are taken along the process: issuing warrants, holding initial appearances, and conducting preliminary hearings.

Determining Probable Cause

A judge or magistrate of the court may be called on to make a determination of whether there is probable cause to arrest someone before the arrest takes place. Or the judge may have to make a postarrest determination that there is probable cause to hold the suspect for further court action. Whether this task is done before or after arrest, however, the judge must perform it in all criminal cases except those originated by a grand jury indictment. This is to ensure that an accused is not prosecuted without a judicial review of the charges and a determination that the probable cause standard has been met prior to prosecution. In the words of the Supreme Court, "The Fourth Amendment requires a judicial determination of probable cause as a prerequisite to extended restraint on liberty following arrest."[1] It should be pointed out that it does not matter whether the restraint consists of being held in jail, released on bail bond, or released on one's own recognizance (ROR). Even the ROR suspect is generally subjected to restraints on his or her liberty in the form of conditions on the release.

Issuing Warrants   Earlier we discussed the matter of arresting suspects with or without warrants. In those cases where police request an arrest warrant from a magistrate, they are in effect asking the court to find probable cause for the arrest before the arrest is actually made. The magistrate, usually a lower-court judge, requires a sworn statement from the officer about the facts the officer has regarding the alleged offenses of the accused. If the officer's information is based on personal observation and firsthand knowledge, so much the better. On the other hand, if the information is based on the report of someone else, then one of two things must be provided: (1) the identity of the informant or complainant or (2) if it is a confidential informer whose identity is to be kept secret, some information from the applying officer about the reliability of that CI. Reliability may be established by stating that a number of previous tips resulted in cases being solved or that the CI's previous information resulted in convictions.

If the judge is satisfied that there is sufficient probable cause to arrest the suspect, the judge issues a warrant, which any officer may serve. Probable cause to arrest and hold an accused on a specific charge is thus established in advance. If the exact name of the accused is not known, the warrant may be issued to arrest "John Doe" of such and such a description.

The same process is involved in obtaining search warrants from a magistrate, and the magistrate must find that there is probable cause to believe that evidence of a crime will be found in the named premise. Similarly, applications for warrants to place bugs or wiretaps must provide the magistrate with sufficient grounds to find probable cause that the conversations to be overheard are related to specific criminal activities.

Initial Appearance   The **initial appearance** of the accused follows the arrest by forty-eight hours or less in virtually all states and at the federal level. The initial appearance serves several purposes: to make certain the suspects understand their rights; to inquire as to whether they will apply for the services of a public defender or court-appointed attorney; and even to accept pleas to certain minor offenses that do not require grand jury or prosecutorial charging. Here we are concerned, however, about the use of the initial appearance as a means of determining probable cause to hold the accused for further action. This is necessary in all cases in which arrests were performed without court-issued warrants, that is, without a prior determination of probable cause. Usually the facts contained in the booking report are sufficient for the judge to determine that probable cause exists, but in some instances, and in all cases before a few courts, the arresting officer must be present to report the facts. If the arresting officer, or a representative of the prosecutor is not present or is not prepared to argue that probable cause exists, judges may often give them more time to come forward with their facts. Meanwhile, the accused may be held temporarily.

The determination of probable cause at initial appearance does not involve an adversary process. It is a judicial determination and is made administratively without presentations by any defense counsel. It is meant to ensure only that accused persons are not being held capriciously and that they are not being held for an unreasonable period of time without charges being made clear to them. It is thus similar in function to grand jury proceedings.

Preliminary Hearing In many cases the court's involvement in probable cause determination extends beyond the initial appearance. As we noted earlier in our discussion of the prosecutor (Chapter 7), in cases involving felony charges, a preliminary hearing is often held to determine whether there is sufficient probable cause to continue the state's case (to bind over the defendant) and to prevent unwarranted pretrial detention. In simplified terms this is the purpose of the preliminary hearing. There is little more about it that is simple. As Kamisar and his colleagues point out, there is a "tremendous variation in the structure of the preliminary hearing as it is conducted throughout the country. These variations are found in almost every feature of the preliminary hearing."[2] Some of these variations, which can have a great deal of significance for the defendant, are discussed in the following paragraphs.

1. The availability of the preliminary hearing. As previously indicated, the preliminary hearing is not always available in all cases. At both federal and state levels, a prior indictment almost always nullifies the requirement of a preliminary hearing. In addition, in a few cases where probable cause has already been determined by a magistrate, prosecutors may bypass the preliminary hearing with the direct filing of an information. In Florida, for example, no preliminary hearing is required in such cases if the information is filed within twenty-one days of arrest. In most states where felony prosecutions are permitted by information, bindover at a preliminary hearing is required prior to the filing of the information with the trial court.

2. Limitations on scope of the hearing. There may be considerable variations as to just what can take place during the preliminary hearing. Kamisar and his colleagues refer to

> ... whether the magistrate may consider otherwise inadmissible evidence (e.g., hearsay or illegally seized evidence), whether he may judge the credibility of witnesses, whether he may consider "affirmative defenses" presented by defense, and whether the leeway granted the defense counsel in cross-examining prosecution witnesses and in subpoenaing of other witnesses generally approximates, or is considerably narrower than, that granted at trial.[3]

3. Evidentiary standard governing "bindover" decision. The standard used by magistrates to make their bindover decision may range from the same probable cause that justifies the issuing of an arrest warrant to the much more stringent standard used by a trial judge in determining whether there is sufficient evidence to send a case to the jury. Note that this latter standard still falls somewhat short of the beyond-every-reasonable-doubt requirement necessary for conviction by a trial judge or jury.

4. Impact of bindover decision. For those cases in which a preliminary hearing precedes a grand jury indictment, the jury is in no way limited by the bindover. It may refuse to indict or indict for any charge it feels is warranted. Where prosecution is initiated by information, the prosecutor is usually limited to the charges stipulated in the bindover decision. In some states the prosecutor may also charge the defendant with any other offense disclosed by the evidence at the preliminary hearing.

5. Impact of magistrate's order of dismissal. The magistrate's decision to dismiss charges at the preliminary hearing has little legal impact. In such instances prosecutors may take the matter to a grand jury—where they most often get what they want—refile an information (where permissible), or refile the complaint and attempt to obtain a bindover at a subsequent preliminary hearing, preferably before a different magistrate. While there may be little legal impact on the continuing of the state's case, the practical effects are often quite different. In most jurisdictions the prosecutor will pursue only special cases—usually those in which additional evidence is obtained or the magistrate's ruling is considered clearly erroneous.

6. Timing. Where the preliminary hearing exists, hearing dates vary anywhere from two days to several weeks after the initial appearance. Most states, however, have some law or rule specifying the timing of the preliminary hearing.

Despite the variations in the nature and importance of the preliminary hearings, keep in mind that they all have in common the function of allowing the judge to decide what should be done with a defendant pending further action. The preliminary hearing thus fits in with the issuance of warrants and initial appearances as judicial means for determining whether there is sufficient probable cause to believe the accused committed a crime and whether there should be any restraints on his or her pretrial liberty.

Assuring Appearances by the Defendant

In addition to establishing that there is probable cause to hold someone for possible prosecution, the court performs another essential task in the arrest and charging stages of the criminal process: that of establishing conditions to assure the appearance of the accused during the adjudication stage. There are basically three methods used: bail, the highly controversial preventive detention, and pretrial release programs.

Bail For the accused person who has no desire to remain in jail pending action against him or her by the criminal justice system, the most common method of obtaining freedom is through **bail.** This is a sum of money the accused turns over to the court in exchange for release. The custom of posting money or property to assure the future appearance of defendants is another of those inheritances from England. While the Constitution does not specifically grant the right of bail—mentioning only that "excessive bail shall not be required"—state and federal law have firmly established it in all but capital cases.[4]

It is a general practice of courts to establish standard schedules of bail for misdemeanors and some felony offenses and to have these schedules posted in police stations and jails. Persons being booked may post the scheduled bail and be released immediately. Those who cannot afford the amount or who are being booked on felony charges not covered on the schedule must await their initial appearances in court. If the magistrate then finds probable cause to hold the accused, and the offense is one for which bail is allowable, then the magistrate sets a formal bail amount.

The amount of bail set at or after the initial appearance varies tremendously from place to place, and within any one place it depends on several factors. In addition to consideration of recommendations from the prosecution, defense attorney, police, bondsmen, and others, magistrates who set the amount of bail for specific defendants may ask themselves any of the following questions:

In some jurisdictions those awaiting trial are held in jail for months.

How serious is the offense with which the accused is charged by the arresting officer or the prosecutor?

Does the accused have a criminal record, and, if so, what is the nature of that record?

What is the known record of the accused in terms of employment or school attendance?

What are the family ties of the accused?

Is the accused a fugitive from justice or is there an outstanding warrant for his or her arrest?

How substantial is the probable cause regarding the offense for which the accused is now appearing?

What is the likely financial burden of bail requirements to the accused?

Does the accused have more to gain by jumping bail, that is, by failing to appear and forfeiting the bail amount?

These are the criteria the judge may consider, but observers generally agree that those used most regularly are seriousness of the offense and the accused's criminal record. Also, the relative strength of the evidence is often considered after the preliminary hearing reveals something about the case.[5]

Many people have criticized what they believe to be an undue and undesirable focus on these particular criteria. They generally feel that the setting of bail should reflect the likelihood that the defendant will appear for trial and little else. George Cole feels that "little or no attempt" is generally made to "consider the personal characteristics of the defendant and to assess the probability that he will appear for trial."[6] He contends that not only is the ideal purpose of bail to assure the presence in court of the defendant but that this "is the sole legally stated purpose upon which the decisions concerning bail are to be made in the United States."

> *Along with our assumption that the accused is innocent until proved guilty, the belief exists that he should not suffer hardships awaiting trial. Bail should not be used as punishment, for the accused has not been found guilty. Rather, he should be allowed to live with his family, to maintain community ties, and to prepare his defense. The amount of bail to be posted should therefore not be based only on the seriousness of the crime, but should consider the suspect's entire personal and social situation as it bears on the likelihood of his appearance.[7]*

There is an ironic conclusion to be drawn from this statement of the ideal basis on which to establish bail: poor persons who become defendants generally have much worse personal and social situations than those who can afford to put up bail. Their family lives and community ties tend to be tenuous at best, and their employment picture tends to be bad or nonexistent. By the ideal above, therefore, it would appear that such poor people should have higher bails set than those for wealthier defendants who tend to have stronger family, community, and occupational ties.

Kaplan and Waltz view bail as "the law's pragmatic method of compromise between the principle that a man is innocent until proven guilty and the obvious fact that a large portion of the defendants in criminal proceedings are well on the way to being convicted."[8] They further contend that there is a fallacy in the assumption that an accused who puts up bail will appear in court rather than forfeit the bail amount:

> *It is difficult to envision a bail so large as to guarantee a man's returning for trial which he has reason to believe will result in his death or lengthy imprisonment. The horns of the dilemma are that (a) if a man has enough money to put up bail, the chances are that his bond will not guarantee his*

appearance at trial; and (b) if he does not have the money, the setting of bail will be irrelevant to his appearance since he will not be able to make bail at all.[9]

As we have said, the most common practice in setting bail is to consider the record, if any, of the accused in addition to the reason for the current arrest. It is not possible in many places for the court to gather and consider information about the defendant's character, home life, employment, and other personal factors. In the absence of such information, the court often cannot make an intelligent judgment about the likelihood of the accused's disappearance.

Some Effects of Bail Bail may or may not assure the appearances of defendants, but it seems to have had three effects: penalizing poor defendants relative to those who can afford the bail, costing cities and counties a lot of money to keep in jail those who cannot make bail, and producing the phenomenon of the private bail bondsman.

The impact on poor defendants who cannot afford bail (or bond) is multifaceted according to studies. For one thing, it keeps many of them in jail, where they are mixed with those convicted of crimes. Some jails house more persons awaiting trial than persons serving sentences, and it is generally agreed that most county and city jails are miserable places in which the misery is intensified by overcrowding. In some places those awaiting trial are held for months and may lose jobs and even families in the process. Howard James contends that in many parts of the United States, police use the arrest-jail-bail system to "usurp the authority of the court and punish those arrested."[10] In other words, the bail system inflicts punishment on some defendants who may later be dismissed or acquitted. This may appear to some to be a form of abstract justice. Unfortunately, even from that perspective its effects are discriminatory since many of the worst — that is, violent or career — criminals can pay their way out.

A final cost to defendants who remain in custody appears to be a lessened chance of dismissal or acquittal when compared to those who gain release. A study was done by Eric Single of defendants in New York City who were charged with either misdemeanors or felonies during the first six months of 1971. He found that of those defendants held in jail because they could not make bail, a higher percentage were convicted and sentenced to jail or prison, and their sentences were longer than those who were bailed out prior to disposition of their cases. He found these facts to hold true for defendants regardless of the severity of the original charges, the nature of the evidence, the family situations, employment pictures, prior criminal records, or the amount of the bail.[11]

Not only is there an impact on the individual who cannot raise bail but there is also an impact on cities and counties in terms of the enormous cost of housing pretrial defendants. A study done several years ago pointed out that Philadelphia was spending $1.3 million a year to house those awaiting disposition at the cost of $4.25 per person per day. Most jail costs are now in the range of $8 to $10 a day. The same study pointed out that cities, counties, and states also would bear larger welfare costs than would otherwise be the case since many families must do without the breadwinner who is in jail.[12]

The final effect of bail that we will discuss is the **bail bondsman,** the private entrepreneur who provides, in return for a fee, a bond that promises payment of bail to the court in the event the client flees to avoid prosecution. The fee is set at from 5 to 20 percent of the bail amount. Bail bondsmen see themselves as private businesspeople who provide a vital public service. Not only do they enable people to obtain release who cannot afford to put up bail, but they also pursue bail jumpers for whom they posted the bond. In some courts they become part of the courthouse crowd and even operate in the courtrooms themselves. Howard James found examples of bondsmen and attorneys referring business to each other, and he played a personal role in getting chief judges to ban bondsmen from the courtrooms in Pittsburgh and Philadelphia.[13]

Cole has pointed out that bondsmen may withhold their services arbitrarily, thus the bail system may in effect place control of the jail keys in their hands.[14] Kaplan has noted that bondsmen often demand property or liens on property as collateral for their loans to clients and seize that property should the accused flee. Bondsmen are also often "forgiven" in cases of client flight—that is, the bail is not ordered forfeited by the court.[15] When the bondsmen are threatened with substantial forfeits, they may track down missing clients with methods beyond those permitted law enforcement agencies. One bondsman is quoted as saying: "The person on bail actually belongs to us. We don't have to go through all that legal stuff like extradition."[16]

James notes that some judges think of bondsmen as "vultures," and a study of Detroit judges found many of them setting very low bonds on vice crime cases, in part to deny income to bondsmen. One judge noted that a defendant's money "should be spent on supporting families and paying attorney's fees rather than filling the bondsmen's tills."[17]

Preventive Detention While critics of the bail system have focused largely on the often crushing effects of pretrial detention on the defendant, there is the perhaps equally serious problem of persons committing further crimes while out on bail. Society has long struggled with the dilemma of protecting the right of an accused to pretrial liberty while protecting society itself from the actions of the career criminal, the recidivist (repeat offender), and the dangerously violent offender. As the President's Commission on Law Enforcement said, "The bail system recognizes ensuring appearance at trial as the only valid purpose for imposing bail, but society also has an important interest in securing protection from dangerous offenders who may commit crimes if released before trial."[18]

One response to this problem of the pretrial release of the dangerous offender has been what we may refer to as **preventive detention.** This means holding an accused person in jail without bail for a crime that would normally be bailable if the person were not considered dangerous. In general, states have not established formal programs of preventive detention. Instead, judges have frequently set money bail so high as to have the practical consequences of no bail at all. Such practice has been criticized by some as being unconstitutional or at least a violation of the spirit of the constitutional prohibition against excessive bail. Others have defended it as a necessary means for dealing with a significant problem facing society.

Several studies show that many offenders out on bail in felony cases commit further crimes and that some do so specifically to cover bail costs and attorney fees. The studies conclude that career criminals generally consider bail a routine cost of doing business. As a result, Congress in 1970 gave authority to the district court in Washington, D.C., to order persons to be detained without bail if it was determined that they were dangerous. Under this statute a judicial officer could order pretrial detention in these situations: for a person charged with a dangerous crime if there was no way that the safety of the community could be assured; for a person charged with a crime of violence if that person had been previously convicted (in the last ten years) of a violent crime or if out on bail or probation; for a person charged with any offense if that person, for purposes of obstructing justice, threatens, injures, or intimidates (or attempts to) any prospective witness or juror. The magistrate has to hold a pretrial detention hearing and make a determination under the provisions above.[19]

Opinion as to the effectiveness of this preventive detention statute has been divided. In 1972 a study on preventive detention was conducted by the Vera Institute (named after the wife of New York City industrialist Louis Schweitzer) and the Institute of Criminal Law of Georgetown University. The study concluded that the D.C. project had failed to demonstrate its effectiveness or necessity. The report noted that of six thousand felony arrests in the first ten months, preventive detention was urged by the prosecutor for only twenty persons. The court ordered detention of ten of these but was subsequently overruled on appeal in five.[20] But while these figures can be taken as evidence that preventive detention was unnecessary, they can also be interpreted as demonstrating the judiciousness with which it is invoked. They certainly indicate that the fears of some that there would be wholesale detention of suspects were unfounded. There is support in some quarters for expanding the practice.

While such figures portray the failure of D.C.'s prevention detention program to some, others reach an opposite conclusion:

> *The District of Columbia experiment in preventive detention has had initial success. The fact that the United States attorney moved to detain only seven persons between February and July of 1971 indicates that proper care and judgment can be shown in this matter. Limited preventive detention may have a collateral benefit far greater than the actual results of detaining a few hapless defendants. It may help to lessen the oppressive fear of crime that hangs so heavily over the American society and in inhibiting the life of American cities.*[21]

In 1975 a study sponsored by New York City's Criminal Justice Coordinating Council declared that the emphasis on rehabilitation as an alternative to prosecution and prison was a "failure" and urged the adoption of new measures, including preventive detention.[22]

On the whole, formal preventive detention programs have rarely been alternatives open to magistrates across the nation. The same effect is frequently achieved through the setting of a high bail, but statutory authorization for no bail detention, in other than capital cases, simply has not come about.

Pretrial Release Programs That many persons, including criminal justice officials, are coming to recognize the costs of bail and pretrial detention—not only to defendants but to the system as well—is reflected in various reforms that have been initiated throughout the country. One is the establishment of court-operated bonding systems. Most promising, however, is development of the pretrial release programs. Kalmanoff observes:

> *As the traditional system of money bail became the subject of increasing criticism during the 1950s, reformers began to experiment with and develop alternatives to pretrial detention. Such alternatives ... have included a wide range of possibilities from citations in lieu of arrest to specialized diversion programs for alcoholics, drug addicts, and the mentally ill.*[23]

Remember, it is the function of the court to determine the pretrial status of the accused. Therefore, any of the programs discussed in the following paragraphs must generally have the express approval of the court.

Release on personal recognizance (ROR) has been with us since colonial times. Only recently, however, has it become an institutionalized feature of the criminal justice process. In 1961 the Vera Foundation (later called the Vera Institute) developed a project in which foundation employees screened those arrested and jailed and advised judges as to who could be released on their own recognizance without bail. Its success was so apparent that it was soon taken over by the city's probation department and operated on a citywide basis. It has allowed thousands of persons per year to remain at large while awaiting disposition of their cases, saved millions of dollars in jail costs, and demonstrated that few persons—less than 2 percent—fail to appear in court.[24]

Hundreds of cities and counties have adopted similar release programs, many with the support of LEAA grants, and the general pattern has been the same: huge savings in jail costs, the freeing of jail space for convicted persons, rates of nonappearance lower than for those placed on bail or bonded out by bail bondsmen, and the damaging of fewer lives of those arrested.

The key to success with such programs lies, of course, in the screening process through which candidates for ROR are selected. First, those accused of serious felonies are ineligible. Interviews and background checks of those arrested deal with such matters as the previous record of the accused, the length of residence in the community, the family life, and the employment record. In other words, the screeners use criteria that should be used for setting bail but rarely are.[25]

A magistrate must agree to each release of an accused on his own recognizance. In addition to the recommendation of the probation department or whatever agency operates the ROR program, the views of police and prosecutors are generally considered. All these inputs may be made part of the formal screening process, and where all parties agree to the release, the judge's decision may be **pro forma,** that is, a mere formality. Nevertheless, the formal responsibility for determining the pretrial status of the accused rests with the court.

At the federal level the Bail Reform Act was adopted in 1966. It was the first fundamental change in the federal bail system since its inception in 1789. Federal judges have several options: they may release an accused on his or her own recognizance on a promise to appear on an unsecured appearance bond; they may release the accused to other persons (or organizations) with conditions on travel and behavior; they may require an appearance bond with a deposit of up to 10 percent of the normal bail; or they may require custody during certain hours of the day. While the act thus liberalizes pretrial conditions for many federal arrestees (except those held on capital offenses), it also increases penalties for those who fail to appear.[26]

Still another approach to changing the traditional pattern of arrest, booking, and bail is the use, on minor misdemeanor charges, of citations or summonses in lieu of arrest. There are basically two categories of this type of release program: **field citation** and **station house citation.** In the first type, an offender is issued a citation (similar to a traffic ticket) on the spot or sent a **summons** (court order to appear) for the date of arraignment. This technique enables an accused person to avoid any confinement prior to arraignment and possible trial. The station house citation calls for taking an offender to the station house but releasing him immediately after booking. It allows for "more thorough identification, questioning, and observation of the accused" than does field citation. Both techniques are said to result in better treatment of a person accused but not yet found guilty and in a cost savings for the city or county. Unfortunately, perhaps, neither program's use has been widespread.[27]

Alcohol detoxification programs allow chronic drunks to " 'dry out' under medical and psychological care, in a situation that avoids the hardships of jail." Rather than being hauled off to jail and possibly subjected to the entire process of booking, detention, and trial, the chronic drunk can receive some of the help he so obviously needs.[28]

In drug diversion programs the basic idea is to divert the offender out of the criminal justice process in favor of rehabilitation in some program suited to that purpose. Usually this means entry into a community treatment program. Other diversion and pretrial release programs may apply to the mentally ill and prostitutes.[29]

ADJUDICATION: PRETRIAL ACTIVITIES

In the period between the filing of formal charges by the prosecutor or grand jury and the opening of a trial, several activities take place. Basically, there are three of these that involve the court: arraignment, the holding of hearings on any motions by the attorneys, and the conducting of conferences and negotiations that may lead to a plea of guilty.

Arraignment

Arraignment is the procedure in which the defendant is brought before the bench and the formal charges contained in the information or indictment are read to him. (As pointed out earlier, the initial appearance and arraignment are combined for minor offenses in which a police citation serves as the charging instrument.) The defendant is asked if he or she is represented by counsel. If not, the defendant is not allowed to plead to charges that could result in a jail sentence. Pleas can be accepted to charges resulting in fines. An opportunity is afforded those unrepresented to retain an attorney or an attorney is appointed by the court.

Once counsel is provided and present, the defendant is asked to plead to the charges. The options normally are guilty, not guilty or, in some jurisdictions, nolo contendere. In a few places, however, there are other possible pleas: **standing mute,** which results in an entry of a not guilty plea by the court; **not guilty by reason of insanity,** which in some states is not allowed, though an insanity defense is; **once in jeopardy,** which consists of asserting that the defendant has already been tried for this offense and is being subjected to double jeopardy; and **former judgment.** The last is in accordance with the laws of a few states that do not permit a state trial of someone previously tried on a federal offense arising from the same criminal incident.[30]

If a defendant enters a guilty or nolo contendere plea, the judge must decide whether or not the plea is voluntary and if it is entered by the defendant with full knowledge of its implications, including the development of a criminal record and a possible jail or prison sentence. In addition, the judge must make certain to the best of his ability that the plea is accurate and the result of fair process. It should be in accordance with the facts of the case and with the law as it applies to those facts, and it should not result from any threats, promises, or pressures from either attorney.[31]

To make a judgment about the nature of a plea, trial judges ask a series of questions. Should they then have doubt as to whether the plea is a proper one, they may refuse to accept it. If they are satisfied that the plea is acceptable, they complete the adjudication of the defendant and move the case into the sentencing stage. The judge then imposes sentence immediately or sets it to take place at a future date, often after a presentence investigation.

Hearings on Motions

A plea of not guilty results in the setting of a date for trial. Before a trial is held, however, there are usually several motions entered by counsel. Most of these come from the defense, but prosecutors file some, too. The number and type of motions entered depend, of course, on the nature of the case, especially its seriousness and complexity. Whatever the motion, the role of the court is to decide whether it should be granted or denied. Whichever way the judge rules, it can have a major impact on the outcome of the case.

There are several motions that are common in major felony cases. In the following sections we will discuss each of them in turn.

Motion for Discovery The defense in criminal cases has an interest in knowing what evidence and witnesses will be introduced at any trial of the defendant. In most states the defense has a right of **discovery,** that is, the right to examine the physical evidence, evidentiary documents, and lists of witnesses in the possession of the prosecutor. A few states do not recognize such a right, usually on the grounds that defendants already have sufficient advantages in the process and that full discovery of state evidence enables the defendant to shape a story to fit the case.[32]

In states where there is a right to discovery, the extent and meaning of the right varies. Some allow full examination of the entirety of the state's case including the right to **depose** (question under oath) state witnesses. A few states provide for **reciprocal discovery**—that is, the right of prosecutors to examine the evidence to be used by the defense as well as that of defense to examine state's evidence. In many states this reciprocity is opposed by defense attorneys on the grounds it compromises the right of defendants under the Fifth Amendment to protection from self-incrimination.

Whatever the law of the state (and at the federal level as well) the judge must take motions for discovery under advisement and either deny the motion or issue an order to the appropriate attorney to make the evidence available.

Motion for Change of Venue A motion for a change of venue is a request that the trial be moved from the county, district, or circuit in which the crime was committed to another venue, or place. The case does not come under the jurisdiction of another court—the original trial court simply moves with the case, keeping it within its jurisdiction.

Either defense or prosecution may move for change in venue, and the grounds for such motions are that the defendant cannot obtain a fair trial in the original place. If there has been substantial publicity about the case, either side may claim that it has been prejudicial and that this makes it impossible to pick an impartial jury. In small communities the reason may be that most people know the victim, defendant, or both personally.

The judge may reject the motion when first put, but grant it later after an attempt to pick a jury or other subsequent developments indicate a move is required.

Motion for Suppression Ever since the 1914 decision of the Supreme Court in *Weeks* v. *United States*, which established the Weeks exclusionary rule, it has not been permissible to use illegally seized evidence in a federal criminal trial.[33] In 1961 the rule was extended to state criminal trials in *Mapp* v. *Ohio*.[34] Ever since then defense attorneys have filed motions with trial courts seeking the **suppression of evidence**, a court ruling that evidence cannot be used at trial. The grounds for such a motion must be that the evidence was obtained through illegal search and seizure. It is then up to the judge to decide whether or not the search and seizure was conducted legally and the evidence thus admissible. If it is not, the judge orders it suppressed.

Confessions are also subject to suppression if they were obtained in violation of the Supreme Court's decisions in the *Escobedo* and *Miranda* cases.[35] If the judge finds that a verbal admission or signed confession was obtained from the defendant by means that did not constitute a voluntary waiver of his right to remain silent, with full knowledge of the implications of giving a confession, then the judge should order the admission or confession suppressed. Recently, the court ruled that the suppression can be lifted if the defendant takes the stand during trial and denies his participation in the crime. Under cross-examination, the prosecutor may attack the credibility of the defendant's denial by reading the confession.[36]

Motion for Severance of Defendants Cases which involve more than one person charged with participation in the same crime may result in situations in which the interests of one or more defendants would be best served by separate trials. This would be especially true where one person's defense will consist of placing the blame on a codefendant. The judge may grant a motion to **sever defendants** in such cases, especially where any one defendant will insist on a trial by jury.

Motion for Severance of Charges The prosecutor in most jurisdictions may consolidate related offenses into a single case against a defendant. If a criminal commits the same offense several times within a period of time—say a number of burglaries within a week—he may be charged with multiple counts within a single case. The same is true if the accused commits a number of different crimes within a single incident—say a burglary, followed by an assault, followed by the theft of a vehicle for a getaway. Often it is in the interest of the defendant to respond to all charges within the same case, but sometimes it is not. If the prosecutor files a single case, but the defendant wants to use different defense tactics to respond to each charge—such as take the stand on one but not on another—a motion for **severance of charges** may be filed.

Motion for Continuance Frequently near the beginning of a trial, a motion is made by the prosecutor or defense to postpone trial opening to some future date. In some cases the trial judge may also order a **trial continuance**, even in the absence of an attorney's motion, because of an overcrowded docket (calendar).

When either prosecution or defense moves for a continuance, it is often because of their inability to adequately prepare for trial in the time allotted. This inability to meet the original trial date may be due to such reasons as the failure to find witnesses, the failure of the evidence lab to return evidence and reports, the difficulty of obtaining satisfactory discovery of the other side's evidence, illness or other indispositions of the defendant or witness, or the sheer inability of the attorney to begin trial due to other case commitments.

For the defense, we may add another reason. They frequently delay to enhance their client's chances in a trial. Rosett and Cressey note that some

> ... *of the less reputable members of the private criminal defense bar are retained by their clients more for their ability to "buy time on the street," to keep their clients free on bail, than for their prowess in the courtroom. Some defense lawyers use ingenious technical stalls, even when there is no hope of acquittal, because they know old cases are settled more cheaply than fresh ones.*[37]

Motion to Determine Sanity At any time before or during a trial, the defense can move for a determination of the sanity of the defendant. Judges may also initiate such proceedings on their own. The prosecutor, defense attorney, and even the court may choose psychiatrists or psychologists who test the defendant and prepare reports and testimony to be given at a sanity hearing, generally held before a judge without a jury. An adverse ruling by the judge—that is, one in which the judge rules the defendant is capable of standing trial—can result in the insanity defense being used at trial. A ruling that the defendant is insane usually results in the defendant being committed to a mental health facility for treatment. The case can be held open until he is able to stand trial, or it can ultimately be dismissed if he is committed for an extended period.

Motion for Reduction of Bail The defense may move for reduction of bail or an ROR if the defendant is unable to pay the amount or if the fee and demands for security by bondsmen cause undue hardships. During hearings on the motion, defense attorneys may offer information relating to those factors (such as job, family, or community ties), which the judge may not have had opportunity to consider at initial appearance or arraignment. Prosecutors may oppose or acquiesce in a reduction.

Motion for Dismissal A motion for judicial dismissal of charges may be made by the defense where it can be argued that the case is weak or has been weakened by previously granted motions for suppression. The issue may also be taken up by the judge on his or her own. In places where prosecutors are not given full authority to issue a nolle prosequi, they must seek judicial dismissals of cases or charges they wish to drop. Charges dismissed during the pretrial state generally may be reinstated since no jeopardy is attached in the pretrial process, but there are practical if not legal limits to how many times a charge may be filed, dismissed, and then refiled. A legal limit in some states, for example, is set by their speedy trial rules (e.g., 180 days for a felony, 90 days for a misdemeanor).

Pretrial Conferences

It is a general policy of many judges to call both sides' attorneys in for a **pretrial conference** to establish various ground rules about how the trial will be conducted. Each attorney informs the court about how many witnesses they expect to call, how many pieces of evidence will be entered, and generally how long they expect presentation of their respective cases to take. Each attorney may also stipulate, or agree, to certain testimony or evidence the other plans to admit, thus avoiding controversy over these matters during trial. In general, then, the purpose is to plan the trial so that time is saved once it opens.[38]

Another purpose of judge-called pretrial conferences may be for the judge to encourage, or even participate in, plea negotiations so that trial can be avoided. The role of the court in these negotiations and their outcomes varies greatly from place to place, and even from judge to judge within a court.

The Court and Negotiated Pleas

As we have already established, the most frequent method of conviction is by a guilty plea. Also, most of these are the result of plea negotiations between prosecution and defense. The role of the court in these plea negotiations varies from place to place and judge to judge.

Participation by Judges in Plea Negotiations The level of involvement by the trial judge in negotiations ranges from direct participation to pro forma ratification of an agreement reached by prosecutor, defense attorney, and defendant. Newman observed such variation in involvement in a 1969 study. He noted:

The judge in Michigan is more often directly involved in the decision to reduce the charge. It is ordinarily accomplished in open court with the judge initiating the reduction in some cases and in all instances being fully aware of the process and agreeing to it. In Kansas the trial judge is usually confronted with the accomplished fact of a lesser charge at the time of arraignment. Most judges are fully aware of the practice and support it but report "no alternatives but to go along with the county attorney or his deputy" once the bargain has been made.[39]

While most judges are likely to fall closer to the second example, Kalmanoff notes that "many judges do participate ... and often coerce both sides into a bargain."[40]

There are serious questions frequently raised as to what role, if any, judges should play in encouraging or otherwise participating in plea negotiations. In 1967 the President's Crime Commission saw the judge's role as being an "independent examiner" of the plea bargain rather than a direct participant. The judge's role is a delicate one, for it is important that he carefully examine the propriety of the agreement without undermining his judicial role by becoming excessively involved in the negotiations.

The judge's role is not that of one of the parties to the negotiation, but that of an independent examiner to verify that the defendant's plea is the result of an intelligent and knowing choice. The judge should make every effort to limit his participation to avoid formulating the terms of the bargain. His power to impose a more severe sentence than the one proposed as part of the negotiation presents so great a risk that defendants may feel compelled to accept his proposal.[41]

The American Bar Association has stated flatly that "the trial judge should not participate in plea discussions."[42] As a San Francisco committee on crime report noted: "The federal rule in several jurisdictions holds that judicial intervention in plea negotiations in federal cases is inherently coercive and may not be permitted."[43]

The San Francisco committee also offered several reasons why judges' roles in plea negotiations should be carefully examined:

1. *A judge who has participated in plea bargaining ... may form an opinion about the merits of the case, and this opinion could conceivably influence his rulings on pretrial motions or on evidential issues at trial.*
2. *Where a judge is participating in plea negotiations, there is an inherent temptation to try the merits of the case in chambers, unguided by constitu-*

tional requirements of a public hearing, right to confront witnesses, and even without the requirement that a record of the proceedings be kept....

3. To the extent that the courts engage directly in plea negotiations, they will come to be seen, in the public eye, less as impartial tribunals ... and more as components of an entire system which can function only by securing guilty pleas from those accused of crime.[44]

The San Francisco study did indicate that defense attorneys in that city favored judicial participation in plea negotiation. Some of their reasons include the following:

1. Having a judge present during plea discussions does away with the uncertainty which is most prevalent during discussions: When a judge is present, the defendant's attorney knows precisely what sentence the defendant will receive in return for a guilty plea.

2. Most frequently, the judge will require the prosecutor to present a realistic appraisal of its case against the defendant. This forces the prosecution to abandon any bluffs which may remain in the case by way of overcharging or by way of hinting to produce witnesses who will not in fact appear at trial.[45]

Judges do participate in plea negotiations in San Francisco, but the process has some built-in protections: judges indicate recommended sentences based on facts developed at preliminary hearings, make the recommended sentences conditional on a pre-sentence investigation report in felony cases, and refrain from presiding in trials of cases they have unsuccessfully mediated.[46]

Judicial Review of Negotiated Pleas While the role of most judges in plea negotiations falls short of active participation, their involvement with the subject remains an important one. As we have already noted, when the court is confronted with a plea of guilty from a defendant, the judge is responsible for ascertaining three things: (1) whether it is a voluntary plea, that is, made in the absence of coercion of any kind or inducements in the form of promises of a lighter sentence; (2) whether the defendant has full knowledge and understanding of the consequences, those being the maximum punishment to which he or she could be sentenced and the fact that he or she would then have a criminal record; and (3) whether the charge to which the defendant pleads is accurate, that is, corresponds to the facts of the case as known by the attorneys and the judge. If the judge determines that the answer to any of these questions is no, he is called upon to reject the plea and insist upon a trial.[47]

In determining whether a plea is voluntary and its implications understood by the defendant, trial judges must question the defendant in open court. Many judges go to great length to assure that the defendant has not been coerced into a guilty plea (voluntariness) and that he fully understands how it will affect him (knowledgeability). Some judges make only a superficial attempt to meet these requirements, merely asking the defendant whether he or she is, in fact, guilty as charged. States' rules on the intensiveness of a judge's effort to get at the nature of the plea vary considerably, though it is settled law that they must at least go through this public questioning of the defendant.[48]

Even in those situations where the trial judge makes an effort to get at the question of voluntary and knowledgeable pleas, such a determination is not always that easy. While prosecutors and defense attorneys may avoid direct threats or promises of light sentences to obtain guilty pleas (and some do not abstain from even these acts), most plea bargains obviously involve an understanding regarding the relative sentences likely for a plea versus a trial conviction. Then there are situations in which the maximum penalty—for example, death—is so terrible that no specific threats or inducements to plead are necessary. The Supreme Court has rejected claims that the possibility of a death penalty brings about an involuntary plea.[49] Justice White said in *Brady v. United States* that there is no reason to reject a plea "motivated by the defendant's desire to accept the certainty or probability of a lesser penalty rather than face a wider range of possibilities extending from acquittal to conviction and a higher penalty authorized by law."[50] Even bad advice or erroneous information from attorneys that can be interpreted by defendants as threats—for example, that if a trial is held, a coerced confession will be used—has been ruled an inadequate basis for rejection of a conviction by plea.[51]

As a result of these decisions, Rosett and Cressey reach the conclusion that "as long as the defendant has a lawyer, the prosecutor does not publicly beat him in the courtroom, and the judge asks the right questions and receives the predictable answers, the arranged guilty plea is now beyond challenge."[52]

If there is controversy over the meaning and required extent of plea voluntariness and knowledgeability by the defendant, there is even more controversy over the third aspect of judicial review of guilty pleas: determination that the charge(s) to which the defendant has pled fit the facts of the case. Presumably, if the judge finds that the plea is inaccurate, he is supposed to reject it even if its voluntariness and the defendant's knowledge of the consequences are beyond question. But how far should a judge go in reviewing the facts of the case following a plea? What process should be used by the judge to determine what the true facts and evidence are? Upon what basis can a judge find a plea inaccurate and unacceptable?

Newman found two unique methods being used to determine plea accuracy. A number of courts in Michigan were using pre-sentence reports prepared by probation officers (in advance of formal adjudication) in which they were ordered to focus "on evidence tending to prove or disprove the accuracy" of the pleas. In some Wisconsin courts Newman found post-plea hearings being conducted in which the defendant had to take the stand and offer testimony as to how he committed the crime to which he was pleading.[53] Earlier we noted that in San Francisco judges use transcripts of the preliminary hearing as an acceptable record of the facts of a case in conducting their plea bargaining sessions.

Impact of Sentencing on Plea Negotiations Aside from any impact judges might have on plea negotiations through their direct participation or plea review, there is the impact that can stem from sentencing patterns. Weimar, in a recent study, found that

Even after statistically controlling for such variables as seriousness of offense, strength of case, and characteristics of the defendant, those defendants who are convicted by a jury are likely to receive a more severe sentence than defendants who plead guilty.[54]

Kalmanoff suggests that such disparity in sentencing may actually

... encourage innocent defendants to plead guilty to crimes on the theory that even if the average risk favors a trial, the odds for an individual defendant are less favorable. In other words, the risk of a serious penalty may be avoided in favor of the certainty of a modest one.[55]

Judges may engage in such sentencing disparities for a variety of reasons, but at least three have been suggested. The first is the judge's lack of knowledge about the seriousness of the crime. When a defendant pleads, the judge does not get as good an opportunity to realize the seriousness as when there is a trial. A second reason is the judge's suspicion that a defendant who goes to trial, testifies in his defense, but yet is convicted, is guilty of perjury. The third is the judge's belief that "a demand for trial is in reality only a defense tactic aimed at delay. According to this view, those who do not engage in delay tactics should be rewarded and those who do should be punished."[56]

It should be clear from the above discussion that the court, through its judges, can, and often does, have significant impact on the process and outcome of plea negotiations. With the large number of cases decided in this fashion, the impact on dispositions of criminal cases becomes even more significant.

Assuming that a defendant does not enter a guilty plea, he or she will go to trial on a date set by the trial judge. The nature of the criminal trial will be explored in the next chapter.

TEST YOURSELF

Define these key terms:

bail bondsman
ROR
reciprocal discovery
severance of defendants

Answer the following questions:

1. What steps are usually taken at an initial appearance?

2. What two criteria are most commonly used by judges to determine what bail, if any, should be set?

3. What is "preventive detention," and why is it controversial?

4. Name and explain five motions attorneys may make prior to trial.

5. What two questions must a judge obtain answers to before accepting a plea of guilty from a defendant?

NOTES

1. *Gerstein* v. *Pugh*, 420 U.S. 103 (1974).
2. Yale Kamisar, Wayne R. LaFave, and Jerold H. Israel, *Cases on Modern Criminal Procedure*, 4th ed., (St. Paul: West Publishing, 1974), pp. 958–81 and 991–93.
3. Ibid., p. 959.
4. *Carlson* v. *Landon*, 342 U.S. 524 (1952). See also John Kaplan, *Criminal Justice* (Mineola, N.Y.: Foundation Press, 1973), p. 180.
5. Gilbert B. Stuckey, *Procedures in the Justice System* (Columbus, Ohio: Merrill, 1976), p. 44; and Kaplan, *Criminal Justice*, pp. 304–6.
6. George F. Cole, *Politics and the Administration of Justice* (Beverly Hills, Calif.: Sage, 1973), pp. 43–44.
7. Ibid., pp. 42–43.
8. John Kaplan and Jon Waltz, as quoted in Kaplan, *Criminal Justice*, p. 297.
9. Ibid.
10. Howard James, *Crisis in the Courts*, rev. ed. (New York: McKay, 1971), p. 114.
11. Eric W. Single, "The Consequences of Pre-Trial Detention," unpublished paper, as discussed in George F. Cole, *The American System of Criminal Justice* (N. Scituate, Mass.: Duxbury Press, 1975), pp. 288–90.
12. Daniel J. Freed and Patricia M. Wald, *Bail in the United States* (Washington, D.C.: Government Printing Office, 1964), pp. 39–45.
13. James, *Crisis*, pp. 115–17.
14. Cole, *American System*, p. 285.
15. Kaplan, *Criminal Justice*, pp. 306–7.

16. James, *Crisis*, p. 117.
17. Ibid., p. 115. See also Kaplan, *Criminal Justice*, pp. 305–6.
18. President's Commission on Law Enforcement and Administration of Justice, *Task Force Report: The Courts* (Washington, D.C.: Government Printing Office, 1967), p. 39.
19. D.C. Code, 1967 ed., supp. IV (1971), 84 stat. 644–50.
20. Nan C. Bases and William F. McDonald, "Preventive Detention in the District of Columbia: The First Ten Months," in et al., *Criminal Procedure*, pp. 790–92. See also Kaplan, *Criminal Justice*, p. 324.
21. Lewis Katz et al., *Justice is the Crime: Pretrial Delays in Felony Cases* (Cleveland, Ohio: Case Western Reserve University, 1972), pp. 174–175.
22. "Prison Reform Plan Called Failure," *New York Times*, 10 August, 1975, pp. 1 and 24.
23. Alan G. Kalmanoff, *Criminal Justice: Enforcement and Administration* (Boston: Little, Brown, 1976), p. 189.
24. James, *Crisis*, pp. 119–20.
25. Ibid., pp. 120–24. See also Kaplan, *Criminal Justice*, pp. 312–15.
26. Public Law 89-465, 89th Congress 5.1357, 80 stat. 214. See also Hall et al., *Criminal Procedure*, pp. 782–86.
27. Kalmanoff, *Criminal Justice*, pp. 189–91.
28. Ibid., p. 192.
29. Ibid., pp. 193–95.
30. Stuckey, *Procedures*, pp. 49–53.
31. Donald J. Newman, *Conviction: The Determination of Guilt or Innocence without Trial* (Boston: Little, Brown, 1966), chaps. 1 and 2.
32. Stuckey, *Procedures*, pp. 121–23.
33. 232 U.S. 383 (1914).
34. 367 U.S. 543 (1961).
35. *Escobedo* v. *Illinois*, 378 U.S. 478 (1964); and *Miranda* v. *Arizona*, 384 U.S. 438 (1965).
36. *Oregon* v. *Hass*, 419 U.S. 714 (1975).
37. Arthur Rosett and Donald R. Cressey, *Justice by Consent: Plea Bargains in the American Courthouse* (Philadelphia: Lippincott, 1976), p. 22. See also Ronald J. Waldron et al., *The Criminal Justice System* (Boston: Houghton Mifflin, 1976), p. 201.
38. Rosett and Cressey, *Justice by Consent*, p. 22.
39. Newman, *Conviction*, p. 92.
40. Kalmanoff, *Criminal Justice*, p. 231.
41. President's Commission, *Task Force Report: Courts*, p. 13.
42. American Bar Association, *Standards Relating to Pleas of Guilty* (Chicago: American Bar Association, 1968).
43. San Francisco Committee on Crime, *Reports on the Courts*, in Kaplan, *Criminal Justice*, pp. 430–32.
44. Ibid.
45. Ibid.
46. Ibid.
47. Hazel Kerper, *Criminal Justice System* (St. Paul, Minn.: West Publishing, 1972), p. 294.
48. *McCarthy* v. *United States*, 394 U.S. 459 (1969); and *Boylsin* v. *Alabama*, 395 U.S. 239 (1969).
49. *Brady* v. *United States*, 397 U.S. 742 (1970); and *Parker* v. *North Carolina*, 397 U.S. 790 (1970).
50. 397 U.S. 742 (1970).
51. *McMann* v. *Richardson*, 397 U.S. 770 (1970).
52. Rosett and Cressey, *Justice by Consent*, p. 62.
53. Newman, *Conviction*, pp. 14–20.
54. David Weimar, "Inequity in Plea Bargaining: A State Policy Perspective," in Kalmanoff, *Criminal Justice*, p. 230.
55. Kalmanoff, *Criminal Justice*, p. 230.
56. Ibid.

CHAPTER 11
Courts: Trial and Sentencing

OUTLINE

PRETRIAL DECISIONS
   Place of Trial
   Trial Date
   Trial by Judge or Jury?
   Trial by Jury
      Jury Size
      Jury Selection
      Jury Member Alternates and Sequestering

TRIAL PROCEDURE
   Opening Statements
   Presentation of the State's Case
      Types of Evidence and Witnesses
      Examination of Witnesses
   Presentation of the Defense's Case
   Rebuttal and Surrebuttal
   Closing Arguments
   Jury Charge and Deliberations
   Court Adjudication

SENTENCING STAGE
   Purposes of Criminal Sanctions
   Sentencing Alternatives
      Types of Sanctions
      Sentence Severity
      Alternatives to Sentencing by Judges
   Sentencing Procedures
      Pre-sentence Investigations
      Attorney Recommendations
      Jury Recommendations
      Pronouncement of Sentence
   Sentencing Disparities
   Sentencing Reform

ENVIRONMENT OF CRIMINAL COURTS
   Impact of Community
   Impact of Government
   Impact of Other Criminal Justice
       Components

OBJECTIVES

After reading this chapter the student should be able to:

Discuss the stipulations of the Constitution as to the location of a trial and what a defendant can do to change that location.

Discuss the right of an accused to a speedy trial and explain how that right has been developed by court rulings and state statutes.

Discuss the right of a defendant to trial by jury and the pros and cons of choosing between that and trial by a judge.

Describe the process of jury selection.

Discuss the use of alternates during a trial to replace regular jury members.

Define and discuss the concept of jury sequestering.

List and describe each of the basic steps in the process of a criminal trial.

Describe each of the several types of evidence and witnesses that may be introduced.

Name and discuss five theories advanced as to the purpose of criminal sanctions.

Discuss the sentencing alternatives for trial courts in terms of sanction type and severity.

List some of the constraints that may exist on the court's power to increase or decrease sentence severity.

Define the concepts of definite, indefinite, indeterminate, concurrent, and consecutive sentencing.

Discuss several sources of recommendations that a judge may receive prior to the sentencing of a defendant.

Discuss the issue of sentencing disparities and suggestions for sentencing reform.

Describe the nature of the three sources of environmental influence on criminal courts.

KEY TERMS

court or bench trial
sequester
prejudicial error
real evidence
testimonial evidence
relevant evidence
competent evidence
direct evidence
hearsay evidence
expert witness
lay witness
redirect
recross
resting of a case
directed verdict
rebuttal
surrebuttal
jury charge
jury foreman
hung jury
adjudication
retribution
incapacitation
deterrence
special deterrence
general deterrence
rehabilitation
restitution
incarceration
probation
fine
concurrent sentencing
consecutive sentencing
penal code
definite sentence
indefinite sentence
indeterminate sentence
mitigating and aggravating
   circumstances
sentencing disparities
mandatory minimum law
inherent power doctrine

☐ Few cases go to trial in the United States relative to the total number of criminal cases disposed. Nevertheless, as we have pointed out, trial practices, procedures, and results have an importance beyond the specific cases tried. They establish the background against which other cases are processed. They determine the rules of evidence, the patterns of convictions versus acquittals and dismissals, and the patterns of postconviction sentencing. These rules and behavior patterns are known by prosecution and defense attorneys who engage in the pretrial maneuvers and negotiations by which most cases are disposed.

Even if a trial affected only the defendants tried, this would be sufficient reason to consider the process. Significant numbers of cases are tried, the fates of many defendants are decided, and the cases that do go to trial are generally ones in which the guilt or innocence of the accused and questions of fact and law are closely contested.

PRETRIAL DECISIONS

Before a trial actually gets underway, many decisions must be made. Several of these can be of great importance to one or all of the participants in a case. Matters to be decided are the place of the trial, the date of trial, and whether the trial will be by judge or jury.

Place of Trial

For most cases (particularly misdemeanors) the location of the trial is a settled point and not even subject to question. The Sixth Amendment to the Constitution and law in all states provide that the location (venue) is to be within the state and district "wherein the crime shall have been committed." Trials will be held according to this dictate unless the defendant requests and is granted a change of venue. Such a request, based on the claim that a fair and impartial trial cannot be assured in the district where the crime was committed, is frequently made but seldom granted. It is within the judge's prerogative to make this decision.

Trial Date

The Sixth Amendment to the Constitution requires that every "accused shall enjoy the right to a speedy and public trial," and state constitutions reflect the same right. It is the court's duty to see that this right of the defendant is not violated. In fulfilling this duty courts operate under a great deal of flexibility as to just what constitutes a "speedy trial." Cohn points out that "the Supreme Court has made several rulings on the subject in its attempt to interpret the Sixth Amendment right to speedy trial in federal courts" and has "looked at the situation in the states."[1] The end result has still produced nothing more than general guidelines and principles, and state trial courts have been left to work within the framework of whatever requirements their states have set. Of this situation the American Bar Association has noted:

> Most states have enacted statutes setting forth the time within which a defendant must be tried following the date he was arrested, held to answer, committed, or indicted, and it is these statutes which have received principal attention. If a statutory violation is found, there is seldom any inquiry into the alleged constitutional denial; and if the statute has not been violated, it is typically assumed that the constitution is satisfied. There exists considerable variety and uncertainty in these statutes on such matters as when the time begins running, what defendants are covered, and what the consequences of excessive delay are.[2]

Trial by Judge or Jury?

If a defendant decides to go to trial, the next decision to be made is whether that trial will be conducted before a judge or jury. In some places the decision may be dictated by state requirements that do not permit the jury trial to be waived at all or permit it to be waived only in misdemeanor cases. Some states permit waiver in all except capital cases.[3] Where defendants have a choice, they may base their decisions on various factors.

The factors influencing the defendant toward trial by a judge (**court or bench trial**) include these: the crime may be so heinous or well publicized as to make it difficult to get an unemotional jury; the nature of the defense may be too complex or technical for lay persons to comprehend or accept; the assigned trial judge may have an overall record perceived as more likely to be favorable to the defendant than would a jury. Stuckey adds:

> The general appearance of the defendant may be such that a jury may become more prejudiced against him. The defendant may have a serious past criminal record subjecting him to possible impeachment should he take the witness stand in his own defense, and the probability of the jury convicting the defendant on his past record rather than on the evidence contended in the present charge is great. Or the defendant may be a part of an organized criminal syndicate, or minority group of which local feeling is against, and the jury

may convict the accused by association rather than on the facts of the case. A judge is considered less inclined to be affected by any of these situations than a jury [emphasis added].[4]

If a trial judge is assumed to be more favorable by some defendants, still others frequently choose trial by jury. Perhaps they believe, as the Supreme Court stated in *Duncan v. Louisiana* (1968), that the jury gives them "an inestimable safeguard against the corrupt or over-zealous prosecutor and . . . the compliant, biased, or eccentric judge" and provides them with the benefit of a jury's commonsense judgment over the "more tutored but perhaps less sympathetic reaction of the single judge."[5] More likely, many defendants simply recognize that odds for acquittal are better with a jury than a judge. Kalven and Zeisel found juries to be significantly more lenient than judges. Their study showed the total conviction rate by juries to be 64.4 percent and that for judges 83.3 percent.[6] Some defendants may also feel that their judge has a reputation of being hard on criminals in general or on those who commit the crime with which they are charged.

Trial by Jury

Assuming that a defendant is to be tried before a jury, we can note that the nature of that jury may not be exactly the same from place to place. Juries may vary not only in size but in the method of member selection, use of jury member alternates, and jury sequestering.

Jury Size Due to some reason rooted deep in the past, the most common jury size in criminal trials has been twelve. In some states, however, trials may be conducted before smaller juries. While no state presently allows for less than a twelve-member jury in capital cases, the number may vary for other felony and misdemeanor cases. The practice in Florida of providing six-person juries for all but capital cases has been upheld by the U.S. Supreme Court. In the Court's opinion, the Sixth Amendment right to trial by jury does not include a right to a jury of any particular size. The Court noted also that the fact that no state allows less than twelve persons to legitimize the imposition of the death penalty indicates sufficient concern by the states for the rights of defendants. Rather than interpret the Sixth Amendment in such a fashion as to "forever dictate the precise number which can constitute a jury," the Court felt it best to leave such considerations to Congress and the states.[7]

Jury Selection Before trial may begin, a jury must be selected. Recall that each attorney (prosecution and defense) participates in a voir dire, or questioning of the members of the jury panel. The purpose of the questioning supposedly is to allow each attorney to see if a prospective juror is likely to be fair and impartial. Few observers of the process deny that the real thrust is toward obtaining a jury as partial to one's own side as can be obtained. Accordingly, the practice of jury selection seems to approach an art if not a science. Questions, which may simply be part of a selection strategy that includes observation and background studies, have become endless in variety, and it is not uncommon to see many of them aimed at the construction of psychological profiles for each prospective juror.

Those panel members (from which the final jury will be selected) not satisfying an attorney may be removed through the use of peremptory challenges. Each side is allotted a number of these challenges, allowing it to discharge a panel member simply as a matter of right.

In addition to removal by peremptory challenge, panel members may be discharged for cause. If, under questioning by attorneys or the judge, a person is thought to be too biased or prejudiced to serve impartially, he or she may be challenged for cause and dismissed. There is no limit on the number of challenges for cause. Only those panel members surviving both types of challenges may end up as part of the trial jury.

Jury Member Alternates and Sequestering There are two remaining questions with respect to the role of juries in criminal trials. One is whether alternates may be seated in the jury box and used to replace jurors who become incapacitated during the trial. Some states allow the substitution to be made at any time prior to the start of jury deliberations. Others permit it at any time before the verdict is reached, though alternates do not participate in the deliberations unless and until the regular juror is discharged. The rule to be followed is usually determined by law or rules of procedure and is not a matter for the judge's decision.

The other question concerns whether the jury should be **sequestered,** or locked up, during trial and deliberations. A sequestered jury is one in which the members are kept together, fed and housed by the court, and not allowed contact with outside persons for the duration of their duty. Sequestering of a jury can take place for the entire trial, for the period of deliberation, or not at all. The trial judge must decide which procedure is advisable in the light of such factors as the notoriety of the case, the right of defendants to a fair trial, and the hardships sequestering adds to the burden of jurors. It is generally done only if the judge views it as an absolutely essential step.[8]

TRIAL PROCEDURE

The procedure used in criminal trials is more generally agreed on throughout the United States than almost any other aspect of the criminal justice process. One does not find the sorts of wide variations in the conduct of trials that we have found in the areas of charging, uses of pretrial hearings and conferences, and judicial acceptance of guilty pleas. The trial process consists of the following steps:

1. opening statements by prosecution and defense attorneys
2. presentation of the state's case
3. presentation of the defense case
4. possible rebuttal of defense case and surrebuttal by defense
5. closing arguments by prosecution and defense attorneys
6. jury charge
7. jury deliberation and verdict

Trials by judge would differ very little from the process above except for those steps relating to a jury.

Opening Statements

Attorneys for each side have an opportunity to make an opening statement to the jury. Though there is a great deal of freedom as to what is said in these statements, several limitations do exist: statements are not to be portrayed by either attorney as evidence, prosecutors cannot refer to evidence that they know is inadmissible, and prosecutors cannot comment on any prior criminal record of the defense. Both of the latter two acts are serious errors on the part of the prosecutor. They are considered to be **prejudicial errors** and can result in a mistrial or a reversal of conviction upon appeal.[9]

After certain preliminary activites are taken care of—for example, impaneling the jury and reading the information or indictment—opening statements commence. Generally, the prosecution will go first, although this is normally a matter of custom rather than requirement. The defense may choose not to make any statement, depending on the strategy it has decided to pursue. The situation might be such, for example, that the defense has not yet constructed its defense (waiting to see the state's case) or is simply not willing to reveal it. In any case, defense does not have to make an opening statement and failure to do so should not have any impact on the outcome of the case.

In making its opening statement, the prosecution attempts to provide the jury (or judge) with an outline of the case and how it intends to prove beyond a reasonable doubt that the defendant did commit the crime with which he or she has been charged. The case outline will generally include a description of the crime, the defendant's role in it, and the evidence and witnesses to be presented. A successful presentation by the prosecutor will prepare the jury for the case to follow.

Should the defense choose to make an opening statement, it will usually describe how it plans to show that the state has no case against the defendant. It is not uncommon for the defense attorney to discuss the meaning of the principle of presumption of innocence and the requirement that the prosecution must prove the defendant guilty of the crime charged beyond a reasonable doubt. Again and again defense may return to the theme that the burden of proof rests entirely on the state and that this proof must be beyond a reasonable doubt.

Presentation of the State's Case

In the adversary process of a trial, it is the prosecution that presents the case first. During this portion of the trial, the prosecution's task is to prove its case by the questioning of witnesses and the presentation of evidence. Since there are various types of evidence and witnesses, some basic distinctions should be made clear.[10]

Types of Evidence and Witnesses **Real evidence** consists of physical objects. It is the weapon used in the crime, the merchandise stolen, the clothing worn by the victim or the assailant, the film or book alleged to be pornographic, the fingerprints relevant to the case. Such real evidence may be either the original object or a facsimile or duplicate. The latter includes photographs of the crime scene, models of the room or building where the crime occurred, and plaster casts of footprints or tire tracks. Duplicates and facsimiles are admitted only where the original evidence either is not available or is not in usable form.

Testimonial evidence is the sworn, verbal statements of witnesses. All real evidence is accompanied by testimony from someone qualified to explain and discuss it, normally police officers or others who discovered and processed the evidence.

Relevant evidence is evidence that is necessary to prove or disprove a fact at issue in the trial. Evidence that is related to matters of fact not at issue, or that cannot properly be brought before the court, is said

Witnesses are of vital importance in criminal trials since they provide sworn testimonial evidence.

to be irrelevant or immaterial. Such evidence usually includes information about the background of the defendant that is not considered necessary to tie him to the crime in question but could prejudice the jury or court about the character of the defendant. Defense attorneys will object to the admission of evidence they consider irrelevant, and the judge must rule on its admissibility.

Competent evidence is testimony presented by a competent witness. An incompetent witness may be someone too young, too ill, or too feebleminded, or someone with a criminal record. Again, defense attorneys will object to the use of incompetent witnesses by the prosecution, and the judge must rule on the matter.

Evidence that is obtained by a witness through firsthand knowledge or observation is known as **direct evidence. Hearsay evidence** is a statement that a witness obtained secondhand and indirectly. Hearsay evidence is not acceptable in court unless it is judged to be an exception to the hearsay rule. Such exceptions may include any admissions by the defendant or statements made by dying persons to the testifying witness.

An **expert witness** is one who is usually not a direct observer of the incident (crime) in question but who can present opinions about evidence based on his or her training, education, and experience in professionally dealing with such matters. Stuckey describes the expert witness as "an individual who has knowledge and skill in a particular field which is beyond the knowledge of the average man on the street." It is a person who "gives the judge and jury the benefit of his knowledge, often in the form of an opinion, to assist them in arriving at the truth of a matter."[11] Evidence technicians, psychologists, criminologists, and others may be used as expert witnesses.

Lay witnesses or nonexpert witnesses are persons who can testify about some aspect of the case based upon what they have personally seen, heard, or felt. These witnesses are not permitted to offer opinions as to what they conclude from their personal knowledge, however.

It is the duty of the court to decide whether the type of evidence offered is proper for admission and whether a witness qualifies as an expert. At the trial's conclusion, it will be the duty of the jury (or judge) to evaluate witnesses and evidence in terms of whether they contribute to proving the guilt of the accused.

Examination of Witnesses In addition to physical evidence, an important aspect of the prosecutor's case is the presentation of witnesses. Whether these witnesses are lay or expert, the procedure is generally the same. First, each witness is required to take an oath or to affirm that he or she will "tell the truth, the whole truth, and nothing but the truth." After this, the witnesses are put under the direct examination of the prosecution. The prosecution asks those questions that it feels will best bring out the testimony and evidence it wants the jury or court to hear. During the prosecution's questioning, the defense may frequently object to questions about matters it thinks are irrelevant or beyond the competence of the witness or questions that seem to be leading the witness to an opinion or conclusion.

After questioning by the prosecution, the defense is allowed to cross-examine the witness. The defense attempts to poke holes in the testimony or discredit it in some way. If inconsistencies in the testimony or damaging information about the witness can be brought out, the witness may be impeached (his or her testimony devalued). Depending on any number of factors, the defense counsel may choose to pass up cross-examination. The prosecution may follow any cross-examination with more questions of its own—a **redirect**. The defense may also question again— a **recross**.

When the prosecution has presented each witness and gained the entry of every piece of real evidence it thinks necessary to prove the guilt of the defendant, it tells the court that the state or prosecution **rests** that is, has finished its presentation.

Following presentation of the state's case, it is common for the defense to move that the judge enter a judgment of acquittal on the grounds that the state failed to prove its case—that is, a defense motion for **directed verdict**. Should the judge agree, "he has the authority to take the case out of the hands of the jury and enter a judgment of acquittal, which is a bar to any further action against the defendant on the crime charged."[12] In some states this may vary, with the judge directing the jury to return a verdict of not guilty. In some states there may be even more variation, with juries being allowed to continue the trial and return a verdict of guilty. In no instance is the judge allowed at this point to enter a judgment of conviction or direct a verdict of conviction.

Presentation of the Defense's Case

Among the decisions the defense attorneys have to make during the conduct of a trial are two very important ones. Should the defense present a case at all? If a case is presented, should the defendant take the stand and testify in his own behalf? With reference to the first question, defense counsel may believe that either the prosecution's case has been so poor or the defense's case is so vulnerable to prosecution attack that it is best to rest immediately. The hope may be that the court or jury will have sufficient reasonable doubt of the defendant's guilt to bring in a verdict of acquittal.

As for the defendant taking the stand, he, of course, is not required to do so. He is protected by the Fifth Amendment's guarantee against self-incrimination not only from having to testify but also from the prosecution being able to comment on or otherwise use that fact as an indication of probable guilt.[13] If the defendant takes the stand, he is treated like any other witness and is subject to cross-examination by the prosecutor. Also like any other witness, he may not refuse to answer any proper questions.

Whatever the defense does, on conclusion of its case, it announces that "the defense rests." This is usually followed by another motion for a directed verdict of acquittal. If granted, the trial comes to an end. If not, it continues.

Rebuttal and Surrebuttal

After presentation of the defense case, the prosecution is entitled to put on a **rebuttal** of any points the defense made. Prosecutors do not avail themselves of this opportunity very often because of the limitations placed on the introduction of any new witnesses or evidence and their desire to avoid what could appear to be prosecutorial overkill. In some states the defense is entitled to a **surrebuttal,** the defense's rebuttal to a prosecution rebuttal.

After both sides have rested their case, there is normally a recess while attorneys prepare closing arguments and perhaps work with the judge in the preparation of jury instructions.

Closing Arguments

The order of closing arguments is basically the same as in the presentation of evidence and testimony: the prosecution presents its statement first, the defense follows, and the prosecution may offer a rebuttal. Variations in this procedure may exist from place to place.

Whatever else they may accomplish, closing arguments give each side an opportunity to summarize the evidence and testimony offered during the trial and to tie everything together in a clear picture of the crime and the defendant's role in it. The prosecution obviously attempts to paint a picture of guilt, with the defense striving for the opposite view.

In delivering its statement the prosecution has a great deal of freedom in content but faces some restrictions. As Stuckey notes, the prosecution may emphasize those points that strongly indicate guilt and may display any evidence already introduced. A prosecutor may explicitly state "that in his opinion the evidence clearly proves the defendent is guilty of the crime charged," but he will have committed a serious error (prejudicial) should he state or indicate that "from facts in his personal knowledge, he knows the defendant to be guilty, implying that he has information not brought forth during the trial."[14]

Defense attorneys have very few real restrictions on their closing arguments. While it is considered improper for an attorney to appeal to the emotions or sympathy of a jury, the defense, unlike the prosecutor, who is under a threat of committing a prejudicial error, stands to lose little by doing so.

> Technically the same rules of conduct which apply to the prosecuting attorney are applicable to the defense, but since his misconduct is not appealable if the defendant should be acquitted, the defense attorney often engages in considerable freedom in his arguments.[15]

Jury Charge and Deliberations

Upon completion of each side's closing arguments, the next step generally calls for the judge to instruct the jury in the law relevant to the case it is to decide. The **charge to the jury** will review the appropriate rules of evidence and clarify, insofar as possible, the legal meaning of the reasonable doubt standard the jury must use in reaching a verdict. It has been pointed out that attempts to interpret or clarify the standard have often resulted in even more confusion. In some states, for example, it is required that a defendant be proven guilty "beyond a reasonable doubt and to a moral certainty." (Florida is one such state.) In any case, the jury is to be made aware of this standard and the law applicable to the case before them.

It is quite common for both prosecution and defense to participate in this phase of the trial by furnishing to the judge (orally or written) their thoughts on specific instructions that should be included or excluded from the jury charge. There is significant debate as to how much understanding of these often complex and technical instructions a jury really has, but law itself, nevertheless, requires that such instructions be given.

After they are duly charged by the judge, members of the jury retire to the jury room to reach a verdict. During this period members are kept together and prohibited from communicating with anyone but a court bailiff or the trial judge. Should deliberations continue longer than one day, the jury may be sequestered in a nearby motel or hotel. Here they will be isolated from other guests and kept from reading newspapers or watching television accounts of the trial.

One of the first activities of the jury will be to select a **foreman.** This person is considered the jury spokesperson, may act as moderator in group discussions, and signs the form on which the jury delivers its verdict to the court.

Juries are permitted to examine pieces of physical evidence and any documents introduced during the trial. Most states allow jurors to take notes during the trial if the judge permits it. It is not, however, a very common practice.

Most states require verdicts to be unanimous, but the Supreme Court has ruled that it is not necessary. Consistent with its position that juries may consist of less than twelve persons, it is the Court's view that "a substantial majority" of jurors is sufficient to find guilt beyond a reasonable doubt. Again, there is nothing sacred in the number of twelve, except when dealing with a possible death penalty.[16] Whether the Court will permit four out of six to convict is not yet clear, but nine out of twelve is permissible.

Whatever the requirement for a decision, if the jury cannot agree in sufficient numbers on a verdict, it is said to be a **hung jury.** After urging it to keep trying, and keeping the jurors at their deliberations for as long as possible, the judge must eventually accept such developments and declare a mistrial. This puts the case back to its pretrial status. The prosecutor is usually faced with a decision as to whether to retry the case or drop (nolle prosequi) charges. Another possibility, however, is that the defendant will offer to plea to reduced charges, and the prosecutor, who may have rejected such an idea prior to the trial, may now accept it.

Court Adjudication

When the jury has reached a verdict, the foreman communicates it to the court. If the verdict is not guilty, the judge will normally discharge the defendant. Exceptions would occur where there are additional cases pending against the defendant or he has time to serve for a previous conviction. If the verdict is guilty, the next step is formal adjudication by the court.

Adjudication is that point where, upon receiving the jury's verdict of guilty or a guilty plea, the judge renders the judgment of the court as to the defendant's guilt or innocence. In most instances he accepts the jury verdict and formally adjudicates the defendant guilty. In many places the judge may withhold actual adjudication or court conviction pending a pre-sentence investigation or for some other reason. The judge may do so, for example, under the provision that if the defendant stays out of trouble during a period of time, actual adjudication will never take place and thus no conviction be shown on the defendant's record. Judges may also modify the verdict of the jury, finding a defendant guilty of a lesser charge or crime or setting aside the guilty verdict in favor of acquittal. They may not, of course, adjudicate a defendant guilty who has been found innocent by a jury.

At this point it is well to remind ourselves that all through this process the judge has been responsible for serving justice and particularly for protecting the rights of the defendant. Judges should never hint to a jury that their sympathies lie with either side. They should treat the legitimate motions, objections, and other behavior of each attorney with deferrence. On the other hand, they should keep firm control of the trial and not allow zealous attorneys or disruptive defendants to hinder the progress and overall fairness of the process. Judges may be called on to make many decisions on points of law and procedure in the course of a trial, and they should know the law well enough so that they do not have to recess the trial to study and decide minor points. Presiding over most trials, especially misdemeanor trials, can become a repetitive and even boring task. Some judges find it very difficult to even pretend to be interested in the proceedings. It is crucial, however, that judges conduct fair trials. To the extent that they cannot or will not, justice is not served, and the rights of both defendants and the public are jeopardized.

Formal adjudication by the court pushes the defendant into the next stage of the criminal process: sentencing.

SENTENCING STAGE

Whatever has gone on prior to this point, the defendant is now faced with a moment that can have a great impact on his or her life. Defendants may, with just a few words from a judge, find themselves subjected to anything from a fine to death, depending on the nature of the crime. Sentencing can also be important to more than just the defendant. There are some who contend that patterns of sentencing have more impact on the prevalence or scarcity of crime than anything done by police, prosecutors, or juries—that is, that lenient sentencing patterns encourage crime and tough sentencing patterns discourage crime. There are frequent political attacks made on the "softness" of judges in their sentencing decisions, whereas some social critics point out that sentences in the United States are more harsh than in any other western nation. The subject of sentencing, then, has long been a source of debate.

Purposes of Criminal Sanctions

In the levying of a sentence on someone convicted of a crime, the court may be reflecting any one of several purposes of criminal sanctions. While society has never clearly and systematically expressed its goals or objectives of sanctions, a number of themes have been advanced. The most prominent of these include retribution or revenge, incapacitation or isolation, deterrence, and rehabilitation. Sometimes restitution is added to the list.[17]

The theory of **retribution** asserts that the state shall act as the instrument of the community's collective revenge against those who break its laws. It rests on the notion of "an eye for an eye, a tooth for a tooth," but it also incorporates the concept that victims of crime cannot be allowed to exact their own personal revenge on offenders. The state acts as agent for the victim and for society as a whole.

Many social critics view revenge as a base or uncivilized motive for criminal sanctions, even when performed in an institutionalized framework on behalf of society and following due process. Others assert, however, that revenge is a natural and unavoidable motive for human action and that the criminal justice system directs it into legitimate and controlled channels.

The theory of **incapacitation** is behind any sanction that physically disables the offender from committing further crimes. It is the basis for such practices as cutting off the hands of thieves and the sterilization or castration of rapists. More civilized means of incapacitation amount to forms of isolation. Banishment and deportation are old forms, and imprisonment is the modern means of accomplishing this goal.

The theory of **deterrence** asserts that sanctions should serve to dissuade persons from committing crimes. There are two types of deterrence: **special**, in which the individual offender is caught, punished, and thus deterred; and **general**, in which the general punishment of offenders causes other would-be offenders to desist from the commission of crimes. Whether or not such a theory is valid, Kalmanoff contends that it is currently "the major justification for the punishment of crimes."[18]

The theory of **rehabilitation** rests on the belief that persons who commit crimes have certain motives that are susceptible to discovery, treatment, and alteration. It is more than just a matter of persuading the offender that "crime doesn't pay," it is a matter of converting the offender into a person who understands the error of his ways, and who no longer desires to commit crimes. The ultimate goal, therefore, is to achieve a long-term modification of the offender's behavior and to reintegrate him or her into lawful society. This theory is behind countless programs involving psychiatry, counseling, education, vocational training, job placement, and medical treatment.

An on-again-off-again theory is that of **restitution**—that is, of requiring the offender to directly compensate the victims of his crimes for the inconvenience, hardship, or suffering his actions may have caused them. It is more applicable to property offenses than those involving violence, and it may range from returning stolen property or repairing damage to payment of sums judged to be the value of the deprivation caused. This theory has never been an explicit or widely used basis for sentencing in the United States, but some judges have used it in handling specific cases and it is being discussed more and more in connection with proposals for systems of victim compensation.

It is not our purpose at this point to analyze each of these theories in terms of specific means used to realize them, or in terms of logical difficulties inherent in each, or even in terms of relative successes and failures in attempts to achieve any of them. These points will be addressed in Chapter 12. We have discussed them briefly because they undoubtedly underlie the sentencing behavior of many judges and are constantly a source of public debate.

Sentencing Alternatives

Whatever theory of sanctions might motivate the sentencing of a defendant, there are a number of sentencing alternatives available to the court. The alternatives are products of penal codes enacted by legislative assemblies (whether state or Congress) plus the facilities and programs provided in the corrections component of the criminal justice system. Sentencing alternatives can be seen from two perspectives: the type of sanction and its severity. The sentence pronounced must address both matters.

Types of Sanctions Basically there are three types of sanctions from which the court may choose: incarceration of the individual in a prison, jail, or other residential facility; placing the individual on probation; or imposing a fine of a specified amount.

With **incarceration** the convicted offender may be sentenced to a period of time in a federal or state prison, a county or city jail, a community corrections center, or any one of a variety of other facilities in which offenders reside.

An offender may also be placed on **probation.** In this case he or she remains physically at large yet within the jurisdiction of the court for a period of time. Judges may attach conditions of probation to which the offender must adhere or risk revocation of the probation and subsequent resentencing to some period of incarceration. Most probationers are supervised by probation officials, who are required to report any violations of conditions to the court. The conditions themselves often go beyond mere avoidance of further criminal behavior, and judges generally enjoy wide latitude in imposing special conditions on offenders designed to prevent them from committing the same violation again. Avoidance of alcohol is a common condition.

The imposition of a **fine** may be in lieu of or in addition to incarceration or probation. A typical sentence, for example, may be "thirty days or thirty dollars." Fines are the traditional means of dealing with most traffic violations and many misdemeanors. The use of fines has been somewhat curtailed in recent years since the Supreme Court ruled that the inability to pay a fine shall not result in a longer period of incarceration than would normally be imposed for the same offense.[19] Thus it is difficult for courts to enforce the collection of fines from the kinds of petty offenders who used to be routinely fined and ordered to work off their fines in jail.[20]

Sentence Severity The court's sentencing decision must stipulate not only the type of sentence but its severity as well. For the fine, severity is expressed in terms of the amount of money the defendant must pay. For probation it means the length of time served in that capacity as well as any conditions imposed. For incarceration it again means length of time to be served.

The court is normally given a great deal of discretion in determining just how severe a sentence will be, but the court does operate within the parameters of various state sentencing provisions. These may relate severity to the type of crime, establish limits on felony incarcerations, call for mandatory periods of incarceration for certain crimes, require that multiple incarceration sentences be served consecutively or concurrently, and the like.

It is the practice in most states for a distinction to be made in sentencing for misdemeanor and felony crimes. The penalty for a misdemeanor usually cannot exceed one year in jail or a $1000 fine. While the court is generally free to choose probation over one or both of these, it is not free to impose any greater penalty for a single-charge conviction. This does not, however, prohibit the court from using all or a portion of the penalty for convictions on each of several charges or crimes. In most places the court also has the choice of deciding whether multiple sentences are to be served **concurrently** (simultaneously) or **consecutively** (back to back). For felony crimes the court is able to impose penalties of a much greater severity.

Assuming that the court wishes to impose a sentence of incarceration on a convicted offender, it does so within limits set out in state **penal codes,** or criminal statutes. These codes vary from state to state and range from allowing the exercise of great discretion by the court to the allowance of no discretion at all. Frank Miller has suggested that state sentencing provisions may be placed into the following classifications:[21]

1. Maximum and minimum terms fixed by the court: Within this classification the court is able to set forth both the maximum and minimum number of years that an offender must serve within the limits allowed by law. As an example, the law may set the penalty for armed robbery at five years to life and the court is free to impose any sentence within those limits (ten to twenty, fifteen to life, etc.). This classification offers the most flexibility to the court. Parole eligibility is usually determined by the minimum period established in the sentence.

2. Maximum term fixed by statute, minimum term fixed by the court: In these states (just two) the judge has to levy the maximum term set by statute but may fix the minimum term. In one of the states, Hawaii, the court must place its minimum sentence at a sufficient distance from the maximum as to assure that a "reasonable period" of time exists between the two. The parole board may then release an offender at any point within this reasonable period.

3. Maximum and minimum term fixed by court, but minimum not to exceed a certain fraction of maximum: In a few states the law requires the court to adhere to a certain gap between the minimum and maximum terms of incarceration. For example, in Pennsylvania the minimum may not exceed one-half the maximum sentence imposed and in several states it may not exceed one-half the statutory maximum.

4. Maximum term fixed by the court, minimum fixed by law: The most common kind of provision, this approach enables the court to set the maximum as high as the law allows but leaves the minimum, if any, to parole authorities. Here, as an example, the court might sentence a defendant to a term not to exceed ten years. The maximum is thus set, with the minimum being left open.

5. Statutory maximum and minimum term to be imposed by the court: Under this approach the legislature sets both the maximum and minimum sides of the term and the court has no choice but to levy that sentence. From the court's point of view, this is one of the most inflexible and restrictive kinds of state sentencing provisions. It takes away court discretion and places the responsibility of determining the length of incarceration in the hands of a parole board. Such extreme restriction on the court exists only in about six states.

While the classifications above generally cover the variety of state sentencing provisions relating to incarceration, one more frequently sees the same thing expressed in such terms as definite, indefinite, and indeterminate sentencing.

Definite sentencing refers to those sentences that are for a specified period of time, with no minimum-maximum spread. Known also as "straight" or "flat time" sentencing, where used it allows the court absolutely no flexibility as to sentence length. Because of this inflexibility, Stuckey notes, the definite sentence "has all but disappeared from the justice system."[22] Newman, however, suggests that it is a common sentence for misdemeanors but "nowhere found as a general feature of felony sentencing structures."[23]

Indefinite sentencing refers to those situations where the court sentences a defendant to a prison term of some length between a fixed maximum and a fixed minimum established by law. The term served is indefinite in that the actual date of release is determined by an administrative agency, normally a parole board. All the first four Miller classifications are versions of indefinite sentencing.

An **indeterminate sentence** is very much like the indefinite sentence in that from the prisoner's standpoint he is not given a definite range of time to be served. It differs by allowing the court only to sentence the offender to prison and by allowing it not to set any actual term. "The term is fixed by a parole board, according to the convict's progress toward a rehabilitative goal. The term may be extended or terminated at a parole board's discretion. There is usually a statutory limit on the prison time to be served, but the limits are extremely high."[24]

There is another point to be noted regarding the length of a sentence. If an offender is convicted of more than one charge or crime, the issue arises as to whether sentences for each conviction are to be served concurrently (at the same time) or consecutively (one after the other). Most state courts have the power to decide which way it will be.[25]

As a summary of the varied sentencing provisions described above, we present the observations of Newman.

> It is difficult to state with precision the most typical or prevalent sentencing structure, for there are often different provisions within jurisdictions from one offense to another.... The sentencing alternatives possible with a case involving burglary may be different from those provided by statute for cases of armed robbery. And minimum or maximum sentences provided by law for burglary in one state may not be the same as provisions in neighboring states.... However, it can be said in most jurisdictions for most crimes judges have some choice among alternative types and lengths of sentences.[26]

There is, without question, sufficient judicial discretion to result in vast sentencing disparities. This we will discuss a bit later.

Alternatives to Sentencing by Judges To those constraints upon the power of judges to exercise discretion in the levying of sentences, we must add another: in some jurisdictions juries participate in or actually make the sentencing decision. Most of those allowing jury sentencing, however, limit it to serious felony cases.[27] In a few places juries offer the judge recommendations in cases involving a possible death penalty, but the judge makes the final decision. In California until recently the judge decided whether the sentence would include incarceration but an adult authority, independent from the court, determined for how long.[28]

The practice of jury sentencing is frowned upon by many people. The American Bar Association suggests that "jury sentencing in non-capital cases is an anachronism" and recommends that it be abolished. The bar expressed concern about the disparity in jury sentencing, the lack of knowledge that the jury might—and often is not entitled to—have about the defendant, and the effect that a jury's control over sentencing might have on its rendering of verdicts.[29]

Sentencing Procedures

Before imposing a sentence, the judge in most courts receives additional information or recommendations from other officials. These sources include pre-sentence investigation reports by probation officers, recommendations from the attorneys involved in the case, and perhaps a recommendation from the jury.

Pre-sentence Investigations For felony convictions, most states provide for the conduct of a pre-sentence investigation by the probation officers attached to the court. The preparation of these reports may vary from state to state, from court to court, and even with the background and training of the officer doing the report. They generally contain information on the defendant's family life, educational record, employment history, peer group relations, and any criminal history. Whether the report contains a specific recommendation for sentencing depends again on the court or the office preparing the report.[30]

It has been widely urged that pre-sentence investigations be required in all criminal cases or at least in those involving possible incarceration of the defendant.[31] It is hoped that such requirement would reduce some of the disparity in sentencing practices. Judges, however, are free to ignore the contents of such investigation reports and any recommendations they contain. Such investigations are rare for misdemeanors.

Attorney Recommendations The attorneys for prosecution and defense have at least one of two opportunities to submit information or recommendations to the sentencing judge. They may contribute to the preparation of the pre-sentence report and they may also make comments about sentencing to the judge both in open court and in any pre-sentence conference the judge may call. Of course, in the process of plea negotiation, the attorneys may have indicated to the defendant a sentence he can expect to receive in return for a plea of guilty, and they may discuss this directly with the judge, especially in those courts where judges participate in the negotiation process itself.

Judges have varying attitudes regarding the impact of attorney's recommendations on sentencing and especially on the matter of suggested sentences for negotiated pleas. Rosett and Cressey assert that the judge

> ... shares in a framework of understandings, expectations and agreements that are relied upon to dispose of most criminal cases. As does the prosecutor or a defense attorney, he can deviate from this consensus slightly; otherwise he threatens the whole working structure of the courthouse. When he strays too far from expectations by imposing a sentence either substantially more lenient or more severe than the one agreed on by the defendant, defense lawyer, and prosecutor, it becomes more difficult for the prosecutor and defense counsel to negotiate future agreements.[32]

In order to expedite the bargaining process, some judges in the busiest courts may acquiesce completely in the arrangement of allowing attorneys to speak on their behalf in discussing sentences with defendants. Some judges, however, resent the process and what it does to their authority. Even these judges, though, are not likely to deliberately frustrate such negotiations by rejecting the recommendations of attorneys. In cases that go to trial, judges are usually much freer to impose the sentence they think proper.

Jury Recommendations The procedure for receiving a jury recommendation involves a postconviction hearing at which the jury hears evidence of **mitigating and aggravating circumstances.** These are circumstances concerning the defendant and the crime, which indicate the defendant's motives and state of mind at the time of the crime and which might indicate whether he or she deserves harsh or merciful treatment. Once the jury deliberates and offers a recommendation, the judge may either accept or reject its conclusion. Jury recommendations are required in capital cases in those states whose capital punishment penalty procedures meet Supreme Court requirements.[33]

Pronouncement of Sentence Sentence is pronounced by the judge to the defendant standing before the bench. Defendants are generally asked if they have anything to say before sentence is pronounced. If the conviction is the result of a guilty plea, the judge asks the questions designed to assure the voluntariness and accuracy of the plea (as discussed earlier). Then the judge pronounces sentence.

Sentencing Disparities

As we have noted, despite some restraints judges do exercise considerable discretion in the area of sentencing. In the eyes of many critics, they have had too much. In recent years the sentencing behavior of judges has come under strong attack.

Marvin Frankel, himself a federal appellate judge, argues that "the almost wholly unchecked and sweeping powers we give to judges in the fashioning of sentences are terrifying and intolerable for a society that professes devotion to the rule of law."[34] He goes on to say that the result "is a wild array of sentence judgments without any semblance of the consistency demanded by the ideal of equal justice," adding, "it could not be otherwise under our nonsystem of so-called laws prescribing penalties."[35]

Frankel's despair is supported by the findings of Richard Singer and Richard Hand. Their survey uncovered vast differences among the states in their penal codes, especially with respect to credit for time spent, defendants convicted of two or more offenses, and provisions for habitual offenders—sometimes labeled "career criminals." They write:

> This situation, of course, is appalling. Although it deals with many problems, a rational system of sentencing should be among the most important of priorities, if only because it is a measure of the values and quality of our society. Yet our survey failed to discover any concern in most states about the subjects we reviewed—subjects critically important to thousands who are sentenced to prison or placed on parole or probation.[36]

Countless examples can be provided of **disparity in sentences**, that is, the sentencing of similar offenders who commit similar offenses to terms of widely varying disparity. There are also many examples of some offenses that violate the moral norms of a community (e.g., possession of small amounts of marijuana) resulting in long prison terms, while well-placed white-collar criminals rarely are incarcerated, regardless of how many thousands or even millions of dollars they have stolen through clever, nonviolent means.

Sentencing Reform

The inequities in sentencing are due not only to the inequities and inconsistencies in state penal codes but also to the behavior of judges who operate within these codes. The problems have not, obviously, gone unnoticed, and several routes are being taken in an effort to realize greater consistency. Only a few can be briefly mentioned here.

Several states have adopted variations of the American Law Institute's Model Penal Code. This model provides for the establishment of classes of offenses, setting penalties for each class, then classifying specific crimes within the categories provided.[37]

Some states have adopted, or are considering, **mandatory minimum laws** that provide that all persons who commit specific types of crimes (e.g., those in which a firearm is used) must be sentenced to and actually serve a minimum period in prison. Florida has recently adopted such a law for the use of firearms in crimes.

Some courts are operating sentencing councils in which judges meet once a week or so to review each other's cases and make recommendations about the sentence. The actual decision is left to the judge who handled the case.[38]

Over twenty states permit appellate review of sentences (as distinct from a review of entire cases) and those capital punishment laws approved by the Supreme Court include appellate review of the death sentence as a matter of right. The advantage to sentence review is that unfair sentences do not result in complete retrials but simply a resentencing in keeping with the findings of the appellate court.[39]

Two other proposals that have not been adopted anywhere but are interesting are these:

1. use of mixed tribunals in which other professionals, such as psychologists, sociologists, and educators, join the judge in rendering a sentence decision[40]
2. retention of jurisdiction over imprisoned offenders by the sentencing court and the ability of that court to modify a sentence when the situation warrants it[41]

There is no absolutely perfect sentencing policy or procedure. Nor are there any in sight. As long as conflicting goals are adhered to, the penal codes will be a source of dissatisfaction and cries of "injustice" will be heard from some segments of the community. Furthermore, there will always be a contest between the objectives of providing equity in sentencing and of individualizing sentences to fit the circumstances and the defendant. Finally, judges are not likely to be willing to give up their right to make the ultimate determination of sentence.

ENVIRONMENT OF CRIMINAL COURTS

The reader will recall that throughout the book we have stressed the importance of the environment of a system. We have noted its impact upon both police and prosecutor and the constraints it places upon them in the performance of their tasks. It should be clear that criminal trial courts and their judges also operate within an environment that places varied constraints on the manner in which they deal with criminal cases and defendants. While judges exercise widely different degrees of discretion from court to court, case to case, and task to task, no judge is "totally free to act solely on the basis of his personal views. Rather he must consider the expectations of them."[42]

As with other criminal justice components, trial courts are subject to influences from at least three levels: community, other government agencies and branches, and other agencies within the criminal justice system. Input from each of these elements within a court's environment helps to shape what courts and judges are able to do and what they actually do.

Impact of the Community

Citizens have both direct and indirect ways of letting courts know how they feel. Responses to public opinion polls and letters to the editor are vehicles for expressing themselves indirectly. More direct means include voting, where judges are elected, and the verdicts of citizens who sit on trial juries. Of course, courts often receive contradictory signals from citizens. Indirect channels usually carry messages expressing dissatisfaction with the failure of courts to convict criminals or to sentence them harshly enough. On the other hand, Kalven and Zeisel have found that judges convict about 20 percent more defendants than juries do and that juries are more likely to bring nonlegal values into play and are more willing than judges to give defendants the benefit of the doubt.[43]

While judges are not supposed to be influenced by public opinion in handling specific cases, many cannot help but reflect popular attitudes when they come to the bench and be responsive to public expectations in their overall conduct. Large municipal courts tend to provide judges with more anonymity and isolation from the public than would be the case in small cities, towns, and rural areas. Judges in the latter courts are more likely to be prominent political figures with close ties to certain segments of the community.

Impact of Government

While criminal courts enjoy a good deal of authority within their realm of concern, they have little direct power in the political arena. As indicated, they receive input from a multitude of sources within their environment that influences their output, but they do not have a large impact upon other elements or components of government. Their relative weakness politically is reflected in the generally small share of the budgetary pie that courts receive from legislative bodies. Of all money appropriated for criminal justice for all levels of government in 1974, only 12 percent went for "judicial activities," with law enforcement receiving 57 percent and corrections almost 22 percent.[44]

Because they cannot wheel and deal for funds like bureaucratic agencies of the executive branch, courts have frequently voiced what might be called the **doctrine of the inherent power** of the courts. The essence of the doctrine is that courts are entitled to the support (budget) they require if mandated functions are to be performed. The argument, in short, is that the Constitution and the legislature require certain functions to be performed and thus must back this up with the necessary financial support.[45]

Not only does the legislative branch of government have an impact upon trial courts through its control of funding but also through its creation of law. As we previously pointed out, it is the legislative assembly which creates substantive law and it is this law which sets forth the definitions of crimes and the penalties for violations. The legislature may also be the source for all or some of the rules of procedure governing the operation of a court. It might, for example, require a presentence investigation before sentencing, set speedy trial requirements, or establish the number of peremptory challenges each side may use in jury selection. All in all, the legislative branch of government can be said to have a solid impact on criminal trial courts.

The executive branch of government also has impact upon the trial court. Its impact may be somewhat direct through the appointment of judges by the governor or more indirect through the legal opinions of the attorney general on points of law and procedure. In addition, attorneys from the office of attorney general usually represent the state or prosecution in any appeal of a trial court ruling. An appeal of a ruling favorable to the prosecution thus places the fate of the judge's decision in the hands of an assistant attorney general and an appeal of a ruling favorable to the defense places his position under attack by the attorney general's office.

Also part of the government's impact on trial courts is an institution within the judicial branch of government—the appellate court. When a state court of last resort or the Supreme Court sets forth new legal principles, trial courts are expected to abide by the new rules. In addition, these courts are the only agencies of government which have the direct authority to decide a trial court has erred, to void its decision, to order a case retried, or to order resentencing of an individual. Judges are generally more sensitive to this possibility than to criticism and attack from any other quarter.

Impact of Other Criminal Justice Components

The dependence of trial courts upon other criminal justice agencies for their caseload is complete. Law enforcement officers and prosecutors initiate the cases, and courts have no authority to interfere with this activity. The nature of the output from these sources, whatever its quantity and quality, becomes the input for trial courts. It is the court's working material.

While it is appropriate to note the dependence of trial courts on other criminal justice components for basic input in the form of cases, we should also note the overall interdependence that each component shares in the processing of cases and defendants. Once a case is placed before the court, it has virtually complete authority to dispose of the matter. Its output, other than acquittals and dismissals, becomes input for the corrections component. Feedback from the successes and failures of this component may, in turn, furnish new input for all other components, including the courts.

TEST YOURSELF

Define these key terms:

sequester
relevant evidence
hearsay evidence
jury charge
hung jury
concurrent sentencing
indefinite sentence
aggravating circumstances

Answer the following questions:

1. Explain three reasons why a defendant might choose to be tried without a jury.

2. What is the standard of proof in a criminal trial?

3. What is the difference between "real" and "testimonial" evidence?

4. Explain the two types of witnesses used in criminal trials and the different purposes served by each.

5. What precisely is adjudication and when does it occur?

6. Give the five possible situations that may be established by penal code settings of minimums and maximums for felony incarceration.

7. What are sentencing disparities and how do they occur?

NOTES

1. Alvin W. Cohn, *Crime and Justice Administration*, (Philadelphia: Lippincott, 1976), p. 184.
2. American Bar Association, *Standards Relating to the Administration of Justice*, (Chicago: ABA Project on Standards for Criminal Justice, 1974), p. 272.
3. Gilbert B. Stuckey, *Procedures in the Justice System*, (Columbus, Ohio: Merrill, 1976), p. 91.
4. Ibid.
5. 391 U.S. 145 (1968).
6. Harry Kalven and Hans Zeisel, *The American Jury* (Boston: Little, Brown, 1966), pp. 56 and 60.
7. *Williams v. Florida*, 399 U.S. 78 (1970).
8. Stuckey, *Procedures*, pp. 153-65.
9. Ibid., p. 167.
10. Ibid., pp. 169-70 and 178; Hazel Kerper, *Criminal Justice System* (St. Paul, Minn.: West Publishing, 1972), pp. 306-12; and Alan G. Kalmanoff, *Criminal Justice, Enforcement and Administration* (Boston: Little, Brown, 1976), pp. 251-53.
11. Stuckey, *Procedures*, p. 169.
12. Ibid., p. 179.
13. *Griffin v. California*, 380 U.S. 609 (1965).
14. Stuckey, *Procedures*, pp. 186-87.
15. Ibid., p. 188.
16. *Apodaca v. Oregon*, 406 U.S. 404 (1972).
17. For a discussion of these different theories see Herbert L. Packer, *The Limits of the Criminal Sanction* (Stanford: Stanford University Press, 1968); Leonard Orland and Harold R. Tyler, ed., *Justice in Sentencing: Papers and Proceedings of the Sentencing Institute for the First and Second United States Judicial Circuits* (Mineola, N.Y.: Foundation Press, 1974), pp. 3-17; John Kaplan, *Criminal Justice* (Mineola, N.Y.: Foundation Press, 1973), pp. 9-29; Cohn, *Crime*, pp. 269-83 and 304-10; and Kalmanoff, *Criminal Justice*, pp. 313-20.
18. Kalmanoff, *Criminal Justice*, p. 318.
19. *Williams v. Illinois*, 399 U.S. 235 (1970).
20. Stuckey, *Procedures*, pp. 231-32.
21. Frank W. Miller, *The Correctional Process* (Mineola, N.Y.: Foundation Press, 1971), pp. 973-76.
22. Stuckey, *Procedures*, p. 221.
23. Donald J. Newman, *Introduction to Criminal Justice*, (Philadelphia: Lippincott, 1975), p. 244.
24. Kalmanoff, *Criminal Justice*, pp. 320-21.
25. Kerper, *Criminal Justice*, p. 332.
26. Newman, *Criminal Justice*, pp. 239 and 264.
27. Ibid., p. 235.
28. Kerper, *Criminal Justice*, fn. p. 330.

29. American Bar Association, *Standards for the Administration of Criminal Justice, Sentencing Alternatives and Procedures* (Chicago: American Bar Center, 1967), pp. 43-47.
30. Newman, *Criminal Justice*, pp. 246-47.
31. National Advisory Commission on Criminal Justice Standards and Goals, *Corrections* (Washington, D.C.: Government Printing Office, 1973), p. 18.
32. Arthur Rosett and Donald R. Cressey, *Justice by Consent: Plea Bargains in the American Courthouse* (Philadelphia: Lippincott, 1976), p. 81.
33. *Gregg* v. *Georgia, Proffitt* v. *Florida,* and *Jerek* v. *Texas,* 96 Sup. Ct. (1976).
34. Marvin E. Frankel, *Criminal Sentences* (New York: Hill & Wang, 1972), p. 5.
35. Ibid., p. 7.
36. Richard G. Singer and Richard Hand, "Sentencing Computation: Law and Practices," *Criminal Law Bulletin* 10 (May 1974), pp. 321-22.
37. Kerper, *Criminal Justice,* p. 328, and American Law Institute, *Model Penal Code,* proposed draft (1962).
38. Frankel, *Criminal Sentences,* pp. 69-74.
39. Ibid., pp. 75-85.
40. Ibid., pp. 74-75.
41. NACCJSG, *Corrections,* p. 173.
42. David W. Neubauer, *Criminal Justice in Middle America* (Morristown, N.J.: General Learning Press, 1974), p. 102.
43. Kalven and Zeisel, *American Jury,* pp. 56-62.
44. Calculated from statistics provided in Law Enforcement Assistance Administration, *Expenditure and Employment Data for the Criminal Justice System, 1974* (Washington, D.C.: Government Printing Office, 1976), p. 21, table 2.
45. Ernest Friesen, Edward C. Gallas, and Nesta M. Gallas, *Managing the Courts* (Indianapolis: Bobbs-Merrill, 1971), pp. 95-100.

PART V
Corrections

CHAPTER 12
Corrections: Functions and Structure

OUTLINE

HISTORY OF CORRECTIONS
    Criminal Treatment in Ancient Times
    Criminal Treatment in England
    Development of Criminal Treatment in the United States
      Prison Development
      Evolution of the Death Penalty
      Development of Parole
      Development of Probation
      Other Correctional Programs

FUNCTIONS OF CORRECTIONS
    Traditional Functions
      Retribution
      Deterrence
      Incapacitation
      Rehabilitation
    Recently Emerging Functions of Corrections
      Restitution
      Reintegration
    Corrections Goals: Mixed Purposes

STRUCTURE OF CORRECTIONS
    Institutions
      Jails
      Federal and State Correctional Institutions
      Prison Organization and Administration
    Community-Related Corrections
      Parole
      Probation
      Community Treatment Centers and Programs

OBJECTIVES

After reading this chapter the student should be able to:

Discuss the meaning of "corrections."

Outline and describe the treatment of criminal offenders from ancient times through colonial America.

List the various stages of prison development.

Discuss the history of capital punishment.

Describe the development of parole, probation, and other correctional programs.

Discuss the four traditional functions of corrections in terms of the meaning of each and give arguments for and against each.

Describe two recently emerging functions of corrections.

Discuss the purposes and conditions of jails.

Describe those factors that influence or determine the assignment of offenders to specific correctional institutions.

Outline the basic structure of the federal corrections system.

Discuss the variations in organization and administration of corrections institutions.

Describe two of the major components of many institutions: custody and treatment.

Discuss the importance of inmate organization.

Discuss the meaning and purpose of parole.

Describe the operations of parole boards.

Discuss the organization, roles, and importance of parole supervisors or officers.

Discuss the meaning and purpose of probation.

Describe the functions of probation officers.

List and describe the variety of programs referred to as community corrections.

KEY TERMS

corporal punishment
capital punishment
Pennsylvania and Auburn prison models
penitentiary
parole
probation
work release
halfway house
community corrections center
furloughs
retribution
deterrence
special or specific deterrence
general deterrence
incapacitation
rehabilitation
restitution
reintegration
jail
maximum, medium, and minimum security institutions
custodial staff
treatment staff
parole board
parole officer
probation officer
institution- versus noninstitution-related community treatment programs
reentry services program
guided-interaction programs (GIPs)
halfway-in house

☐ We move now to another component of the criminal justice system, corrections. It is here, according to some, that "the successes and failures of the criminal justice system are measured."[1] It is an area of recognized importance but also one that has generated considerable debate and controversy. Its importance and the nature of the debate surrounding it can be seen in the following discussion of corrections history, functions, and structures.

To talk about the nature of corrections in the criminal justice system, we must have some idea of the term's meaning. To some it is a philosophy of handling those persons convicted of a criminal offense—doing something for or against them. To others it is a process through which an offender travels from conviction to reentry into society. For yet others the term refers to the variety of institutions and programs to which an offender can be assigned upon conviction. We see no need to argue over such distinctions. We view corrections as a system encompassing all these things. Perhaps the best description of the term is offered by Newman:

The term "corrections" encompasses almost all postconviction and postsentencing interventions with offenders. In its broadest sense, corrections involves the use of such techniques as fines, jail sentences, imprisonment, probation, parole, and various combinations of incarceration and community supervision. Correctional systems are complex organizations, comprising much more than probation and parole field services and a few prisons. Modern correctional systems employ a wide variety of programs, facilities, and techniques for the classification, processing, treatment, control, and care of their charges. Within the ambit of correctional services are hospitals for the criminally insane, group counseling programs, work-release projects, halfway houses, farms, forestry camps, diagnostic centers, schools, factories which produce goods for state use, special programs for narcotic addicts, sex deviates, and physically ill prisoners, and even geriatric programs for those who become old and senile while under sentence. Maximum-security prisons are administratively linked with medium- and minimum-security facilities, with reformatories for young felons, and with training schools for juvenile delinquents. There are separate facilities and programs for female offenders, and the vast network of centralized prisons and other facilities is often incorporated with a wide variety of community-based institutions and programs.[2]

HISTORY OF CORRECTIONS

As the description by Newman indicates, we have a rather complex corrections system in this country. Its roots are in the distant past and its development closely intertwined with the history of corrections in other countries, especially England. In general, history shows the movement from times when capital and corporal punishment constituted society's primary reaction to crime to the present acceptance of not only more humane forms of punishment but also a broader conception of corrections than just punishment alone.[3]

Criminal Treatment in Ancient Times

While we owe much of our early system of corrections to England, that country's treatment of criminal offenders really reflected centuries of societal reaction to crime. In ancient times punishment was clearly the dominant, if not sole, philosophy of criminal treatment. While some might apply the terms "cruel and unusual" to one or more forms of current punishment, they seem more apt for such ancient practices as beheading, hanging, throwing from a cliff, burning or burying alive, drowning, stoning, and crucifixion. A most unusual punishment was devised by the Romans for the killing of a parent. "Offenders were placed in a sack which contained also a dog, a cock, a viper, and an ape and then thrown into the water."[4] **Corporal punishment,** involving bodily injury, discomfort, and degradation, was also widespread. Fines and banishment (exile) were additional penalties that were often used.

Criminal Treatment in England

The philosophy that punishment is the most appropriate treatment for criminal offenders continued into the Middle Ages. In fact, in England capital and corporal punishments were not only still practiced but their use even increased. Capital punishment became the penalty for a growing number of offenses, many of which were quite minor in nature. In addition, as Cohn notes, the methods of imposing the death penalty became, if possible, even more cruel. These included hanging, boiling, drawing and quartering, breaking bones on the wheel, and sawing to pieces.

> *Drawing and quartering was sometimes administered by hitching a horse to each leg and arm of the offender and then leading the four horses in opposite directions, thus pulling the victim to pieces. Under the penalty of breaking on the wheel, the prisoner's arms and legs were propped upon a wheellike platform and were broken in several places with an iron bar. The mangled body was then turned rapidly until the victim eventually died. Sawing in pieces was also administered by English executioners. The victim was usually hanged by his feet and sawed in two vertically by two executioners.*[5]

Corporal punishment included flogging (public whipping), branding (use of a hot iron to burn some symbol of the crime's nature into an offender's flesh), mutilation (bodily injury), the ducking stool (repeated submersion in water), and the stock and pillory (locking of offender's arms, legs, and head into a wooden brace). The idea behind such forms of punishment was not only to inflict discomfort and pain but to subject the offender to public humiliation. Keep in mind that all these methods of punishment were generally no more severe than the means of determining guilt or innocence (recall our discussion of trial by ordeal and battle in Chapter 8).

While many of these methods of punishment continued into early modern times, England generally began to move toward more humane criminal treatment. As Cohn notes, "The number of offenses for which capital punishment was prescribed in England grew until it reached 350 in 1780" but dropped over the next fifty years to only 17. Hanging became the sole method of capital punishment and the use of corporal punishment decreased. Prisons at first were constructed for short-term confinement, but by the end of the eighteenth century, they were also used for long-term imprisonment. "Between 1820 and 1861," says Cohn, "the British criminal code was completely transformed.... Many of the cruel and unusual punishments were removed from the law codes during this period of legal overhaul."[6]

Development of Criminal Treatment in the United States

As could be expected, much of England's criminal procedure was brought to America by the early settlers. Consequently, punishment was the dominant philosophy of treatment and was, throughout most of the colonial period, as severe as it had been in the mother country. **Capital punishment**—taking of the accused's life—was widespread and applied to a large number of both major and minor offenses, for example, treason, murder, rape, burglary, heresy, breaking and entering, robbery, arson, forgery, counterfeiting, perjury, striking a parent, adultery, piracy, and flight from servitude. Corporal punishment was also widespread and included the use of stocks, pillory, whipping, branding, and the ducking stool. Some lesser offenses drew fines with the provision of corporal punishment upon nonpayment.[7]

Imprisonment as a means of punishment was unusual during colonial times. Barnes notes:

> There were two institutions in existence, the combination of which later produced the modern prison. They were the jails, or prisons of the time, and the workhouses. The jails or prisons were chiefly used for the detention of those accused of crime pending their trial and for the confinement of debtors and religious and political offenders. They were rarely used for the

incarceration of what were regarded as the criminal classes.... The workhouses ... were utilized almost solely to repress vagrants and paupers and were not open for the reception of felons.[8]

There was very little in the way of significant change in criminal treatment during the colonial years. The Quaker colonies of West Jersey and Pennsylvania did experience a period of time during which the death penalty was replaced by imprisonment for all serious crimes except murder and treason. This, however, did not continue for long and any lasting reforms largely awaited American independence.

Once out from under the domination of England, America began its efforts at reform along enlightenment principles. By 1820 most states had changed their criminal codes to reflect a philosophy of more humane criminal treatment. The use of capital punishment was not only drastically reduced but generally limited to first-degree murder. Corporal punishment was replaced by less severe penalties such as fines and imprisonment.[9] Let us look at some of these developments.

Prison Development Prison development has moved from a complete absence of reform and rehabilitation to a point where reform and rehabilitation are not only widely espoused but attempts at implementation have been made. Duffee and Fitch suggest that we have gone through five phases of prison development, as outlined in the following paragraphs.[10]

1. Early prison system, 1790–1830. In this stage there was no real attempt at reform of the offender and prison was just a place to punish.
2. Pennsylvania and Auburn prison models, 1830–1870. This period saw adoption of prison models designed to replace punishment as the sole or dominant philosophy of criminal treatment, with a philosophy of reformation through penitence (hence the term **penitentiaries**). One model sought penitence through total individual isolation and silence (Pennsylvania). The other allowed inmates to work and eat together under a strict rule of silence (Auburn). The latter became the model for other state prisons. By the end of this period, however, most states employed only distorted versions of the Auburn system. The model had failed in theory and in practice. Prisoners, say Clare and Kramer, were now generally " 'herded together,' where they were often morally corrupted and psychologically and physically harmed by each other." Further, because of the desire to maintain prisons as self-supporting institutions, the emphasis on work became such that inmates became virtual slaves of the state.[11]
3. Post-Civil War reform, 1870–1900: This period is marked by the

attempt to implement prison reforms proposed in the National Prison Association's "Declaration of Principles" (1870). The principles called for an emphasis on humane treatment and rehabilitation of the offender. They advocated such specific things as a classification system for offenders, educational and vocational training, indeterminate sentencing (no fixed term of imprisonment), and the chance to earn conditional release (parole).[12] Out of these principles came the reformatory system. Designed to help rehabilitate all offenders, it eventually failed because it was never applied to most adults (comprising the bulk of the prison population) and because it became virtually no more than a conventional prison for young offenders. Barnes points out that the system of discipline was repressive and did not provide the psychological surroundings necessary for the success of rehabilitation.[13]

4. The industrial prison, 1900–1935: This period is characterized by an extreme emphasis on prison self-support and very little thought of rehabilitation. In most respects it was a return to the prison of a century before with emphasis on custody, punishment and hard labor. Once the opposition of labor unions and economic conditions forced an end to the sale of prison-made goods on the open market, the prison became simply an institution of custody and punishment. Conditions were notoriously bad in almost all prisons, and the prisoner could be faced with everything from a lack of bathroom facilities to extreme cruelty and harassment by other prisoners and prison officials.[14]

5. The contemporary prison: Many observers of prison development have characterized the last four decades or so as the period of the contemporary prison. It is seen by some as a time when prisons have generally accepted a new penology that emphasizes rehabilitation and the individual needs of each inmate. Duffee and Fitch describe it as a period "when prison administrators began to implement some of the reform models proposed in Cincinnati in 1870."[15] Clare and Kramer contend that while many unsolved problems remain in the field of corrections, recent years have seen significant changes achieved by proponents of the new penology of rehabilitation:

> The last twenty years have seen a great revival of interest in the development of rehabilitation programs. As a result of this interest, there are now more therapy, recreation, and education programs within correctional institutions than at any other time in our history. There have also been significant improvements in classifying and segregating various types of prisoners, in creating special facilities for different types of offenders and in the extended use of probation and parole. Following the example of the federal government and the state of California, most states have established sophisticated governmental units (state departments of corrections) that control and coordinate all institutional parole functions. Thus, services are administered more efficiently and duplication of effort is reduced.[16]

Not everyone views the contemporary prison in as favorable a light as Clare and Kramer—citing such problems as the continuing use of obsolete facilities, the increase of tensions and violence in prisons (especially of an interracial nature), and the overall failure of rehabilitation programs to yield measurable results. However, even the severest of critics have generally agreed that there has been progress in the development of prison systems and that most prisons have abandoned inhumane treatment as a matter of policy. The current state of American prisons will be dealt with later in our discussion of the structure and process of the corrections system.

Evolution of the Death Penalty The increasing concern during postcolonial America with humanizing conditions within institutions of confinement and the decreasing severity of punishment has been matched by development concerning capital punishment. Public executions have been abandoned, the last one occurring in 1936. Electrocution was introduced in 1890, supposedly as a more humane method of execution to replace hanging. The number of offenses punishable by death has decreased to that of first-degree murder. By 1967 the number of executions had steadily dwindled to only three and not another one took place until 20 January 1977.[17]

In 1972 the Supreme Court ruled that all existing capital punishment laws were a violation of the Eighth Amendment's prohibition of "cruel and unusual punishment" because of the inconsistent way in which these laws had been administered by the various states.[18] A number of states then revised their capital punishment laws, and in 1976 the Supreme Court again reviewed the death penalty. It found the new laws of Georgia, Florida, and Texas acceptable because they provided adequate flexibility in sentencing and appellate review of each sentence. Several states had their laws struck down because they had made capital punishment mandatory for specific crimes.[19] As of this writing, scores of prisoners are on various death rows throughout the United States and many states are still struggling with the problem of how to design a constitutionally acceptable capital punishment code and procedure.

Development of Parole **Parole** is a form of release that may be granted to a prisoner after he or she has completed some portion of a sentence in a correctional institution. It is not to be confused with probation (involving no serving of time in an institution) or formal release upon completion of a sentence.

The origin of parole may be found in a number of sources. One of these is the work of Captain Alexander Maconochie who introduced into England's penal system (1840) the idea of allowing prisoners to earn "marks" in order to gain early release. Some years later Sir Walter Crofton adapted this concept to Irish prisons. He set up a system whereby a prisoner could, after serving satisfactory terms in first a conventional prison and then an intermediate one, gain conditional release ("ticket of leave"). Violation of this conditional pardon could return the offender to prison. Police supervision of those issued the tickets became routine and the principle of parole supervision was established.[20]

In America the first real use of parole came with the creation of the reformatory system. Adopted at the Elmira Reformatory in 1876, each parolee had to submit plans for employment and upon release "continued under the jurisdiction of the prison for . . . six months and was ordered to report to a guardian upon arrival at his place of employment." By 1945 every state had some form of parole legislation,[21] and today every state, the District of Columbia, and the federal government have parole for both adults and juveniles.

Development of Probation As alternatives to imprisonment and corporal and capital punishment, other corrections approaches have developed over the years. Among these is **probation.** Recall that probation is a form of quasi freedom (or quasi detention) within which persons may remain at large so long as they obey conditions imposed by the sentencing court and probation authority.

The origin of probation in America lies in the work of a Boston cobbler, John Augustus. As early as 1841 Augustus began bailing out of Suffolk County Court many offenders who could not afford to pay their own bail. His goal was to help those worthy of reform. To do this Augustus would bail out an offender, help him obtain a job, and report on his progress toward reformation to the court before sentencing. This would often result in the judge levying only a small fine instead of a jail or prison sentence.[22]

In performing these unselfish and humanitarian acts, Clare and Kramer note, Augustus "did several things which have become characteristic of the present day probation system." These were the development of the concept of acceptable risks for probation (first offenders and "those who gave promise of adopting acceptable behavior"), the pre-sentence investigation into an offender's background, and supportive supervision—not only making impartial reports to the court but helping the offender obtain education or employment—"the essence of contemporary probation officers' functions."[23]

The efforts of Augustus did not result in a speedy adoption of probation by states. The first adoption did not occur until 1878 in Massachusetts, and few other states followed suit. By 1900 the number of adoptions stood at only five. It was not until 1956 that probation became a program of criminal treatment in every state. The progress for juveniles was somewhat more rapid, with every state providing probation by 1925.[24]

Other Correctional Programs Other alternative corrections programs and efforts have appeared in this country, some very recently. **Work release,** in which incarcerated persons are allowed to work outside the institution that houses them, appeared in 1913 in Wisconsin but became popular throughout the nation only in the 1950s. **Halfway houses,** in which offenders are housed within the community but under some form of supervision, appeared in the nineteenth century in New York and Philadelphia, but they are a recent development in most places.[25] **Community corrections centers** and programs for prison **furloughs** (time off to visit families) are of even more recent vintage and are still waiting for acceptance among officials and the public. These programs, as well as probation, parole, and other previously discussed methods of criminal treatment, will be dealt with again later in this and the next chapter.

FUNCTIONS OF CORRECTIONS

Of all of the components of the criminal justice system, it is corrections that perhaps generates the most controversy when the question of functions or purposes is raised. Since corrections is the end toward which the rest of the system operates and the point at which criminal sanctions are formally applied and society imposes its will on those judged to have violated its laws, it is indeed ironic that there is so much disagreement about what is supposed to occur and over what approach best serves the interests of society.

Traditional Functions

There are four generally recognized goals or functions of corrections to which various degrees of support have been given: retribution, deterrence, incapacitation, and rehabilitation.

Retribution Many persons hold that the basic goal of corrections is **retribution.** This means punishment of the offender for the crime he has committed and to an extent that matches the impact of the crime upon its victim (e.g., person, class of people, corporation). In effect the

Retribution? Incapacitation? Deterrence? Rehabilitation?

state is expected to be the agent of vengeance on behalf of the victim and to make the offender suffer at least as much as did the victim. The differences between old-fashioned personal revenge and state imposed retribution are twofold. For one thing, punishment by the state is supposed to be more rational or more in keeping with the true nature of the crime. The second difference is that punishment is imposed by an agency of the state rather than the victim or the victim's relatives and friends. Thus punishment becomes legitimized and made part of the state's overall concern with the protection of its citizens.

Debate over retribution as a function has been intense. There are those who contend that it is "backward looking," concerned only with repaying the offender for his past behavior and not with any effect on his or others' future. It is also argued that some forms of punishment may actually make the offender more dangerous or more likely to commit another crime. Some people also argue that retribution does little or nothing for the victim. It does not bring back the dead, heal physical wounds, or restore lost property. Herbert Packer contends also that retribution standing alone is a nonutilitarian objective and that punishment becomes utilitarian only when linked to the prevention or reduction of crime.[26]

Proponents of retribution not only reject many of the arguments of those opposing it but offer some of their own. To those who argue that it does nothing for the victim, it is replied that punishment of the offender provides at least some measure of psychological satisfaction to the victim. It is further argued by some that crime offends society and that punishment of the criminal results in a symbolic satisfaction that helps maintain social order and support for the justice system. Above all else, some say, retribution is, in and of itself, a desired goal of corrections. Those who break the law must be punished.

Deterrence The goal of **deterrence** can be stated as the attempt to prevent future crimes. It has two aspects: **special or specific deterrence**, which is the effort to prevent a particular offender from committing further acts of crime, and **general deterrence** which is aimed at discouraging others from criminal behavior by making an example of the offender being punished. This function is forward looking in the sense that it is concerned with future behavior rather than the past behavior of offenders. It is tied up with punishment, of course, since the idea is to instill a certain fear in the offender and in other potential offenders. It also assumes that a certain rationality is involved in criminal acts and that people will consider the consequences in deciding whether or not to commit a crime. Finally, it depends on sentences and punishments being swift, sure, severe, and publicized if they are to have the desired effect.

One other point should be made about the goal of deterrence. It is possible to determine whether specific deterrence has worked, but it is very difficult to establish the effectiveness of general deterrence. We have no way of knowing how many crimes were not committed out of consideration and fear of the consequences. Recently Florida enacted a statute that provides that all persons convicted of certain crimes involving the use of firearms are subject to a mandatory minimum sentence of three years in prison. The number of reported armed burglaries and robberies declined significantly over the following months. To some it is logical to argue that the new law deterred persons from committing these crimes. On the other hand, other crimes not covered by the mandatory minimum law declined and economic conditions generally improved during the same period. How, then, is anyone to estimate the deterrent effect of the law, since other factors may also have contributed to the decline in these crimes?

There has always been a heated debate over the deterrent effect of capital punishment. Studies have been conducted using various methods in an attempt to establish that there is or is not a deterrent effect, and the results have been inconsistent and inconclusive. The basic problem with all such studies is that the researcher cannot hold other factors constant that could affect the results—factors such as cultural attitudes, social patterns, and economic activities. In the case of capital crimes, there is an additional problem: most murders and rapes are acts of rage or passion in which offenders do not consider the consequences of their acts, a prerequisite to the success of deterrence.

It is also pointed out that rational crimes, such as embezzlement, fraud, forgery, and professional thefts, are not punished consistently or severely enough to establish a general deterrence.

Incapacitation Throughout much of history **incapacitation** of an offender generally consisted of such corporal punishments as branding a symbol of the crime committed into a visible part of the flesh (for example, "T" for thief) or cutting off a thief's fingers or hand. The purpose, of course, was to make it difficult, if not physically impossible, for an offender to commit further crimes. As corporal punishments were abandoned, isolation through confinement became the basic means of incapacitation.

Persons who favor prison terms for criminal offenders may do so for several reasons. For some it is a matter of specific deterrence, preventing the offender from committing any further crime for at least the time he or she is incarcerated. Others speak of incapacitation's impact on crime deterrence in general. Yet others see it as a means of punishment or retribution.

One of the arguments against incapacitation concerns the matter of deterrence. While admitting that incapacitation may prevent an offender from committing another crime against members of the public during the length of confinement, critics point out that it does not usually prevent crimes against other inmates. As Duffee and Fitch put it: "Incapacitation merely changes the location of the next crime rather than reducing the probability of the next crime."[27] While the idea of criminals committing crimes against other criminals may be acceptable to many people, to some it only adds to the probability that an offender will leave prison more inclined to commit another crime. Marvin Frankel, author of a book on criminal sentences and a United States district judge for the Southern District of New York, has stated:

> *Some of our best and toughest ... minds have discerned for a long time that lengthy prison sentences ... may have just the opposite effect from what was intended. They may tend in a variety of ways to promote rather than reduce*

crime. . . . *Responsible judges know the huge extent to which prisons breed crime rather than quell it.*[28]

Frankel suggests that each judge must calculate costs along with benefits as he or she sentences, and this means being aware of the nature of prison life and what "the steadily corrosive influences of the prison's negative values" can do to an inmate constantly exposed to them. He states:

> *Every society has its culture, and "the society of captives" . . . is not excluded. The acculturation that goes on behind walls is often deep, vicious and ineradicable. The man imprisoned for up to a few years may resist or recover. The long-termer eventually released again into the community is likely to rejoin us as one of our most assuredly dangerous (and very possibly, cunning and undetectable) neighbors.*[29]

To these discussions we can add the position held by many people that incapacitation without rehabilitation may also contribute to the potential for a criminal to commit another crime upon release. Kalmanoff suggests that severe criminal behavior may be engendered by the lack of rehabilitation and subsequent release to the experiences of unemployment, poverty, job discrimination, or racism.

Aside from all the arguments based on the impact of incapacitation on an offender, there may be raised a question of cost. In general, the average cost per offender per year has run about eight to ten times as much for institutionalization as for community treatment programs (e.g., probation or parole).[30] In support of alternatives to prison, such as probation, Frankel has argued: "The defendant on probation, if he merits the opportunity, supports himself and his family. Instead of costing us every year the price of a college education to be maintained in prison (plus welfare for his family), he costs the much smaller expenses of supervision."[31]

Rehabilitation While each of the other goals of corrections has enjoyed some level of support over the last several decades, the most widely touted goal has been that of **rehabilitation.** Basically, rehabilitation can be defined as the altering of an offender's attitude so that he will not want to commit further crime. Whereas deterrence seeks by external means to dissuade persons from committing crimes, rehabilitation aims at producing changes within the offender. It is based on the premise that criminals are sick and that it is the task of corrections to cure them. To accomplish this task the corrections system's programs have included medical treatment, counseling, education, job training, employment, and others. These have been offered not only within jails and prisons but during parole, probation, and programs such as work release.[32] In most penal systems in the United States, offenders have been required to take part in some rehabilitation program.

Though rehabilitation has been a goal of corrections subscribed to by many people within the corrections system, the criminal justice system, the academic world, and the general public, it has not been without its critics, particularly during the last several years. Mounting criticism has led to such recent declarations as "the model has come under increased scrutiny,"[33] ". . . now under more intense attack than ever before,"[34] and, "there's a revolution going on inside prisons. . . . It's a revolution in the way prisons are run and the purposes they serve. What's causing this change is a growing disillusionment with what once was viewed as a main task of prisons: the rehabilitation, or reform, of criminals."[35]

An August 1975 article by the *U.S. News and World Report* credits a 1971 book by Quakers with being "the beginning of the big change in attitudes on rehabilitation." In this book the Quakers, who had pioneered in the concept of offender reform, concluded that the penitentiary system was a failure and that "this reformist prescription is bankrupt."[36] In 1974 the crime rate in America reached its highest point in fourteen years, prompting Attorney General William Saxbe, among others, to lash out at rehabilitation programs. Noting that he had once been a supporter of such programs, Saxbe then declared rehabilitation to be a "myth," at least for violent criminals. Instead of more of such programs, what was needed was more punishment, which would act as a deterrent to crime.[37]

In 1970 Dr. Robert Martinson, hired by New York state, completed a study of all the research that had been done on 231 of the rehabilitation programs existing in the United States between 1945 and 1967. Perhaps disturbed by Martinson's findings, the state refused to publish the report or allow Martinson to do so. Finally, in the spring of 1974, he was able to publish a summary of his findings and "the article landed like an artillery shell on much of the corrections community." Basically, it concluded that rehabilitation had been a failure. As Martinson put it: "With few and isolated exceptions, the rehabilitative efforts that have been reported so far had no appreciable effect on recidivism" (committing another crime). While Martinson's study has been attacked as having a number of significant weaknesses—for example, time period (pre-1967), number and scope of rehabilitation programs examined—it has been a significant factor in an intensive debate over the nature of rehabilitative programs and the desired functions or goals of our corrections system.[38]

The most severe criticism of rehabilitative programs is that they simply have not worked. Many observers of the corrections system have taken the position that rehabilitation efforts have not had the highly expected impact on either reforming criminals or reducing crime. Recidivism rates, in short, have not been significantly altered, and crime has shown a continual increase despite a great deal of effort or emphasis on rehabilitation. Cole notes, in fact, that California, where the rehabilitative model has probably been the most completely incorporated, has one of the nation's highest recidivism rates.[39]

What has gone wrong with the rehabilitative model? Perhaps, say some, it was doomed from the beginning because we proceeded on the theory that each criminal was sick and needed to be cured, yet we did not really know how to adequately diagnose and treat the causes of crime. In explaining why the federal penal system would no longer emphasize rehabilitation as its primary goal for prisons, Norman Carlson, director of the U.S. Bureau of Prisons, stated: "The unfortunate truth of the matter is that we don't know very much about the causes or cures for crime. For a long time, we said we did—or kidded ourselves that we did. But I think a new sense of reality is now sweeping over the entire criminal justice system of this country." Carlson noted that rehabilitation programs would not be discontinued in federal prisons but offered only on a voluntary basis. Several states have considered following the federal prison lead.[40]

Hans Mattick, criminologist and former assistant jail warden, contends that rehabilitation reflects society's view that crime is a lower-class phenomenon and that if

> ... only the criminal had a job, could read and was mentally healthy, he'd be O.K., like us—middle class. But the Watergate criminals were literate, had jobs and weren't crazy. We've just been working under a warped sense of reality. Too often, we put a mugger in a wood-shop course and all we get when he's through is a mugger who can cut wood.[41]

Some critics and defenders of rehabilitation have argued that its failure can be attributed in large part to the environment in which it often must operate—prisons. It is felt that most prisons offer neither the conditions nor atmosphere conducive to rehabilitation success. Says Robert McColley, commissioner of the Maryland Division of Corrections:

> If corrections were given the opportunities and the resources, it could work.... But most correctional institutions... are dealing with modernistic concepts in obsolete facilities. It's like putting a Cadillac engine in a Model T Ford. Most correctional institutions are seriously overcrowded, so you're doing more warehousing than rehabilitation. Under the system we're now operating, no, rehabilitation is not working.[42]

Another problem with rehabilitation has been that of knowing whether rehabilitation is working for a given offender. Practice has been that the inmate is released from prison (or whatever program he is in) when it has been decided that he is rehabilitated. Because of the inability to really evaluate an individual's level of rehabilitation, "many offenders have learned to exploit rehabilitation as a 'con game'."[43] "It's turned prisons into drama schools."[44] William Nagel, executive director of the American Foundation in Philadelphia and former New Jersey prison official, notes that he and other prison administrators once believed that it was possible to determine the point at which an offender was rehabilitated and ready for release. "As it turned out... we didn't have the skills to determine when a guy was ready. The slick and the con-wise were the prisoners released first. It began to be a con game and we lost as much as we won."[45]

To some, particularly prison administrators, talk of the failure of rehabilitation is not only premature but wrong. A number of prison administrators and others find it hard to believe that rehabilitation programs have had no effect on recidivism. They question also the validity of measuring rehabilitation effectiveness by looking at recidivism rates, "since there are so many other factors that determine whether an offender resumes a life of crime."[46] Further, many prison administrators not only defend their prison programs but feel that they do not need to prove the success of rehabilitation programs in order to "justify the existence of prisons." A survey of prison administrators shows that 48 percent believe the "primary purpose of their institutions is to protect the public from the men and women locked inside of them.... Only... 24 percent cite rehabilitation as their primary goal."[47]

Recently Emerging Functions of Corrections

In addition to the various goals of retribution, deterrence, incapacitation, and rehabilitation, two others have recently emerged: restitution and reintegration.

Restitution The concept of **restitution** calls for an offender to compensate his victim for loss or damage to property and person. In this country it has not enjoyed widespread acceptance and, when used, has rarely been in cases involving crimes against persons. Restitution is most likely to be found in cases of worthless checks, minor property offenses, and vandalism involving juveniles. When it is used, it often occurs as part of a diversion effort in which there is no conviction.

The use of restitution has perhaps been limited at this point by a recognition that in many cases an offender "does not have an ability to make restitution and even if placed on probation or ordered to jail with work release privileges, most criminals could, at best, make only partial restitution for their delinquent acts."[48] In addition, it has been generally felt that the serving of prison time is sufficient restitution for an offender to make. While use of restitution has been limited, it is a concept that is being given a great deal of thought and many more victims may someday realize compensation for crimes against their property and person.

Reintegration Another goal emerging within the past few years is that of **reintegration.** This refers to the phased reentry of an offender into society rather than the usual abrupt reentry at the end of a prison sentence. Its appearance as a distinct function of corrections seems due to the recognition that almost all offenders who serve prison time are released back into society and to the increasing belief in the failure of traditional rehabilitation programs. The philosophy behind reintegration is that rehabilitation cannot be achieved with most offenders within the confining, controlling, artificial environment of institutions such as prisons. It is felt that most offenders in institutions cannot learn to function lawfully in society except through the maintenance of outside contacts and phased reentry into society.

The emphasis on reintegration has spurred greater interest in community corrections programs and in various forms of furloughs, work releases, and other means of establishing and maintaining ties with family, friends, jobs, and other positive elements of the community.

Corrections Goals: Mixed Purposes

We have discussed each of the corrections goals as if they were largely unrelated to one another. This is not the case. Each has some relation to the others, be it complementary or conflicting. Retribution, for example, is closely linked to incapacitation; deterrence, when it occurs, would likely result from incapacitation or punishment. Some feel that rehabilitation and other goals such as retribution and incapacitation are basically incompatible. Others believe that rehabilitation cannot be achieved without some degree of isolation and punishment.

In practical terms, what does this mean to the corrections system of today? It means that society attempts to accomplish its goal of reducing crime and protection of citizens through a corrections system that has no clearly articulated mandate in terms of specific goals. As Newman observes:

All these goals infuse corrections today, so that in any sentence, whether to prison or probation, the drama of multiple objectives is played out on all lev-

els.... *In short, though the place where sentence is served may range from the community to a maximum-security prison, the purposes of the sentence ... apply simultaneously, though with some differences in emphasis and priority. Not all of the rules and regulations of a prison are designed solely to punish, nor are all the conditions and restrictions of probation directed to rehabilitation and reintegration. Conditions of all sentences reflect a mixture of purposes, often conflicting and not easily reconciled.*[49]

STRUCTURE OF CORRECTIONS

The corrections system consists of many different agencies and organizations at every level of government. We will examine the structure of corrections by grouping all agencies and programs into two general categories: institutions of confinement and community-based corrections. Among the institutions are local jails, state and federal corrections institutions, and special purpose facilities such as mental hospitals and alcohol detoxification centers. Within the category of community-based corrections, we will consider pretrial diversion, parole, probation, and newer types of facilities and programs designed to emphasize reintegration of the offender into the community.

Institutions

Jails A **jail** is defined as a locally administered institution that has the authority to hold persons for forty-eight hours or longer. There were 3,921 jails in the United States in 1972, and they housed well over 140,000 persons at any one time. The vast majority of jails (over 70 percent) housed 20 or fewer inmates and less than 390 had a capacity of 250 inmates or more. The Northeast had the fewest jails (231) of any of the four sections of the country, but it tended to have larger facilities than other sections. The South had by far the most jails (1,865) and the largest jail population of any section (over 55,000).[50] See Table 12.1.

Institutions are facilities within which convicted persons are incarcerated or confined for short or extended periods of time. Most attempt to provide some sort of treatment.

Jails are used for two basic purposes: as a means of detaining persons awaiting trial, other judicial disposition, or transfer to another institution, and as a correctional institution for persons sentenced to a term of one year or less. Usually less than half of those in jail are there to serve a sentence. Many have not been convicted of a crime and are awaiting trial or adjudication. The remaining persons are in jail pend-

TABLE 12.1 Jails and Inmates, by Section of the U.S.

	Jails	Inmates	Jails with Fewer than 21 Inmates	Jails with 21–249 Inmates	Jails with 250 or More Inmates
Total	3,921	141,588	2,901	907	113
Northeast	231	27,362	91	117	23
North Central	1,153	23,516	970	167	16
South	1,865	55,461	1,356	475	34
West	672	35,249	484	148	40

Source: Department of Justice, *The Nation's Jails* (Washington, D.C.: Government Printing Office, 1975), pp. 1–2.

ing further court disposition or transfer to another corrections institution.[51] It is clear, therefore, that jails are basically places of custody for most inmates and do not perform corrections functions for most residents.

Upon examination it is apparent that most jails are neither staffed nor equipped for more than custodial purposes. Virtually every authority on the nation's jails agrees that the vast majority of them are wretched places. Frank Prassel says they are "the worst means of confinement in America," and declares that jails can be called "the most disgraceful feature of corrections in all of criminal justice."[52]

Hassim Solomon points out that the jail's problems are generally in four areas. The first problem area is that the majority of them mix all types of prisoners—convicted and pretrial, alcoholics, drug addicts, the physically and mentally ill, first offenders, and hardened criminals and recidivists. In this respect many jails are like the old English gaols. The second problem area is the organizational structure, which, Solomon points out, is an obstacle to reform. Jails are secondary concerns of local police departments, primarily county sheriffs. Local politics and citizen lack of interest often mean the jails are ignored. The needs of their inmates often take second place to holding down jail costs. The third problem is the age and condition of most physical plants used as jails. Many are little better than cages, and they are usually overcrowded, some to intolerable levels. The final problem area is staffing, both in terms of quantity and quality. Not only are the guards often too few, most are untrained and many are otherwise unfit. There is also a lack of professional medical and rehabilitative staff, especially in the smaller facilities.[53]

There are, of course, exceptions to the picture above, especially in progressive metropolitan areas. We are personally familiar with the progressive jails operated by the Orlando Police Department and the Orange County Sheriff's Department in Florida. It is also true that the Law Enforcement Assistance Administration is encouraging improvements in the physical facilities of jails, the training of staff, and the introduction of rehabilitative and reintegrative programs in jails. Solomon points out that since jails are at the community level, they have the potential to become vital parts of the community corrections movement.[54] Kalmanoff adds that the location of jails within their communities and the fact that most of their convicted inmates do not require maximum or even medium security facilities make jails advantageous institutions for the use of work release and other reintegrative methods.[55]

Presently most states exercise little or no authority over local jails. About 40 percent of the states provide some form of supervisory or inspection services to local jails, and a few states have authority to require changes in operations. Very few (about a half dozen) states provide subsidies to local jails, and in even less are local jails under full state control.[56]

The two major organizational changes being urged and considered are the placement of jails under the authority of state corrections agencies and the development of regional jails that would be large enough to provide proper treatment facilities. There are problems with any change, of course. Regionalized facilities make transportation of prisoners and booking of arrestees more time-consuming and expensive. It is also possible for state or regional takeovers to interfere with local initiatives for reform. With respect to most jails, however, almost any change would be an improvement.

Federal and State Correctional Institutions Should an offender commit a crime that warrants some period of institutionalization other than a local jail, he or she may be confined in one of many correctional institutions around the country. The institution to which each offender is assigned will depend on a number of factors. These range from the sex of the offender to the nature of the crime committed.

1. The nature of the crime. In referring to the nature of the crime, we mean two things: whether it is a violation of state or federal law and whether it is a felony or misdemeanor. With regard to the first, each governmental level has its own corrections system containing a variety of institutions in which offenders may be confined for varying lengths of time. We will discuss both federal and state systems shortly.

The distinction between felonies and misdemeanors is, as we have indicated, based on the seriousness of the crime. Recall that a misdemeanor is generally a minor offense, which can draw a fine or a short period in confinement (usually less than one year). Felonies are more serious crimes, with possible penalties being much more severe. At the state level misdemeanants frequently serve their time in some facility (for example, jail) operated by local authorities, while felons are always sent to a state institution. In many states misdemeanants and felons may be incarcerated in the same facility. Except for maximum security penitentiaries, the federal corrections system is basically the same.

2. The length of the sentence. At both federal and state levels, the length of a sentence plays a role in designating the institution in which an offender is to be confined. Within the federal prison system, for example, offenders sentenced to greater than five years serve their time in maximum security penitentiaries housing only felons; a two-to-five-year sentence is served in a medium security correctional institution housing felons and misdemeanants; lesser sentences are served in prison camps under minimum security.

3. The age of the offender. Although there is some variation among states regarding the age at which an offender is classified as an adult, most states and the federal corrections system make some provision for separation of youthful and adult offenders.

4. The sex of the offender. A number of states and the federal systems have some coeducational institutions, but most are limited to one sex only.

5. The level of security needed. Inmates are also classified according to security risks and at both levels, federal and state, are assigned to appropriate institutions. Thus at both levels we find maximum, medium, and minimum security institutions. A **maximum security facility** is defined as one in which the security is maximized both inside and around the perimeter. The **medium security facility** usually features strong fenced perimeters but less in the way of internal restrictions and control over inmates. **Minimum security** generally means very little security at all, internal or external.

6. First-time offense. Though it may be only one of several factors, the past record of an offender is frequently a determinant of the correctional institution to which he or she is assigned. A number of states, for example, have designated one or more institutions as being principally for first offenders—for example, Georgia has two institutions that house primarily first-offense felons and misdemeanants between the ages of 20 and 25 years; Texas has several such units, one primarily for older first offenders, one for ages 17 to 21, and two with no age limit.

Prisons can be classified according to the level of security maintained—maxium, medium, or minimum.

7. Special needs and treatment programs. After diagnostic evaluation by screening and placement personnel, offenders may be assigned to an institution whose facilities are designed to meet some special need—physical or psychological—or provide some program of treatment to aid in rehabilitation and reintegration into society. In speaking of facilities designed to meet special needs, we mean those that attempt to deal with offender problems such as alcohol or narcotics addiction, physical handicaps, and mental illness (e.g., the Illinois Menard Psychiatric Center for the mentally ill and sexually dangerous persons in need of mental treatment).

In addition to these specialized types of facilities, correctional systems often may designate one or more of their institutions to provide vocational and educational training for offenders. New York's Coxsackie Correctional Facility, for example, is described as designed for "felons and misdemeanants, . . . usually 16–19 years of age, and more hopeful male offenders who are likely to profit from a program offering varied vocational training activities and intensified academic and related trade studies."[57] Arizona's Fort Grant Training Center is characterized as a "remedial, high school, vocational and college level educational facility."[58]

The federal corrections system, under the jurisdiction of the Department of Justice, is operated by the Federal Bureau of Prisons, established in 1930 by Congress. The bureau has the responsibility for "the safekeeping, care, protection, instruction, and discipline of all persons charged or convicted of offenses against the United States." To accomplish this task, the federal corrections system utilizes forty-seven different institutions ranging from penitentiaries to halfway houses. These include six maximum security penitentiaries housing male felons serving a sentence of greater than five years, a dozen medium security "federal correctional institutions" containing felons and misdemeanants serving terms of two to five years, with several facilities being limited to specific age groups (for example, 18-25), three medium security "metropolitan correctional centers" designed for felons and misdemeanants serving sentences of two to five years, two medium security "detention centers" (one for aliens), one "medical center" (felons and misdemeanants, medium security), three medium security "reformatories"—two for youthful offenders and one for females—four minimum security "prison camps" for felons and misdemeanants, and four "federal youth centers" (felons and misdemeanants).[59]

There are many adult institutions of confinement other than county or local jails that fall under state authority. In about half the states, the agency responsible for administering correctional services (parent agency) has a department rank within the structure of state government. In the remaining states it is found within a department containing other state services—for example, social services.[60]

The 1974 *Census of State Correctional Facilities* shows that there were 592 institutions for adults, containing 187,982 inmates. Most of these institutions, over 67 percent, were what we commonly think of as "prisons," though in reality very seldom called that. They housed over 90 percent of all confined inmates (169,241). As Table 12.2 shows, there were also 33 classification or medical centers providing some service (diagnostic or medical) to 9,766 offenders and 158 community centers (8,975 inmates). The census also found that 39 percent of all institutionalized inmates were in maximum security confinement, 34 percent in medium security, and 27 percent in minimum security.

State corrections systems around the country vary considerably in the nature of their programs and facilities. Some systems are simple,

TABLE 12.2 Summary Statistics on State Correctional Facilities for Adults, January 1974

	Number of Facilities	Number of Inmates
Total	*592*	*187,982*
All prisons	401	169,241
Classification or medical centers	33	9,766
Community centers	158	8,975

Source: American Correctional Association, *Juvenile and Adult Correctional Departments, Institutions, Agencies, and Paroling Authorities* (College Park, Md.: American Correctional Association, 1975), p. 258.

containing only one institution of confinement for adults; others are more complex in both number and variety. Some of the differences can be seen in the brief descriptions of adult institutions within three state corrections systems: Mississippi, Rhode Island, and Texas (see Table 12.3).

Though corrections systems differ considerably from state to state, they do offer a much greater selection of programs and institutions than were available at any other time in this country's history. As Chamelin, Fox, and Whisenand note: "This offers the total prison system a greater flexibility that permits greater treatment than has ever existed before."[61]

Prison Organization and Administration It is difficult to offer even the briefest description of the internal structure of correctional institutions because the organization and administration of each varies with purpose, size, population, and degree of custody. It is not, for example, likely to be the same for a huge maximum security prison as it is for a minimum security conservation camp or honor farm. It will assuredly be different for the small facility that places almost sole emphasis on treatment than for the large, often overcrowded institution that must place substantial stress on custody and security.

In addition to factors such as size, purpose, population, and custody, the organization and administration of an institution will depend on the personality, competence, and institutional goals of its administrator and administration.

The title of the chief administrator of the many corrections institutions varies not only from state to state but often within a specific corrections system. The most common title is that of superintendent, followed closely by warden. Other titles less frequently used include director, administrator, and supervisor.

Whatever the title, the administrator of a corrections institution has certain duties to perform. These may include public relations, budget preparation and administration, personnel management, and administration of the institution's various programs. To accomplish these things the administrator may delegate responsibility to others, such as a deputy, associate, or various department heads.

Chamelin, Fox, and Whisenand suggest that a prison's important departments will include these:

... *(1) custodial; (2) school programs; (3) classification system; (4) chaplain and the religious program; (5) hospital and dental services; (6) industries; (7) farm; (8) chief engineer and maintenance department; (9) business manager...; (10) psychiatric and mental health services...; (11) recreation; (12) library...; and (13) administrative services such as accounting, personnel, and record office....*[62]

TABLE 12.3 Mississippi, Rhode Island, and Texas State Corrections Systems

System	Institution	Average Population	Inmates Housed
Mississippi (1975)	Mississippi State Penitentiary	2,163 males 83 females	Male and female; felons; age limit: 18 and up
Rhode Island (1973)	Awaiting trial facility	99	Males; felons, misdemeanants, and others; age limit: 18 and up
	Admission and orientation unit	25	Same as above
	Maximum security facility	260	Same as above
	Medium security facility	50	Same as above
	Minimum security facility	50	Same as above
	Adult correctional institution, women's division	25	Female; felons, misdemeanants, and others; age limit: 18 and up
	Work release unit	33	Felons, misdemeanants, and others; age limit: 18 and up

Source: American Correctional Association, *Juvenile and Adult Correctional Departments, Institutions, Agencies, and Paroling Authorities* (College Park, Md.: American Correctional Association, 1975).

TABLE 12.3 (continued)

System	Institution	Average Population	Inmates Housed
Texas (1973)	Huntsville unit	1,885	Male; primarily older first offenders. Treatment center for mentally irresponsible and mentally deficient
	Diagnostic unit	674	Males; felons; age limit: 17 and up
	Central unit	730	Males; felons, primarily first offenders
	Clemens unit	1,072	Males; felons, primarily first offenders
	Coffield unit	889	Males; felons; minimum security unit for inmates of nonviolent crimes, work release program
	Darrington unit	811	Males; felons; primarily for recidivists under 25
	Eastham unit	1,553	Males; felons; general population with priority for certain handicapped recidivists
	Ellis unit	1,612	Males; felons; maximum security unit
	Ferguson unit	1,553	Males; felons; first offenders; age limit: 17–21
	Goree unit	614	Female; felons; work release program
	Jester unit	872	Males; felons; work release program
	Mountain view unit	250	Females; felons
	Ramsey unit	1,903	Males; felons; primarily for recidivists over 25
	Retrieve unit	722	Males; felons; primarily for recidivists over 25
	Wynne unit	1,585	Males; felons; maximum security unit for physically handicapped, work release program

The number, types and importance of an institution's departments will generally depend, of course, on the previously mentioned factors of size, purpose, population, and degree of custody maintained.

For many corrections institutions the two major components of organization are those that are responsible for custody and treatment. The **custodial staff**—primarily guards and their officers—are generally organized along military lines similar to that of police departments. Their tasks include enforcement of rules, prevention of escapes, prevention and control of riots, moving inmates from place to place, and handling of emergencies that arise. The **treatment staff** is composed of professionals who operate some mix of the following programs: psychiatric sessions, group therapy, vocational training, education at various levels, work release programs, conjugal visits by members of the inmates' families, coordination of councils and committees of inmates, and behavior modification through the use of drugs or other methods of treatment. Figure 12.1 shows an organization chart for a typical large maximum security institution and indicates some of the concerns of not only the custody and treatment components but of others as well.

Within many institutions there are two parallel organizations: the formal one of the authorities and employed personnel and the informal one of the inmates. While the first is responsible for formal operation of a facility, most observers agree that the latter is also an important factor in the way many institutions are run. Chamelin, Fox, and Whisenand assert, in fact, that inmates "run the routines of prisons in most institutions," performing "the clerical mechanics of cell changes, work assignment changes, and many other routine procedures." They do so "primarily at the default of the administration and staff."[63]

It has also been pointed out that it would be difficult to keep order or perform any other function without at least tacit understandings between staff and inmates. Guards may overlook some violations of rules and permit the informal inmate organization to function in order to obtain cooperation in keeping the peace and conducting the day-to-day activities. This may be, in short, one form of institutional control.

Community-Related Corrections

By community-related corrections we mean all those corrections efforts which involve keeping the offender out of an institution of confinement. This means that the offender is allowed to have some degree of freedom of movement and to maintain ties with family, occupation or schooling, and with at least some of his or her friends. Included are parole, probation, and a variety of other programs designed to rehabili-

FIGURE 12.1 Organization of Prison Staff and Functions

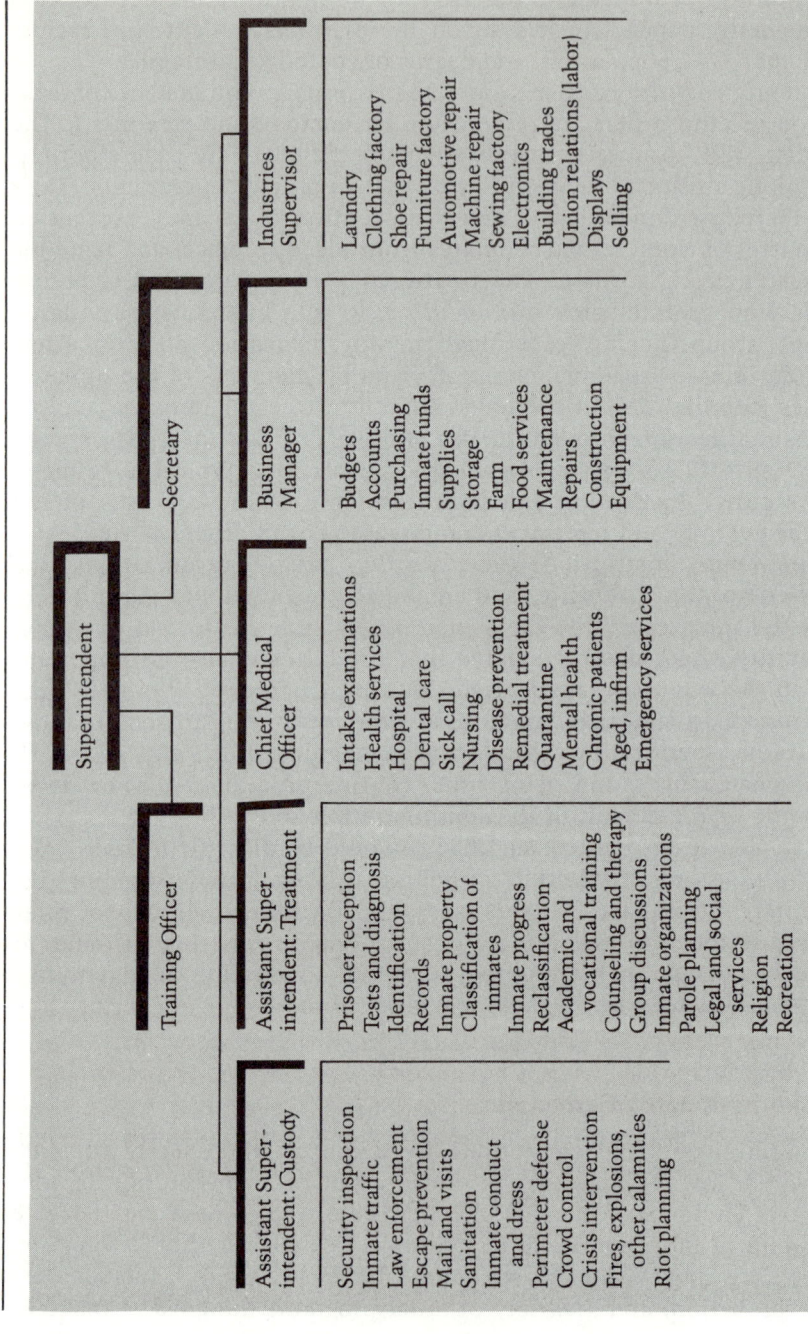

Source: Clarence Shrag, *Crime and Justice: American Style* (Washington, D.C.: Government Printing Office, for National and Mental Health, 1971), p. 193.

tate the offender or reintegrate him with the law-abiding elements of the community.

Parole As we pointed out before, parole is the corrections subsystem operated at the state and federal levels in which prisoners are released—usually prior to the completion of the term to which they have been sentenced—but are placed under the supervision of an officer who works for the parole authority. The offender is allowed to remain at large so long as he reports regularly to the parole officer and abides by a list of conditions agreed upon at the time of release. Violations of these conditions may be grounds for revocation of parole and the return of the offender to prison to complete his full term. Persons who complete their term of sentence without revocation are released from all controls.

Organizationally, parole has two major components: the parole board, which makes the critical decisions concerning parole status for offenders, and the field supervisors or parole officers, who are responsible for working with and supervising the parolees.

While it may vary from state to state, **parole boards** are said to perform four basic functions: selection and placement of prisoners on parole; overseeing the operation of field supervisors; discharging from parole offenders completing their sentences or showing that they are no further risk; and determining whether parole should be revoked in cases of apparent violation of parole conditions.[64]

Parole boards range in size from three to twelve, with the most common sizes being three and five. About 80 percent of all states' boards fall into these two categories.

In about half the states (twenty-nine), the District of Columbia, and at the federal level, parole board members are full-time personnel. All but one of the remaining states (twenty) employ only part-time members. One state utilizes a mixture of both.

As for organizational status, most parole boards are completely autonomous agencies. This means that they are independent from the corrections system in terms of their paroling authority. In general, board members are appointed by a state's governor and are responsible only to him or her. Where there is some tie between a parole board and the corrections system, it is often just financial or administrative and not likely to affect the board's independence. In several states, however, the situation is somewhat different: the Indiana Parole Board reports to the commissioner of corrections, who in turn reports to the governor; the chairman of the Maryland Board of Parole reports to the deputy secretary for Public Safety and Correctional Services; Michigan's parole board members are civil service employees of the Department of Corrections; and Ohio's Adult Parole Authority is a part of the Division of Parole and Community Services. In Wisconsin:

> ... the Secretary of the Department of Health and Social Services is the paroling authority for the state. The Parole Board, which is made up of ten full-time members, is a part of the Secretary's executive staff and exists to advise and make recommendations to the Secretary on all matters pertaining to adults and juveniles in Wisconsin correctional facilities.[65]

The location of a parole board within a corrections system does not necessarily, of course, lead to a loss in independence of paroling authority, but it would appear to offer a greater potential for doing so than would a completely autonomous status.

The front-line organization of a state's parole system consists of field supervisors, or **parole officers.** Within the overall objectives of parole, these officers have several specific tasks: supervising or monitoring the behavior of parolees; exercising some control over that behavior by warning the parolee of possible violation of parole conditions and by recommending revocation when appropriate; and providing guidance and counseling services to those under supervision—a task that frequently may mean assisting in the location of suitable employment.

Organizationally, parole services or supervision most often fall within a state's corrections system.[66] It may be directly under a state department of corrections or part of a corrections component within a state department that also provides other public services. In Oregon, for example, parole supervision is located in the Corrections Division of the Department of Human Resources. In South Dakota it is a matter handled at the state level by the Office of Adult Corrections, which is within the Division of Corrections in the Department of Social Services. In at least a dozen states, parole supervision is entirely independent from the corrections system. In these places it is generally within the jurisdiction of the state's paroling authority, for example, Board of Paroles and Pardons, Board of Pardons and Parole, Probation and Parole Board, or Department of Parole and Probation. Pennsylvania has a somewhat unusual setup in that a state board of probation and parole handles parolees with more than two years to serve and county probation departments supervise all others (less than two years).

Parole officers themselves have a variety of backgrounds, training, attitudes, and previous experience. While the first parole officers were generally retired police—and many still are today—persons trained in social work are moving more and more into the field. To a degree it has resulted in the predictable clashes between those with field experience (on-the-street training) and those with academic training.

The importance of parole as one method of dealing with criminal offenders should not be underestimated. In recent years about 70 percent of prisoner releases have been into parole status, and state-by-state comparisons show that the figures range from 100 percent in New Hampshire to 7 percent in Wyoming.[67] Most of the large states release three-quarters or more of their prisoners through parole. So despite increased talk in some states of abolishing parole due to problems such as parolee recidivism, parole is likely to be with us for a while. The simple fact of life is that corrections institutions can handle only so many persons and parole is far cheaper than continued institutionalization.

Probation Probation can be defined as a status that does not involve an offender's confinement or incarceration but does subject the offender to certain conditions. Even though the offender is free from custody, the courts retain jurisdiction during the probationary period and can resentence him to jail or prison should the terms and conditions of probation be violated. The offender thus has his liberty restrained and in most cases is subject to supervision by probation officers. Probation is now available in every state (and at the federal level) for felony crimes and in all but nine states for misdemeanors. Where it exists, it is employed in the vast majority of misdemeanor cases and well over half of all felony ones.

In recent years there has been a revival of John Augustus's original concept of probation as a preadjudication process in the form of various diversion programs. Whether these programs utilize the established probationary departments and services or employ their own supervisory personnel, they involve deferment of prosecution or adjudication and substitution of a probationary status for an agreed-to period of time.

While parole seeks to rehabilitate offenders and further their reintegration into the community, probation attempts to prevent the disintegration that can result from incarceration, even for short periods of time. Probation is supposed to provide positive support for the maintenance of family ties, continued or new employment, educational efforts, and other worthwhile activities within the community. The hope is not only that families will remain together and the welfare rolls be spared the wives and children of those institutionalized but also that the offender will be more likely to avoid future crimes. From the criminal justice system's point of view, probation is also a very inexpensive means of handling thousands of offenders who probably should not be institutionalized anyway.

There is a great deal of variation around the country in the way probation is organized. We will describe three variations here: vertical, horizontal, and probation-parole linkage.

Vertical variation simply means that the responsibility for probation services may rest at any one of several levels of government and sometimes at more than one. In general, probation programs and agents are organizationally under some state-level agency, such as a department of corrections, but in a handful of states there is local control, such as county probation departments, and sometimes a mixture of both. As an example of the latter situation, Kansas's Department of Corrections is responsible for probation services in 100 counties; 5 counties provide their own and so also do 3 cities.

Vertical variation in probation systems may refer not only to organizational location but to the actual operation of probation services as well. That is, in a number of states, probation may fall within the responsibility of a state department such as corrections but be operated at some lesser level. In Maine, for example, there is a Division of Probation and Parole, within the Bureau of Corrections, which provides field services to four districts. In Michigan the Bureau of Field Services, a part of that state's Department of Corrections, administers probation. The state is divided into six districts and one region. Supervisors oversee the county and state probation and parole agents within the districts.

Not only may probation services be provided at different levels of government but there are horizontal differences as well. This means that at any level of government, probation services can be located within the judicial or executive branches or be independent of either. In three or four states the courts administer probation programs. Approximately ten states utilize an independent government agency such as a State Board of Probation and Parole. The largest number of states (about thirty) place responsibility for probation services within a department of the executive branch, most often the Department of Corrections. Also, as we noted under vertical variations, in a few states the county runs all probation programs.[68] Duffee and Fitch assert that for the most part judges like and trust probation officers who work for nonjudicial departments.[69]

A third variation concerns whether or not probation is organizationally linked with parole. Most states combine these two obviously similar programs within a single framework. About a dozen or so states do not.

As with parole, the front line organization of a state's probation system is made up of field supervisors, or **probation officers.** Probation officers have two important responsibilities or functions to perform: preparation, at the request of the sentencing court, of a pre-sentence investigation report (PSI) and supervision of those on probation. Recall that the PSI is designed to acquaint the court with sufficient information about the offender and his background—social, occupational, and criminal—to help determine an appropriate sentence. It may also contain the probation officer's recommendations for sentencing. The officer's recommendation may be based on any of several factors, such as the nature of the offense, prior record, employment history, age, family history, marital status, and defendant's attitude, or simply whether the officer feels that he can work with the offender. Whatever the recommendation, it is likely to have significant impact on the judge's sentencing decision.[70]

Probation supervision is much like that of parole. It involves not only the supervision or monitoring of probationers but the provision of guidance and counseling as well. In addition, the probation officer may find it necessary to recommend that the probation status of a probationer be revoked and that he or she be subjected to a term in prison. Chamelin, Fox, and Whisenand describe the task of the probation officer:

> *Supervision included not only case work and counseling assistance in employment and personal planning but enforcement functions as well. It is a type of treatment—supervision. The probation officer must use the resources of the community successfully in order to be effective in each of his many cases. He has to know employment possibilities, personnel managers, vocational guidance agencies, child care or welfare agencies, child guidance clinics, mental hygiene clinics, social group agencies, vocational rehabilitation counselors, and all other persons who may be a help in rehabilitating the offender.*[71]

Community Treatment Centers and Programs Probation and parole are well-established and, by now, traditional correctional programs. There is a wide variety of other corrections efforts that are less traditional, generally more experimental in nature, and less widespread in use. There are basically two sets of categories into which these programs can be divided. One set deals with whether the program is **institutional**—that is, made part of an overall corrections effort that includes institutionalization for at least part of the offender's sentence—or **noninstitutional**—that is, serving as an alternative to any incarceration. The other categories have to do with whether the program is residential or nonresidential in nature. That is, does it require offenders to live in a corrections facility, house, hotel, barracks, or other residential building, or does it allow them to live in the community?

An example of an institution-related and usually residential program is the halfway house for offenders who have completed part of their sentences in a prison and where attempts are made to orient them toward a law-abiding life in the community. An example of institution-related but nonresidential treatment is, in addition to parole, a **reentry services program** through which offenders are given more intensified counseling, employment assistance, and other services.

Noninstitutional residential facilities are generally called community corrections centers. Among the noninstitutional and nonresidential programs are probation, special supervision projects, and so-called **guided-interaction programs** (or GIPs) that tend to specialize in treating persons with alcohol, drug, and other behavioral problems.

The differences between these categories are not precise. The National Advisory Commission on Criminal Justice Standards and Goals commented that the line between community-based or noninstitutional programs and those related to institutions is "blurring substantially."[72] This is especially true for programs that are under the administration of jail authorities. There are also corrections centers that offer both residential and nonresidential programs. We will look briefly at the two most common examples of these newer community corrections efforts: halfway houses and community corrections centers.

Hassim Solomon has defined halfway houses as "any relatively small facility, either residential or nonresidential, usually located in or close to the city." He adds that offenders participate in the daily life of the community and live under "comparatively free conditions." They are met, however, with certain expectations on their behavior, especially in terms of undergoing a "group experience" and adjusting to productive life.[73] Halfway houses have existed in a few places for many years (there were prototypes in New York and Chicago in the late nineteenth century) and have assisted many men and women leaving prisons. Their spread throughout the country has occurred within the past few years.

An even more recent development is the addition of **halfway-in houses** and programs to the older halfway house treatment (halfway-out). Halfway-in houses are for those considered too risky for regular probation but not deserving of institutionalization.

Duffee and Fitch point out that halfway houses serve many purposes, including providing a place to live for those who are released from institutions with no place to go, offering drug, alcohol, and psychiatric treatment programs, and providing a decent place for detaining persons prior to adjudication.[74]

Solomon describes community corrections centers as "community-based institutions, located in a selected neighborhood in an effort to reduce the isolation from community services and other resources."[75] McCartt and Mangogna treat community corrections centers as being virtually synonymous with halfway houses. They write: "There is no single definition or description which can possibly be devised at this time which would adequately encompass the wide range of facilities which call themselves or which are called halfway houses or community treatment centers." They point out that intake criteria, length of stay, treatment goals, types of clients served, services offered, and characteristics of the staff and physical plant are too diverse to permit a "unified, capsulized definition."[76]

Vetter and Simonsen comment that a "truly integrated Community Correctional Center" would encompass all the functions performed by so-called halfway houses, jails, and other local correctional programs."[77]

McCartt and Mangogna note that there are several different "populations" served by community-based residential facilities. First there are the mandatory releasees and parolees who have "always been and still are being served" by halfway houses. Second are probationers who are considered too risky to be placed on the normal at-large probation status. Third are the prereleasees who have not yet been placed on parole or given their release from prison. Fourth are those awaiting sentencing by courts, who are subject to study and diagnostic services (as part of the pre-sentence investigation to aid the court in deciding sentence). Fifth are juveniles, a group we will consider separately. Sixth are those with "special difficulties," such as drug abuse, alcoholism, and psychiatric problems. Seventh are those released on bail prior to a charging decision by the prosecutor or prior to adjudication. Finally, there is the use of such facilities for those diverted from the system in return for their agreement to undergo some form of correctional program.[78]

Because of the wide variety of programs being offered through these facilities, the various points along the criminal justice process at which community corrections can be invoked, the varied populations of offenders who are handled, and the degree of change in each of these matters, it is not possible to sketch a precise picture of the structure of community corrections. It is only possible to state the general nature of such efforts and point out the differences between these efforts and the traditional programs of probation and parole. Whereas the latter are laregely efforts to provide some general guidance and supervision of offenders who are at large, the newer programs are intended to provide intensive and specialized treatment of and assistance to specified offenders. The basic goal of all such programs is to enable or compel offenders to reintegrate themselves into the community as law-abiding citizens.

TEST YOURSELF

Define these key terms:

corporal punishment
Auburn prison model
work release
special deterrence
incapacitation
custodial staff
reentry services

Answer the following questions:

1. What were some early methods of capital punishment and corporal punishment?

2. What were the five stages of development of prisons and the central goal of prisons within each stage?

3. Name four problems that plague most American jails.

4. Along what lines can most prison staffs be divided?

5. What are the specific functions of parole boards?

6. Why is community corrections a difficult phenomenon to describe?

NOTES

1. Neil C. Chamelin, Vernon B. Fox, and Paul M. Whisenand, *Introduction to Criminal Justice* (Englewood Cliffs, N.J.: Prentice-Hall, 1975), p. 287.
2. Donald J. Newman, *Introduction to Criminal Justice* (Philadelphia: Lippincott, 1975), p. 289.
3. For good but brief statements of the historical development of corrections, see Paul K. Clare and John H. Kramer, *Introduction to American Corrections* (Boston: Holbrook Press, 1976), pp. 27-95; Alvin W. Cohn, *Crime and Justice Administration* (Philadelphia: Lippincott, 1976), pp. 291-304; David Duffee and Robert Fitch, *An Introduction to Corrections: A Policy and Systems Approach* (Pacific Palisades, Calif.: Goodyear, 1976), pp. 114-25; and Chamelin, Fox, and Whisenand, *Criminal Justice*, pp. 289-99. For a more extensive coverage of the subject, see Christopher Hilbert, *The Roots of Evil: A Social History of Crime and Punishment* (Boston: Little, Brown, 1963); Harry E. Barnes, *The Story of Punishment*, 2d ed. rev. (Montclair, N.J.: Patterson Smith, 1972); John Lawrence, *A History of Capital Punishment* (New York: Citadel Press, 1969); and Harry E. Barnes and Negley K. Teeters, *New Horizons in Criminology*, 2d ed. (Englewood Cliffs, N.J.: Prentice-Hall, 1955).

4. Cohn, *Crime*, p. 293.
5. Ibid., pp. 295-96.
6. Cohn, *Crime*, pp. 297-99.
7. Harry E. Barnes, *The Repression of Crime: Studies in Historical Penology* (Montclair, N.J.: Patterson Smith, 1969), pp. 88-9.
8. Ibid., p. 84.
9. Cohn, *Crime*, p. 300.
10. Duffee and Fitch, *Corrections*, p. 118.
11. Clare and Kramer, *American Corrections*, pp. 46-60.
12. Barnes and Teeters, *New Horizons*, p. 425; and Clare and Kramer, *American Corrections*, pp. 65-77.
13. Barnes, *Repression*, p. 426.
14. Hilbert, *Roots of Evil*, pp. 168-81; Clare and Kramer, *American Corrections*, pp. 81-87.
15. Duffee and Fitch, *Corrections*, p. 124.
16. Clare and Kramer, *American Corrections*, pp. 90-91.
17. Department of Justice, *National Prisoner Statistics Bulletin* (Washington, D.C.: Government Printing Office, 1974), p. 18. Gary Gilmore was executed by firing squad in Utah.
18. *Furman* v. *Georgia*, 408 U.S. 238 (1972).
19. *Gregg* v. *Georgia*, *Proffitt* v. *Florida*, *Jurek* v. *Texas*, *Woodson* v. *North Carolina*, and *Roberts* v. *Louisiana*, 96 Sup. Ct. (2 July 1976).
20. Barnes and Teeters, *New Horizons*, pp. 418-25; see also Cohn, *Crime*, pp. 409-12; and Duffee and Fitch, *Corrections*, p. 221.
21. Duffee and Fitch, *Corrections*, p. 222; Barnes and Teeters, *New Horizons*, pp. 566-72.
22. Barnes and Teeters, *New Horizons*, pp. 553-54.
23. Clare and Kramer, *American Corrections*, p. 261.
24. Harry E. Allen and Clifford E. Simonsen, *Corrections in America: An Introduction* (Beverly Hills, Calif.: Glencoe Press, 1976), p. 120.
25. Duffee and Fitch, *Corrections*, pp. 249 and 255-56.
26. Herbert L. Packer, *The Limits of the Criminal Sanction* (Stanford: Stanford University Press, 1968), p. 36.
27. Duffee and Fitch, *Corrections*, p. 8; and Kalmanoff, *Criminal Justice*, pp. 317-18.
28. Marvin E. Frankel, "An Opinion by One of Those Soft-Headed Judges," *New York Times Magazine*, 13 May 1973, p. 42.
29. Ibid.
30. Kalmanoff, *Criminal Justice*, p. 318-19.
31. Marvin E. Frankel, "Big Change in Prisons: PUNISH, NOT REFORM," as quoted in *U.S. News and World Report*, 25 August 1975, p. 21.
32. Kalmanoff, *Criminal Justice*, p. 319.
33. George F. Cole, *The American System of Criminal Justice* (N. Scituate, Mass.: Duxbury Press, 1975), p. 358.
34. Richard Kwartler, "Rehabilitation," *Corrections Magazine* 1 (May/June 1975), p. 2.
35. "Big Change," p. 21.
36. Ibid., p. 22.
37. See Michael S. Serrill, "Is Rehabilitation Dead?" *Corrections Magazine* 1 (May/June 1975), pp. 3-7.
38. Ibid.
39. Cole, *American System*, p. 354.
40. Norman Carlson, as quoted in "Big Change," p. 21.
41. Hans Mattick, as quoted in "Big Change," p. 22.
42. Robert McColley, as quoted in "Is Rehabilitation Dead?" p. 22.
43. Kalmanoff, *Criminal Justice*, p. 325.
44. "Big Change," p. 21.
45. William Nagel, as quoted in "Is Rehabilitation Dead?" p. 29.
46. "Is Rehabilitation Dead?" p. 4.
47. "Is Rehabilitation Dead?" p. 10.
48. Duffee and Fitch, *Introduction to Corrections*, p. 74.

49. Newman, *Criminal Justice*, pp. 290-91.
50. Department of Justice, *The Nation's Jails* (Washington, D.C.: Government Printing Office, 1975), pp. 1-2.
51. Department of Justice, *Survey of Inmates of Local Jails: Advanced Report* (Washington, D.C.: Government Printing Office, 1973), p. 17.
52. Frank R. Prassel, *Introduction to American Criminal Justice* (New York: Harper & Row, 1975), p. 214.
53. Hassim M. Solomon, *Community Corrections*, (Boston: Holbrook Press), pp. 227-28. See also Department of Justice, *Nation's Jails*, pp. 4-16.
54. Solomon, *Community Corrections*, pp. 225 and 229-38.
55. Kalmanoff, *Criminal Justice*, p. 373.
56. Duffee and Fitch, *Corrections*, p. 130; and George T. Felkenes, *The Criminal Justice System* (Englewood Cliffs, N.J.: Prentice-Hall, 1973), p. 264.
57. American Correctional Association, *Juvenile and Adult Correctional Departments, Institutions, Agencies, and Paroling Authorities* (College Park, Md.: ACA, 1975), p. 111.
58. Ibid., p. 7.
59. Ibid., pp. 188-91.
60. Ibid., pp. 250-57.
61. Chamelin, Fox, and Whisenand, *Criminal Justice*, p. 353.
62. Ibid., p. 360.
63. Ibid., p. 386.
64. Solomon, *Community Corrections*, p. 191.
65. ACA, *Correctional Departments*, p. 178.
66. Ibid.
67. Department of Justice, "Prisoners in State and Federal Institutions for Adult Felons," *National Prisoner Statistics Bulletin*, no. 47 (Washington, D.C.: Government Printing Office, 1972), pp. 22-23.
68. ACA, *Correctional Departments*.
69. Duffee and Fitch, *Corrections*, p. 198.
70. Chamelin, Fox, and Whisenand, *Criminal Justice*, pp. 33-34.
71. Ibid., p. 335.
72. National Advisory Commission on Criminal Justice Standards and Goals, *Corrections* (Washington, D.C.: Government Printing Office, 1973), p. 224.
73. Solomon, *Community Corrections*, p. 224.
74. Duffee and Fitch, *Corrections*, p. 256.
75. Solomon, *Community Corrections*, p. 287.
76. John M. McCartt and Thomas J. Mangogna, *Guidelines and Standards for Halfway Houses and Community Treatment Centers* (Washington, D.C.: Government Printing Office, 1973), p. 6.
77. Harold J. Vetter and Clifford E. Simonsen, *Criminal Justice in America* (Philadelphia: Saunders, 1976), p. 333.
78. McCartt and Mangogna, *Guidelines and Standards*, pp. 26-31.

CHAPTER 13
Corrections: Processes and Environment

OUTLINE

PRE-SENTENCE ACTIVITIES BY CORRECTIONS AGENCIES
    Diversion from Formal Criminal Justice Processing
    Pre-sentence Investigations

PROBATION
    Restrictions on and Conditions of Probation
    The Role of the Probation Officer
        Types of Probation Officers
        Caseworkers versus Social Workers
        Reality of Probation Case Loads
    Revocation of Probation
    Termination of Probation

INSTITUTIONALIZATION
    Reception
    Classification
    Treatment
        Custody and Control
        Rehabilitative Programs
    Informal Processing of Inmates
    Rights of Prisoners
        Prisoner Rights to Due Process
        First Amendment Rights
        Rights Relative to Treatment

PAROLE
    Parole Selection
    Period of Supervision

COMMUNITY CORRECTIONS
    Institutional Programs
    Halfway Houses
    Intensive Intervention Programs

ENVIRONMENTAL INFLUENCES ON CORRECTIONS
    Physical Environment
    Community Influences
    Government Influences
        Court Decisions
        Government Grants
    Relations with Other Components

OBJECTIVES

After reading this chapter the student should be able to:

Describe the activities of corrections agencies in pre-sentence stages of the criminal justice process.

Discuss the conditions judges may impose on probationers.

Compare and contrast various types of probation officers.

Discuss the process of probation revocation.

Discuss the steps in formal processing of inmates in institutions.

List and describe various rehabilitative approaches used in institutions.

Describe what happens during inmates' informal processing through the inmate subculture.

Discuss various aspects of prisoners' rights as delineated in leading court decisions.

Describe the process by which prisoners are selected for parole.

Discuss the process of parole revocation.

Describe various types of community corrections programs.

Describe various ways citizens influence corrections.

Discuss the impact courts are having on correctional institutions.

Discuss the relationship between corrections agencies and other criminal justice components.

KEY TERMS

diversion
probation officers as:
   law enforcers
   time servers
   therapeutic agents
   synthetic officers
   caseworkers
   social workers
technical violations
institutionalization
prisoner classification
control and custody
reality therapy
guided group interaction
psychodrama
behavior modification
work furloughs
home furloughs
prisonization
parole revocation
halfway-out centers
halfway-in centers
intensive intervention program

☐ In this chapter we will examine the process of corrections in terms of both the various alternatives available and the steps taken toward the ultimate release of the offender. We have designated the corrections stage as following that of sentencing by the trial court. Some commentators point out that corrections agencies and objectives are involved at earlier stages of the criminal justice process. There are at least three specific ways in which this happens: defendants can be diverted into corrections programs by agreeing to bypass adjudication and sentencing; jails are used to detain many persons following their arrest; and probation agencies prepare pre-sentence investigation reports for use by courts prior to sentencing. Despite these considerations, the full range of corrections processes is open only following the sentencing of offenders.

Because of the wide variety and overlapping character of corrections efforts, it is difficult to establish any logical order in which they should be considered. We have already said that they can be divided into the two broad categories of institutionalization and community-related corrections. Institutionalization includes two more specific tracks: incarceration in local jails and imprisonment. Community-based corrections include those to which a person can be directly sentenced (probation and community corrections center programs) and those which follow imprisonment (halfway houses and parole).

PRE-SENTENCE ACTIVITIES BY CORRECTIONS AGENCIES

Corrections agencies, especially probation departments and programs, often become involved in cases before the accused is sentenced. In some cases they assume responsibility for persons diverted from traditional processing. In others they perform a pre-sentence investigation of defendants and prepare a report for use by sentencing judges.

Diversion from Formal Criminal Justice Processing

One of the more recent innovations in criminal justice is the **diversion** of persons from the full process and into some form of community-based activity or corrections program. By this we do not mean the dropping of defendants or cases, which has always taken place, but the process by which formal charges are withheld or deferred by the prosecutor or court in return for a formal commitment by the defendant to a certain period of supervised activity. The President's Commission on

Law Enforcement pointed out that diversion serves two purposes: providing "reintegrative services necessary to rehabilitate many of the minor offenders" in a "noncorrectional setting" and providing "specialized treatment of a noncriminal nature" to persons with special problems, such as alcoholism.[1] The commission uses the terms "noncorrectional" and "noncriminal" to describe the nature of the diversionary efforts, and it is true that many of the specific programs and agencies are private or, if governmental, not part of the criminal justice system. On the other hand, insofar as the progress of those diverted is supervised, and insofar as criminal cases against them can be reactivated, it is fair to label their status as being within the scope of corrections.

Because diversion involves placing restraints on people's liberty without a conviction, Donald Newman notes that a major problem "is that it bypasses many of the formal criminal law safeguards"—that, in fact, "some diversionary practices are deliberately utilized to avoid challenge and to bypass proof—and the question remains of whether the gains are worth the costs."[2]

Diversion normally involves the defendants' waiving their right to trial and informally admitting guilt in return for the avoidance of prosecution and possible conviction and less acceptable correctional treatment. So long as they abide by the terms of their agreement and meet the requirements of the program, the original charges are deferred. When the term of their commitment runs out—usually within a year—they are released and the pending charges formally dropped. If, on the other hand, they fail in the program, they can be reinserted in the formal criminal process and be subject to possible conviction and sentencing. Due to this threat, due to the screening that results in the selection of persons who are generally rehabilitatable, and due to the more intensive work done with diverted persons (as opposed to the loose supervision given those placed on formal probation), these diversion efforts tend to be more successful—as well as cheaper—than completion of the formal process. That there are practical problems and legal dangers is undeniable. In view of the alternatives in an overburdened system, most practitioners and defendants, given the opportunity, seem willing to accept the costs.

Pre-sentence Investigations

Earlier we discussed the pre-sentence investigation reports prepared by probation officers for use by sentencing judges. We noted that such investigations dealt with the character, social background, and previous offense record, if any, of the accused. They are used in almost all jurisdictions in cases that could result in imprisonment.

Probation officers are generally responsible for conducting these investigations and writing the reports. The officers use many resources, including criminal histories, employers' records, school documents, and interviews with anyone who could shed light on the background and behavior of the accused. The prosecutor and law enforcement officers who worked the case may also be consulted.

There are differences between states or localities in the precise contents of such reports, and often judges may indicate what they want and do not want in them. One difference arises in whether the officer should include a direct opinion about the accused and a recommendation as to sentence. Some judges depend on this, some consider it, and some reject it as improper.

A major issue involving these reports is whether there should be disclosure of the contents of reports to defendants and others besides the judge. The Supreme Court has never ruled that a defendant has a right to see the report or challenge its contents. As a practical matter or one of rules of procedure, however, it is revealed to the accused and both attorneys in many states. The argument against its disclosure is usually based on the effect it would have on the willingness of persons to provide information and comments for such reports. The National Advisory Commission on Criminal Justice Standards and Goals rejected this argument, however, when it called for "full disclosure, without exceptions as to confidentiality."[3]

PROBATION

Among the correctional alternatives open to the court, the first we will consider is probation. Allen and Simonsen comment that probation "is a process which provides the judge with an alternative disposition that results in an improved status for the offender within a subsystem of the criminal justice system."[4] Newman observes that "probation is seen as a lenient sentence," and agrees that it is when compared to incarceration, but he adds, "it *is* a sentence and not simply a dismissal of the case."[5]

Probation may result from a sentence to prison that is suspended by the judge in lieu of a period of supervised probation, or it may be the status to which the offender is directly sentenced by the judge. The length of the probationary term may be shorter or longer than the appropriate prison or jail term would have been. State laws vary on this point.

Restrictions on and Conditions of Probation

Very serious offenses, especially homicide and rape, are generally outside the permissible limits for probation. We say generally because there are rare cases in which guilty pleas to either forcible rape or manslaughter result in sentences to probation. Probation is normally not assigned to offenders who repeat a felony offense, but there are some cases in which this is done. Beyond these guidelines, the restrictions vary greatly and an offense that would never result in probation in one place may virtually always result in probation elsewhere. This is especially true of some vice crimes such as possession of certain drugs. Newman points out that legislatures have been of little help in setting limits.[6]

Aside from the matter of what offenses can result in probation, there is the matter of conditions placed on the probationer. Allen and Simonsen assert that rules concerning the conditions cannot be made a set of "standard operating procedures," and that courts should tailor the conditions to the needs of the offender and his situation.[7]

Eugene Czajkoski notes that courts usually are responsible for setting probation conditions and that probation departments are generally forbidden from doing so. He also notes that the conditions must be in writing but may still contain rather vague provisions, such as "stay away from disreputable places," or "avoid undesirable associates." Beyond the problem of vague conditions are the conditions that "become substitutes for certain formal judicial processes."[8] For example, the probationer may be ordered to provide support for named dependents or pay restitution to the victim of his or her offense. While these conditions may be appropriate in some cases, persons with grudges against the offender may seek to use the court's power to set conditions that give personal satisfaction.

Kerper and Kerper point out that probation is a status to which offenders must agree, and if they do not like or cannot live with the conditions established by the court, they can refuse probation and accept the incarceration instead.[9] Kerper and Kerper note that courts have ruled that some conditions are illegal, and they cite a California appellate court ruling that probably represented prevailing attitudes when it prohibited conditions which (1) had no relationship to the offender's crime; (2) related to conduct which is not illegal; and (3) required or forbade conduct which is not reasonably related to the offender's possible future criminal behavior.[10] Appellate courts have ruled out certain conditions: those that cannot be met within the probationary period, banishment, requiring persons to attend church, and denying chronic alcoholics the right to drink. On the other hand, they had upheld quite a list of conditions. Kerper and Kerper provide the following list of unusual but accepted conditions:

> A requirement that a 23-year-old defendant afflicted with syphilis, who had pleaded guilty to rape of a 13-year-old girl, submit to vasectomy was upheld. A requirement that a 9-year-old child live apart from her family until she was 18 was upheld, as were conditions that probationer remain within a specified place; that probationer not violate any law of the state or the United States; that probationer who was guilty of crimes growing out of a demonstration against the war not participate in demonstrations; that defendant who was convicted of selling LSD submit himself and his property to search and seizure at any time by law enforcement officers; that defendant not have a telephone in his home or upon any property under his control, where he had been convicted of bookmaking activities carried on by telephone; that defendant avoid use of alcohol in any form. A Texas court has stated that generally a probationer's liberty is conditioned upon conduct above that required of the ordinary citizen.[11]

Newman observes that "unusual, even weird, special conditions on probationers ... can be fairly easily remedied by appellate courts, if the offender is sufficiently outraged, resolute, and otherwise able to bring an appeal."[12]

The Role of the Probation Officer

The probation officer inherits the offender complete with the conditions he or she must obey. These officers come from varied backgrounds and with widely differing preparation for their duties, but it is fair to say that many are poorly or barely qualified. Relatively few have a master's degree in social work—the standard most authorities seem to agree on—and many have no college degree. They are thrust into a difficult role of balancing the need to assist the offender with the need to prevent further transgressions and to obtain the offender's compliance with the court's conditions. Blanchard notes that the probation officer may play any of several roles: employment agent, vocational counselor, marital counselor, school counselor, junior-grade psychoanalyst, father confessor, and law enforcement officer.[13]

Types of Probation Officers Carl Klockars has written of the importance of "the role which the officer sets for himself and the logic and rationale he develops to explain what he does or what he ought to do." He delineates four identifiable types of probation officers: the **law enforcers** who "stress the legal authority and enforcement aspects of their role"; the **time servers** who "are nearly the functional equivalent of the law enforcers," but who meet their job responsibilities minimally and methodically while awaiting their retirement; the **therapeutic agents** who make sincere efforts to improve the life-style and conditions of probationers through frequent and supportive contacts with them; and the **synthetic officers** who set for themselves "the active task of combining the paternal, authoritarian and judgmental with the therapeutic." The latter, therefore, seek a middle ground between control and assistance in their relationships with probationers.[14]

Caseworkers Versus Social Workers In examining the role of probation officers one may set forth another distinction in terms of the form of assistance offered the probationer. On the one hand there are **caseworkers** who focus almost all their attention on their own contacts with and assistance to those under their supervision. Their emphasis is on rehabilitating the offender through counseling and application of psychological or psychiatric techniques. On the other hand, there are the **social workers** who tend to view their function as one of reintegrating the offender with the community. Their approach emphasizes less direct work with the probationer and can be compared to a resources management approach. These officers maintain contacts with other private and public agencies and organizations whose resources can be tapped to provide jobs, educational opportunities, and other services, including counseling, to probationers.[15]

The approach of the social worker seems to be the direction in which probation is moving, since it not only emphasizes the newer goal of reintegration of the offender but is based on a more realistic view of both the credentials and training of probation officers and the demands of their case loads. Under existing conditions probation officers cannot adequately counsel and assist each probationer, and they should not be expected to. Also, there appears to be less conflict between enforcement and referral functions than between enforcement and counseling functions. Social service does not necessarily depend on development of a virtually unattainable level of mutual trust and openness—a prerequisite for successful therapeutic treatment. The National Advisory Commission on Criminal Justice strongly recommends that probation become a "goal-oriented service delivery system" and that the role of probation officers be changed "from caseworker to community resource manager."[16]

Reality of Probation Case Loads The heavy case loads of probation officers have often been cited in corrections literature, and case loads of over one hundred probationers per worker are common.[17] The standard that is frequently suggested is fifty or fewer per officer, but achieving this is rare in practice. Case loads are usually also undifferentiated, that is, not divided and assigned on the basis of the relative risk involved with each offender.

The supervision and assistance that most persons on probation receive is generally conceded to be very thin, to say the least. One probation officer may have spoken for most of his colleagues when he was asked about the level of supervision: "We keep track of them; but we don't supervise them. We theoretically know where they are. We know that they are on probation and that is about the most we can do."[18]

As we mentioned earlier, however, there is little or no evidence that lightening the case load per officer results in any real improvement in the behavior of offenders in terms of recidivism. There is a legitimate question as to whether the fact that many probationers commit further crimes amounts to a failure of probation or a failure of the probationer. That question can only be answered if changes are made other than mere reductions in offender-officer ratios.

Revocation of Probation

Probation is considered a privilege rather than a right, and this is demonstrated by the types of conditions that can be placed on probationers, as discussed above. It is also reflected in the means that may be used to determine whether or not the probationer has violated the terms and conditions of his status and the procedures used to revoke the probation and resentence the offender to jail or prison.

Kerper and Kerper write that the rights of probationers vary with whether or not they were convicted. That is, are they on probation as a result of diversion, or are they on probation following adjudication and sentencing? Convicted probationers lose the rights any other convicted person loses. The important question is whether the probationer is subject to searches and other investigative techniques that are different from those to which free citizens can be subjected—for example, warrantless searches of their persons. Kerper and Kerper find that this situation varies from state to state.[19]

The grounds for revocation of probation include more than the commission of another crime, although they obviously include that. The other grounds are referred to as **technical violations.** Revocation on these grounds requires that some illegal conduct be shown, but this is obviously a vague requirement. Of course, violation of a specific condition of probation is sufficient grounds, but perhaps also is marginally illegal conduct not specified in the conditions. "In New York, failure to appear before the court upon notice is a violation for which probation can be revoked although this condition does not specifically appear in the sentence."[20]

Czajkoski asserts that while revocation is performed by the judge, "it is the probation officer who initiates the revocation action and largely controls it." This "hegemony of the probation officer in probation violation proceedings" is what casts him in "a quasi-judicial role."[21] It is the probation officer who files the report of a violation with the court and thus acts in the charging capacity. The probationer must be notified of the hearing and the nature of the charges, and he is entitled in many states to the same right to counsel that pertains to a trial. The proceedings, however, are more informal, and evidence seized by means not tolerable in a trial may be used. The probation officer may act as prosecutor at the hearing. The hearing does not result in a finding of guilt or innocence but merely that the probationer's status is or is not revoked. If it is, then either the court must resentence the offender or, if probation followed suspension of an original sentence, reimpose that sentence. The offender then goes directly to jail or prison.

Termination of Probation

Probationary sentences may be terminated prior to the expiration of the probationary period. The court may act on a recommendation by the probation officer to permit early release of the offender, or it may allow the full period to run out, in which case the offender is automatically released.

INSTITUTIONALIZATION

The incarceration of an offender into a jail or prison is what we mean by **institutionalization.** We have already described the conditions within most jails and made some observations about prisons in an earlier chapter. Our discussion of the process of institutionalization here is focused on state prison systems, though some of what is said relates at least partially to large county jails.

There are several steps in the formal processing of inmates within institutions. They include reception, classification, treatment, and release. As we will see, the term "treatment" covers virtually anything that is done within the institution to which inmates are assigned.

Reception

Institutional reception begins for most offenders within city or county jails. Many defendants are incarcerated pending disposition of their cases and sentencing. To those convicted the experience they undergo in jail constitutes their introduction to institutionalization. Duffee and Fitch point out that the importance of inmates' experiences with earlier stages of the criminal justice process "should not be underestimated" in determining their receptivity to subsequent corrections processing.[22]

The next step for most inmates is the diagnostic center operated in most state correctional systems. There inmates are interviewed by a committee of staff members and given a battery of tests to attempt to determine their mental and emotional conditions and their aptitudes for various programs of treatment.[23] The prisoners may also be briefed by staff members about how to get along or serve their time in a way that will be the least difficult for all concerned.

Classification

Prisoner classification is the interviewing and testing of inmates to determine the level of security required for each of them and the kind of treatment to be employed. If the state operates institutions of various security levels (maximum, medium, and minimum), classification personnel may even choose the place in which the prisoner will be incarcerated.

Vetter and Simonsen point out that classification has a different meaning for the prison's staff than it does for the inmates. For the staff classification serves to construct a plan that will result in the correction of the inmate. For most inmates classification results in a plan of what they must do to be pronounced releasable. Classification, in short, points the way out.[24] Most observers agree that classification often results in a plan that is best for the institution or within its capabilities rather than what is most suitable for the inmates. Thus if the inmate is a skilled baker, he is placed in the kitchen even if what he really needs is a basic education and the kitchen work interferes with classes.[25]

It is often pointed out that classification must be an ongoing or recurring process so that any progress the inmate makes may be taken into account and adjustments made in his treatment plan. Duffee and

Inmates may be briefed about how to serve their time, in the way that will be the least difficult for all concerned.

Fitch also make the point that inmates should be involved in proposing their own plans and deciding their own classifications. They thus will be positively rewarded for genuine achievements rather than simply going through the motions of meeting expectations placed upon them by others. Some systems are experimenting with so-called mutual agreement programming, which incorporates this concept.[26]

Treatment

The term "treatment" is used to cover all the official programs and activities conducted on behalf of an institution's inmates. Depending, of course, on the output of the classification process, a prisoner is subject to various levels of custody and control by the guards or correctional officers. He is also put through various attempts to rehabilitate him, and he is offered graduated levels of services and privileges designed to reward and encourage him.

Custody and Control As has been pointed out, the intensity of efforts to **control** and keep **custody** of inmates differs with the type of facility. In a maximum security prison the control function is considered paramount, and prisoners are subject to constant surveillance and repeated head counts and searches. Yet total control by guards is impossible, and some interpersonal relations between guards and inmates is necessary. Prisoners perform important functions, including cleaning and maintaining the prison, preparing and serving the food, working in any prison industries, and performing routine clerical and other chores. The custodial staff's power over inmates is never complete, claim Duffee and Fitch. Many guards are susceptible to corruption by inmates with the "right" contacts outside, and most are concerned about the chances of a riot and the possibility of their coming under the control of the inmates they are guarding.[27]

The issue of the use of force by guards is a difficult one in terms of both the extent to which it should be used and the extent to which it is. Corporal punishment, especially whipping, was liberally applied in the nineteenth century. Allen and Simonsen assert that force is now customarily used only in "quelling disturbances." They quote John Palmer as having stated the five conditions under which it is permissible to employ force: (1) self-defense, (2) the defense of others, (3) the enforcement of prison rules, (4) prevention of escapes, and (5) the prevention of crimes within the prison.[28] These guidelines are quite broad, however, and they do not deal with what degree or level of force is acceptable. Shall guards be allowed to use the same level of force being used by inmates or only enough to subdue them? Overreaction and too much force can be disastrous; incidents can escalate into riots, and suppression of rebellions can lead to several—and perhaps unnecessary—deaths and many injuries. The violent suppression of the rebellion at Attica in New York in 1971 is an illustration of the excesses that can result when corrections officers are allowed to join troopers in conducting an assault, a role for which they were not trained or equipped.[29]

Other forms of corporal punishment, such as beatings, may still be common in a few prisons.[30] Prison institutions tend to be brutalizing to the staff as well as the prisoners, and the fact that prisons' populations are increasingly made up of violent, dangerous, and incorrigible offenders to the exclusion of the more stable personalities cannot be helping that situation.

The American Corrections Association adamantly opposes corporal punishment, saying flatly that "it should never be used under any circumstances."[31] Whippings were practiced as late as 1961 but were outlawed by a U.S. Eighth Circuit Court of Appeals decision in which Justice Harry Blackmun argued that they violate the Eighth Amendment prohibition of "cruel and unusual punishment."[32]

Regardless of the level of force that might be employed in a prison, maintaining order and custody are the primary concerns of prison authorities. In maximum security and most medium security institutions, it may be emphasized at the expense of other goals such as rehabilitation.

Rehabilitative Programs Approaches to rehabilitative programs can be divided into two categories: those aimed at altering offenders' values or attitudes and those designed to improve inmates' skills and potential to become productive citizens.

Among the attempts to deal with the offender's attitudes are the following four approaches:

1. Reality therapy: This approach assumes that offenders are irresponsible people, and that they will develop a sense of responsibility through emotional links with the counselor.[33]

2. Guided group interaction: This form of group therapy involves open discussions of their problems by inmates. The leader is expected to encourage a free give-and-take and to adopt a permissive but noncondoning role.[34]

3. Psychodrama: The assumption employed here is that some inmates cannot or will not reveal their innermost feelings unless they can do so within the context of playing a part in a drama. The "plays" are generally not scripted, and participants are encouraged to ad-lib their parts so that they express themselves fully.[35]

4. Behavior modification: The most recent development in offender treatment is based on the assumption that attempts to get at deep-seated causes for deviant behavior are not as effective as simple rewards for good behavior and punishments for bad behavior. The specific techniques employed may include tranquilizing drugs or electric shock therapy.

Solitary confinement and whipping as punishment for disruptive or criminal behavior can be considered crude forms of behavior modification. The newer techniques involve establishing more direct controls over the minds of inmates. The liberal use of drugs under the guise of treatment may be a means of assuring control over the inmate, rather than a means of helping him. Objections to various behavior modification techniques led to the abandonment of specific types of treatment by the federal prison system.[36]

Among the criticisms of all psychiatric and psychological approaches to the rehabilitation of inmates is that all require an assumption that the offenders are sick and need help. Thus this help is imposed on them. The National Advisory Commission on Criminal Justice pointed out that there is a "Catch-22" involved—that officials are saying: "We know you're sick. If you deny you're sick, you're really sick. But if you acknowledge that you're sick, then you must be really sick or you wouldn't admit it."[37]

Observers now largely agree that many inmates go through the motions of being treated simply because it is the only way to get out of prison. But should inmates be allowed to reject treatment? This question is being debated today and will be recalled when we deal with inmates' legal rights.

There are basically two efforts aimed at improving the skills and potentials of offenders to earn them places as productive and law-abiding members of society.

1. Academic education: Some inmates are illiterate and are offered very basic educational programs. Others are given the chance to earn high school diplomas. A few institutions even bring in college professors and make it possible for inmates to obtain bachelor's degrees from nearby colleges.[38]

2. Vocational training: Offering vocational training programs is one of the most traditional of all rehabilitative efforts in prisons. Depending on the size of the facility and other factors, prisons may train inmates in any of several occupational areas. The emphasis in men's prisons, however, has been on heavy industrial work and selected crafts such as furniture making. Women's prisons have stressed development of homemaking skills. In many cases the vocational training program has been geared more toward producing goods for the state (license plates are the prime example) than training the inmates for real employment opportunities on the outside.

In addition to these traditional educational and training programs, some institutions are striving to develop inmates' skills and potentials as participants in the economy and the political life of the community. A few have experimented with "pseudo-economies" in which inmates earn credits they can save, invest, or spend. The savings are turned into cash at the time of their release. Inmates' councils have emerged in several institutions, especially in the medium and minimum security prisons.

Earlier experiments with inmate self-government, including the operating of their own judicial systems, were abandoned either because of internal breakdowns or because of outside pressures. Many administrators today are opposed to any political organization among inmates, and none allow a council to become more than a sounding board and a means of formulating and passing along recommendations on certain matters to the staff.[39] The opposition to inmate self-government is based not only on the potential threat to staff authority but on the desire to avoid legitimizing existing inmate power structures in which the strongest and most aggressive prisoners dominate the others.

In addition to programs aimed at the rehabilitation of prisoners, institutions offer services and activities whose purposes are more in the line of simply making prison life more bearable or assisting in the prisoner's reintegration into society. These are generally privileges that can be withdrawn from individuals, and some of the more important ones are as follows:

1. Recreation: Most prisons provide some opportunity for recreational activities by inmates. Some even have gymnasiums, and in some there are team sports, even contests between teams from different prisons.
2. Visitation privileges: All prisons offer visitation privileges to inmates. Some medium and minimum security institutions are allowing inmates to receive members of their families in private rooms or buildings, that is, conjugal visits. This privilege is not extended to maximum security facilities, however.
3. **Work furloughs:** More and more institutions are permitting selected inmates to accept jobs in private firms outside the institution or are actually placing them in these positions. In some cases this means the inmate returns to the institution each night; in other cases he may return only on weekends.
4. **Home furloughs:** Still another innovation in some systems is the home furlough through which selected offenders are allowed occasional visits to their families or even friends. This is more common than allowing spouses private conjugal visits within institutions and may be the only means of bringing family members together where conjugal visits are not possible.

Other services, which may seem routine to outsiders but which are essential to the maintenance of morale and the inmates' well-being, are medical services, food service, laundry service, and mail service. In large institutions there are also shops or stores, pharmacies, and other facilities that cater to the needs of the inmates.

Informal Processing of Inmates

By its very nature, a total institution provides for all the needs of inmates and subjects them to an artificial environment. This environment leads to what some call the **prisonization** of inmates: the development of an inmate subculture complete with delineated roles and power structure and the existence of an argot or special language. How any one offender fits into the inmate subculture, of course, varies with the individual, the nature of the institution, and his fellow inmates. Gresham Sykes studied a maximum security prison and found that the denials of self-esteem, liberty, security, love, and heterosexual relations lead to dehumanization of inmates. He noted that imprisonment weakens links with family and friends and heightens the prisoners' alienation from the values of free society while he adapts to those of inmate society.[40]

It is often stated that one of the most frightening aspects of prison life is the denial of normal sex and the resultant incidents of homosexual rape. Allen and Simonsen comment, however, that the assumption that rape is common may be exaggerated. They assert that masturbation is probably the most universal outlet for sexual desires. Consensual homosexuality is common, however.[41] In women's prisons family life is dupli-

Visitation privileges are among the services offered to make prison life more bearable.

cated, with stronger aggressive women becoming "husbands" and more feminine women becoming "wives" and with older women becoming the "mothers" of younger inmates. Esther Heffernan found that these families served not only emotionally supportive functions but served in economic and socialization capacities as "distributive centers for many of the products of the system, as well as the source of much of the motivation to participate in the system."[42]

Stanton Wheeler observed that the effects of prisonization varies with inmates and the phase of their institutional careers. It appears that the effects are greatest in the middle stages of the offender's processing and are minimal near the time of release.[43]

It is often observed that prisons are institutions that teach crime and that many offenders who are released are more skilled and more hardened criminals than when they went in. If this is true, it means that the inmate subculture—the informal processing—has more impact than the formal processing administered by the staff. To the extent that the custodial staff of a prison allows some leeway for the operation of the inmate power structure in order to keep order, they probably contribute to the negation of the institution's stated goals. They may have little or no practical choice in the matter due to the physical and other limitations under which they try to work.

Rights of Prisoners

Some discussion must be directed toward the topic of the rights of prison inmates. As they go through the period of their incarceration, inmates are obviously not in a position to exercise the full range of rights guaranteed by the Constitution to free citizens. On the other hand, courts no longer take the position they once did that prisoners have abandoned their rights upon entering these institutions. In 1961 the Supreme Court made its first break with the traditional "hands off" doctrine and started the development of a body of law dealing with the rights of prisoners and the corresponding obligations and prerogatives of prison authorities.[44]

We cannot examine the current state of prisoners' rights in any detail but can only touch on some major areas of concern: due process rights within the prison, First Amendment rights, and rights relative to prison treatment programs.

Prisoner Rights to Due Process What is due process within a prison setting? There is no clause in the Constitution over which there has been more litigation and debate than the due process clause of the

Fourteenth Amendment, and the environment of a prison raises peculiar difficulties. Basically, prisoners have been found to have a substantive due process right to know the rules of the prison, the violation of which can lead to their punishment.[45] What a prisoner's procedural rights are when accused of violating those rules is the subject that has generated more litigation than any other. They are certainly not the same as judicial procedural rights.[46] The nature of procedural rights was at issue in the appellate courts of the country until the Supreme Court issued its decision in *Wolff* v. *McDonnell*.[47] Robert Plotkin notes that the Court "attempted to strike a balance" between inmates and authorities and summarizes its decision as follows:

> *The Court held that prisoners are constitutionally entitled to a hearing prior to punishment but then proceeded to place limits upon that hearing which, many prisoners' advocates contend, vitiate the hearing. A prisoner is now entitled to prior written notice of any proposed disciplinary action and may appear before a hearing to rebut those charges. He may present documentary evidence and call his own witnesses when the tribunal determines that allowing him to do so would not be unduly hazardous to the institution. The decision must be rendered in writing and must be available for review by other officials or agencies. The prisoner is not, however, entitled to confront and cross-examine his accusers, and he is not entitled to counsel or counsel substitute. Further, the Court provided no guidance for the selection of an impartial hearing tribunal.*[48]

The decision was not the final word on the subject by any means, and the Court itself recognized this, noting that it will review subsequent cases and the current decision "is not graven in stone."[49]

Another matter related to due process is that of prisoners' access to lawyers and courts. The courts have said that prison authorities cannot impair an inmate's right to seek a writ of habeas corpus. Such a writ orders the authorities to deliver the prisoner to the court, and an application for the writ allows the prisoner the opportunity to make allegations concerning violations of human rights. Courts have also said prisons must provide reasonable opportunities for inmates to have access to lawyers or law-trained inmates or to law books to assist them in writing petitions to the court.[50]

First Amendment Rights Over the years prisons have censored incoming and outgoing mail of prisoners, restricted their reading materials, controlled their granting interviews to the press, allowed only censored prison newspapers, and resisted their attempts to form associations or organizations. All these restrictions are, of course, based on the interest of security. Courts have begun to try to limit what authorities can do in the way of restricting these activities. But the Supreme Court recently refused to stipulate that prisoners have First Amendment rights per se. In a case dealing with censorship of prisoner's mail, the Court ruled that outsiders who communicate with prisoners have the right to correspond with inmates, that censorship of mail must be restricted to that necessary for security, and that prisoners be told when their mail is being censored.[51]

Plotkin notes that the failure to say whether prisoners have First Amendment rights throws several other decisions that had dealt with speech, press, religion, and assembly into doubt, but he observes, "For the first time, actions of wardens are subject to higher authority."[52]

Rights Relative to Treatment Courts have been very reluctant to deal with issues of prisoners' rights to treatment programs or their right to refuse specific forms of treatment. Since correctional institutions serve sometimes conflicting functions (punishment and deterrence versus rehabilitation or reintegration), courts have not required prisons to provide treatment to all prisoners. On the other hand, in the words of Plotkin, "the courts do recognize that the total absence of programs, or the unequal, discriminatory use of existing programs, may be unconstitutional."[53] Prisoners can be forced to work, and there are no real rights connected with it. As for behavior modification techniques, courts have not ruled on them in general, though experimental brain surgery to which a prisoner had "consented" was blocked in Michigan.[54]

There is also the issue of whether or not general prison conditions violate the Eighth Amendment protection against "cruel and unusual punishment," and there have been landmark cases in this area. Their nature is so broad, however, that they will be taken up in the section dealing with the relation of corrections agencies to their environment.

In this discussion of the processing of offenders through institutions, we have dealt with formal steps and the informal aspects of prison life, and we have made note of the development of notions concerning the rights of inmates. Prisons, their purposes, and their conditions are the subject of intense debate, and there are many differences among various prisons and prison systems. This has been, by necessity, a brief overview of a complex subject.

PAROLE

To be paroled means to be released from incarceration but placed under certain conditions and the supervision of a parole officer. The officer is supposed to assist the offender in his or her reintegration into community life but is also supposed to enforce the conditions and report any violations of those conditions by the parolee. Parole is an aspect of corrections, and the parolee is still, at least technically, not at full liberty.

It can be said that parole really consists of "two systems in one" and that the parole process has two separate phases: that which culminates in the making of a decision on whether or not to parole the offender and that period during which the offender is on parole, that is, under the supervision of his or her parole officer.[55]

Parole Selection

The decision as to whether or not to parole an offender follows two other steps: the determination as to the eligibility of inmates and the hearing before the parole board or hearing examiners hired to conduct them.

The eligibility of inmates for parole is determined by the staff of the parole authority by calculating a date based on the terms of the sentence as well as credit for "good time." The former may include "credit for time served" awarded by the sentencing judge to defendants who awaited their adjudication in jail. The latter refers to time subtracted from the period of minimum service due to the good behavior or progress of the inmate.[56]

Once a prisoner becomes eligible, a file that has been assembled on his or her case is prepared for consideration by the board. That file contains raw data on any or all of the following matters: the offense for which the person was sentenced; the offender's personal background; the overall criminal record of the inmate; the institutional record, that is, the record of his or her formal processing and an evaluation of the inmate's responses to it; a parole plan, that is, the activities the inmate intends to engage in or has lined up on the outside; and a recommendation from the prison staff concerning readiness for parole.[57]

David Stanley observes that while members of a parole board may feel that they have the "terrible power" to play God with the lives of inmates, "the premises and the proceedings are on a decidedly lower level."[58] The length of any inmate's hearing may vary anywhere from twenty-five minutes down to four minutes. Usually it is sheer caseload size that determines how much hearing time can be used for each case.

As for what is said at parole hearings, it usually includes a brief question or comment from each member or examiner present and may resemble an inquisition, a counseling session, or both.[59] Stanley comments that a strong case can be made for abolishing formal hearings since in most cases the board already knows what it will do and in the marginal cases the latent hostility and tension render the hearing "an ineffective way to elicit information, evaluate character traits, and give advice, all of which parole boards try to do." Hearings will probably continue, however, because of our nation's tradition of giving everyone a chance to state his or her case, and both the prisoners and authorities want them to continue.[60]

The parole board usually renders an immediate decision on each case, and it is generally one of three: to grant parole, to continue in prison and reconsider at some future time, or to continue in prison until expiration of the inmate's maximum term. Notification of the prisoner occurs anywhere from immediately to six weeks hence. The wait can be almost unbearable, a negative decision the cause of much bitterness, and a positive one the cause of elation.[61]

It is strongly recommended that the decision be communicated to inmates without delay. Most observers also agree that the criteria for parole and reasons for refusal should both be explicit and made known to the inmate.[62] Duffee and Fitch point out that how an inmate performs during his incarceration often depends on his understanding and expectations concerning parole. Thus the inmate should be informed of what he must do to earn parole, when he may reasonably expect to be paroled, and what to expect on the outside once he is paroled.[63]

Period of Supervision

After pointing out positive effects that parole expectations may have on inmates during incarceration, Duffee and Fitch note that there can also be negative effects. The period of institutionalization may be crippling in terms of the parolee's ability to cope with life on the outside. If the formal and informal processing have caused or enhanced a sense of dependency or inferiority, and if it has intensified contempt for society and authority, then the parolee will probably fail the parole period and wind up back in prison.[64]

The dual function of parole officers—to help parolees while at the same time protecting society from them—has already been mentioned. In most respects the process of completing the parole period and the relationship between the parolee and the supervising officer are very similar to those of probation.

Like probation, parole carries certain conditions which parolees are expected to observe. They are commonly aimed at the reform as well as the control of the parolees. In most states conditions may include special ones designed for particular persons. But whether general or special, the conditions must be treated by parolees "as if they were laws."[65]

The number of contacts between parole officers and their assigned parolees can be as many as four a month at first. The type of contact can vary between an office visit by the parolee, a visit by the officer to the parolee's home or job, or a phone call. The last type is, of course, the least effective, and office visits are the principal means used.[66]

Obviously the more trusting and open the relationship between the parties, the more effective parole will be. As with probation officers, however, parole officers adopt different styles of interaction with parolees, based on the officers' perceptions of their role. It is difficult for enforcement style supervisors to establish openness with their charges; on the other hand, officers who emphasize assisting parolees may be accused of ignoring parole violations and their duty to protect the public.

Parolees who get into trouble may lose their parole status through **parole revocation,** depending on the seriousness of allegations against them and the parole office's standards. The violation may range from a technical one—that is, breaking one of the special rules applied to that person—to an outright criminal act. The response of the parole officer may range from a reprimand to an attempt to have parole revoked. The practice of jailing parolees for a few days is fairly common. It is attacked by many as an abuse of parole powers, but many parole officers consider it a good therapeutic measure which may prevent full revocation.[67]

Formal parole revocation involves several steps: (1) the detention of the parolee in jail; (2) a preliminary hearing to determine whether there is reasonable ground to suspect the parolee of a violation; and (3) a full revocation hearing.[68] Unlike a probation revocation hearing, which occurs before the judge who sentenced the offender, the parole revocation hearing is conducted by the parole board or its designated hearing officers. In short, the decision is made by the people who made the original decision to parole.

The Supreme Court ruled in 1972 that parole revocation hearings must meet the following requirements:

> . . . (a) written notice of the claimed violation of parole; (b) disclosure to the parolee of the evidence against him; (c) opportunity to be heard in person and to present witnesses and documentary evidence; (d) the right to confront and cross-examine adverse witnesses (unless the hearing officer specifically finds good cause for not allowing confrontation); (e) a "neutral and detached" hearing body such as a traditional parole board, members of which need not be judicial officers or lawyers; and (f) a written statement by the factfinders as to the evidence relied on and the reasons for revoking parole.[69]

The Court did not decide whether defense counsel need be present, and in a later case it ruled that parole boards could use their discretion on the matter.[70]

Stanley notes an overwhelming inclination on the part of parole boards to accept the parole officer's recommendation. He also points out, however, that officers and board members agree that fewer revocations are the result of technical violations. He says: "Revocations are increasingly rare except for new crimes, cases of absconding, and cases of prolonged and eventually intolerable uncooperativeness."[71]

Assuming the offender has satisfied the conditions of his parole, in most states he can be discharged from parole even before his full sentence expires. Thirteen states, however, insist on parole status continuing until the full term expires.[72] Where discharge before full service occurs, it is the parole board that examines the reports of parole officers and determines which offenders will be discharged early.

Discharge from parole — or from prison, for that matter — does not necessarily mean that the offender becomes a totally free or full-fledged citizen again. In over half the states offenders continue to be denied the basic rights that were stripped from the offender at the time of his or her conviction. Generally, convicts are prohibited from voting, holding office, entering into contracts, filing suits, holding occupational licenses, or receiving insurance, pensions, or other benefits.[73]

COMMUNITY CORRECTIONS

In addition to probation and parole, there are many different kinds of community-based corrections agencies and programs. There is no such thing as a community corrections process due to the tremendous variety of programs, purposes, and activities. It is possible only to mention a few predominant types.

Institutional Programs

Recall that among institutional treatment programs are several community-related efforts including work release, study release, and other furloughs. These are generally efforts to deinstitutionalize selected individuals and begin their reintegration into the community prior to their parole or release.

Work release and study release programs generally involve inmates who are housed separately from the more securely held prisoners, in minimum security facilities where possible. Jobs or enrollment in schools or colleges are prearranged. The inmates leave the residential facility for the day, attend their classes or jobs, then return in the evening.

Performance on work or study release is often used to evaluate the inmate's readiness for parole, and the work or study release is not intended as a substitute for parole. The experience is helpful to many inmates since it begins their reintegration into the community, enables them to support dependents as well as themselves, and may also enhance the offender's sense of self-worth and dignity.

Naturally there are risks involved since people do "escape"—that is, fail to return. This risk keeps many cautious corrections systems from adopting such programs. Hassim Solomon comments that the programs have "demonstrated beyond doubt that, despite these minimal failures, institutional supervision and opportunity for offenders to perform economic as well as social roles have an extremely favorable effect in the resocialization of offenders."[74]

Halfway Houses

Halfway houses are used in two ways: as halfway-out centers for persons being released from prison and as halfway-in centers for those who would otherwise be sent to prison.

In serving as centers for those halfway out of prison, **halfway-out** houses have been employed for those who are released following the expiration of their terms, for those who are placed on parole, for those about to be released (whether on parole or due to expiration of their terms) and for those already released who have difficulty adjusting to normal life. The latter use may avert the need to resort to parole revocation in many cases.

Whether the offender is in a postrelease or prerelease status, the centers offer a variety of treatment programs. These usually include group therapy sessions designed to deal with special problems offenders have after having been through institutionalization. Participation in the governance of the facility may be employed as means of assisting offenders to gain self-respect and a sense of responsibility. Some centers, such as the Alternative House in Houston, Texas, are geared specifically to handle those with drug abuse problems.[75] Most halfway houses are more generalist in nature, however.

As **halfway-in** facilities, centers may service probationers who are considered too risky to place on normal probation, with its loose supervision, or who are in need of specific types of treatment that probation officers cannot provide. Those who are diverted from prosecution may also be placed in or agree to enter halfway houses. Those who cannot make bail and who should not be kept in jail but are too risky to re-

Halfway houses may provide a variety of treatment programs, including group therapy sessions.

lease on their own recognizance may also be found in these centers waiting for adjudication or sentencing. For those convicted but awaiting sentence, the staff of a halfway house may perform a study and diagnosis of the offender and prepare all or part of a pre-sentence investigation report for use by the sentencing judge.[76]

Many of those who are residents or clients in a halfway-in status are public drunkenness or drug abuse offenders. For such persons these halfway houses may serve either as places where rehabilitation occurs or simply as more humane temporary residences than the "drunk tanks" of local jails.

Intensive Intervention Programs

Still another community corrections effort may consist of what are called **intensive intervention programs** of various types. Like halfway houses, these programs may be used for persons on probation, parolees, or as an alternative to institutionalization. These are distinguishable from traditional probation and parole by the intensity of supervision and treatment. They differ from halfway houses in that they do not house offenders. The types of programs offered may run from therapeutic and behavior modification orientations—the casework approach—to the provision of services in line with the social work or resources management approach.

One of the most popular techniques is guided group interaction. Mentioned earlier as being used in prisons, this involves group sessions in which offenders discuss their own and others' experiences and attitudes. The group leader encourages the development of a group culture through which members may even impose discipline on one another. The group may even decide when one of their members is ready for release from correctional treatment.[77]

It cannot be said with certainty that any one community corrections approach works any better than the others. It can be said, however, that they offer corrections officials and sentencing judges useful and less expensive alternatives to incarceration and that they offer the opportunity to offenders to be treated humanely and to achieve guided integration with the community. Since the vast majority of incarcerated offenders eventually are placed at large anyway, it makes good sense to try alternatives to institutionalization for many and to provide means of easing the reentry of institutionalized persons into society for the others.

What must be avoided is the overloading of these new programs, a danger to which other reformist efforts have surrendered. There is a tendency for any successful program to be inundated with people until it becomes bureaucratized and loses the individuality of treatment that made it successful in the first place. As prisons fill up with the violent and incorrigible, we will probably expect community corrections to handle everyone else. If so, they will most likely go the way of too many probation and parole programs and, before them, the prisons. Handling the load will become the chief concern. If that happens, the only sense in which community corrections will work will be as providers of a less expensive way of putting offenders through corrections.

ENVIRONMENTAL INFLUENCES ON CORRECTIONS

Correctional institutions and programs are no different from other components of the criminal justice system in that they exist and operate within an environment that largely determines what they are able to do by providing various inputs. These inputs include demands, supports, and a good share of apathy. The demands include the laws and policies corrections officials are expected to abide by and enforce; community and political expectations about how the corrections agency will carry out its responsibilities; and, of course, the offenders turned over to them for processing. The supports consist of the money, staff, and other resources provided to corrections to carry out those responsibilities. As for apathy, it appears that corrections suffers more than any other component from a lack of community and political concern.

It can be argued that the output the community receives from corrections, especially the character of offenders released, accurately reflects the various inputs corrections receives from the community. There are two sides to this argument, however. One side argues that the high recidivism rate of those released from incaceration, probation, or parole demonstrates that the "coddling" that offenders receive fails to deter them from future crimes. The other side argues that the harshness and "inhumanity" of jail and prison conditions produces more hardened and bitter criminals. Either side may then argue that corrections receives far too little support to meet the demands placed upon it. There is no one, it seems, who argues that the demands are reasonable, supports are adequate, and the output acceptable.

We will take a look at the influences on corrections from several sources: its physical environment, the community and its citizens, the other agencies of government, and the other components within the criminal justice system.

Physical Environment

Corrections institutions tend to be located in rural areas, or at least away from population centers. While the original purpose was to protect inmates from outsiders, in the interest of protecting the community, society now dictates that corrections facilities be remote and that they be secure. Virtually every observer agrees that the prisons themselves are generally ghastly places. Most of the plants are very old and depressing, and the physical conditions are made even worse by the overcrowding that exists in most institutions. Allen and Simonsen comment: "Nothing can substitute for an actual visit to or confinement in one of these monuments to man's triumph of external control over internal reform."[78] Only in recent years has interest in prison architecture been revived and serious efforts been made to design and build humane facilities.

It is true, of course, that institutions of the medium and minimum security type are generally less oppressive in design and accommodations and that some facilities attempt to be pleasant. The Illinois State Penitentiary at Vienna, for example, is modeled after a village with a town square.[79]

By their very nature, most community corrections centers are not isolated from population centers. Neither are they depressing places, as a rule. Though some are converted military barracks, others are houses and former motels, and the conditions are far superior to jails or prisons.

Community Influences

It is often said that the community's general attitude toward corrections is "out of sight, out of mind." Most citizens are unconcerned about prison conditions or most other aspects of corrections. They seem not to care about anything connected with corrections except that they do not want a facility located in their neighborhood.

Tom Wicker is a *New York Times* reporter who was deeply involved in the negotiations during the Attica uprising and distressed by the means of its suppression. He said recently that he saw no increase in public concern as a result of that incident. He commented:

> *You take a fellow out in Queens with three locks on his door. He's going to work every day, maybe moonlighting at two jobs, doing the best he can. I just do not expect that fellow to be very sophisticated about his corrections philosophy. He's scared. And what does he want? He wants more people in prison and he wants them kept there longer.*[80]

He explained that he tried to convince people that the high cost of prisons and their failure to rehabilitate people should offend their sense of self-interest since they were paying for it. He concludes: "Self-interest is a very powerful motivating force, but it's not as powerful as fear. And people are afraid. And they just want those criminals locked up."[81]

But not all citizens are fearful or apathetic about conditions in institutions or corrections. There are citizens' groups and organizations working to correct the problems, and Michael Serrill divides them into two camps: abolitionists and pragmatists. Abolitionists, led by the National Council on Crime and Delinquency, want prisons phased out of existence over a period of time. Most of them recognize, however, that this is unlikely in the foreseeable future.[82] The pragmatists, such as Wicker and Norval Morris, want reforms, not in the form of more emphasis on rehabilitation but in the form of shorter terms that are mandatory for more offenders and more humane institutional surroundings.[83]

Government Influences

The generalizations we made about formal and informal influences from government agencies on law enforcement and other components apply to corrections as well. Legislative bodies enact laws and appropriate funds; executives make policy and issue directives; and the appellate courts issue rulings which affect the ways in which corrections officials and agencies conduct business. It is with regard to the role of appellate courts, however, that corrections has undergone the most dramatic change in the past few years.

Court Decisions The abandonment of the traditional hands-off position that courts had taken toward corrections has already been noted in the discussion of prisoners' rights. The transition from lack of involvement to direct court participation in corrections policymaking has taken very few years. Its most sweeping aspect involves court interpretations of the Eighth Amendment's prohibition of "cruel and unusual punishment" and the application of those interpretations to entire prisons or prison systems. The Supreme Court has never given a definitive interpretation of the clause, and there is nothing very unusual about terrible prison conditions. Nevertheless, lower federal courts have ruled that certain prisons or prison conditions are unconstitutional.

The two leading cases are *Holt* v. *Sarver* and *Pugh* v. *Locke.* In *Holt* a federal district court declared the entire Arkansas penal system unconstitutional, saying:

> *The concept of "cruel and unusual punishment" is not limited to instances in which a particular inmate is subjected to a punishment.... In the Court's estimation confinement itself within a given institution may amount to cruel and unusual punishment ... where the confinement is characterized by conditions and practices so bad as to be shocking to the conscience of reasonably civilized people....*
> *However constitutionally tolerable the Arkansas system may have been in former years, it simply will not do today as the twentieth century goes into its eighth decade.*[84]

Following this decision, and its affirmation by the Court of Appeals for the Eighth Circuit, many inmate lawsuits were filed. In Alabama a class action suit was filed in federal district court using an old federal statute that allows any citizen to file a federal civil suit against any state official who violates his civil and constitutional rights. U.S. District Court Judge Frank Johnson heard arguments that included an admission by the attorney for the corrections system that plaintiffs' rights were violated but that the system did not have the funds to remedy the conditions. The judge found that imprisonment in Alabama *in itself* constituted cruel and unusual punishment. He ordered the state to meet forty-four guidelines with detailed standards covering such matters as living conditions, classification, protection of inmates from violence, and the provision of opportunities to participate in rehabilitation and other programs. Under living condition requirements the judge included sixty square feet of cell space per inmate, a change of linen once a week, three nutritious meals a day, adequate clothing and sanitary conditions, and a pest control program. Never before had a judge ordered specific conditions met in a correctional facility.[85]

Governor George Wallace reacted by saying it would cost between $40 million and $100 million to meet the standards and accused the judge of trying to turn prisons into "hotels."[86] Judge Johnson's decision does leave open the question of how far federal courts can go in ordering compliance with very specific guidelines designed to meet constitutional standards that are vague at best. In any case, there will surely be more such suits and similar decisions to come.

Government Grants Another direct source of government influence on corrections is the Law Enforcement Assistance Administration and its grants of funds to innovative corrections programs. The LEAA has recently placed a higher priority on corrections than on other components and is stressing diversionary programs, alternatives to incarceration, and the whole gamut of community corrections efforts. More will be said of the LEAA later, but it is appropriate to say that it offers corrections officials the federal "carrot" while the courts are beginning to wield the "stick."

Relations with Other Components

Corrections depends on the other components for its input of offenders, and the other components depend on corrections to process them. Of all the components corrections has the least to say about what it does with its input. Corrections cannot reject cases or offenders in the way that law enforcement agencies can decline to arrest, prosecutors can refuse to charge, and the courts can dismiss cases. Corrections officials cannot say no. They are required to carry out the sentence of the court (or the terms of the diversionary agreement) regardless of the resources or facilities they have at their disposal. They do have some control over how soon they alter the status of an inmate to one of parole, and releases can usually be speeded up if necessary. Generally speaking, however, the capacity of corrections has little to do with how many offenders they are expected to handle. That is part of the reason corrections has come under severe attack in some courts.

As for specific sets of relationships, probation departments obviously work very closely with—if they are not administered by—trial courts. There is a give and take in this relationship since courts depend on probation departments to conduct pre-sentence investigations and submit reports, and the work load of probation is determined by the judges' sentencing patterns.

Probation and parole officers often depend on law enforcement agencies to assist them in controlling probationers and parolees. Probation revocations generally require prosecutors to participate in the hearings. On the other hand, diversionary programs, whether administered by law enforcement, prosecutors, or courts, often involve the probation agencies and depend on their resources.

Prison officials often have to call on law enforcement agencies to assist in capturing escapees or in suppressing riots within the institutions. Local jails, for the most part, are administered by police departments and sheriffs' offices, so their dependency on another component is almost total.

Community corrections programs may be administered and operated by almost any government agency, including the trial court. Their relationship to state-level corrections departments varies. Halfway houses obviously work closely with and partially depend on parole boards and parole officials.

The relationships and patterns of interaction are virtually infinite in their variety. Nevertheless, corrections is totally dependent on the other components for its work load. The successes that corrections programs have with some offenders ease the work loads of the other agencies. The failures, as has been pointed out, come back to haunt the entire system again. They are a form of negative feedback. It is interesting to note, too, that the offenders who commit further crimes are seen more often as the failures of corrections than as failures of other components. Thus they are viewed as the output of the final component rather than as the output of the entire criminal justice system.

The corrections component is torn by conflicting demands and expectations. Its purposes are the least clear of any component. Yet the purposes or functions of the other three rest on the ultimate issue of what to do with the offenders who are caught, prosecuted, and convicted. Without a better notion of what we are supposed to do in the final stage, the others may appear to be rather pointless.

TEST YOURSELF

Define these key terms:

diversion
technical violations
guided group interaction
prisonization
halfway-in centers

Answer the following questions:

1. Who sets conditions under which persons are placed on probation? Are there limits to what the conditions can require?

2. What has probation officer case loads to do with the success or failure of probationers?

3. Describe the stated purpose of prisoner classification. What is too often the reality?

4. What rights do parolees have in hearings which could result in revocation and their return to prison?

5. Into what three groups can citizens be divided regarding their attitude toward prisons? Which group is the largest?

6. What have courts done about prison settings that they believe to constitute cruel and unusual punishment?

NOTES

1. President's Commission on Law Enforcement and Administration of Justice, *Task Force Report: Corrections* (Washington, D.C.: Government Printing Office, 1967), p. 22.
2. Donald J. Newman, *Introduction to Criminal Justice* (Philadelphia: Lippincott, 1975), p. 391.
3. National Advisory Commission on Criminal Justice Standards and Goals, *Corrections* (Washington, D.C.: Government Printing Office, 1973), p. 189.
4. Harry E. Allen and Clifford E. Simonsen, *Corrections in America: An Introduction* (Beverly Hills, Calif.: Glencoe Press, 1976), p. 122.
5. Newman, *Criminal Justice*, p. 261.
6. Ibid., p. 263.
7. Allen and Simonsen, *Corrections in America*, p. 128.
8. Eugene H. Czajkoski, "Exposing the Quasi-Judicial Role of the Probation Officer," *Federal Probation* XXXVII (September 1973), pp. 11-12.

9. Hazel Kerper and Janeen Kerper, *Legal Rights of the Convicted* (St. Paul, Minn.: West Publishing, 1974), p. 250.
10. Ibid., p. 256.
11. Ibid., p. 257.
12. Newman, *Criminal Justice*, p. 300.
13. Robert E. Blanchard, *Introduction to the Administration of Justice* (New York: Wiley, 1975), p. 263.
14. Carl B. Klockars, Jr., "A Theory of Probation Supervision," *Journal of Criminal Law, Criminology and Police Science* 63 (1972), pp. 550-52.
15. NACCJSG, *Corrections*, pp. 320-23.
16. Ibid.
17. See President's Commission, *Task Force Report: Corrections*, p. 173.
18. San Francisco Committee on Crime, *Report on Adult Probation in San Francisco* (1970), p. 19, as quoted in John Kaplan, *Criminal Justice: Introductory Cases and Materials* (Mineola: Foundation Press, 1973), p. 517.
19. Kerper and Kerper, *Legal Rights*, p. 260.
20. Ibid., p. 262.
21. Czajkoski, "Exposing," p. 13.
22. David Duffee and Robert Fitch, *An Introduction to Corrections: A Policy and Systems Approach* (Pacific Palisades, Calif.: Goodyear, 1976), p. 133.
23. Ibid., pp. 133-34.
24. Harold J. Vetter and Clifford E. Simonsen, *Criminal Justice in America: The System, the Process, the People* (Philadelphia: Saunders, 1976), p. 272.
25. Ibid.
26. Duffee and Fitch, *Corrections*, pp. 135-36.
27. Ibid., pp. 142-43.
28. Allen and Simonsen, *Corrections in America*, p. 231.
29. Ibid., pp. 231-32.
30. Alan G. Kalmanoff, *Criminal Justice: Enforcement and Administration* (Boston: Little, Brown, 1976), pp. 375-77.
31. See Allen and Simonsen, *Corrections in America*, p. 234.
32. *Jackson v. Bishop*, 404 F.2d 517 (8th Circuit, 1968).
33. Duffee and Fitch, *Corrections*, p. 150.
34. Blanchard, *Administration of Justice*, p. 258.
35. Duffee and Fitch, *Corrections*, p. 152.
36. "U.S. Ends Project on Jail Inmates," *New York Times*, 6 February, 1974, p. 12.
37. NACCJSG, *Corrections*, p. 199.
38. See Duffee and Fitch, *Corrections*, p. 156; and President's Commission, *Task Force Report: Corrections*, p. 183.
39. See Duffee and Fitch, *Corrections*, pp. 161-63.
40. Gresham Sykes, *The Society of Captives: A Study of a Maximum Security Prison*, (Princeton, N.J.: Princeton University Press, 1958), pp. 63-83.
41. Allen and Simonsen, *Corrections in America*, pp. 153-55.
42. Esther Heffernan, *Making It in Prison: The Square, the Cool, and the Life* (New York: Wiley, 1972), pp. 88-107.
43. Stanton Wheeler, "Socialization in Correctional Communities," in Lawrence Hazelrigg, ed., *Prison within Society: A Reader in Penology* (Garden City, N.Y.: Doubleday [Anchor Books] 1969), p. 150.
44. See Kerper and Kerper, *Legal Rights*, pp. 278-79.
45. Ibid., pp. 301-2.
46. Ibid., p. 305.
47. 418 U.S. 539 (1974).
48. Robert Plotkin, "Recent Developments in the Law of Prisoners' Rights," *Criminal Law Bulletin* 11 (July-August 1975), p. 407.
49. Ibid.
50. Ibid., pp. 408-10.
51. *Procunier v. Martinez*, 416 U.S. 396 (1974).
52. Plotkin, "Prisoners' Rights," p. 416.

53. Ibid., pp. 416-17.
54. Ibid., pp. 421-23.
55. See Allen and Simonsen, *Corrections in America*, p. 371.
56. See David T. Stanley, *Prisoners Among Us: The Problems of Parole* (Washington, D.C.: Brookings Institution, 1976), p. 32.
57. Ibid., pp. 48-50.
58. Ibid., p. 34.
59. Ibid., pp. 34-37.
60. Ibid., pp. 43-44.
61. Ibid., pp. 44-46.
62. See Kenneth C. Davis, *Discretionary Justice* (Urbana, Ill.: University of Illinois Press, 1971), p. 65; National Council on Crime and Delinquency, "Parole Decisions: A Policy Statement," *Crime and Delinquency* 19 (April 1973), p. 137; NACCJSG, *Corrections*, p. 422.
63. Duffee and Fitch, *Corrections*, pp. 232-33.
64. Ibid., p. 234.
65. Stanley, *Prisoners Among Us*, pp. 82-84.
66. Ibid., pp. 96-99.
67. Ibid., pp. 105-6.
68. *Morrisey v. Brewer*, 408 U.S. 471 (1972).
69. Ibid.
70. *Gagnon v. Scarpelli*, 411 U.S. 778 (1973).
71. Stanley, *Prisoners Among Us*, pp. 112-13.
72. Ibid., p. 120.
73. Kerper and Kerper, *Legal Rights*, p. 20.
74. Hassim M. Solomon, *Community Corrections* (Boston: Holbrook Press, 1976), pp. 307-8.
75. Ibid., pp. 249-50.
76. Ibid., pp. 243-44.
77. Ibid., p. 268; and Duffee and Fitch, *Corrections*, pp. 271-72.
78. Allen and Simonsen, *Corrections in America*, p. 150.
79. See Solomon, *Community Corrections*, pp. 81-83.
80. Tom Wicker as quoted in Michael S. Serrill, "Critics of Corrections Speak Out," *Corrections Magazine* 2 (March, 1976), p. 22.
81. Ibid.
82. Ibid., pp. 3-8 and 21.
83. Ibid., pp. 21-26.
84. 309 F. Supp. 362 (E.D. Ark, 1970).
85. See "Alabama Prisons," *C.J. Bulletin* (Cincinnati, Ohio: W. H. Anderson, 1976), pp. 1-4.
86. "The Snake Pits," *Newsweek*, (26 January, 1976), p. 43.

PART VI
Juvenile Justice

CHAPTER 14
The Juvenile Justice System

OUTLINE

HISTORICAL TREATMENT OF JUVENILE OFFENDERS
    Adult Status for Juvenile Offenders
    Parens Patriae
        A Philosophy of Treatment
        Juvenile Court
        A New Vocabulary
    Due Process for Juvenile Offenders
        In re Gault
        Other Court Decisions
        Post-*Gault* Due Process

PROCESS OF JUVENILE JUSTICE
    Juvenile Justice System versus Juvenile Court
    Juvenile Delinquency Defined
    Law Enforcement and Juveniles
        Detection of Delinquent Acts
        Law Enforcement and Juvenile Offenders
    Juvenile Court
        Intake
        Filing of Petition
        Juvenile Detention
        Adjudicatory Hearings
        Disposition

JUVENILE CORRECTIONS
    Probation
    Juvenile Institutions
    Juvenile Aftercare (Parole)

OBJECTIVES

After reading this chapter the student should be able to:

Discuss the nature and significance of the three historical periods of juvenile justice.

Outline differences in vocabulary utilized in juvenile and adult justice systems.

Explain the significance of the Supreme Court decisions of *In re Winship* (1970) and *McKeiver* v. *Pennsylvania* (1971).

Discuss the progress of juvenile courts in assuring juveniles of the due process rights set forth in *Gault*.

Explain how the juvenile system of justice and the juvenile court differ in scope.

Describe the ways in which juvenile delinquency is defined and discuss the debate over which acts should be labeled "delinquent."

Describe the sources of complaints against juveniles that bring them to the attention of those in the juvenile justice system.

Describe the various ways in which police can deal with juvenile offenders.

Outline the structure of juvenile courts.

Describe the nature of juvenile court intake, including the alternative decisions available.

Describe the petition for adjudication of delinquency.

Define and discuss juvenile detention, adjudicatory hearings, and disposition hearings.

Discuss the disposition alternatives available to juvenile court judges.

Describe juvenile probation, both informal and formal.

List and describe the various types of institutions for juvenile delinquents.

Describe the rationale, release authority, and responsibility for juvenile aftercare.

KEY TERMS

parens patriae
delinquent juvenile
dependent child
neglected child
status offenses
juvenile court
juvenile court intake
adjudicatory hearing
petition
detention
dispositional hearing
social history report
informal probation
formal probation
state training schools
outdoor-style institutions
group homes
halfway houses
shelters
juvenile aftercare

☐ To this point our discussion has centered basically on the criminal justice system for adults. While the justice system for juveniles is not an entirely separate one, it is different enough to warrant a special discussion. As Vetter and Simonsen note: "The juvenile is tried in a separate set of courts, a different vocabulary pertains to him and there is a different philosophy underlying the administration of juvenile justice."[1] In this chapter we will discuss these and other differences.

HISTORICAL TREATMENT OF JUVENILE OFFENDERS

Treatment of juvenile offenders has varied during the history of America. There have been essentially three different periods of treatment. The first period we have labeled *adult status* because few distinctions were made between juvenile and adult offenders. The second we call **parens patriae** because of the acceptance of a philosophy that state courts had the power to act as the parents of juvenile offenders and protect their welfare as part of the effort to cure and save them. The third period we refer to as "due process" because of Supreme Court requirements that juveniles be granted the rights of due process that they had lost under the doctrine of **parens patriae.** (See Table 14.1).

Adult Status for Juvenile Offenders

As indicated, during this period, lasting essentially until the beginning of the twentieth century, few distinctions were made between juvenile and adult offenders. The juvenile was generally as subject to the harshness of the criminal system as an adult, and recall that it was a system that indeed was harsh. In New Jersey, for example, as late as 1828 a "boy of thirteen was hanged for an offense committed when twelve years of age."[2] U.S. Supreme Court Justice Abe Fortas points out that the **parens patriae** period of juvenile treatment was brought about by reformers who "were appalled by adult procedures and penalties, and by the fact that children could be given long prison sentences and mixed in jails with hardened criminals." He further notes that

TABLE 14.1 Historical Treatment of Juvenile Offenders

Before 1899:	1899–1967:	1967–present:
Adult status	*Parens patriae*	Due process

... at common law, children under seven were considered incapable of possessing criminal intent. Beyond that age, they were subjected to arrest, trial, and in theory to punishment like adult offenders. In these old days the state was not deemed to have authority to accord them [juveniles] fewer procedural rights than adults.[3]

Parens Patriae

This period introduced for the juvenile offender not only a new philosophy of treatment but a new institution and a new vocabulary as well. The philosophy was that of *parens patriae*; the institution, the juvenile court; and the vocabulary, a list of terms designed to reflect the separation of juvenile and adult systems.

A Philosophy of Treatment As we indicated, reformers were upset by what they thought to be rather harsh treatment of juvenile offenders. In the words of Justice Fortas:

They were profoundly convinced that society's duty to the child could not be confined by the concept of justice alone. They believed that society's role was not to ascertain whether the child was "guilty" or "innocent," but "what is he, how he became what he is, and what had best be done in his interest and in the interest of the state to save him from a downward career." The child—essentially good, as they saw it—was to be made "to feel that he is the object of the state's care and solicitude," not that he was under arrest or on trial. The rules of criminal procedure were therefore altogether inapplicable. The apparent rigidities, technicalities, and harshness which they observed in both substantive and procedural criminal law were therefore to be discarded. The idea of crime and punishment was to be abandoned. The child was to be "treated" and "rehabilitated" and the procedures, from apprehension through institutionalization, were to be "clinical" rather than punitive. These results were to be achieved ... insisting that the proceedings were not adversary, but that the state was proceeding as parens patriae.[4]

Juvenile Court As part of the means to carry out the new philosophy of juvenile treatment, a new institution was created—the juvenile court. While "separation of children from adults was carried into the court process in limited form as early as 1861 in Chicago, and by the 1890s a handful of states had authorized special handling of children by the courts," the first juvenile court was established in Cook County, Illinois, in 1899.[5] By 1945 all states had adopted some form of juvenile court system.

As indicated above, the court's task was not to determine the guilt or innocence of a child but understand and deal with him "as a wise parent would deal with a wayward child." Accordingly, the judge exercised virtually unlimited discretion in the handling of juvenile offenders and due process rights for those referred to the court were practically nonexistent. The court setting was highly informal, private and nonadversary in nature. It was felt that defense lawyers and harsh confrontations of accuser and accused were not needed or were detrimental to the achievement of the court's goal of helping the juvenile offender rather than determining his or her guilt and levying punishment. In fact, notes Cole, "Even the vocabulary and physical surroundings of the juvenile system were changed so that emphasis would be fixed on the goals of diagnosis and treatment rather than the adjudication of guilt." [6]

A New Vocabulary To accompany the new juvenile justice philosophy, terms used in the adult criminal justice system were modified and adopted. Instead of committing a "crime," and being labeled a "criminal," the juvenile commits a "delinquent act" and is labeled a "delinquent." Instead of being "arrested," the juvenile is "taken into custody." Being held in jail becomes "detention." These and other changes in terminology can be seen in Table 14.2 and will come up again as we focus on the process of juvenile justice.

Due Process for Juvenile Offenders

While some criticisms of the juvenile court's operation under the philosophy of **parens patriae** existed from its inception, it came under concerted attack with a Supreme Court decision in 1967. Because of the state of Arizona's treatment of a young boy named Gerald Gault, the U.S. Supreme Court received the case that has meant the most significant change in juvenile justice in over seventy-five years.

In re Gault The Gault story and the Supreme Court decision in *In re Gault* is of such importance that we present substantial portions verbatim from the majority opinion written by Justice Abe Fortas:

> On Monday, June 8, 1964, at about 10 A.M., Gerald Francis Gault and a friend, Ronald Lewis, were taken into custody by the Sheriff of Gila County [Arizona]. Gerald was then still subject to a six months' probation order which had been entered on February 25, 1964, as a result of his having been in the company of another boy who had stolen a wallet from a lady's purse. The police action on June 8 was taken as the result of a verbal complaint by a neighbor of the boys, Mrs. Cook, about a telephone call made to her in which the caller or callers made lewd or indecent remarks. It will suffice for pur-

TABLE 14.2 Comparison of Significant Juvenile and Adult Justice Terminology

Juvenile Term	Adult Term
Delinquent act	Crime
Delinquent child	Criminal
Take into custody	Arrest
Detention	Holding in jail
Petition	Accusation or indictment
Adjudicatory hearing	Trial
Dispositional hearing	Sentencing
Probation	Probation
Commitment	Sentence to imprisonment
Shelter	Jail
Aftercare	Parole

Source: Harold J. Vetter and Clifford E. Simonsen, *Criminal Justice in America*, pp. 346-47; © 1976 by the W.B. Saunders Company, Philadelphia, Pa. Reprinted by permission.

poses of this opinion to say that the remarks or questions put to her were of the irritatingly offensive, adolescent, sex variety.

At the time Gerald was picked up, his mother and father were both at work. No notice that Gerald was being taken into custody was left at the home. No other steps were taken to advise them that their son had, in effect, been arrested. Gerald was taken to the Children's Detention Home. When his mother arrived home at about 6 o'clock, Gerald was not there. Gerald's older brother was sent to look for him at the trailer home of the Lewis family. He apparently learned then that Gerald was in custody. He so informed his mother. The two of them went to the Detention Home. The deputy probation officer, Flagg, who was also superintendent of the Detention Home, told Mrs. Gault "why Jerry was there" and said that a hearing would be held in Juvenile Court at 3 o'clock the following day, June 9.

Officer Flagg filed a petition with the court on the hearing day, June 9, 1964. It was not served on the Gaults. Indeed, none of them saw this petition until the habeas corpus hearing on August 17, 1964. The petition was entirely formal. It made no reference to any factual basis for the judicial action which it initiated. It recited only that "said minor is under the age of eighteen years, and is in need of the protection of this Honorable Court; and that said minor is a delinquent minor." It prayed for a hearing and an order regarding "the care and custody of said minor." Officer Flagg executed a formal affidavit in support of the petition.

On June 9, Gerald, his mother, his older brother, and Probation Officers Flagg and Henderson appeared before the Juvenile Judge in chambers. Gerald's father was not there. He was at work out of the city. Mrs. Cook, the complainant, was not there. No one was sworn at this hearing. No transcript or recording was made. No memorandum or record of the substance of the proceedings was prepared. Our information about the proceedings and the subsequent hearing on June 15 derives entirely from the testimony of the Juvenile Court Judge, Mr. and Mrs. Gault and Officer Flagg at the habeas corpus proceeding conducted two months later. From this it appears that at the June 9 hearing Gerald was questioned by the judge about the telephone call. There was conflict as to what he said. His mother recalled that Gerald said he only dialed Mrs. Cook's number and handed the telephone to his friend, Ronald. Officer Flagg recalled that Gerald had admitted making the lewd remarks. Judge McGhee testified that Gerald "admitted making one of these lewd statements." At the conclusion of the hearing, the judge said he would "think about it." Gerald was taken back to the Detention Home. He was not sent to his own home with his parents. On June 11 or 12, after having been detained since June 8, Gerald was released and driven home. There is no explanation in the record as to why he was kept in the Detention Home or why he was released. At 5 P.M. on the day of Gerald's release, Mrs. Gault received a note signed by Officer Flagg. It was on plain paper, not letterhead. Its entire text was as follows:

> "Mrs. Gault:
> "Judge McGhee has set Monday June 15, 1964 at 11:00 A.M. as the date and time for further Hearings on Gerald's delinquency
> "/s/ Flagg"

At the appointed time on Monday, June 15, Gerald, his father and mother, Ronald Lewis and his father, and Officers Flagg and Henderson were present before Judge McGhee. Witnesses at the habeas corpus proceeding differed in their recollections of Gerald's testimony at the June 15 hearing. Mr. and Mrs. Gault recalled that Gerald again testified that he had only dialed the number and that the other boy had made the remarks. Officer Flagg agreed that at this hearing Gerald did not admit making the lewd remarks. But Judge McGhee recalled that "there was some admission again of some of the lewd statements. He — he didn't admit any of the more serious lewd statements." Again, the complainant, Mrs. Cook, was not present. Mrs. Gault asked that Mrs. Cook be present "so she could see which boy that done the talking, the dirty talking over the phone." The Juvenile Judge said "she didn't have to be present at that hearing." The judge did not speak to Mrs. Cook or communicate with her at any time. Probation Officer Flagg had talked to her once — over the telephone on June 9.

At this June 15 hearing a "referral report" made by the probations officers was filed with the court, although not disclosed to Gerald or his parents. This listed the charge as "Lewd Phone Calls." At the conclusion of the hearing, the judge committed Gerald as a juvenile delinquent to the State Industrial School "for the period of his minority that is, until 21, unless sooner discharged by due process of law." An order to that effect was entered. It recites that "after a full hearing and due deliberation the Court finds that said minor is a delinquent child, and that said minor is of the age of 15 years."[7]

The Gaults attempted to have the commitment decision set aside but their efforts were rejected by both the superior and supreme courts of Arizona. The U.S. Supreme Court heard the case and on May 15, 1967, rendered its historic decision. Briefly, the Court held that juveniles are entitled to certain procedural rights such as notification of charges, right to counsel, right to confrontation and cross-examination of witnesses, and protection against self-incrimination.

The Court, speaking through Justice Fortas, very forcefully pointed out to those of the juvenile court system that "neither the Fourteenth Amendment nor the Bill of Rights is for adults alone."[8] Recognizing the good intentions and motives behind the philosophy of *parens patriae*, the Court nevertheless noted that it had "led to a peculiar system for juveniles, unknown to our law in any comparable context" and that "the Constitutional and theoretical basis for this peculiar system is—to say the least—debatable."[9]

At this point we will use the words of Justice Fortas to further describe the Court's deep dissatisfaction with the juvenile court system at that time:

Ultimately, however, we confront the reality of that portion of the Juvenile Court process with which we deal in this case. A boy is charged with misconduct. The boy is committed to an institution where he may be restrained of liberty for years. It is of no constitutional consequence—and of limited practical meaning—that the institution to which he is committed is called an Industrial School. The fact of the matter is that, however euphemistic the title, a "receiving home" or an "industrial school" for juveniles is an institution of confinement in which the child is incarcerated for a greater or lesser time. His world becomes "a building with whitewashed walls, regimented routine and institutional hours. . . ." Instead of mother and father and sisters and brothers and friends and classmates, his world is peopled by guards, custodians, state employees, and "delinquents" confined with him for anything from waywardness to rape and homicide.

In view of this, it would be extraordinary if our Constitution did not require the procedural regularity and the exercise of care implied in the phrase "due process." Under our Constitution, the condition of being a boy does not justify a Kangaroo court. . . . The essential difference between Gerald's case and a normal criminal case is that safeguards available to adults were discarded in Gerald's case.

. . . If Gerald had been over 18, he would not have been subject to Juvenile Court proceedings. For the particular offense immediately involved, the maximum punishment would have been a fine of $5 to $50 or imprisonment in jail for not more than two months. Instead he was committed to custody for a maximum of six years. If he had been over 18 and had committed an offense to which such sentence might apply, he would have been entitled to sub-

stantial rights under the Constitution of the United States as well as under Arizona's laws and Constitution. The United States Constitution would guarantee him rights and protections with respect to arrest, search, and seizure, and pretrial interrogation. It would assure him of specific notice of the charges and adequate time to decide his course of action and to prepare his defense. He would be entitled to clear advice that he could be represented by counsel, and, at least if a felony were involved, the State would be required to provide counsel if his parents were unable to afford it. If the court acted on the basis of his confession, careful procedures would be required to assure its voluntariness. If the case went to trial, confrontation and opportunity for cross-examination would be guaranteed. So wide a gulf between the State's treatment of the adult and of the child requires a bridge sturdier than mere verbiage, and reasons more persuasive than cliché can provide.[10]

Other Court Decisions Following its declaration of due process rights for juveniles in *In re Gault*, the Supreme Court further expanded these rights in 1970. In the case of *In re Winship*, the Court concluded that a juvenile may be declared delinquent only after a judge is convinced of delinquency "beyond a reasonable doubt." The standards of proof prior to this decision, a civil evidence standard, required only a "preponderance" of evidence to establish delinquency. Speaking for the majority, Justice Brennan stated:

The same considerations which demand extreme caution in fact-finding to protect the innocent adult apply as well to the innocent child.... We conclude, as we concluded regarding the essential due process safeguards applied in Gault, that the observance of the standards of proof "beyond a reasonable doubt" will not compel the states to abandon or displace any of the substantive benefits of the juvenile process.... In sum, the constitutional safeguard of proof beyond a reasonable doubt is as much required during the adjudicatory stage of a delinquency proceeding as are those constitutional safeguards applied in Gault—notice of charges, right to counsel, the rights of confrontation and examination, and the privilege against self-incrimination.[11]

It should be noted that while the Supreme Court has drastically expanded a juvenile's due process rights, it has not made these rights as complete as those for adults. While a few states provide for juries in juvenile cases, the Supreme Court ruled in *McKeiver* v. *Pennsylvania* that this is not a constitutional right. The Court made it clear—as it had in *Gault*—that its expansion of due process rights should not destroy the juvenile court's ability to operate in an intimate, informal, and protective fashion in the adjudicating of juvenile delinquency. Requirement of the jury as a "matter of constitutional precept" might do just that. The Court stated:

The imposition of the jury trial on the juvenile court system would not strengthen greatly, if at all, the fact-finding function, and would, contrarily, provide an attrition of the juvenile court's assumed ability to function in a unique manner. It would not remedy the defects of the system. Meager as has been the hoped-for advance in the juvenile field, the alternative would be regressive, would lose what has been gained, and would tend once again to place the juvenile squarely in the routine of the criminal process.[12]

Post-Gault *Due Process* The Supreme Court decisions in *Gault* and subsequent cases may have required for juveniles many of the due process rights enjoyed by adults, but as Ted Rubin has noted, "Supreme Court decisions are not self-executing." He compares *Gault* with the Court's school integration decision of 1954 *(Brown v. Board of Education of Topeka)* in terms of the slowness in implementation: years after *Gault* the Court's due process requirements are ignored in many communities. The requirements are met only in those courts, Rubin suggests, "where there is strong judicial respect for law, strong judicial leadership in demanding that court procedures adhere to law, and where organized defense counsel services along with prosecutor offices have assigned effective counsel to this court."[13]

Taking the requirement in *Gault* that a juvenile court judge must advise each child of his or her right to a lawyer (private or court appointed if the family is unable to afford one), Rubin contends that some judges have rigorously followed it, some have "waffled" on it, and many have simply ignored it. Judges range from those who will not consider any case without counsel present to those where "less than 10% of children are represented." Rubin suggests that juvenile courts have ways to discourage representation.[14] And Cole states:

The lower social status of the offender's parents, the intimidating atmosphere of the court, and judicial hints that the outcome will be more favorable if a lawyer is not present are reasons the procedures outlined in Gault *are not demanded. The litany of "treatment," doing what's right for the child," and "working out a just solution" may sound enticing, especially to people who are unfamiliar with the intricacies of formal legal procedures.*[15]

Despite the lack of progress toward implementation of the *Gault* decision in many places, Rubin points out that prior to *Gault* some states had overhauled their juvenile codes and after *Gault* many other states did also. Thus juvenile law reform is essentially "an incomplete achievement and an ongoing process." Rubin's overall assessment is that "the future is clear: law and due process are here to stay in the juvenile court; prosecution and defense counsel have become permanent members of the court's case of characters; rehabilitation efforts will be pursued within a legal context."[16]

THE PROCESS OF JUVENILE JUSTICE

Quite often, discussions of juvenile justice become primarily or exclusively discussions of juvenile court. The two concepts, however, are not really the same and it is important, we believe, to make a distinction between them.

Juvenile Justice System versus Juvenile Court

Simply put, the juvenile justice system is much broader than the institution of juvenile courts and the court is, in fact, just one component within the total system. Juveniles who enter the justice system often never reach the jurisdiction of the juvenile court because charges against them are dismissed or they are diverted from any — or further — entry into the justice process. Even where the court does decide the disposition of a juvenile case, once it has completed its task, other elements within the system continue to make decisions affecting the child: "probation supervision decisions, discipline and treatment decisions in the training school, discretionary release from training school and juvenile parole supervision and revocation decisions."[17] The point, again, is that the system and process of juvenile justice is broader in nature than the concept of juvenile court.

Though more narrow in one sense than the juvenile justice system, so too is the juvenile court much broader in another sense. By this we mean that it generally has jurisdiction over a broader range of juveniles than does the justice system. The juvenile justice system is concerned basically with those children who fit into a category called **delinquent**. Delinquent juveniles are those who commit acts that if committed by an adult would be crimes or certain other acts that would be unlawful only if committed by a juvenile (status offenses). Juvenile courts not only have jurisdiction over delinquents but over those who may be **dependent, neglected,** or in the process of being adopted.[18] The terms dependent and neglected apply to those children suffering from parental neglect, abuse, abandonment and the like. Miller and his colleagues point out that in some states the juvenile court jurisdiction even "extends to making custody decisions about children whose parents are separated or divorced."[19] Thus the juvenile court handles not only the delinquency case that falls within the scope of the juvenile justice

FIGURE 14.1 Relationship of Juvenile Court to the Juvenile Justice System

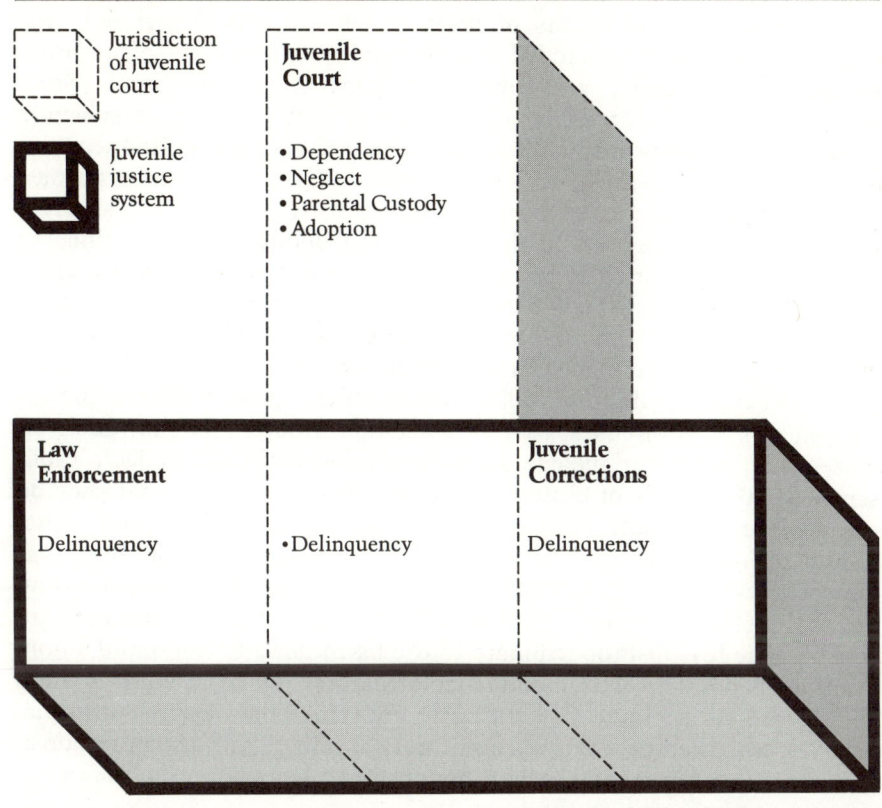

system but also matters outside of it as well. (See Figure 14.1.) Cole points out that of those children referred to juvenile courts, about 75 percent are delinquency cases, about 20 percent are dependency and neglect, and about 5 percent "involve special proceedings such as adoption."[20]

Juvenile Delinquency Defined

Though we have already set forth a definition of delinquency, it is an area of such controversy and debate as to warrant further discussion. Basically, delinquent acts are of two kinds. The first kind involves those acts committed by juveniles that, if committed by an adult, would be a crime. These run the gamut from felonies such as murder and burglary to misdemeanors such as shoplifting and vandalism. The second kind involves **status offenses** which are acts illegal only for children. These have included such behavior as violation of curfews, truancy, use of alcohol and tobacco, running away from home, being ungovernable or incorrigible, consensual sexual behavior, disobeying authority, and waywardness.[21] In about half the states, delinquency is defined in terms of those acts in the first category plus violation of a previous order of the juvenile court. Status offenses fall into a separate nondelinquency category. In the other states delinquency is defined to include both categories of behavior—violations of adult criminal codes and status offenses. A few states within the latter group may be labeled "mixed" because some status offenses are included in delinquency and some are placed in a separate category.[22]

The debate over defining delinquency centers principally on the inclusion of status offenses. Many people and groups feel that such offenses should not be labeled as delinquent because this subjects thousands and thousands of children each year to punishment that they do not deserve. The National Council on Crime and Delinquency points to the rehabilitative philosophy of juvenile courts and contends that "imprisonment or detention of a status offender serves no humanitarian or rehabilitative purpose." Instead it is "unwarranted punishment, unjust because it is disproportionate to the harm done by the child's noncriminal behavior." The council feels that the juvenile court system should use its coercive powers fairly and efficiently against criminal behavior threatening to the community's safety and leave responsibility for the unacceptable but noncriminal behavior of children to noncoercive community services:

> Use of family counseling and youth service bureaus and increasing educational and employment opportunities would be more beneficial than depending on juvenile courts. . . . The result of giving jurisdiction over noncriminal behavior to the juvenile court is that a disproportionate share of available resources is applied to youth who pose no criminal danger to society. With the continued acceleration of juvenile crime, we can ill afford to waste these meager resources. The juvenile court should be the agency of last resort for antisocial—i.e., criminal—conduct. Its efforts and sanctions should be reserved for serious criminal conduct. . . . Noncriminal conduct should be referred to social agencies, not to courts of law.[23]

A recent article on juvenile delinquency in the *Book of the States, 1976-77* suggests that the trend is toward either abolishing court jurisdiction over status offenders or separation of these offenders from those charged with the commission of adult crimes. Another trend has been to recognize differences between "juvenile delinquents" and "dangerous juvenile offenders" and to increasingly treat the latter as adults instead of children.[24]

Before leaving this subject of defining delinquency, it must be noted that age is also part of each definition. States may set a minimum age below which the child cannot be classified as a delinquent and a maximum age above which he or she must be treated as an adult offender. The most common maximum age is eighteen, with several states as high as twenty-one. Those states establishing lower age limits vary greatly, with the lowest being generally eight years old.[25] Most states provide for the waiver of juveniles to adult court upon the commission of various serious offenses.

Law Enforcement and Juveniles

The process of juvenile justice runs from the point where someone detects an act thought to be delinquent and brings it to the attention of the juvenile justice system to the final disposition of the matter in juvenile court. Some juvenile offenders will be processed along the entire path; others will leave it at varying points. We begin our discussion of the juvenile justice process with the detection of delinquent acts and a look at the role played by law enforcement agencies.

Detection of Delinquent Acts Before a child can enter or be a potential for entrance into the juvenile justice process, a complaint must be brought against the child charging the child with the commission of some act that could be judged to be delinquent. Complaints may come from police officers who apprehend a juvenile committing a delinquent act or from others such as parents, truant officers, school officials, neighbors, and victims of an offense.[26]

Law Enforcement and Juvenile Offenders Matters of delinquency brought to the attention of police by police officer observation or reports from other sources such as parents, school officials, and victims may be dealt with in a number of ways. As with adults the police exercise a great deal of discretion at this point. The officer apprehending a juvenile offender or investigating a report of delinquency may decide that there is no case of delinquency and thus no further action is warranted, may take the child into custody, or may reprimand the child for his or her behavior and then release the child. In Denver, Colorado, for example,

> . . . the juvenile justice process . . . generally begins with the investigation of an offense by a policeman in the field. If a juvenile is apprehended for the commission of an offense, the investigating officer (invested with the power of discretion) can release the child on the spot, release the child after a lecture, or refer the suspect to the Delinquency Control Division of the Denver Police Department (DCD).[27]

"Referring the suspect" means taking the child into custody and carrying him or her to the central office of the DCD.

Estimates are that police account for about 90 percent of all diversion of juvenile offenders from the justice system and most of that occurs with the officer in the streets.[28] Cole suggests that "in neighborhoods where law enforcement officials have developed strong relationships with the inhabitants, violators may be dealt with by giving warnings to the juveniles and notifying their parents."[29]

Depending on a number of factors such as the seriousness of the offense, the youth's prior record, and perhaps his or her attitude at the time of police contact, the police officer may decide to take a juvenile into custody. Coffey points out that at this point the officer must be certain the child understands his rights, the intent to take him into custody, the cause for custody, and the officer's authority to take him into custody. "Moreover," says Coffey, "all the legal complexities of, among others, *probable cause, stop-and-frisk, warrants* . . . apply to juvenile as well as adult arrests."[30]

The juvenile may be taken to the police station, where, again, a decision will be made on whether the matter needs further attention or can be eliminated from the justice process. Many police departments have special juvenile sections (e.g., bureaus, divisions) to make such decisions.[31] The decisions made at this point may include releasing the juvenile outright (on his own or to parents), releasing the juvenile to parents pending further investigation, referral to a social agency, or referral to juvenile court.

Of those juveniles taken to the police station, most are diverted out of the system through referral or release. Estimates are that only about one-third are referred to juvenile court.[32] In Denver, police intake officers within the Delinquency Control Division estimated that about two-thirds of all youths apprehended and referred to them are given a lecture and released in the custody of their parents or guardians.[33]

Juvenile Court

There is, in every county in the United States, a court that has jurisdiction over juvenile matters. Quite commonly we refer to these as

juvenile courts. It should be noted, however, that all courts handling juvenile matters do not formally bear that name nor are these courts always organizationally separate from other courts. Both the court's name and structure take various forms. In some places it is a separate juvenile court for a specified geographical area (for example, Denver and Boston juvenile courts). In some states there are statewide juvenile courts and "juvenile offenses are considered exclusively by juvenile court judges in the various districts of that state"[34] (for example, Utah and Connecticut). Some states have juvenile offenders handled by family courts (for example, Delaware and Rhode Island). The more common situation is for juvenile offenders to be dealt with by a court that falls within the jurisdictional boundaries of a state's highest or lowest general trial court. In Florida, for example, there are juvenile divisions of the state's circuit courts. There are, notes Rubin, other variations. These range from juvenile divisions within probate court (e.g., Michi-

Throughout the United States there are courts that have jurisdiction over juvenile matters.

gan) to mixed situations in which the location of the juvenile court within the court structure varies from district to district.[35]

Intake Referral of a juvenile by police (or others) to juvenile court does not automatically (and not even generally) lead to formal action by the court. As Clare and Kramer point out, procedures may vary from court to court, but referrals to the juvenile court generally are first considered by an intake officer. The purpose of **intake** is to screen cases to determine which ones can be settled through informal means and which ones need the formal attention of the court. During this period the intake officer, frequently a probation officer who may be assigned to the case from start to finish,[36] may hear the report of the officer having taken the juvenile into custody, question (if the need exists) the juvenile about his identity or location of parents,[37] or simply conduct informal discussions among himself, the child, and the parents.[38] Again, the purpose of the intake period and intake conferences is to see if an informal adjustment can be made in order to avoid further and formal court proceedings.[39]

After careful consideration the intake officer makes his or her decision. If the matter is to be handled informally, the officer may reprimand and lecture the child or the parents and then release the child with no restrictions. Or the officer may refer the child or the family to a community social service agency for counseling. Other alternatives include requiring periodic reports by the juvenile for several months (informal probation) or making some other informal adjustment. If informal adjustment is deemed as unsuitable or if the child or the parents deny the charges, the intake officer decides that formal treatment by the court is necessary.

Filing of Petition Assuming that formal action by the juvenile court is necessary, the next step would be an **adjudicatory hearing** at which the court decides upon the question of delinquency. For this to occur, a **petition** must be filed with the court. This is the document, equivalent to an information in the adult criminal process, containing the nature of the charges against the juvenile offender. It is "an application for the court to act in the matter of a juvenile apprehended for a delinquent act."[40] Fox notes that juvenile court acts vary as to who may file the necessary petition. This may range from the intake or probation officer to the district or state attorney's office to, in some places, practically anyone.[41] In Florida, as an example of how the petition is handled, the Division of Youth Services sends its filing recommendations and the juvenile offender's case file to the state attorney's office where the decision to file or not file is made. The state attorney's office may accept or reject the youth services office recommendations, for it has final control over the decision.

Juvenile Detention During the period of time from initial custody of a juvenile to the holding of an adjudicatory hearing by the court, juvenile offenders may, under law, be held in **detention.** This is allowed if juveniles are potential runaways, cannot remain in their home for some reason, must be held for another jurisdiction, or present a distinct danger to themselves or someone else. Where it exists detention will likely be in a juvenile detention facility. In some places, however, juveniles are held in county or city jails. A few places forbid detention of juveniles in adult jail facilities. Despite this, it still occurs in places throughout the country.[42] In some courts detention in any facility is not allowed without a detention hearing within the juvenile court.[43] More notes:

> In the judicial area, many states have established detention hearing provisions, either mandatory, or on request after notice of the right to a hearing. These hearings must be held promptly after admission to detention—usually within 24 or 48 hours—and have served as an important screening device to reduce detained populations.[44]

Adjudicatory Hearings One of the most important functions of juvenile court is to hear the facts of a case and decide if an accused juvenile offender is delinquent. This takes place at the adjudicatory hearing. The juvenile court judge presides over what, since *Gault,* may closely resemble a trial in an adult criminal court. A few states even provide for juries in juvenile cases. As we noted, however, there is no constitutional right to a jury hearing. Counsel may be present for the juvenile and he or she enjoys other previously mentioned rights such as confrontation of witnesses and the standard of proof of "beyond a reasonable doubt."

After hearing the case the judge may dismiss the case or make a finding of delinquency. Should it be the latter, a date will be set for a dispositional hearing.

Disposition The purpose of a **dispositional hearing** is for all of the interested parties—judge, probation officer, prosecutor, defense attorney, and the child's parents—to get together and decide what is best for the child. These hearings have generally retained much of the informal nature that pervaded the courts prior to *Gault.* After listening to all those concerned, the judge must make the final disposition decision.

Most juvenile court judges have a wide range of dispositional alternatives available to them. To aid them in making a choice between alternatives, a **social history report** is prepared, usually by a probation officer. The report, similar to an adult pre-sentence investigation report, is the product of an intensive investigation into a juvenile's "background, family relations, mental and physical health, school performance, work record, and prior delinquent history."[45] Kerper notes that the report is generally started much earlier—upon the decision to file a petition—but is not read by the judge until completion of the adjudicatory hearing and a judgment of delinquency. To decide on an appropriate disposition, however, the judge is said to rely heavily on the report.[46]

Those dispositions handed down by the judge may include the following: (1) probation; (2) commitment to the state correctional authority for placement in an institution; (3) placement in a "foster home, a group home of some kind, or a child-serving institution which may specialize in the 'treatment' of specific kinds of youths, such as those who are handicapped, emotionally disturbed, or in need of special and remedial assistance;"[47] (4) dismissal, with or without reprimand; (5) fine; and (6) restitution. Cole describes another alternative: in the juvenile system certain cases are "continued without a finding" for an indefinite period. Although the label "delinquent" is not conferred, the court holds this in abeyance for possible use should a youth misbehave while under the informal supervision of a probation officer.[48] Selection of a particular disposition by the court will, of course, be influenced by available state or community resources. It should be noted again that for very serious crimes a juvenile may, in most jurisdictions, be tried in an adult criminal court.

JUVENILE CORRECTIONS

Juvenile corrections involves a range of possibilities similar to that for adult offenders. Included are forms of probation, institutionalization, and parole.

Probation

Of those juveniles referred to juvenile court, the single most frequent disposition is that of probation. Chamelin, Fox, and Whisenand point out that about half of the 900,000 cases referred to juvenile courts each year are "held open, dismissed, or adjusted in some way." About

50,000 of the remaining group are committed to institutions, and about 400,000 receive formal or informal probation.[49] Probation may be generally defined as the permitting of a juvenile offender to remain free in the community but under supervision of a probation officer and usually under certain specified conditions or restrictions. As indicated earlier, however, there are two kinds of probation.

Informal probation occurs during the court intake phase and prior to any filing of a petition. It is, as we earlier pointed out, one of the ways in which the court intake officer (frequently a probation officer) makes an informal adjustment of the case. The National Advisory Commission on Criminal Justice noted:

Informal probation, another method of nonjudicial handling of juvenile cases coming to the attention of the court, permits informal supervision of young persons by probation officers who wish to reserve judgment regarding the necessity for filing a petition until after a child has had the opportunity for some informal treatment.[50]

The commission suggested that informal probation had the advantages, among others, of avoiding "the stigma of a delinquent record and a delinquent reputation," and being "less costly than formal probation."[51]

Formal probation is one of the disposition alternatives available to the court after a formal finding of delinquency. It allows the juvenile who has been adjudicated delinquent to remain free in his or her community but under the supervision of a probation officer and under court-ordered conditions. There is substantial variation from place to place as to the nature of the probation supervision provided and to the conditions attached to probation. In some jurisdictions probation may be highly structured, with many regular contacts between the juvenile and the probation officer. In other jurisdictions exactly the opposite may be true.[52] Conditions may range from virtually none to a great many. They have frequently included school attendance, curfew, nonassociation with law violators, remaining in a specified locality (for example, the offender's community), reporting regularly to the probation officer, and obeying all laws. Failure to abide by court-ordered conditions can result in probation revocation and the placement of the juvenile in a state correctional institution. As Kerper points out, this is not usually done for minor violations of probation conditions but for the commission of another offense, leaving the court jurisdiction, or failing to report regularly to the probation officer.[53]

Probation supervision of juveniles, unlike that for adults, is largely a local affair. In twenty-six states and territories, probation is entirely local and in most others (nineteen) it is a combination of state and local. In only a few places does the state alone assume responsibility for probation services.[54] (See Table 14.3.)

Juvenile Institutions

There are a variety of institutions in which a juvenile may spend some time during his or her contact with the juvenile justice system. We have mentioned the detention center, which is generally locally operated and serves primarily as a temporary place of confinement for juveniles awaiting court action. Most juveniles judged delinquent and committed are assigned to **state training schools.** With few exceptions these are operated by the state. So, too, are the **outdoor-style institutions** such as ranches, forestry camps, and farms, which also are basically for delinquent youths. **Group homes** and **halfway houses** are frequently run by probation departments and "tend to be specialized institutions which are used for those youngsters needing special kinds of services and programs. These generally are much closer to the youngsters' homes and communities, so many ... attend regular schools or are employed, but live at the facility." **Shelters** do not generally house delinquent youths but are geared more toward those that are dependent or neglected.[55] Table 14.4 shows these different state and local correctional institutions and the numbers of juveniles in each. Of the 794 facilities mentioned in the table, 367 (46 percent) are operated at the state level, with the remaining 427 (54 percent) operated by cities or counties.

As we noted above, most (about 60 percent) institutionalized juvenile delinquents are sent to state training schools. While some of these

TABLE 14.3 Locale of Responsibility for Juvenile and Adult Probation Services

	Juvenile	Adult
Local	26	9
State, District of Columbia, territories	8	32
State and local	19	12

Source: American Correctional Association, *Juvenile and Adult Correctional Departments, Institutions, Agencies, and Paroling Authorities* (College Park, Md.: ACA, 1975), p. 250.

TABLE 14.4 Summary Statistics on State and Local Public Correctional Facilities for Juveniles (30 June, 1973)

	Number of Facilities	Number of Juveniles
Total	794	45,694
Training schools	187	26,427
Detention	319	10,782
Ranches, forestry camps, and farms	103	4,959
Reception and diagnostic centers	17	1,734
Group homes	90	889
Halfway houses	59	713
Shelters	19	190

Source: American Correctional Association, *Juvenile and Adult Correctional Departments, Institutions, Agencies, and Paroling Authorities* (College Park, Md.: ACA, 1975), p. 259.

are undoubtedly fine institutions, assessments of most have been very critical. Coffey contends that "the general failure of the training school is almost universally admitted."[56] Chamelin, Fox, and Whisenand assert:

> *The juvenile training school has been an enigma to correctional people for a long time. The recidivism rate is higher than it is in adult institutions, giving rise to the notion that the earlier a person gets into the criminal justice system, the longer he will stay in it. Whether by selection of the poorest risks for socialization or by conditioning in associating intimately with other delinquents for long periods of time, the principle holds true. There is reason to believe that both occur, reinforcing each other.*[57]

Vetter and Simonsen note that "Many state training schools are not much more than miniature reformatories," and "represent the most expensive and least successful method of handling juvenile offenders."[58]

Critics call for more nonjudicial alternatives such as diversion and the use of halfway houses, foster homes, and the like. Massachusetts, in fact, became so dissatisfied with its training schools that it simply abolished them and placed all occupants into residential settings, foster homes, or on parole.[59] Other states are said to be considering similar action.[60]

The length of time that a juvenile will spend in a state training school or other institution will vary from place to place. In general, courts have been able to commit a juvenile to an indefinite period of time, not to extend beyond the legal age of adulthood (eighteen to twenty-one). Some states, however, specify the maximum time that a youth may be held in an institution (for example, Connecticut, New Hampshire, and Washington, D.C., all specify two years).[61] While most states allow indeterminate dispositions (indefinite length) that could amount to many years depending on the age of the youth at confinement, the average stay is from six to ten months.

Juvenile Aftercare (Parole)

Upon release from a state training school or other institution, a young offender is frequently placed into a program known as **aftercare.** This program allows the juvenile freedom within the community but under supervision. Aftercare is another of those terms designed to reflect the differences between adult and juvenile justice. Like many other terms, this one has not been accepted everywhere and thus it is not uncommon to hear instead the term "juvenile parole."

The rationale for aftercare has been described by the President's Commission on Law Enforcement and Administration of Justice:

The rationale for aftercare is simple. Each juvenile must have a carefully planned, expertly executed, and highly individualized program if he is to return to life outside the institution and play a constructive role there. Successful reentry into society is often made difficult both by the effects of institutional life on a juvenile and by the attitudes of the community to which he returns. The aftercare plan for him must take both these factors into account.[62]

The commission pointed out that a good aftercare plan would make use of not only institutional resources but a variety of community resources as well. Further, it should not wait until the release of a juvenile but begin during confinement.[63] Overall, the concept of aftercare is much like that of probation in that both are aimed at prevention of further delinquent acts and the juvenile's adjustment to the varied and often complex demands of community and society.

When institutionalization of a juvenile is for an indefinite period of time, someone has to determine when he or she is ready for release. The releasing authority varies from state to state and can be the director of the institution in which the delinquent is kept, the juvenile court, a youth authority or commission, or some combination of these.

In general, the responsibility for aftercare services (not the decision to release) rests almost exclusively with the state. In only about a half dozen states does responsibility belong entirely at the local level or in the hands of both state and local agencies.

TEST YOURSELF

Define these key terms:

parens patriae
status offenses
dispositional hearing
juvenile aftercare

Answer the following questions:

1. Through what three stages has the juvenile justice process evolved and what was the theme of each?

2. What denials of rights did the Supreme Court say occurred in the *Gault* case?

3. Describe the problems that exist in trying to define "delinquency."

4. How is the way delinquency cases get into juvenile court different from the way criminal cases get into adult court?

5. List the types of institutions that are used for delinquents.

NOTES

1. Harold J. Vetter and Clifford E. Simonsen, *Criminal Justice in America* (Philadelphia: Saunders, 1976), p. 343.
2. Herbert H. Lou, *Juvenile Courts in the United States* (New York: Arno Press and the New York Times, reprint edition, 1972), pp. 13-14.
3. *In re Gault*, 387 U.S. 1 (1967).
4. Ibid.
5. Alan R. Coffey, *Juvenile Justice as a System* (Englewood Cliffs, N.J.: Prentice-Hall, 1974), pp. 36-37.
6. George F. Cole, *The American System of Criminal Justice* (N. Scituate, Mass.: Duxbury Press, 1975), p. 434.
7. *In re Gault*.
8. Ibid.
9. Ibid.
10. Ibid.
11. *In re Winship*, 397 U.S. 358 (1970).
12. *McKeiver* v. *Pennsylvania*, 403 U.S. 528 (1971).
13. H. Ted Rubin, "The Eye of the Juvenile Court Judge: A One-Step-Up View of the Juvenile Justice System," in Malcolm W. Klein, ed., *The Juvenile Justice System* (Beverly Hills, Calif.: Sage, 1976), pp. 136-37.
14. Ibid.
15. Cole, *American System*, p. 438.
16. Rubin, "Juvenile Court Judge," pp. 137-38.
17. Frank Miller et al., *The Juvenile Justice Process* (Mineola, N.Y.: Foundation Press, 1971), p. 1153.
18. Ibid.

19. Ibid.
20. Cole, *American System*, p. 436.
21. Hazel Kerper, *Criminal Justice System* (St. Paul, Minn.: West Publishing, 1972), pp. 388-89; and Board of Directors, National Council on Crime and Delinquency, "Jurisdiction over Status Offenses Should Be Removed from the Juvenile Court," *Crime and Delinquency* 21 (April 1975), p. 97.
22. Council of State Governments, "The States and the Criminal Justice System," *The Book of the States: 1976-77*, (Lexington, Ky.: Council of State Governments, 1976), p. 407.
23. NCCD, "Jurisdiction," pp. 98-99.
24. Council of State Governments, "The States," p. 408.
25. American Correctional Association, *Juvenile and Adult Correctional Departments, Institutions, Agencies, and Paroling Authorities* (College Park, Md.: ACA, 1975).
26. Kerper, *Criminal Justice*, p. 389.
27. Lawrence E. Cohen, *New Directions in Processing of Juvenile Offenders: The Denver Model* (Washington, D.C.: Government Printing Office, 1975), p. 11.
28. Andrew Rutherford and Robert McDermott, *Juvenile Diversion* (Washington, D.C.: Government Printing Office, 1976), p. 27.
29. Cole, *American System*, p. 436.
30. Coffey, *Juvenile Justice*, p. 63.
31. Paul K. Clare and John H. Kramer, *Introduction to American Corrections* (Boston: Holbrook Press, 1976), p. 10.
32. Cole, *American System*, p. 436.
33. Cohen, *Denver Model*, p. 13.
34. Rubin, "Juvenile Court Judge," pp. 133-34.
35. Ibid.
36. Clare and Kramer, *American Corrections*, p. 15.
37. Kerper, *Criminal Justice*, p. 390.
38. Cole, *American System*, p. 437.
39. Sanford J. Fox, *Juvenile Courts* (St. Paul, Minn.: West Publishing, 1971), p. 26.
40. Vetter and Simonsen, *Criminal Justice*, p. 347.
41. Fox, *Juvenile Courts*, p. 27. As of 1 January 1972, 92 percent of the states plus the District of Columbia showed no restrictions on who may file a petition. Michael J. Hindelang et al., *Sourcebook of Criminal Justice Statistics* (Washington, D.C.: Government Printing Office, 1976), p. 142.
42. National Council on Crime and Delinquency, *Criminal Justice Newsletter* 8 (14 February, 1977).
43. Hindelang et al., *Sourcebook*, p. 138.
44. Harry W. More, ed., *Principles and Procedures in the Administration of Justice* (New York: Wiley, 1975), p. 333.
45. Kerper, *Criminal Justice*, p. 392.
46. Ibid.
47. Alvin W. Cohn, *Crime and Justice Administration* (Philadelphia: Lippincott, 1976), p. 333.
48. Cole, *American System*, pp. 438-39.
49. Neil C. Chamelin, Vernon B. Fox, and Paul M. Whisenand, *Introduction to Criminal Justice* (Englewood Cliffs, N.J.: Prentice-Hall, 1975), pp. 348-49.
50. National Advisory Commission on Criminal Justice Standards and Goals, *Corrections* (Washington, D.C.: Government Printing Office, 1973), p. 255.
51. Ibid.
52. Cole, *American System*, p. 439.
53. Kerper, *Criminal Justice*, p. 395.
54. *ACA Correctional Departments*, pp. 250-57.
55. Cohn, *Crime*, pp. 336-37.
56. Coffey, *Juvenile Justice*, p. 128.

57. Chamelin, Fox, and Whisenand, *Criminal Justice*, p. 375.
58. Vetter and Simonsen, *Criminal Justice*, pp. 361-62.
59. ACA, *Correctional Departments*, p. 80.
60. Vetter and Simonsen, *Criminal Justice*, pp. 361-62.
61. ACA, *Correctional Departments*, pp. 25, 31, and 102.
62. President's Commission on Law Enforcement and Administration of Justice, *Task Force Report: Corrections* (Washington, D.C.: Government Printing Office, 1967), pp. 141-54.
63. Ibid.

PART VII
Toward a True System

CHAPTER 15
Innovations in Criminal Justice

OUTLINE

THE PARTIAL NATIONALIZATION OF CRIMINAL JUSTICE
    The Warren Court and Criminal Justice
    The President's Crime Commission
    Federal Legislation Since 1968
        Omnibus Crime Control and Safe Streets Act
        Crime Control Act of 1973
        Juvenile Justice and Delinquency Prevention Act
    The LEAA: Progress and Controversy
        Structure of the LEAA
        Programs of the LEAA
        Criticisms of the LEAA
    The National Advisory Commission on Criminal Justice Standards and Goals
        National Advisory Commission Recommendations
        Impact of NACCJSG Recommendations

INNOVATIONS WITHIN CRIMINAL JUSTICE COMPONENTS
    Law Enforcement
        Police Professionalization
        Innovations in Dealing with Crime and Other Services
    Prosecutors
        Education and Training
        Special Crime Programs
        Prosecution Standards
        Management Tools and Assistance
    Courts
    Corrections
        Professionalization of Staff
        The Des Moines Project and Its Impact

TOWARD A TRUE SYSTEM OF CRIMINAL JUSTICE
    Criminal Justice Information Systems
    Legislation and Code Revisions

OBJECTIVES

After reading this chapter the student should be able to:

Describe the federal legislation, especially the Omnibus Crime Control and Safe Streets Act, that broadens the federal role in criminal justice.

Outline and describe the structure and key programs of the Law Enforcement Assistance Administration.

Discuss the controversies surrounding the LEAA and its programs.

List the key recommendations of the National Advisory Commission on Criminal Justice Standards and Goals, and explain the importance of the project.

Discuss the innovations within law enforcement.

Discuss the innovations within prosecution.

Discuss the innovations within trial courts.

Discuss the innovations within corrections.

Describe the innovations and trends relevant to the entire criminal justice system.

Cite some indications that a true system of criminal justice is emerging.

KEY TERMS

categorical grants
block grants
discretionary grants
opportunity costs
external costs
professionalization
lateral entry
police unionization
job actions
affirmative action
team policing
neighborhood watch programs
crisis intervention
blind assignment of cases

☐ In this final section we will examine recent and current developments in the field of criminal justice with a focus on those changes that can truly be said to be departures from the traditions or practices of the past. In some cases the innovations are based on new ideas or concepts, but in other cases the changes amount to attempts to realize ideals that have been around for a long time. We will look at the changes in the environment of the criminal justice system that have given impetus to the innovations within the system, especially the shift in the role of the federal government, and then survey the innovations themselves. We are especially concerned with the attempts to break down or overcome the effects of fragmentation and the movement toward integration of the various components and agencies and the realization of a true system of criminal justice.

THE PARTIAL NATIONALIZATION OF CRIMINAL JUSTICE

Up to the 1960s it could safely be said that criminal justice was almost completely the responsibility of state and local governments. Federal criminal statutes were limited in their coverage, federal assistance to local law enforcement was generally in the areas of training and the processing of evidence, and the Supreme Court concerned itself with only the most notorious of violations of constitutional rights by state and local authorities. Then came the revolution.

The Warren Court and Criminal Justice

The revolution began with decisions of the Supreme Court in a series of cases appealed from various states. Many of the most important of these decisions came in the years 1961 through 1966, and these have already been discussed at various points earlier in this text. The importance of these cases goes beyond their individual impact on criminal processes—it encompasses the fact that the Supreme Court has become a permanently active part of the environment of the criminal justice system. Whatever decisions the Court makes in the current and upcoming years, it cannot return to its former isolation from and ignorance of the operations of law enforcement agencies, criminal trial courts, and correctional institutions and agencies. The meanings of the constitutional provisions have been clarified and nationalized—that is, made common for all authorities and all defendants. Even if the Court narrows the applications or meanings of its former pronouncements, and the pendulum swings in favor of police and prosecutors and against the interests of defendants, we will not return to the days when the law and the rights of the accused were whatever the local or state officials wanted them to be.

The emergence of standards of due process common to all states and localities is part of the movement toward a true system of criminal justice in America. It may have, in fact, stimulated many of the other steps that have been taken in this direction, especially those that seek to overcome organizational fragmentation between federal, state, and local agencies.

The President's Crime Commission

In 1967 a presidential commission released a report based on months of work by several task forces established to study and report on various aspects of crime and justice in the United States. The President's Commission on Law Enforcement and the Administration of Justice was the first such commission to examine the subject since 1931. Its report, *The Challenge of Crime in a Free Society*, was backed up by detailed reports from separate task forces, which studied the police, the courts (including prosecutors), corrections agencies and programs, and selected special topics such as juvenile delinquency, organized crime, and science and technology.[1] Experts from many fields, including law, sociology, economics, and public administration, participated in or contributed to the effort, and the government disseminated the results throughout the country.

The commission's reports contained descriptive and analytical materials and recommendations for action to improve the system. These recommendations ran the gamut from major organizational and structural overhauls to revisions of penal codes, and from changes in procedures to steps to develop more professionalism among agency personnel. In the year following the issuance of these reports, Congress took action.

Federal Legislation Since 1968

Omnibus Crime Control and Safe Streets Act In 1968 Congress passed and the president signed a sweeping act that made some changes in the federal criminal justice process. Its real importance, however, lay in its assumption of a broad federal responsibility for encouraging changes in the administration of justice at the state and local levels. Since 1965 there had been an Office of Law Enforcement Assistance (OLEA) within the Justice Department that offered **categorical**

grants to law enforcement agencies—for example, grants for specific projects to be operated at the local level but expressly approved by OLEA, the granting agency. This very limited three-year experiment was replaced with a large-scale program of **block grants**—awards of blocks of funds to state planning agencies, which were then to use them for state and local projects approved by the state agency. The purposes of this new program were

> ... to: (1) encourage states and units of local government to prepare and adopt comprehensive plans based upon their evaluation of state and local problems of law enforcement; (2) authorize grants to states and local units of government in order to improve and strengthen law enforcement; and (3) encourage the research and development of new methods for the prevention and reduction of crime and the detection and apprehension of criminals.[2]

To administer this program the Law Enforcement Assistance Administration (LEAA) was created and placed within the Department of Justice, absorbing the old OLEA. It set out upon uncharted seas without a captain since its administrator and two associate administrators had to agree on everything before action could be taken.[3] For four years LEAA operated without clear leadership but managed to award almost $2.5 billion in grants.

Crime Control Act of 1973 In 1973 Congress overhauled the LEAA, made the administrator the agency's sole director, and altered the grants process. Since the passage of the Crime Control Act in 1973, the LEAA has required agencies to match only 10 percent of the cost of any action project in its first year. The LEAA (since 1971) has required the match to be in specifically allocated funds and not in facilities or services—a so-called match in kind—but the lowering of the percentage in 1973 encouraged many more agencies to seek funds. The LEAA has also provided up to 100 percent of funding for regional planning units within the states.[4] These smaller planning bodies usually cover several counties.

Juvenile Justice and Delinquency Prevention Act In 1974 Congress passed the Juvenile Justice and Delinquency Prevention Act, which established grants for projects in juvenile justice, and set up the Office of Juvenile Justice and Delinquency Prevention within LEAA. This act contains one condition that goes beyond requiring generalized plans for improvements in the justice system: states that receive funds under this act must abolish the use of detention in cases involving only so-called status offenses by juveniles. The failure of states to apply for the monies available led to a recent decision that states, in order to be eligible, must only show good faith in trying to move toward the realization of that goal.[5] This situation illustrates the kinds of conflicts that abound in proposals to improve the system and the kinds of rules the federal government can seek to impose as a condition of obtaining funds.

The LEAA: Progress and Controversy

From 1969 through 1976 LEAA has pumped $5 billion of federal funds into criminal justice projects. It has also stimulated and overseen some marked changes in the criminal justice agencies and processes within the states. At the same time the LEAA and the programs it has stimulated have been the subject of continuous controversy both within and outside the criminal justice system.

Structure of the LEAA The Law Enforcement Assistance Administration is a bureau of the Justice Department, equivalent organizationally to the Bureau of Prisons, the DEA, the INS, and the U.S. Marshalls. In addition to its several staff or support divisions, the LEAA boasts five operational offices, one of which oversees the activities of the ten regional offices located in major cities throughout the country. As of this writing, however, plans were being made to close the regional offices of the LEAA and concentrate all activities in Washington. (See the organizational chart in Figure 15.1.)

The National Institute of Law Enforcement and Criminal Justice is the research arm of LEAA. It sponsors research into a broad range of topics and produces practical guides and reports for use by agencies and educators. In 1974 the National Institute assumed responsibility for evaluating projects funded with LEAA grants, developing techniques of project evaluation, assisting local agencies in setting up their own evaluation systems, and assessing the overall impact of LEAA on criminal justice in America. It also houses an Office of Technology Transfer that attempts to provide specific advice to agencies on "how to do it." It publishes *Prescriptive Packages*, which attempt to answer the most asked questions, and *Exemplary Projects* brochures, which describe the projects judged to be the most innovative and effective among those funded.[6]

The National Criminal Justice Information and Statistics Service is the data collection and disseminating arm of LEAA. It conducts surveys and publishes its results in several categories of topics, including crime victimization, the populations of jails, prisons, and juvenile detention centers, and expenditure and employment levels for criminal

FIGURE 15.1 Organization of the Law Enforcement Assistance Administration

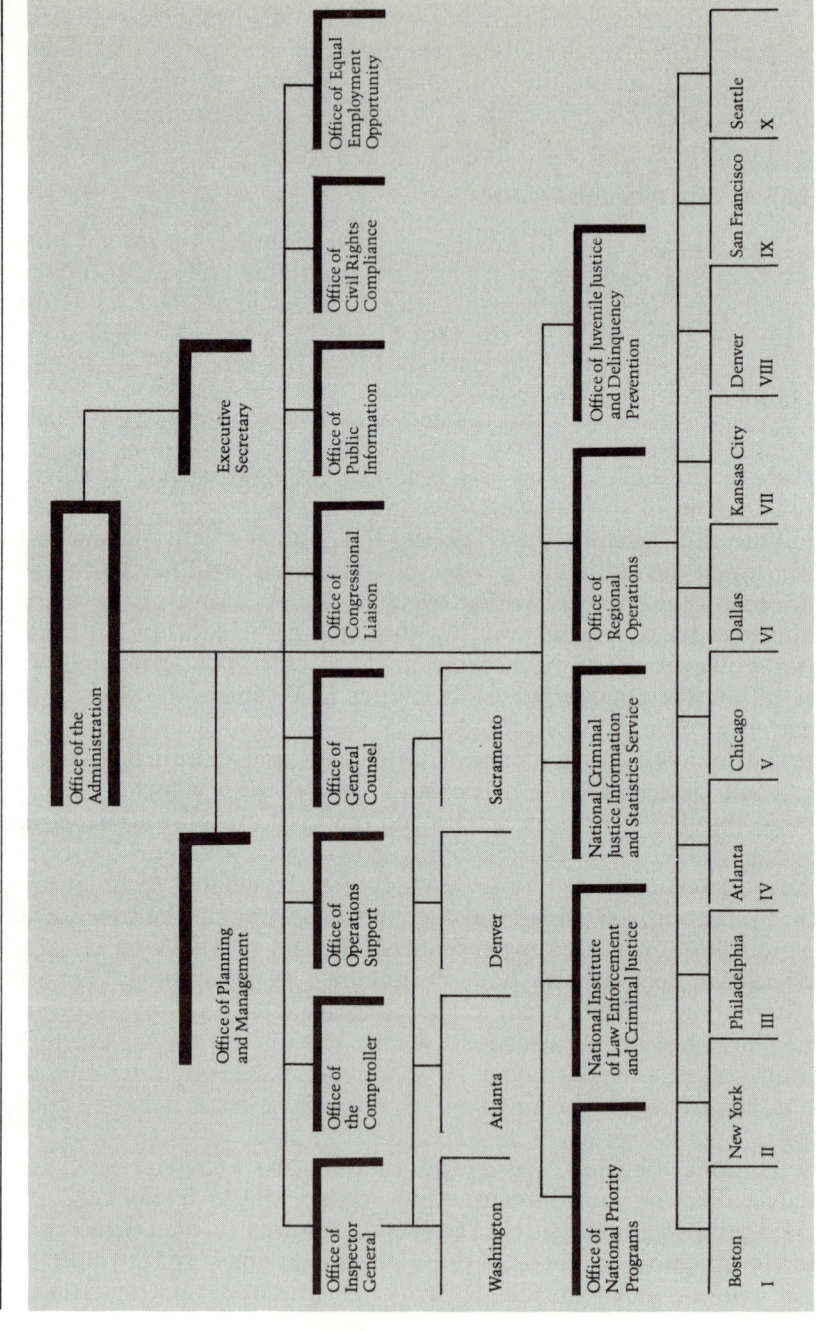

Source: Law Enforcement Assistance Administration, *Orientation Handbook* (Washington, D.C.: Government Printing Office, 1975), p. II-2.

justice agencies. Since 1974 the service has also had the responsibilities of promoting the development of comprehensive criminal justice information systems, the use of electronic data processing in these systems, and the implementation of measures to insure the security of these systems from illicit use in order to protect the privacy of individuals on whom information is stored by these systems.[7]

We will have more to say about research, evaluation, and information systems in connection with innovations within the criminal justice system itself.

Programs of the LEAA   The Omnibus Crime Control and Safe Streets Act declared that "crime is a local problem" requiring local solutions. Thus followed the adoption of the block form of grants to states. State planning agencies, in cooperation with local units of government and regional planning units, are supposed to devise plans that will make the best use of the funds. As Michael Serrill explains:

The theory was that state and local officials, with help from a new breed of college-educated planners and analysts, would sit down together periodically to decide exactly what needed to be done to reduce crime and upgrade the criminal justice systems in their jurisdictions. They would try new and innovative programs, then rigorously evaluate those efforts to see if they were effective. The failures would be thrown out, the successes expanded. The result, it was reasoned by the Act's supporters, would inevitably be a reduction in crime.[8]

Amendments to the act have tightened up the planning requirements, stipulated that localities and regions with 250,000 persons or more should have their own planning units, and even authorized interstate metropolitan or regional boards.[9] Steps in the full process are supposed to include the following: (1) individual agencies submit problem statements and preliminary requests to the responsible regional or state planning agency; (2) the planning board assesses the needs and drafts an annual comprehensive plan containing its goals and priorities; (3) the planning unit is allocated its share of block funds (where regional units exist, they receive shares of the funds the state units receive); (4) requesting agencies whose projects were authorized submit full applications for their share of the funds allocated to the planning units; (5) the applications are scrutinized by planning board staffs; (6) funds are awarded to those agencies whose applications meet specified criteria and who can meet the matching requirements; (7) the planning unit monitors and evaluates implemented projects; (8) the successful projects that require further grant funding are given priority in the next cycle.

State planning agencies devise plans to make the best use of LEAA funds.

In addition to this block grant approach, LEAA has also used a portion of its funds to operate a **discretionary grant program.** This involves direct grants to criminal justice agencies for large-scale projects that deal with specific matters—such as white-collar or organized crime—and that have a high priority but would cost states too large a share of block funds. These projects are listed in a discretionary *Guideline Manual*—a kind of catalog—published each year.

Another program of LEAA is the Law Enforcement Education Program through which college and universities receive funds to cover the tuition and other expenses of criminal justice personnel who are seeking degrees in criminal justice or related programs. The obvious purpose of this effort is to assist in the professionalization of criminal justice personnel. While in-service (working) personnel have first priority, students who intend to pursue careers in the field also receive support on many campuses.

Criticisms of the LEAA As early as its second year of operation, LEAA was being attacked on various grounds. Among the criticisms were that funds were being squandered on projects that had little or nothing to do with reducing crime, that far too much money was going into police hardware such as riot control equipment, that LEAA could not even keep track of what its funds were being spent for, and that state agencies were cheating high-crime areas of major cities in favor of suburbs by distributing funds on a population per capita basis.[10]

Many of these same criticisms were repeated during 1973 and 1976, the years in which Congress was faced with the question of whether or not to extend the life of the agency. Michael Serrill writes:

Many observers now say that LEAA suffered greatly from unrealistic expectations. The program was launched, they say, with the same kind of heady rhetoric characteristic of other Johnson administration social programs. The message was that the crime problem, like the poverty problem, was more a failure of national will than anything else.[11]

Gerald Caplan, director of the National Institute of Law Enforcement and Criminal Justice, commented on this phenomenon in a December 1975 speech:

At the time, when we were about to land a man on the moon, perhaps it did not seem so difficult to purge the nation of its muggers, rapists, thieves, corrupt officials and white-collar criminals.... There was a feeling in the air that, if only some bright people would just work very hard at it, a harvest of plummeting crime rates would ensue.[12]

Crime rates have not, of course, plummeted—or even been much retarded in their growth. LEAA did indeed suffer from the inflated expectations of those who would try to solve problems by "throwing money at them," but it also suffered from circumstances not of its making. Among these are the following: the deliberate placing of responsibility with state agencies for determining needs and priorities; the tendency of officials to spend funds on highly visible projects for which long-term commitments need not be made (in case the federal funds dried up); and the tendency of local and state governments to use federal funds to supplant (substitute for) funds they would have spent for certain projects anyway. Efforts have been made by LEAA and by Congress in new legislation to correct these faults, but the more strings and controls placed on the funds, the less desirable they become. One runs into the complaint that complying with all the conditions placed on would-be recipients and the paperwork required to meet the ever-increasing reporting requirements are so costly or stifling in themselves that the grants are not worth having.

There is also a paradox built into the dual objectives of LEAA: to reduce crime and improve the system. By improving the system, especially in terms of its effectiveness in dealing with offenders, rates of reported crime may in the short run be driven up. The enhanced ability of police to detect it, the increased potency of prosecution, the improved ability of courts to dispose of cases, and the resultant increased willingness of victims and witnesses to report crime would tend to increase the crime rate without any real increase in crime. It could be argued that real crime reduction would not be apparent for a number of years.

Defenders of LEAA make another point: LEAA funds have amounted to only 5 percent of all funds spent by local and state governments for criminal justice. LEAA Administrator Richard Velde has said it is "unrealistic" to expect his agency's funds and activities to have any impact on the national crime rate. He does point out, however, that certain LEAA-sponsored projects seem to be having an effect on certain types of crimes and recidivism in their localities.[13]

The 1976 renewal of LEAA for three more years included provisions designed to force LEAA and states to demonstrate that sponsored projects were successful in reducing crime or improving the system in a measurable way.[14] It will be interesting to see whether the attempts to tighten up will really stop waste or simply make it difficult to fund projects whose benefits are difficult or impossible to tabulate.

One of the most sweeping attacks on LEAA came from the governor of California, Gerald Brown. Through fiscal 1976 California received $425 million in LEAA funds, but Governor Brown believes most of it was wasted. He described LEAA as a "Byzantine pretzel palace" and its projects as "leaf-raking projects for white-collar workers." He says LEAA is a "bureaucratic maze" that is not doing anything useful but is making local officials do a "bureaucratic dance" to obtain funds. Brown is especially vehement in discussing the jargon used by LEAA, calling it "utter gibberish," "gobbledygook," and "subversive of American institutions," because "only the illuminati can understand it."[15] As far as we know, there has been no direct response from LEAA spokespeople regarding the governor's comments on red tape and the use of an elitist jargon. As noted above, new requirements created by the Congress may even add new steps to the "bureaucratic dance."

The National Advisory Commission on Criminal Justice Standards and Goals

The National Advisory Commission on Criminal Justice Standards and Goals (NACCJSG), created in 1971 under the auspices of LEAA, followed up on the President's Crime Commission by drawing up sets of standards for every facet of the criminal justice system and specific goals the commission believed the system ought to strive to achieve. It issued a series of volumes in 1973 dealing, respectively, with the entire criminal justice system, police, courts, corrections, and community crime prevention. We have mentioned several of the recommendations of this commission throughout this text, but a brief overview of some of the more important ones will provide a better impression of the tone of the entire project.

National Advisory Commission Recommendations The NACCJSG urged police departments to take on crime prevention as a high-priority function and to work with citizens and businesses to involve them in securing their properties, reporting suspicious activities, and denying criminal opportunities through architectural design of residential and business buildings. It called for written departmental policies on use of police authority, law enforcement priorities, and treatment of misconduct. The commission urged police to cooperate in efforts to keep people out of the system through various diversionary and treatment efforts. It recommended consolidation of small (ten persons or less) police departments, requiring new recruits to have some college education, setting up special units to work with other criminal justice components, increased use of civilian personnel, and several technical and procedural changes.[16]

The NACCJSG made a number of specific recommendations regarding courts, including prosecution, defense, and court management. It urged tight screening of cases and offenders using standards that would divert many out of the system. Diversion programs, on the other hand, should be used only for those who would benefit from them. In one of its most controversial recommendations, the commission called for the abolition of plea bargaining by 1977 and the development of standards and guidelines for its conduct until the abolition becomes possible. The NACCJSG urged standardization of sentencing, a more limited use of incarceration, but tougher treatment of recidivists and dangerous offenders. Judges should be selected on merit and subject to discipline and removal for conduct short of the crimes required to have a judge impeached. Other recommendations included efforts to professionalize and make a career of prosecution and public defense, the use of modern court and case-flow management techniques, the employment of court administrators, and the unification of state court systems.[17]

For the corrections component the NACCJSG had sixty-three separate recommendations covering every aspect of treatment of convicted offenders. The commission urged full access to courts and the assistance of counsel to inmates who seek to challenge their convictions, sentences, prison conditions, or rights violations. It called on custodial facilities to provide healthful and protective environments to inmates and to allow them religious practices and access to the public. It also called for due process in discipline and grievance procedures. Classification committees should include representatives of the community and should employ agreed-to criteria. The commission also favored well-planned community-based efforts that would involve the full use of existing community resources and services.[18]

The NACCJSG recommendations for the juvenile system included the development of intake criteria and services as well as specific standards for police handling, intake processing, the use of detention, and diversion programs.[19]

The commission addressed other subjects, such as the need for comprehensive planning in criminal justice, consolidation or unification of agencies, methods of evaluating programs, and the need for legislation to correct certain faults in the system and humanize treatment of offenders. A separate volume dealt with various ways in which citizens should be involved in crime prevention and governments should deal with and limit opportunities for corruption.[20]

Impact of NACCJSG Recommendations The publication of the National Advisory Commission's reports on standards and goals set off a flurry of debate on many of its provisions. Most of the specific recommendations were recapitulations of provisions to be found in the reports of the President's Crime Commission and studies done by the American Bar Association, the American Bar Institute, the Judicature Society, the American Corrections Association, the National Council on Crime and Delinquency, and countless other groups. Nevertheless, the fact that these were the recommendations of a government commission, and their adoption by the LEAA as a set of guidelines against which states should draw up their own standards and goals, gave them more impact than those of other groups.[21]

The recommendation that plea bargaining be abolished found many supporters among police officials but was rejected by prosecutors.[22] It is interesting to note, however, that some jurisdictions are adopting standards and criteria for plea bargaining, and others are experimenting with abolishing it for certain classes or types of crimes, such as armed robberies.

A common complaint about many of the standards and goals is that they carry a prohibitive cost. The National Institute of Law Enforcement and Criminal Justice has commissioned a number of cost analyses of the correctional standards to assist states and localities in estimating the financial impact of adopting them. In its treatment of institutional-based programs and parole, the study group even projected costs of incarceration versus parole or probation in terms of two types of costs: **opportunity costs**—that is, lost inmate productivity in the economy—and **external costs** borne by private and public agencies for inmate services such as public health.[23] Thus the intent is to help governments estimate the total costs of various alternatives and not just the direct cost of any one program.

LEAA is obviously serious about promoting standards and goals whether they are the specific ones adopted by the NACCJSG or not. It requires state plans and regional plans to contain statements as to their standards and goals and is supposed to approve only those projects consistent with those standards and goals.

INNOVATIONS WITHIN CRIMINAL JUSTICE COMPONENTS

A number of innovations have been taking place within each of the components of the criminal justice system. A brief look at some of the more important ones will give an impression of current trends.

Law Enforcement

Law enforcement, especially the local police, has undergone considerable change over the past decade or so. There is said to be some resistance to change among many old-line chiefs and even more inertia within the rank and file of departments.[24] Nevertheless, some large and medium-sized departments have attempted dramatic breaks with elements of the past. A number of new approaches and techniques have been introduced, often with the aid of LEAA.

There appear to be two purposes in the changes that are being made. One is to increase the technical and professional capability of police to detect crime and apprehend offenders. The other is to enlist citizens in the fight against crime. The latter purpose is in contrast to the effect, whether intended or not, of the modernization of police that took place in the fifties and sixties, that effect being largely to create greater distance in the relations between police and citizens. The most obvious illustration of this trend was the replacement of beat-walking police with police in cars. Efforts are now being made to overcome the loss of police-citizen interaction without losing the mobility and ability to respond to calls for assistance that cars provide.

Police Professionalization One of the most persistent themes of the past several years has concerned the **professionalization** of police. Morris Cogan has defined a profession in the following terms:

> ... *a vocation whose practice is founded upon an understanding of the theoretical structure of some department of learning or science, and upon the abilities accompanying such understanding. This understanding and these abilities are applied to the vital affairs of man. The practices of the profession are modified by knowledge of a generalized nature and by the accumulated wisdom and experience of mankind, which serve to correct the errors of specialism. The profession, serving the vital needs of man, considers its first ethical imperative to be altruistic service to the client.*[25]

There can be legitimate doubt as to whether any vocation meets all the standards set forth in this definition. There can be substantial doubt as to whether there are more than a handful of law enforcement agencies that consistently serve all these standards. Yet most police officials agree that they establish a goal toward which police service should strive, and most observers acknowledge that law enforcement generally meets certain of the criteria. Requirements for education and training have steadily intensified. Several states have established police standards boards that attempt to set standards of education and training for departments and develop criteria for recruitment, promotion, and raises. Supreme Court decisions have tended to force police to learn rules of evidence, procedure, and defendants' rights as well as to rely on means of solving crimes other than "dragnet" arrests and interrogations. We will look at a number of ways in which police are moving toward professionalism.

With regard to education and training of police, criminal justice programs have appeared on hundreds of college and university campuses within the past ten or so years as the LEAA has funded their creation and subsidized the enrollment of personnel. Many question the need for college educations for street patrol officers, but the resistance, most of it from old-line officers, is being overcome.[26] Others have been critical of many colleges' programs and the quality of their teaching faculty.[27] A truly academic discipline—based on knowledge drawn from sociology, law, public administration, and other fields—is, however, emerging.

More and more departments are setting up and requiring training at police academies. Many put recruits through several hundred hours of training before they are assigned, and in-service officers are being required to put in specified numbers of hours in refresher programs in which they learn new techniques, polish skills, and learn the latest legal and procedural rules. Some of these academies bring in instructors from nearby colleges, prosecuting attorneys, and others whose knowledge is considered useful.

A side effect of police attendance at colleges is the attack this constitutes on the traditional isolation of police officers from other citizens. They mix with other students on campuses and in many classes, and this may tend to relieve some of the societal tension and establish communications between the "fuzz" and the "freaks." Even some academically trained college professors may benefit from the representation of the law enforcement personnel.

Another aspect of professionalism is the ability of persons to obtain employment in any agency or office in the country at a level commensurate with their knowledge, skills, and experience. This is the principle of **lateral entry,** and it is not yet common to police. The President's Crime Commission criticized the "provincialism" of police departments in 1967, and many observers assert that it has not changed. Police must still advance through the ranks within one agency, and an attempt to enter another agency places the officer back at the bottom in seniority and benefits.[28]

While there has been little advancement in lateral entry for officers, many larger departments have begun to hire chiefs from outside. In 1974 the LEAA and the International Association of Chiefs of Police established a Police Chief Executive Committee whose purpose was to research the tenure and recruitment of police chiefs, commanders, commissioners, and the like, and to draw up specific standards and criteria for police leadership, for selection of police chiefs, and for retention of qualified chiefs.[29] A few police executives, including Patrick Murphy, O. W. Wilson, and Robert DiGrazia, have commanded several large departments in their distinguished careers. The controversy continues, however, as to whether a police executive class can emerge that can effectively command various police departments in markedly differing environments, or whether outsiders create more problems than they solve within a given department. Until the problems of lateral entry for police and their leaders are dealt with, however, it can be argued that there is no real police profession in the United States.

A very important development related to the subject of police professionalism is that of **police unionization.** According to a recent estimate, 150,000 of the approximately 600,000 law enforcement officers in the nation are represented by collective-bargaining units. Of this number, 25,000 were in national unions—15,000 as Teamsters and 10,000 in municipal employees unions.[30] The majority of those organized were members of organizations that are not technically unions but have taken on many of their characteristics, such as the Police Benevolent Association or the Fraternal Order of Police.[31] Some cities and counties are required to bargain with one or more of these organizations. Police strikes are generally illegal, but police have found ways to engage in so-called **job actions**—expressions of displeasure short of strikes. Among these are attacks of "blue flu," a situation in which large numbers of officers call in sick and stay off the job.

The subject of unionization of police and collective bargaining is naturally a very controversial one. Some argue that it is fundamentally incompatible with the police role in society and principles of police organization.[32] Still others argue that union organization may stimulate more professionalism among officers than has the traditional administration of police forces.[33] In any case, it is a development not likely to be reversed, and its impact on law enforcement is difficult to predict.

Another topic related to the professionalization of police work is the impact of the Federal Equal Opportunity Act and the requirements of the Equal Employment Opportunity Commission that departments in cities or counties that receive federal funds demonstrate that they do not discriminate against women or minority groups in hiring, assigning, promoting, or compensating police officers. Women have been involved in police work since the nineteenth century, but only recently have women officers joined their male colleagues in street patrol. Police administrators have mixed reactions to this phenomenon. A study of the comparative behavior of policemen and policewomen in Washington, D.C., found some differences in the levels of traffic citations and misdemeanor arrests and a tendency to avoid dispatching women to scenes of violence or potential violence. On the other hand, researchers found no significant differences in felony arrests or overall effectiveness.[34] Increased use of women in all phases of law enforcement seems inevitable and desirable.

Police departments are under great pressure to recruit blacks and other minority group members and to assign and treat them on an equal basis with white officers. Departments with low ratios of nonwhite officers to white officers are expected to engage in so-called **affirmative action** (giving preference to nonwhite applicants) to raise the percentage of nonwhites. Chicago is one city whose department has been ordered to favor nonwhite applicants and achieve a quota.[35] Many officials complain that efforts to hire more nonwhites have failed due to minority groups' antipathy toward police work, and some rank and file white officers complain of reverse discrimination against them. Nevertheless, efforts to improve the role of nonwhites in police work are bound to continue, federal pressure or not.

The final topic relative to police professionalism is the increased employment of civilian personnel to perform various duties within departments. Theoretically, civilians can be used to do anything except perform the searches, arrests, investigations, and other legal functions that require sworn officers. Many departments have hired civilians for clerical, staff, communications, and other work with the notion of releasing more uniformed officers for street and crime-fighting duties at less cost than hiring more sworn personnel. Whether civilians are effective in some of these jobs and whether they jeopardize the security and confidentiality required for police work are matters of debate.[36]

There are, as we can see, many trends in the attempts to improve and professionalize police work in the nation. Some of them appear divergent—that is, aimed in different directions. Their long-run impact remains to be seen. They cannot be viewed separately from other trends in police work, either—those trends concerning the use of innovative techniques of crime fighting and providing other services. These are our next concern.

Innovations in Dealing with Crime and Other Services There is an almost bewildering array of experiments being conducted throughout the country to improve police services and deal more effectively with the crime problem. They range from different ways of assigning patrol units and putting officers back on walking beats to almost total reorganization of police departments using new concepts of administration and responsibility for various aspects of police work. We will deal with only a few of the more important changes.

Some police departments have established special investigative units to deal with particularly serious crime problems. We do not mean SWAT teams, but projects such as the New York Street Crime Unit. This unit employs carefully selected and specially trained officers who utilize plainclothes surveillance and decoy tactics and who are specially equipped with a fleet of taxis, unmarked cars and vans, cameras, and communications gear. They focus on robberies and assaults, including rapes. The unit achieved a significant decrease in target crimes in test areas of the city and was selected as an "exemplary project" by LEAA.[37]

Another approach that has received a good deal of publicity recently is the operation of a "swap shop," which purchases stolen goods from burglars and thieves. After weeks or months of acting as a fence should act, but tape-recording and keeping detailed records of all transactions, the police round up all those who have sold stolen items to their shop. In Washington, D.C., police were able to operate two such shops and stage two massive roundups within months of each other.[38]

Another innovation more sweeping in scope than the others is called

team policing. There are variations on the theme, but the basic concept involves decentralization of police authority and responsibility to quasi-autonomous teams assigned to designated neighborhoods. The concept is called "full-service neighborhood team policing." The team may range in size from twenty to forty persons and should include patrol officers, investigators, other support staff, and team supervisors or commanders.[39]

Team policing involves more than simply reassigning personnel and reorganizing time schedules or shifts. As Paul Whisenand puts it, "team policing is a vast structural-functional change in law enforcement."[40] It involves management principles quite different from those of hierarchy and chain-of-command that have dominated police administration.

Peter Block and David Specht have contrasted traditional police methods with those of team policing. Among the steps that they find to be truly innovative are the adoption of what can be called participatory management (supervisors consult team members in making policy), extended rather than rotated assignments, strong emphasis on community relations by patrol officers through street contacts and attendance at community functions and meetings, and planning at the team level with review by superiors.[41]

The anticipated benefits of team policing are to provide a more effective attack on crime, to reestablish close relationships between citizens and their neighborhood policeman, and to increase the job satisfaction of police officers themselves.[42] The challenge to police officials is to accept the notion of decentralized authority, to allow many officers to be generalists rather than specialists, and to give the concept a chance to work by carefully selecting and training team members, then turning responsibility for most police work over to the teams.

Aside from the dramatic changes required in terms of police administration, team policing also means a dedication to establishing a rapport with the community and becoming a social service agency interested in more than law enforcement and maintenance of order. These latter functions are supposed to be served more effectively as a result of voluntary citizen information and cooperation, which aids the police in crime detection, investigation, and in isolating potentially violent situations.

Team policing has been tried in more than a score of cities. A change in police commissioners led to the abandonment of the effort in Detroit, and it is deemed less than a success in several other places.[43] On the other hand, Holyoke, Massachusetts, Los Angeles, and other cities rated their programs as beneficial to police and citizens and successful in reducing crime. The experiments continue.[44]

There are other projects that focus on police-community relations and crime prevention. These include neighborhood watch programs and crisis intervention training.

In **neighborhood watch programs** police encourage groups of citizens to cooperate in crime prevention—specifically, theft of valuable items—by having them install security and alarm devices and watch each other's homes and apartments for suspicious activities.[45]

In **crisis intervention** police are trained to cope with family and neighborhood quarrels and other situations that hold a potential for violence or crimes. The object is to assure peace without making arrests, thus diverting the matter from the formal process.[46]

No one approach is likely to have a significant impact on crime. The hope that crime can be reduced probably rests on combining all the innovative methods discussed here with the development of professionalism among law enforcement officers, plus successful changes in

Police are placing more emphasis on establishing rapport with the community and becoming a social service agency.

other components and the system as a whole. It is to the other components, beginning with the prosecutor, we now turn.

Prosecutors

There appear to be four innovations of importance taking place in criminal prosecution. They are the development of educational and training programs, the creation of special units within offices to handle selected types of cases, the attempt to articulate standards and policies for charging and plea bargaining, and the movement toward use of management concepts and tools.

Education and Training For years some large offices of prosecution have engaged in limited in-service training of new assistants, and some states have initiated seminars and other programs prosecutors can attend to learn the latest in law, rules, and methods of prosecution. It is only recently, however, that education and training in the fundamentals of prosecution came to be a matter of national concern. The National College of District Attorneys was founded with the assistance of the National District Attorneys Association (NDAA) a few years ago, and its programs have earned accreditation from many state bar associations. The college offers career and executive prosecutors courses in its facilities in the College of Law at the University of Houston in Texas, and it also operates seminars in special topics at various locations throughout the country.[47]

Special Crime Programs Across the country many medium-sized and large offices of prosecution are establishing special units or divisions to handle cases that fall within specified categories of serious crime problems. Many of these units are projects supported with grants from LEAA and assistance from the National District Attorney's Association. The most common areas of concentration are organized crime, economic or white-collar crime, corruption, cargo theft and fencing operations, drug abuse, and offenses committed by career offenders.

One of the earliest efforts of this kind was the creation of the Major Offense Bureau of the Office of the District Attorney for Bronx, New York.[48] The bureau employs twenty-two persons, including nine trial assistants. It uses the checklist illustrated in Chapter 7 to identify offenders who should be diverted from the normal case flow and given special attention by the bureau. The criteria considered include the nature and heinousness of the offense, the prior record of the alleged offender, and the strength of the evidence. Cases flagged for bureau action are prepared for grand jury review within three days, and defendants are arraigned on the very day indictments are filed. Trials are generally conducted within thirty to ninety days in one of two trial divisions of the court set aside to handle these major offenses. According to reports filed with the LEAA, the bureau has achieved the following results:

The MOB has a median time of 97 days from arrest to case disposition compared to a median time of 400 days for other bureaus within the D.A.'s office;

The MOB has an overall conviction rate of 96 percent. Though not strictly comparable to MOB cases, a comparison group selected from the case load of the D.A.'s Supreme Court Bureau has a rate of 84 percent. Similarly, the MOB has a conviction rate at trial of 92 percent, while the comparison group has a 52 percent rate of conviction at trial;

Ninety-four percent of MOB convictions result in sentences of incarceration as contrasted with 79 percent of the comparison group cases. In 1975 the MOB defendant's average maximum sentence was 10 years while the defendant from the comparison group had an average maximum of 3.5 years.[49]

In many offices of prosecution, white-collar crime and fraud programs are being supported by the NDAA through its Economic Crime Project Center. Each issue of the *Prosecutor* carries a section of news dealing with the various economic crime projects operated by prosecutors throughout the country.[50]

Welfare fraud is the latest type of crime to receive special attention, and the NDAA has allied itself with a new National Welfare Fraud Association to mount a coordinated attack on fraud perpetrated by vendors of medical and other subsidized services as well as on recipients who file false claims.[51] The association is made up of prosecutors, investigators, probation officers, and other professionals and interested citizens. The investigations and prosecutions of vendors—such as providers of medical services that receive Medicaid reimbursements—are particularly difficult due to what the association's president, Robert Neilson, points out is the "affluence and prestige that vendors enjoy in a local community."[52]

Prosecution Standards Concern about disparities in charging and the controversy surrounding plea bargaining—especially since the NACCJSG report recommended its abolition—have led prosecutors' offices, state associations of prosecutors, and the NDAA to struggle with the development of articulated standards and criteria for prosecutors to follow. More and more manuals for prosecutors contain specific guidelines and statements of office policy. Now the NDAA has published a document containing a national set of standards and goals for prosecutors.[53] The effort to reduce outright disparity and to provide adequate bases upon which prosecutors can continue to individualize justice will no doubt continue.

Management Tools and Assistance Perhaps the most fundamental change in offices of prosecution is the awakening of prosecuting attorneys to the principles of office management and public administration. Not only must budget requests be prepared and office supplies and equipment be managed, but personnel, the case load and its attendant paperwork must be managed as well. Several years ago the LEAA and NDAA created the Office of Prosecution Management to study prosecution needs and practices and provide technical assistance to offices. In Washington, D.C., the Prosecution Management Information System was developed. It enables the U.S. attorney's office to track cases and defendants, to use quantified criteria in the making of decisions, and to generate statistics on case loads and dispositions. Variations on this type of system have appeared in large and medium-sized offices throughout the United States. A nonprofit association, the Institute for Law and Social Research in Washington, has assumed control of the Prosecution Management Information System, with the mission of developing its full potential as a management and research tool and assisting offices in adapting it to their own needs.[54]

As for the Office of Prosecution Management, it has been succeeded by NDAA's Management, Evaluation, and Contracts Division. This office supplies low-cost technical assistance and other services to prosecutors who are interested in any administrative support, such as writing grant applications, evaluating existing projects, installing new records or filing systems, or having the entire office and all its operations studied and overhauled.[55]

Many of the projects prosecutors are involved in are jointly operated with or dependent on the cooperation of the trial court. These include the development or improvement of information systems, programs to assist victims and witnesses, and programs to divert selected offenders into nontraditional processing (whether that means deferment of prosecution or quicker, more intense prosecution). It is to innovations in the courts that we now turn.

Courts

Many criminal trial courts in the United States are operating largely under nineteenth-century organizational structures and using even older procedures in handling their work load. Courts, among all the components of the criminal justice system, have been the most resistant to change. Changes, however, are coming fast in many states. Some of these have been discussed previously in this text, and we need only point out that trends are established on these matters. They include the further spread of the merit system (Missouri plan) of selecting judges, the reorganization of trial courts in more states into unified or coordinated systems, the adoption of devices other than impeachment for the disciplining or removal of corrupt or unfit judges, and the increasing use of various diversionary processes for selected defendants.

There are innovations we have not discussed, however, which require our attention. They generally fall into the category of court administration and include a number of specific projects and efforts.

As Ted Rubin points out, "a new and important professional is now rapidly joining the court team." According to Rubin:

He is known by different titles, but most typically he is called the court administrator. In different state or local court systems he may also be referred to as a judicial administrator, a court executive officer, a court coordinator, administrative director, or executive secretary to the courts. He may be a state court administrator, with either administrative or a coordinating responsibility for all courts in a state. He may be a trial court administrator with management responsibility for his local court. He may be a criminal court coordinator, managing the criminal division of a general trial court under the supervision of the trial court administrator. He may be a juvenile court administrator.[56]

While there were such professionals in a few courts prior to 1970, it was in that year that the American Bar Association spearheaded a drive to establish the Institute for Court Management in Denver to train court administrators, and the rapid spread of such positions began.[57] A research study sponsored by the American Judicature Society reveals that state court administrators exist in forty-six states, that 56 percent of the administrators are persons with law degrees while only 6 percent of the persons employed have a graduate degree in business or public or judicial administration. Thirty-six percent have had prior experience as lower-court administrators or as judges before assuming their present positions.[58]

The functions of court administrators vary widely, of course, with the level of the court for whom he or she works, the size of the operation, and the desires of the judges served. The authority of court administrators ranges from being mere "go-fers" for judges to having full command of all supportive tasks and all personnel except the judges themselves. The profession is still in its infancy, and its potential is yet to be fully realized. As Rubin notes, the goal cannot be exclusively that of efficiency; the primary function of the court must always be the service of justice. Thus the unique role of court administrators is to assist the court to better serve justice by promoting methods of gaining efficiency that are compatible with due process of law.[59]

There are several specific matters over which court administrators may exercise responsibility and in which innovative techniques are being employed. These include case-flow or calendar management, witness and juror management, planning new courthouses, and managing existing courthouse space.

Probably the most important area for management expertise balanced with requirements of due process is that of case-flow or calendar management. Judges and their administrative staff, together with attorneys and other interested agencies, are trying to design case assignment and management systems that will coordinate the schedules of court personnel, prosecutors, defense attorneys, witnesses (including lay, expert, and police witnesses), jurors, defendants, and the courtrooms themselves.[60] Multi-judge courts use systems that attempt to insure **blind assignment** of cases—that is, systems that seek to prevent either attorney from being able to determine which judge will handle the case.

Many courts, with aid from LEAA or other sources, are setting up offices of witness management. Others are improving their means of selecting and handling persons called for jury service. More and more the lists of potential jurors are being placed in computer banks to insure randomness and quickness of summons. Many courts also put jurors or witnesses into an on-call status, rather than have them sitting for hours in the courthouse, then notify them by phone when their appearance is required. Compensation in the form of fees and travel expenses is increasingly computerized or otherwise made more efficient, too. Many of the witness management projects are operated by the prosecutor's office or public defenders. Others are joint programs in which the court, attorneys' offices, and law enforcement agencies all play key roles, thus enhancing coordination of all their efforts.[61]

Another development is the involvement of court administrators and other agencies in joint efforts to plan new facilities for the courts. The National Center for State Courts and the Council of State Governments have both received LEAA funds to assist states and local governments in their court planning.[62] These efforts go beyond, but include, the planning of buildings, and prototype plans have been produced for the consideration of local officials and architects.

Managing existing space involves coordination of all persons involved in the criminal process, plus all other officials and agencies that use space in the courthouse. In this task court administrators are rarely directors but serve as liaison officers between the courts and the other agencies.[63] On the other hand, they may be given the authority over the use and assignment of the courtrooms themselves.

We have been able to provide only a brief overview of this emerging and fascinating field of court administration. Partly because the courts have remained so firmly entrenched in tradition, administrative approaches that have become common to other components are innovations for this one.

Corrections

It could be argued that the history of corrections has been largely the history of innovations—new ideas, new approaches, new structures, new programs, new techniques, none of which have truly been successful. Either the approaches and ideas have been wrong in the first place, or they have not been given a fair chance to work. Experts have argued and continue to argue this point.

Of course, there has been progress in penology. We no longer give public approval to physical torture or public executions—though a few still call for the latter through the medium of television. Generally we treat inmates poorly, but public policy and court decisions at least call for treating them as human beings. Still, the prisons tend to be barbaric places, the idea of rehabilitation is under severe attack, and the movement toward community corrections programs and facilities runs into understandable fear and resistance on the part of citizens who live in their vicinity.

We have already discussed most of these matters in our chapters on corrections. It remains for us here to discuss only a few of the recent innovations or trends that offer a little hope, however small, for the future.

Professionalization of Staff In recent years the custodial officers in prisons and jails, and those who hold similar positions in residential or detention facilities for either adults or juveniles, have joined police officers in the move toward professionalism. An observer writes: "One can safely say that throughout the eight years of LEAA's existence, there has been no higher priority for the use of its funds than training" for corrections personnel.[64] Grant funds are supposed to be awarded to corrections departments and agencies who insist on eighty hours of training for recruits and twenty hours of in-service training each year for corrections officers and staff. A state showing an effort to comply with this goal will not, however, have its funds cut off.

Some states have established corrections academies similar to those for police. Connecticut's Justice Academy opened in 1972 with the participation of the Departments of Corrections, Adult Probation, and Children and Youth Services. The problem now is to be able to allow personnel the time off needed to attend.[65]

Along with new emphasis on training, other manifestations of emerging professionalism include increased attendance in college and university programs, unionization, and the pronouncement of a code of ethics by the American Correctional Association.[66] Corrections officers seem determined to escape the situation in which they assert they have found themselves in recent years: hated by the inmates, looked down upon by the treatment staff members, and ignored and denied support by the administrators.[67]

The Des Moines Project and Its Impact We have already dealt with community corrections as a concept and have discussed some of its manifestations in probation, parole, halfway houses, community corrections centers, and furlough programs. In Des Moines, Iowa, a project was initiated several years ago, however, that can be labeled innovative in several respects. As presently constituted, the Fifth Judicial District Department of Court Services operates several distinct but closely integrated programs. The units include the following: a release on recognizance unit through which arrested persons who meet a few basic requirements are released pending further court actions; a release with services unit through which offenders who do not meet the requirements for ROR, but who should not be kept in jail or required to put up bail, are released under close supervisions; a pre-sentence investigation unit that performs the PSIs normally engaged in by probation departments; a probation unit; and the residential services unit, which operates two community corrections facilities, a fifty-four-bed unit for men and a sixteen-bed facility for women.[68]

The Des Moines project is innovative in several ways. It combines pretrial with correctional services and programs under a single organizational umbrella. It provides means by which the traditional jail could be emptied of most of those awaiting disposition and many of those convicted who would not normally be placed on probation. It employs a staff with a varied background and imposes few bureaucratic controls on their behavior. It makes possible a completely integrated chain of services and treatment. A key advantage of the project is that the release services, pre-sentence investigation, and probation units share a building and information, thus eliminating duplication, delays, and organizational conflicts normally experienced by competing offices.[69] Another is that clients can be shifted from one unit to another, even if temporarily, to accomplish a specific result. Thus a probationer who fouls up can, without going through a bureaucratic or legal maze, be given a few days in the residential facility or the jail to convince him of the errors of his ways.

The residential facility (known as Fort Des Moines since it is a converted army barracks) is the keystone of the operation. It operates as a detention and corrections facility for those who cannot be released but who should not be simply locked up. It offers better living conditions than prisons, work furloughs, and other privileges—but infractions of the rules can lead to denial of privileges or time in jail or even termination from the program.

Research has demonstrated the success of the Des Moines program. Persons who are selected for its pretrial programs have much lower rates of nonappearance, rearrest, and ultimate conviction than those who remain in jail or on bail; persons who complete its corrections phase have much lower rearrest rates than those treated by traditional means; and the programs saved the district $450,000 over what traditional programs would have cost during 1973 alone.[70] The project has the enthusiastic support of judges and other officials. Its success had led to attempts to replicate the Des Moines project elsewhere. The state of Iowa has been trying to establish similar projects in the other districts, with limited success. Salt Lake City, on the other hand, has struggled with a poorly planned and executed attempt at replication. LEAA pushed the project too quickly, and conflicts between city and state officials also hampered the efforts in Utah.[71]

A successful replication has occurred in Orange County, Florida. An Office of Court Alternatives in Orlando operates a pretrial release program, a residential center (in a former motel), a program of probation with supervision for misdemeanants, and other programs not incorporated within the Des Moines model. These include a pretrial diversion program and a reentry services unit that acts as a community resource center for families of persons who are in state prisons and for inmates who are released from prisons. This umbrella agency is governed by a board of directors, chaired by the county sheriff, which includes representatives of prosecution, defense, the court, other agencies, and citizens, and is administered by a director under the office of the court administrator. It thus crosses all component lines and serves to integrate the criminal justice system of Orange County.[72]

These programs are very appealing. They can be funded largely with LEAA grants while they get organized, establish their operations, and build a record of accomplishment. The fact that they can demonstrate significant savings in per capita client costs makes them attractive to legislators and local government officials. But perhaps their most significant contribution is that they require the cooperation and support of all agencies of criminal justice and yield some benefit to each of them. They thus compel everyone to think in terms of the whole system and to act in concert. This brings us to the issue of whether or not a truly integrated system of criminal justice is emerging in the United States.

TOWARD A TRUE SYSTEM OF CRIMINAL JUSTICE

You will recall that in Chapter 1 we outlined the requirements for a system. Those requirements were as follows: that identifiable parts or components exist to serve certain functions; that these parts fit into an identifiable whole that has characteristic activities and outputs; that the parts or components be interdependent; that an environment be identified for the system as a whole and each component within it; that a flow of activity occur in which each component receives an input that it processes and produces as output, which, in turn, becomes the input of the next component in the chain; and that outputs of components or the system as a whole generate feedback in the environment.

We stipulated that there are four components of the criminal justice system: law enforcement, prosecution, trial courts, and corrections. We offered our views as to what the overall functions of the criminal justice system were and how each component contributes to those functions by attempting to serve certain functions of their own. The flow of activity through the entire system was divided into five stages, and the roles of each component within each stage were discussed. We attempted to emphasize the interactions of the components—the fact that none of them made any sense without the others and the ways they are each affected by what the others do.

On the other hand, references were made to why many refer to a nonsystem of criminal justice. The fragmentation in organization and the conflicts between components were pointed out. We argued, however, that conflicts did not negate the existence of a system. Interdependence is the key. We hope we have made clear throughout this text that interdependence is real. A system does exist. The question is, can the fragmentation and the conflicts be overcome? Is there evidence that a closing of the ranks is taking place? Are criminal justice officials and government officials thinking in systems terms? Are forces at work compelling a trend toward true cooperation and coordination? We answer, "yes."

In this chapter on innovations we have touched on several matters that give support to our position. The importance of the Omnibus Crime Control and Safe Streets Act, the LEAA, the emergence of state and regional planning units, the grants process, and the interagency projects and programs cannot be overemphasized. Even if funds have been wasted in the sense that crime reduction has not been achieved, the whole process has brought the components of the criminal justice system together and forced officials to discuss each other's and their own common problems. It has also promoted an academic discipline and attempts to establish a common set of terms and concepts for purposes of gathering and exchanging data.

There are additional indicators and projects we have not yet covered because they do not fit under any one component but are systemwide in scope. They illustrate and encourage the trend toward a true system. Only the briefest mention of each is possible, but the point will be clear.

Criminal Justice Information Systems

Mention was made earlier of the role of LEAA in encouraging the development of systemwide criminal justice information systems. These systems involve more than the computerization of criminal histories of known offenders, though this is part of the picture. Here we mean systems that store and make available information relating to the processing of individuals and cases through all stages and by all components. These systems are often called Offender-based Tracking Systems, and several states have attempted to design and implement such systems. A complete system should also handle data related to the budgets, personnel, property, space utilization, and other administrative aspects of criminal justice agencies.

Where agencies or components have developed their own data systems and purchased their own computers, the LEAA and state planning agencies are encouraging the establishment of linkages and common data bases. Unfortunately, too many agencies are already committed to narrow, inflexible data systems, and duplication is the rule rather than the exception. But information system development is a pragmatic goal and a means of coordinating the operations of the criminal justice system without necessarily violating the identity or distinct needs of any one component.[73]

Legislation and Code Revisions

Another of the hopeful signs of the past decade or so is the fact that twenty-one states have revised their criminal codes, many of them completely overhauling and consolidating their criminal statutes. Seven states enacted significant revisions during 1974 and 1975.[74] Many states are adopting the framework of establishing classes of crimes with appropriate sanctions for each and then defining each offense in terms of its appropriate class. This tends to decrease the disparity in criminal sanctions that gets built into statutes as each particular chapter or section is written without proper regard for the others.

The Council of State Governments has found that code revisions of recent years illustrate several trends: decriminalizations of selected victimless crimes, attempts at control over or limitations on handguns, the reintroduction of the death penalty in terms acceptable to the Supreme Court, reduction of the sentencing discretion of judges—usually through the enactment of mandatory minimum sentences for certain crimes or career criminals—and the adoption of various plans for compensating victims of violent crimes.[75] The council points out that states are also unifying court systems, consolidating corrections agencies, removing juvenile status offenses from their provisions for delinquency, and promoting the growth of community corrections centers.

The Council observes:

> The criminal justice system is not a unified structure for service delivery; rather it is a collection of independent institutions and agencies carrying out a variety of services and programs. It is not surprising, therefore, that there are several different dynamics for change taking place in the States, some of them mutually compatible and others in conflict.[76]

It finds the two major "dynamics" in law revision to be (1) "the move to make the imposition of criminal sanctions more certain and fair" by changes in sentencing structures and removals of or limitations on the discretion of judges and parole boards and (2) "the continued concern for the rights of individuals who come into contact with criminal justice agencies" reflected in extensions of due process rights to juveniles and adult prisoners.[77]

In all this, however, we are convinced that the legislators are aware that any changes they make in one part of the system affect the operations of all its components. For example, mandatory minimum sentences for selected offenses increase prison populations, which in turn requires the building of more prisons, the provision of alternative correctional programs for other offenses, or the diversion of other offenders from the system altogether. New York state repealed its prohibition of plea-bargaining provisions for drug offenders when it became clear that the entire system—especially law enforcement and prosecution—was being hamstrung in its efforts to deal realistically with the narcotics problem.[78] A major argument for decriminalizing possession of marijuana and some other vice offenses is that it will free criminal justice resources to cope with serious crime. In all this there is an awareness that the parts of the system are interdependent.

We do not anticipate, nor do we desire, a completely integrated or unified system of justice. The elimination of the independence of the components and the creation of a single structure is not the end we advocate. It is not constitutionally permissible to eliminate the separation of the executive and judicial branches, either at the federal or state levels. Total nationalization of criminal justice is certainly not desirable. The states must retain their police powers, and the components must retain their identities. We do not foresee a monolith. We see a system striving to overcome unnecessary conflicts and working toward the realization of a common if ultimately elusive goal—justice.

TEST YOURSELF

Define these key terms:
categorical grants
discretionary grants
lateral entry
neighborhood watch programs

Answer the following questions:

1. What is full neighborhood team policing and what are its implications for police administration?

2. Describe the emergence of administrators and list a few of the responsibilities they might have.

3. Describe and discuss the importance of the Des Moines project.

4. What are some of the indications that criminal justice is moving toward realization of a true system?

NOTES

1. President's Commission on Law Enforcement and Administration of Justice, *The Challenge of Crime in a Free Society* and various task force reports (Washington, D.C.: Government Printing Office, 1967).
2. Omnibus Crime Control and Safe Streets Act, title 1, "Declarations and Principles."
3. Law Enforcement Assistance Administration, *Orientation Handbook* (Washington, D.C.: Government Printing Office, 1976); and Michael S. Sherrill, "LEAA: A Question of Impact, Part I," *Corrections Magazine* 11 (June 1976), pp. 7 and 8.
4. See LEAA, *Orientation Handbook*; and Council of State Governments "The States and the Criminal Justice System," *The Book of the States: 1976–77* (Lexington, Ky.: Council of State Governments, 1976), pp. 402–3.
5. See Serrill, "LEAA: A Question of Impact, Part II, *Corrections Magazine* 11 (September 1976), pp. 34 and 35.
6. LEAA, *Orientation Handbook*, pp. 16–20.
7. Ibid., pp. 22–24.
8. Serrill, "LEAA, Part I," p. 5.
9. Council of State Governments, "The States," pp. 402–3.
10. "Conflicts Beset U.S. Anticrime Agency," *New York Times*, 27 December 1970, pp. 1 and 34.
11. Serrill, "LEAA, Part I," p. 12.
12. Ibid.
13. Ibid.
14. S.2212 signed into law on 15 October 1976. See "Three-Year LEAA Authorization Enacted," *Congressional Quarterly Almanac* (Washington, D.C.: Congressional Quarterly, 1977), pp. 397–98.
15. Serrill, "LEAA, Part II," p. 30.
16. National Advisory Commission on Criminal Justice Standards and Goals: *Police* (Washington, D.C.: Government Printing Office, 1973).
17. NACCJSG, *Courts* (Washington, D.C.: Government Printing Office, 1973).
18. NACCJSG, *Corrections* (Washington, D.C.: Government Printing Office, 1973).
19. NACCJSG, *Courts* and *Corrections*.
20. NACCJSG, *A National Strategy to Reduce Crime* (Washington, D.C.: Government Printing Office, 1973).
21. See remarks by Elliot L. Richardson, attorney general of the United States, at a press conference in Washington, D.C., on 9 August 1973; and policy statement issued by Donald E. Santanelli in 1974, as quoted in American Bar Association, *Comparative Analysis of the Standards and Goals of the National Advisory Commission on Criminal Justice Standards and Goals with the Standards for Criminal Justice of the American Bar Association* (Washington, D.C.: ABA, 1974), pp. ix–x.
22. See, for example, William L. Cahalan, "Comments on the Court's Task Force Report," *Prosecutor* 9 (1973), pp. 125–27.
23. National Institute of Law Enforcement and Criminal Justice, *Cost Analysis of Correctional Standards: Institutional-Based Programs and Parole* (Washington, D.C.: Government Printing Office, 1976), chap. IX.
24. See Paul M. Whisenand, *Crime Prevention: A Practical Look at Deterrence of Crime* (Boston: Holbrook Press, 1977), p. 85.
25. Morris L. Cogan, "Toward a Definition of a Profession," *Harvard Educational Review* XXIII (Winter 1953), p. 33.
26. See National Institute of Law Enforcement and Criminal Justice, *Police Training and Performance Study* (Washington, D.C.: Government Printing Office, 1970), p. 169.
27. See Serrill, "LEAA, Part I," p. 7.
28. President's Commission, *Task Force Report: The Police*, (Washington, D.C.: Government Printing Office, 1967), p. 142; and remarks by Boston Police Commissioner Robert J. DiGrazia at conference on "Improving Resource Utilization in Public Safety," Orlando, Florida, 29 October 1976.

29. Police Chief Executive Committee of the International Association of Police Chiefs, *The Police Chief Executive Report* (Washington, D.C.: Government Printing Office, 1976).
30. "Brethren in Blue: Police, Other Officers in Some States Sign Up with Teamsters Union," *Wall Street Journal*, 5 March, 1976, p. 1.
31. See J. P. Morgan, Jr., and Richard J. Korstad, *Impact of Collective Bargaining on Law Enforcement and Corrections* (St. Petersburg, Fla.: Public Safety Research Institute, 1976), pp. 3 and 4.
32. Detroit Police Commissioner John Nichols, as quoted in Morgan and Korstad, *Impact of Collective Bargaining*, p. 2.
33. Patrick J. Murphy, in remarks at the Southern Regional Conference of the American Society for Police Administration, Orlando, Florida, 28 October 1974.
34. Office of Criminal Justice Programs, "Police Women Study," *Frontline* 2 (September 1973), p. 3.
35. See "Chicago Will Use Quotas for Police," *New York Times*, 27 June 1976, p. 16 and "Chicago Police Warned of Further Hiring Quotas if Discrimination Persists," *New York Times* 10 December 1976, I, p. 24.
36. Morgan and Korstad, *Impact of Collective Bargaining*, pp. 24 and 25. See also Alfred I. Schwartz et al., *Employing Civilians for Police Work* (Washington, D.C.: Government Printing Office, 1975).
37. Andrew Halper and Richard Ku, *New York City Police Department Street Crime Unit* (Washington, D.C.: Government Printing Office, no date), esp. pp. 2 and 107-12.
38. "Full Story on 'Got Ya Again'," *Washington Star*, 7 July, 1976 pp. A-1 and B-4.
39. See J. P. Morgan, Jr., et al., *Full Service Neighborhood Team Policing: Planning for Implementation* (St. Petersburg, Fla.: Public Safety Research Institute, 1975).
40. Whisenand, *Crime Prevention*, p. 91.
41. Peter Block and David Specht, *Neighborhood Team Policing* (Washington, D.C.: Government Printing Office, 1973), p. 2.
42. Morgan et al., *Team Policing*.
43. Block and Specht, *Neighborhood Team Policing*, p. 1.
44. Helen C. O'Malley, *Evaluation Report on the Holyoke Team Police Experiment* (Holyoke, Mass.: Holyoke Police Department, 1973); and Los Angeles Police Department, *Final Evaluation of Team 28 Experiment* (Los Angeles: LAPD, 1974).
45. Whisenand, *Crime Prevention*, pp. 181-84.
46. Ibid., pp. 189-99.
47. National College of District Attorneys, *1976-77 Academic Catalog* (Houston: University of Houston College of Law, 1976).
48. NILE/CJ, *An Exemplary Project: The Major Offense Bureau* (Washington, D.C.: Government Printing Office, no date), esp. pp. 6-8; and Mario Merola, "The Major Offense Bureau: A Blueprint for Effective Prosecution of Career Criminals," *Prosecutor* 11 (January 1976).
49. NILE/CJ, *Major Offense Bureau*, p. 10.
50. See, for example, editors, "Economic Crime Project," *Prosecutor* 12 (April 1977), p. 239.
51. Letter from Robert Rook, NDAA president, in *Prosecutor* 12 (March 1977), p. 164.
52. Robert E. Neilson, "Medical Vendor Fraud," *Prosecutor* 12 (March 1977), p. 166.
53. National District Attorneys Association, *Standards and Goals Project* (Chicago: NDAA, 1977).
54. See copies of *INSLAW, PROMIS Newsletter* (Washington, D.C.: Institute for Law and Social Research).
55. "NDAA Management Studies Save Thousands," *Prosecutor* 12 (March 1977), p. 156.
56. H. Ted Rubin, *The Courts: Fulcrum of the Justice System* (Pacific Palisades, Calif.: Goodyear, 1976), p. 186.
57. Editors, "Profile of the Court Administrator," *Court Systems Digest* vol. #2 (February 1977), pp. 8-9.
58. Ibid., p. 9.
59. Rubin, *Courts*, p. 186.

60. Ibid., p. 188.
61. See, for example, Frank J. Cannavale, Jr., and William D. Falcon, ed., *Improving Witness Cooperation* (Washington, D.C.: Government Printing Office, 1976).
62. Daniel McGillis and Lake Wise, *Court Planning and Research* (Washington, D.C.: Government Printing Office, 1976), pp. 4-5.
63. Rubin, *Courts*, pp. 196 and 198.
64. Serrill, "LEAA, Part II," p. 25.
65. Ibid., p. 26.
66. See American Correctional Association, "Declarations of Principles," *Manual of Correctional Standards*, 3d ed. (College Park, Md.: American Correctional Association, no date).
67. See David Fogel, *We Are the Living Proof: The Justice Model for Corrections* (Cincinnati, Ohio: Anderson, 1975), chap. 2.
68. Roger O. Steggerda and Peter S. Venezia, *Community-Based Alternatives to Traditional Corrections: The 1973 Evaluation of the Fifth Judicial District Department of Court Services—State of Iowa* (Davis, Calif.: National Council on Crime and Delinquency, 1974), pp. 13-20; and Rob Wilson, "Plaudits in Des Moines, but Problems in Salt Lake," *Corrections Magazine* 11 (September 1976), pp. 16-18.
69. Wilson, "Plaudits," p. 18.
70. See Steggerda and Venezia, *Community-Based Alternatives*, pp. 140, 141, and 157.
71. Wilson, "Plaudits," pp. 21 and 24.
72. "Office of Court Alternatives" (Orlando, Fla.: unpublished paper, 1976).
73. For a review of systemwide models for Criminal Justice Information Systems, see J. Chaiken et al., *Criminal Justice Models: An Overview* (Washington, D.C.: Government Printing Office, 1976), chap. 3.
74. Council of State Governments, "The States," p. 404.
75. Ibid., pp. 404-5.
76. Ibid., pp. 413-15.
77. Ibid.
78. "Carey Signs Legislation Easing State Drug Laws" *New York Times* 2 July, 1976, I, p. 10.

Bibliography

Adams, Thomas F. *Introduction to the Administration of Justice.* Englewood Cliffs, N.J.: Prentice-Hall, 1975.

Advisory Commission on Intergovernmental Relations. *State-Local Relations in the Criminal Justice System.* Washington, D.C.: U.S. Government Printing Office, 1971.

Allen, Harry E., and Simonsen, Clifford E. *Corrections in America: An Introduction.* Beverly Hills, Calif.: Glencoe Press, 1976.

Almond, Gabriel. "Political Theory and Political Science," *American Political Science Review*, 60: 869–79, 1966.

American Bar Association. *Comparative Analysis of the Standards and Goals of the National Advisory Commission on Criminal Justice Standards and Goals with the Standards for Criminal Justice of the American Bar Association.* Washington, D.C.: American Bar Association, 1974.

American Bar Association Project on Standards for Criminal Justice. *Administration of Criminal Justice.* Chicago: American Bar Association, 1974.

———. *Prosecution Function and the Defense Function.* Chicago: American Bar Association, 1971.

American Correctional Association. *Juvenile and Adult Correctional Departments, Institutions, Agencies, and Paroling Authorities.* College Park, Md.: American Correctional Association, 1975.

———. *Manual of Correctional Standards*, 3d ed. College Park, Md.: American Correctional Association, no date.

American Law Institute. *Model Penal Code*, proposed draft. Philadelphia: American Law Institute, 1962.

Banton, Michael. *The Policeman in the Community.* New York: Basic Books, 1964.

Barnes, Harry E. *The Repression of Crime:*

Studies in Historical Penology. Montclair, N.J.: Patterson Smith, 1969.
——. *The Story of Punishment,* 2d ed. rev. Montclair, N.J.: Patterson Smith, 1972.
——, and Teeters, Negley K. *New Horizons in Criminology,* 2d ed. Englewood Cliffs, N.J.: Prentice-Hall, 1955.
Bent, Alan E., and Rossum, Ralph A. *Police, Criminal Justice, and the Community.* New York: Harper & Row, 1976.
Bercal, Thomas C. "Calls for Police Assistance," in *Police in Urban Society,* Harlan Hahn, ed. Beverly Hills, Calif.: Sage Publications, 1971.
Bird, Otto A. *The Idea of Justice.* New York: Praeger, 1967.
Black, Henry C. *Black's Law Dictionary,* 4th ed. St. Paul, Minn.: West Publishing Co., 1951.
Blanchard, Robert E. *Introduction to the Administration of Justice.* New York: Wiley, 1975.
Bloch, Herbert, and Geis, Gilbert. *Crime, Man and Society,* 2d ed. New York: Random House, 1970.
Block, Peter, and Specht, David. *Neighborhood Team Policing.* Washington, D.C.: U.S. Government Printing Office, 1973.
Blumberg, Abraham. *Criminal Justice.* Chicago: Quadrangle Books, 1967.
——. *Law and Order: The Scales of Justice.* New Brunswick, N.J.: Transaction Books, 1973.
Breitel, Charles. "Controls in Criminal Law Enforcement," *University of Chicago Law Review,* 27: 427–35, 1960.
Chaiken, J., et al. *Criminal Justice Models: An Overview.* Washington, D.C.: U.S. Government Printing Office, 1976.
Cannavale, Frank J., Jr., and Falcon, William D., eds. *Improving Witness Cooperation.* Washington, D.C.: U.S. Government Printing Office, 1976.
Chamelin, Neil C., Fox, Vernon B., and Whisenand, Paul M. *Introduction to Criminal Justice.* Englewood Cliffs, N.J.: Prentice-Hall, 1975.
Cho, Yong Hyo. *Public Policy and Urban Crime.* Cambridge, Mass.: Ballinger Publishing, 1974.
Clare, Paul K., and Kramer, John H. *Introduction to American Corrections.* Boston: Holbrook Press, 1976.
Coffey, Alan R. *Juvenile Justice as a System.* Englewood Cliffs, N.J.: Prentice-Hall, 1974.
Cogan, Morris L. "Toward a Definition of a Profession," *Harvard Educational Review,* 23:33–50, 1953.
Cohen, Lawrence E. *New Directions in Processing of Juvenile Offenders: The Denver Model.* Washington, D.C.: U.S. Government Printing Office, 1975.
Cohn, Alvin W. *Crime and Justice Administration.* Philadelphia: Lippincott, 1976.
Cole, George F. *The American System of Criminal Justice.* North Scituate, Mass.: Duxbury Press, 1975.
——. *Criminal Justice.* Belmont, Calif.: Wadsworth, 1972.
——. *Politics and the Administration of Justice.* Beverly Hills, Calif.: Sage Publications, 1973.
Committee on Crime Prevention and Control. *New Perspectives on Urban Crime, Spec. 31.* Chicago: American Bar Association, 1972.
Committee on the Office of Attorney General. *Survey of Local Prosecutors.* Raleigh, N.C.: National Association of Attorneys General, 1973.
Council of State Governments. "The States and the Criminal Justice System," in *The Book of the States,*

1976-77. Lexington, Ky.: Council of State Governments, 1976.

Creamer, J. Shane. *The Law of Arrest, Search and Seizure*. Philadelphia: Saunders, 1975.

Cressey, Donald. *Theft of the Nation*. New York: Harper & Row, 1969.

Czajkoski, Eugene H. "Exposing the Quasi-Judicial Role of the Probation Officer." *Federal Probation*, 37:11-12, 1973.

Daley, Robert. *Target Blue*. New York: Delacorte Press, 1971.

Darwick, Norman. "State Police and Highway Patrols," in *The Book of the States: 1974-75*. Lexington, Ky.: Council of State Governments, 1975.

Davis, Kenneth C. *Discretionary Justice*. Urbana, Ill.: University of Illinois Press, 1971.

Duffee, David, and Fitch, Robert. *An Introduction to Corrections: A Policy and Systems Approach*. Pacific Palisades, Calif.: Goodyear, 1976.

Eastman, George, ed. *Municipal Police Administration*. Washington, D.C.: International City Managers Association, 1969.

Easton, David. *The Political System*. New York: Knopf, 1953.

Edelhertz, Herbert. *The Nature, Impact and Prosecution of White Collar Crime*. Washington, D.C.: U.S. Government Printing Office, 1970.

Executive Office of the President. *The Budget of the United States Government: Fiscal Year 1977*. Washington, D.C.: U.S. Government Printing Office, 1976.

Federal Bureau of Investigation. *Crime in the U.S., 1975*. Washington, D.C.: U.S. Government Printing Office, 1975.

Federal Bureau of Prisons. "Prisoners in State and Federal Institutions for Adult Felons," *National Prisoner Statistics Bulletin No. 47*. Washington, D.C.: U.S. Government Printing Office, 1972.

Felkenes, George. *The Criminal Justice System: Its Functions and Personnel*. Englewood Cliffs, N.J.: Prentice-Hall 1973.

Fisk, James G. *The Police Officer's Exercise of Discretion in the Decision to Arrest: Relationship to Organizational Goals and Societal Values*. Los Angeles: Institute of Government and Public Affairs, 1974.

Fogel, David. *We Are the Living Proof: The Justice Model for Corrections*. Cincinnati, Ohio: Anderson, 1975.

Folley, Vern L. *American Law Enforcement*. Boston: Holbrook Press, 1973.

Fox, Sanford J. *Juvenile Courts*. St. Paul, Minn.: West, 1971.

——. "Juvenile Justice Reform: An Historical Perspective." *Stanford Law Review*, 22:1187-1239, 1970.

Frankel, Marvin E. "An Opinion by One of Those Soft Headed Judges," *New York Times Magazine*, pp. 40-45, May 13, 1973.

——. *Criminal Sentences*. New York: Hill & Wang, 1972.

Freed, Daniel J., and Wald, Patricia M. *Bail in the United States*. Washington, D.C.: U.S. Government Printing Office, 1964.

Friedrich, Carl J. *Man and His Government, an Empirical Theory of Politics*. New York: McGraw-Hill, 1963.

Friesen, Ernest, Gallas, Edward C., and Gallas, Nesta M. *Managing the Courts*. Indianapolis, Ind.: Bobbs-Merrill, 1971.

Fuller, Lon L. *Anatomy of the Law*. New York: Praeger, 1968.

Garber, James. "Screening of Criminal Cases and Recommendations," in *Screening of Criminal Cases*. Chicago: National District Attorneys Association, 1973.

Germann, A. C., Day, F., and Gallati, R. J. *Introduction to Law Enforcement and Criminal Justice.* Springfield, Ill.: Thomas, 1968.

Goldstein, Joseph. "Police Discretion Not to Invoke the Criminal Process: Low Visibility Decisions in the Administration of Justice," in *Criminal Justice,* George F. Cole, ed. Belmont, Calif.: Wadsworth, 1972.

Greenwood, Peter W., and Petersilia, Joan. *The Criminal Investigation Process,* Vols. I–III. Santa Monica, Calif.: Rand Corporation, 1975.

——. et al. *Prosecution of Adult Felony Defendants in Los Angeles County: A Policy Perspective.* Washington, D.C.: U.S. Government Printing Office, 1973.

Hall, Livingston, et al. *Modern Criminal Procedure,* 4th ed. St. Paul, Minn.: West, 1973.

Halper, Andrew, and Ku, Richard. *New York City Police Department Street Crime Unit.* Washington, D.C.: U.S. Government Printing Office, no date.

Harding, Allen. *Social History of the English Law.* Baltimore, Md.: Penguin Books, 1966.

Hawkins, Gordon, and Morris, Norval. *The Honest Politician's Guide to Crime Control.* Chicago: University of Chicago Press, 1970.

Hefferman, Esther. *Making It in Prison: The Square, the Cool, and the Life.* New York: Wiley, 1972.

Hilbert, Christopher. *The Roots of Evil: A Social History of Crime and Punishment.* Boston: Little, Brown, 1963.

Hindelang, Michael, J., et al. *Sourcebook of Criminal Justice Statistics.* Washington, D.C., U.S. Government Printing Office, 1976.

Homer, Frederick D. *Guns and Garlic.* West Lafayette, Ind.: Purdue University Press, 1974.

Hopkins, E. Jerome. *Our Lawless Police.* New York: Viking, 1931.

Inciardi, James A. *Careers in Crime.* Chicago: Rand McNally, 1975.

International Association of Chiefs of Police. *Criminal Investigation,* 2d ed. Gaitlersburg, Md.: International Association of Chiefs of Police, 1971.

Irish, Marian D., and Prothos, James W. *The Politics of American Democracy,* 5th ed. Englewood Cliffs, N.J.: Prentice-Hall, 1971.

Jackson, Donald D. *Judges.* New York: Atheneum, 1974.

Jacobs, Herbert. *Justice in America,* 2d ed. Boston: Little, Brown, 1972.

——. *Urban Justice: Law and Order in American Cities.* Englewood Cliffs, N.J.: Prentice-Hall, 1973.

Jacoby, Joan E. *Pretrial Screening in Perspective.* National Evaluation Program Phase I Report. Washington, D.C.: U.S. Government Printing Office, 1976.

James, Howard. *Crisis in the Courts,* rev. ed. New York: McKay, 1971.

Kalmanoff, Alan. *Criminal Justice: Enforcement and Administration.* Boston: Little, Brown, 1976.

Kalven, Harry, and Ziesel, Hans. *The American Jury.* Boston: Little, Brown, 1966.

Kaplan, John. *Criminal Justice.* Mineola, N.Y.: Foundation Press, 1973.

Kelling, George L., and Pate, Tony. *The Kansas City Patrol Experiment: Summary Report.* Washington, D.C.: The Police Foundation, 1974.

Kerper, Hazel B. *Criminal Justice System.* St. Paul, Minn.: West, 1972.

——, and Kerper, Janeen. *Legal Rights of the Convicted.* St. Paul, Minn.: West, 1974.

Kirkham, George F. "A Professor's 'Street

Lessons'," *F.B.I. Law Enforcement Bulletin*, pp. 14-22, March, 1974.

Klockars, Carl B., Jr. "A Theory of Probation Supervision," *Journal of Criminal Law, Criminology and Police Science*, 63:550-52, 1972.

Kravitz, Theodore M. "The Grand Jury: Past, Present, Future," *Missouri Law Review*, 24:318, 1959.

Kroes, William H., et al. "Job Stress in Policemen," *Journal of Police Science and Administration*, 2:145-55, 1974.

Kwartler, Richard. "Rehabilitation," *Corrections Magazine*, 1:2, May/June, 1975.

Ladinsky, Jack. "The Impact of Social Backgrounds of Lawyers on Law Practice and the Law," *The Journal of Legal Education*, 16:128, 1965.

Lafave, Wayne R. *Arrest: The Decision to Take a Suspect into Custody*. Boston: Little, Brown, 1965.

Lasswell, Harold. *Who Gets What, When, How*. New York: World, 1958.

Law Enforcement Assistance Administration. Crime in the Nation's Five Largest Cities. Washington, D.C.: U.S. Government Printing Office, 1974.

—. *Criminal Justice Agencies*, vols. 1-10. Washington, D.C.: U.S. Government Printing Office, 1976.

—. *Criminal Victimization in the U.S., 1973 Advanced Report*, Vol. 1. Washington, D.C.: U.S. Government Printing Office, 1975.

—. *Criminal Victimization: Surveys in Thirteen American Cities*. Washington, D.C.: U.S. Government Printing Office, 1975.

—. *An Exemplary Project: The Major Offense Bureau*. Washington, D.C.: U.S. Government Printing Office, no date.

—. *Guide for Discretionary Grant Programs*, M4500. lc. Washington, D.C.: U.S. Government Printing Office, 1974.

—. *National Prisoner Statistics Bulletin*. Washington, D.C.: U.S. Government Printing Office, 1974.

—. *National Survey of Court Organization*. Washington, D.C.: U.S. Government Printing Office, 1973.

—. *National Survey of Court Organization, 1975 Supplement to State Judicial Systems* Washington, D.C.: U.S. Government Printing Office, 1975.

—. *The Nations Jails*. Washington, D.C.: U.S. Government Printing Office, 1975.

—. *Orientation Handbook*. Washington, D.C.: U.S. Government Printing Office, 1976.

—. *Police Training and Performance Study*. Washington, D.C.: U.S. Government Printing Office, 1970.

—. *Survey of Inmates of Local Jails: Advanced Report*. Washington, D.C.: U.S. Government Printing Office, 1973.

Lawrence, John. *A History of Capital Punishment*. New York: Citadel Press, 1969.

Lee, Capt. W. L. Melville. *A History of Police in England, 1901*. Montclair, N.J.: Patterson Smith, 1971.

Lou, Herbert H. *Juvenile Courts in the United States*. New York: Arno Press, 1972.

Mason, Alphens, T., and Beany, William M. *The Supreme Court in a Free Society*. New York: Norton, 1968.

McCart, Samuel. *Trial by Jury: A Complete Guide to the Jury System*. Philadelphia: Chilton Books, 1964.

McCartt, John M., and Mangogna, Thomas J. *Guidelines and Standards for Halfway Houses and Community Treatment Centers*. Washington, D.C.: U.S. Government Printing Office, 1973.

McGillis, Daniel, and Wise, Lake. *Court Planning and Research*. Washington,

D.C.: U.S. Government Printing Office, 1976.

Meglio, John J. "Comparative Study of the District Attorneys' Offices in Los Angeles and Brooklyn," *Prosecutor*, 5:238, 1969.

Merola, Mario. "The Major Offense Bureau: A Blueprint for Effective Prosecution of Career Criminals," *Prosecutor*, 11:8–14, 1976.

Miller, Frank W. *The Correctional Process*. New York: Foundation Press, 1971.

——. et al. *The Juvenile Justice Process*. Mineola, N.Y.: Foundation Press, 1971.

More, Harry W., ed. *Principles and Procedures in the Administration of Justice*. New York: Wiley, 1975.

Morgan, J. P., Jr., et al. *Full Service Neighborhood Team Policing: Planning for Implementation*. St. Petersburg, Fl.: Public Safety Research Institute, 1975.

——, and Korstad, Richard J. *Impact of Collective Bargaining on Law Enforcement and Corrections*. St. Petersburg, Fl.: Public Safety Research Institute, 1976.

Morris, Mark O. *Field Contact Report*. Oakland, Calif.: Oakland Police Department, 1974.

Morrison, Samuel Eliot. *The Oxford History of the American People*. New York: Oxford University Press, 1965.

Myren, Richard A. "The Role of the Police," in *Critical Issues In Law Enforcement*, Harry More, ed. Cincinnati, Ohio: Anderson, 1972.

National Advisory Commission on Criminal Justice Standards and Goals. *Corrections*. Washington, D.C.: U.S. Government Printing Office, 1973.

——. *Courts*. Washington, D.C.: U.S. Government Printing Office, 1973.

——. *Criminal Justice System*. Washington, D.C.: U.S. Government Printing Office, 1973.

——. *Police*. Washington, D.C.: U.S. Government Printing Office, 1973.

National Archives Service. *U.S. Government Manual: 1975/76*. Washington, D.C.: U.S. Government Printing Office, 1975.

National College of District Attorneys. *1976-77 Academic Catalog*. Houston: University of Houston College of Law, 1976.

National Council on Crime and Delinquency. *Criminal Justice Newsletter*, 8: Feb. 14, 1977.

——. "Jurisdiction over Status Offenses Should Be Removed from the Juvenile Court," *Crime and Delinquency*, 21:97, April, 1975.

——. "Parole Decisions: A Policy Statement," *Crime and Delinquency*, 19:137, April, 1973.

National District Attorneys Association. *Screening of Criminal Cases*. Chicago: National District Attorneys Association, 1973.

——. *Standards and Goals Project*. Chicago: National District Attorneys Association, 1977.

National Pretrial Intervention Center. *Descriptive Profiles on Selected Pretrial Criminal Justice Intervention Programs*. Washington, D.C.: American Bar Association, 1974.

Neubauer, David W. *Criminal Justice in Middle America*. Morristown, N.J.: General Learning Press, 1974.

Neilson, Robert E. "Medical Vendor Fraud," *Prosecutor*, 12: 166, March, 1977.

New York State Special Commission on Attica. *Attica*, New York: Bantam, 1972.

Newman, Donald J. *Conviction: The Determination of Guilt or Innocence Without Trial*. Boston: Little, Brown, 1966.

—. *Introduction to Criminal Justice.* Philadelphia: Lippincott, 1975.

Office of Criminal Justice Programs. "Police Women Study," *Frontline,* 2:3, Sept., 1973.

Packer, Herbert L. *The Limits of the Criminal Sanction.* Stanford, Calif.: Stanford University Press, 1968.

—. "The Police and the Community," *Stanford Law Review,* 22:1314–17, 1969.

Perkins, Rollin M. *Criminal Law and Procedure,* 4th ed. Mineola, N.Y.: Foundation Press, 1972.

Plotkin, Robert. "Recent Developments in the Law of Prisoners' Rights," *Criminal Law Bulletin,* 11:405–33, July–Aug., 1975.

Police Chief Executive Committee of the International Association of Police Chiefs. *The Police Chief Executive Report.* Washington, D.C.: U.S. Government Printing Office, 1976.

Popper, Karl. *The Open Society and Its Enemies,* Vol. 1. New York: Harper Brothers, 1945.

Pound, Roscoe. "Discretion, Dispensation and Mitigation: The Problem of the Individual Special Case," *New York University Law Review,* 35:925–27, 1960.

Prassel, Frank R. *Introduction to American Criminal Justice.* New York: Harper & Row, 1975.

—. *The Western Peace Officer: A Legacy of Law and Order.* Norman, Okla.: University of Oklahoma Press, 1972.

President's Commission on Law Enforcement and the Administration of Justice. *Task Force Report: The Challenge of Crime in a Free Society.* Washington, D.C.: U.S. Government Printing Office, 1967.

—. *Task Force Report: Corrections.* Washington, D.C.: U.S. Government Printing Office, 1967.

—. *Task Force Report: The Courts.* Washington, D.C.: U.S. Government Printing Office, 1967.

—. *Task Force Report: The Police.* Washington, D.C.: U.S. Government Printing Office, 1967.

Pringle, Patrick. *Hue and Cry: The Battle of the British Police.* London: Museum Press, 1955.

Pursley, Robert D. "Leadership and Community Identification Attitudes Among Two Categories of Police Chiefs," *Journal of Police Science and Administration,* 2:414–22, 1974.

Reiser, Martin, "Some Organizational Stresses on Policemen," *Journal of Police Science and Administration,* 2:156–59, 1974.

Rosett, Arthur, and Cressey, Donald. *Justice by Consent: Plea Bargains in the American Courthouse.* Philadelphia: Lippincott, 1976.

Royal Commission on the Police. *Final Report.* London: Her Majesty's Stationery Office, 1968.

Rubin, H. Ted. *The Courts: Fulcrum of the Justice System.* Pacific Palisades, Calif.: Goodyear, 1976.

—. "The Eye of the Juvenile Court Judge: A One-Step-Up View of the Juvenile Justice System," in *The Juvenile Justice System,* Malcolm W. Klein, ed. Beverly Hills, Calif.: Sage Publications, 1976.

Ruchelman, Leonard. *Police Politics.* Cambridge, Mass.: Ballinger, 1974.

—, ed. *Who Rules the Police?* New York: New York University Press, 1973.

Rutherford, Andrew, and McDermott, Robert. *Juvenile Diversion.* Washington, D.C.: U.S. Government Printing Office, 1976.

San Francisco Committee on Crime. *Report on Adult Probation in San Francisco.* San Francisco: San Francisco Committee on Crime, 1970.

———. *Reports on the Courts.* San Francisco: San Francisco Committe on Crime, 1970.

Schafer, Stephen. *The Political Criminal: The Problem of Morality and Crime.* New York: Free Press, 1974.

Schur, Edwin. *Crimes Without Victims: Deviant Behavior and Public Policy.* Englewood Cliffs, N.J.: Prentice-Hall, 1965.

Schwartz, Alfred F., et al. *Employing Civilians for Police Work.* Washington, D.C.: U.S. Government Printing Office, 1975.

Schwartz, Bernard. *The Law in America.* New York: American Heritage, 1974.

Serrill, Michael L. "Critics of Corrections Speak Out," *Corrections Magazine,* II:3-9, 21-26, Sept., 1976.

———. "Is Rehabilitation Dead?," *Corrections Magazine,* I:3-12, 21-32, May/June, 1975.

———. "LEAA: A Question of Impact," *Corrections Magazine,* II:(Part I) 3-12, 17-29, June, 1976; (Part II) 3-12, 25-6, 34-6, 49-50, Sept., 1976.

Shulman, Harry M. "The Measurement of Crime in the United States," *Journal of Criminal Law,* 57:483-92, 1966.

Singer, Neil M., and Wright, Virginia B. *Cost Analysis of Correctional Standards: Institutional-Based Programs and Parole.* Washington, D.C.: U.S. Government Printing Office, 1976.

Singer, Richard G., and Hand, Richard. "Sentencing Computation: Law and Practices," *Criminal Law Bulletin,* 10: 321-22, May, 1974.

Skolnick, Jerome. *Justice Without Trial: Law Enforcement in Democractic Society.* New York: Wiley, 1966.

Smith, Bruce. *The State Police.* Montclair, N.J.: Patterson Smith, 1969.

Solomon, Hassim M. *Community Corrections.* Boston: Holbrook Press, 1976.

Stanley, David T. *Prisoners Among Us: The Problems of Parole.* Washington, D.C.: The Brookings Institution, 1976.

Steggerda, Roger O., and Venezia, Peter S. *Community-Based Alternatives to Traditional Corrections: The 1973 Evaluation of the Fifth Judicial District Department of Court Services—State of Iowa.* Davis, Calif.: National Council on Crime and Delinquency, 1974.

Stuckey, Gilbert. *Procedures in the Justice System.* Columbus, Ohio: Merrill, 1976.

Sutherland, Edwin H. *White Collar Crime.* New York: Dryden, 1949.

Swaton, J. Norman, and Morgan, Loren. *Administration of Justice.* New York: Van Nostrand, 1975.

Sykes, Gresham. *The society of Captives: A Study of a Maximum Security Prison.* Princeton, N.J.: Princeton University Press, 1958.

Teasley, C. E., III, and Wright, Leonard. "The Effects of Training on Police Recruit Attitudes," *Journal of Police Science and Administration,* I:241-48, 1973.

Thorne, Gary F. "The Rural Prosecutor and the Exercise of Discretion," *Criminal Law Bulletin,* 12:305-07. 1973.

Tiffany, Lawrence, P., et al. "Detection of Crime," in *The American Bar Foundation Survey of the Administration of Criminal Justice in the United States.* Boston: Little, Brown, 1967.

Tifft, Larry L. "The 'Cop Personality' Reconsidered," *Journal of Police Science and Administration,* 2: 266-78, 1974.

Tresolini, Rosco J. *American Constitutional Law,* 2d ed. New York: Macmillan, 1965.

———, and Shapiro, Martin. *American Constitutional Law,* 3d ed. New York: Macmillan, 1970.

Turk, Austin. *Criminality and the Legal Order.* Chicago: Rand McNally, 1969.

U.S. Department of Justice and U.S. Department of Commerce. *Expenditure and Employment Data for the Criminal Justice System: 1975.* Washington, D.C.: U.S. Government Printing Office, 1975.

Vetter, Harold J., and Simonsen, Clifford E. *Criminal Justice in America: The System, the Process, the People.* Philadelphia: Saunders, 1976.

Von Moschzisker, Robert. *Trial by Jury.* Philadelphia: Bisel, 1930.

Waldron, Ronald J., et al. *The Criminal Justice System.* Boston: Houghton Mifflin, 1976.

Warner, H. C. "Development of Trial by Jury," *Tennessee Law Review,* 26: 459–67, 1959.

Westley, William A. *The Police: A Sociological Study of Law, Custom, and Morality.* Cambridge, Mass.: MIT Press, 1970.

Wheeler, Stanton. "Socialization in Correctional Communities," in *Prison Within Society: A Reader in Penology,* Lawrence W. Hazelrigg, ed. Garden City, N.Y.: Anchor Books, 1969.

Whisenand, Paul W. *Crime Prevention: A Practical Look at Deterrence of Crime.* Boston: Holbrook Press, 1977.

—, and Cline, James L. *Patrol Operations.* Englewood Cliffs, N.J.: Prentice-Hall, 1971.

Whitehouse, Jack E. "Historical Perspectives on the Police Community Service Function," *Journal of Police Science and Administration,* I:87–92, 1973.

Wilson, James Q. *Thinking About Crime.* New York: Basic Books, 1975.

—. *Varieties of Police Behavior.* Cambridge, Mass.: Harvard University Press, 1968.

Wilson, Jerry. *Police Report: A View of Law Enforcement.* Boston: Little, Brown, 1975.

Wilson, O. W., and McLaren, Ray C. *Police Administration,* 3d ed. New York: McGraw-Hill, 1972.

Wilson, Rob. "Plaudits in Des Moines, but Problems in Salt Lake," *Corrections Magazine,* II: 13–34, Sept., 1976.

Winters, Glenn R., ed. *Judicial Selection and Tenure,* rev. ed. Chicago, Ill.: American Judicature Society, 1973.

Witt, James W. "Non-Coercive Interrogation and the Administration of Criminal Justice: The Impact of Miranda on Police Effectuality," *The Journal of Criminal Law and Criminology,* 64: 320–32, 1973.

Glossary

adjudication That point in the criminal process where a judge renders the official judgment of the trial court as to the defendant's guilt or innocence.

adjudicatory hearing A hearing for a juvenile offender at which the court decides upon the question of delinquency.

affidavit A written statement made or taken under oath before one who is authorized to administer an oath.

aftercare For juveniles; the equivalent of adult parole. (See *parole*).

appeal A request by either defense or prosecution that a case be removed from a lower court to a higher court so that the completed trial can be reviewed by the higher court. Those filing an appeal seek to have a lower court decision altered or reversed.

arraignment A court proceeding in which the defendant is informed of the formal charges against him and asked to enter a plea. This proceeding normally occurs after the issuance of an indictment or information but for certain minor crimes may take place during the initial appearance. (See *initial appearance*.)

arrest Taking a person into custody by authority of law, for the purpose of charging him with a criminal offense.

arrest warrant A document issued by the court ordering law officers to arrest a person.

bail A sum of money or other security that is posted to assure the future attendance of the defendant at every stage of the criminal proceedings. Such money or security is to be forfeited if the defendant does not appear in court as directed. (See *bail bondsman*.)

bail bondsman One who provides, in return for a fee, a bond to the court promising payment of bail in the event the defendant flees to avoid prosecution. (See *bail*.)

bailiff A court's security guard. Functions may include the maintenance of order in the courtroom and its immediate vicinity, custody of defendants on trial, calling of witnesses to the stand, and care and custody of jury members.

bench trial A trial in which a judge hears the trial and renders a verdict; a nonjury trial.

beyond a reasonable doubt The standard of proof used in trial courts to justify conviction of a defendant. It is a standard that requires a presence of facts sufficient to fully convince an ordinary person that a defendant committed the crime charged. (See *probable cause*.)

bindover When probable cause is found to exist at a preliminary hearing, the court orders that the accused be held for trial. The accused thereafter may be eligible for release on bail or under other conditions.

booking The process of officially recording an arrest and identifying the person, place, time, arresting officer, and reason for the arrest. Usually done at a police station.

capital offense One for which the penalty may be the taking of an offender's life.

challenge for cause A motion made by either prosecutor or defense attorney that a prospective juror be dismissed on the grounds that he or she would be unable to reach a verdict based on the evidence alone because of such reasons as personal prejudices and preconceived notions of guilt or innocence. There is no limit on the number of these challenges that can be made or granted. (See *challenge, peremptory*.)

challenge, peremptory The challenge of a prospective juror without cause, that is, without specifying to the court any reason or grounds for dismissal. Both prosecutor and defense attorneys are allowed a specified number of such challenges, the exact number varying from place to place and often with the seriousness of the charge.

change of venue Removal of a trial from one locale to another.

citation An order issued by a law enforcement officer directing that a person appear in court at a later date to answer to criminal charges. Also often refers to that which is issued to traffic offenders and which may require only payment of a fine. (See *summons*.)

continuance, trial The postponement to a later date of a case pending in court.

count Each separate offense listed in a complaint, information, or indictment.

court jurisdiction The authority of a court over a particular class of cases that arise within an assigned geographic area or venue.

courts of appellate jurisdiction Those courts having authority to review and overturn rulings of the lower courts from which a case is appealed.

courts of general jurisdiction Criminal courts having jurisdiction to try all criminal offenses, including felonies, that may or may not hear appeals. These courts are commonly called superior courts, district courts, or circuit courts.

courts of limited jurisdiction Criminal courts having jurisdiction to try only minor criminal offenses. Such courts are usually restricted to misdemeanor cases. Examples of these courts include city and county courts. Sometimes referred to as inferior courts.

courts of original jurisdiction Those courts which have the lawful authority to hear or act upon a case from its beginning and to render a verdict. These courts may be either courts of general jurisdiction or courts of limited or special jurisdiction.

deposition A sworn written record of oral testimony, in the form of questions and answers, made before a public officer and intended to be used for the purpose of discovery or trial of an action in court.

discovery The method by which a party in a case can gain access to information and evidence held by the opposing party. In criminal law the right to discovery is usually reserved for the defendant, but some states allow the prosecutor the same right, or reciprocal discovery.

disposition hearing For juveniles; the equivalent of adult sentencing. It is the point at which the judge makes a final disposition decision such as probation, commitment, or case dismissal.

diversion The suspension at any point of formal criminal processing of an alleged offender and the referral of that person to a treatment program inside or outside the criminal justice system. Successful completion of treatment results in dismissal of the case; violation of conditions set at the time of diversion may result in reactivation of the case.

entrapment The act of officers or agents of the government in inducing a person to commit a crime not contemplated by him, for the purpose of instituting a criminal prosecution against him.

evidence Physical objects or sworn statements that a court may consider in trying a case and upon which a verdict is based.

evidence, direct That which comes from first hand observation by a witness.

evidence, heresay Testimony by a witness as to what someone told him, not what he personally observed. Usually inadmissable in a trial but exceptions can be made.

evidence, real Evidence consisting of physical objects (e.g., weapons, stolen property) as opposed to testimonial evidence.

evidence, relevant Evidence necessary to prove or disprove a fact at issue in a trial. Evidence that is related to matters of fact not at issue, or that cannot properly be brought before the court is said to be irrelevant or immaterial.

evidence, testimonial The sworn, verbal statements of witnesses.

examination, direct The initial questioning of a witness by the attorney who calls him to the stand.

examination, cross Questioning of a witness by the attorney that did not call the witness to testify. This normally occurs after direct examination.

exclusionary rule A rule that any evidence obtained through unlawful means (e.g., illegal search and seizure, illegal lineups) is inadmissable in court.

felony A crime that is considered serious enough to be punishable by death or confinement in a state or federal prison, usually for more than one year. (See *misdemeanor*.)

fine The financial penalty imposed by the court upon a convicted person.

frisk A physical search or "patting down" of a suspect's outer clothing to discover weapons; a quick superficial search.

halfway house A facility in which offenders are housed within the community but under some form of supervision, used generally for offenders just released from prison (halfway out) or offenders considered too risky for probation but not dangerous enough for prison (halfway in).

hung jury A jury that is unable to arrive at a verdict.

immunity A formal promise not to prosecute in exchange for testimony. It is used to encourage a person to answer questions that he might otherwise refuse to answer under his fifth amendment right against self-incrimination.

incarceration Imprisonment in a federal, state, or local corrections institution.

index crimes Seven classes of offenses included by the FBI in part I of its Uniform Crime Reports. They are labeled the "serious" crimes and include criminal homicide, forcible rape, robbery, aggravated assault, burglary, larceny-theft, and motor vehicle theft. (See *Uniform Crime Reports.*)

indictment, true bill of A document by which a grand jury formally files charges against a person. It arises out of matters placed before the jury by a prosecutor. (See *presentment, grand jury.*)

information A document filed by a prosecutor with the court formally charging the accused with a specific crime.

initial appearance The first appearance of an offender in court following arrest. Depending upon the jurisdiction, various procedural steps may be taken at this point. Generally the accused is informed of the charges and of his constitutional rights, such as the right to counsel. Based upon the nature of the offense and often upon other factors, such as the defendant's background, bail may be set or the defendant released on his own recognizance. For many minor crimes, the initial appearance may be used to allow pleas. Where it has not already been established during the securement of an arrest warrant by police, this proceeding may also include a determination of probable cause. The initial appearance should not be confused with a step that comes later in the process—arraignment. The confusion between the two terms stems from the fact that some jurisdictions refer to this first court appearance variously as a "preliminary arraignment," "first arraignment," "arraignment on the warrant," or just "arraignment". (See *arraignment.*)

interrogation, custodial The questioning of a suspect who is in police custody.

interrogation, field In the field (on the street) stopping and questioning by police of a "suspicious" person.

jail A locally administered institution used to detain persons awaiting trial or as a place of confinement for persons sentenced to a term of one year or less.

jury charge Instructions to the jury concerning the law relevant to the case it is to decide. They are read to the jury by the trial judge prior to jury deliberations.

jury, grand A body of citizens within a jurisdiction who have been selected and sworn to investigate criminal activity and the conduct of public officials. They also hear the evidence against an accused person to determine whether there is sufficient evidence to bring that person to trial. (See *indictment* and *presentment, grand jury.*)

jury, petit An ordinary trial jury, as opposed to a grand jury. Its function is to hear a trial and then to reach a verdict. In some places it is used also to recommend or determine sentences.

juvenile court Courts with original jurisdiction over juvenile cases.

juvenile delinquent A juvenile who commits acts that if committed by an adult would be crimes and/or certain other acts that are unlawful only if committed by a juvenile. (See *status offense*.)

law, case Law made by American judges as they interpret statutory and constitutional provisions in cases coming before them.

law, civil That part of law having to do with noncriminal matters—e.g., contracts, wills, marriages, divorces, and adoptions.

law, common A set of general legal principles inherited from England that were the product of judicial decisions made in English courts of law. These principles became precedents for subsequent decisions in English and American courts.

law, constitutional Case or judge-made law arising from appellate cases in which nullification of a statute or executive action is sought on the grounds of its unconstitutionality.

law, criminal That branch of the law which defines crimes and provides the punishment for violations.

law, statutory Law enacted by legislative assemblies—e.g., Congress, state legislatures, county commissions, and city councils. That which is enacted by government institutions at less than the state level may be more generally known as ordinances.

magistrate An inferior judicial office (e.g., justice of the peace) or inferior court judge who handles pretrial matters and who may dispose of minor infractions and misdemeanor cases.

misdemeanor An offense less serious than a felony that is generally punishable by less than one year of incarceration in a county or city corrections facility. (See *felony*.)

mistrial A trial that has been halted and declared void prior to the jury returning a verdict or the judge declaring his verdict in a non-jury trial. This action may occur because of factors such as the death or illness of an essential trial participant, a highly prejudicial error, or most commonly, because of the jury's failure to reach a verdict. (See *hung jury*.)

modus operandi The characteristic method used by a person in the performance of repeated criminal acts. Through study of the mode of operation used in multiple crimes, police may be able to link several crimes to one person.

motion to dismiss A request by the defense to the court that a case be dismissed for some stated reason such as a defective information, violation of the statute of limitations or the failure to prove a case against the defendant.

motion to suppress A request by defense to the judge to have certain state's evidence or an admission by the defendant ruled inadmissable and excluded from trial. (See *exclusionary rule*.)

nolle prosequi The withdrawal or dropping of charges against a defendant by the prosecutor.

nolo contendre A plea by the defendant in which he does not contest the charges against him. While not strictly an admission of guilt, it is the equivalent of such and thus subjects the accused to the same criminal sanctions.

parole A program whereby prisoners are released prior to normal expiration of their sentences but are placed under the supervision of the paroling authority. The offenders retain their freedom as long as they meet the conditions agreed upon at the time of release.

parole board That agency of government

which decides whether and under what conditions to grant a prisoner early release.

parole officer The government employee responsible for working with and supervising offenders placed on parole.

parole revocation The canceling of an offender's freedom enjoyed under parole due to violation of parole conditions set by the parole authority.

penal code State or federal criminal law statutes.

petition, juvenile For the juvenile; the equivalent of the filing of an information against an adult. It is a document filed in juvenile court requesting that the court find a juvenile to be delinquent, a status offender, or dependent.

plea A defendant's formal answer in court to the charges brought against him in a complaint, information, or indictment.

plea bargaining The practice involving negotiation between prosecutor and defendant and/or defense attorney over leniency in treatment in exchange for a guilty plea or cooperation with the government in the prosecution of other offenders. Leniency in treatment may mean a reduction or dismissal of charges or a promise that the prosecutor will recommend a lighter sentence than would otherwise be imposed.

preliminary hearing A hearing before a judge to determine if there is sufficient probable cause to hold or bind over an accused person for trial. It is generally limited to persons arrested on felony or high misdemeanor charges, and is conducted as an adversary proceeding. If the judge orders the release of the accused, it does not, in most places, prohibit the subsequent adjudication of the accused on formal charges.

pre-sentence investigation report A report on the background of a convicted offender for the purpose of aiding the judge in the evaluation of a proper sentence.

presentment, grand jury A charge issued by a grand jury on the basis of its own investigations. (See *indictment*, true bill of.)

probable cause A set of facts and circumstances which would induce a reasonably intelligent and prudent person to believe that an accused person had committed a specific crime. It is the standard of proof required in most jurisdictions for arrest and the beginning of prosecution. (See *beyond a reasonble doubt*.)

probation A form of sentence whereby an offender may remain free of confinement so long as he obeys certain conditions imposed by the sentencing court and probation authority.

probation officer The official responsible for working with and supervising offenders placed on probation.

probation revocation The canceling of an offender's freedom enjoyed under probation due to violation of probation conditions set by the sentencing court and probation authority.

prosecutor An official whose primary function is to represent the people in prosecutions against violators of criminal law. This function is performed by various officials such as district attorneys, county attorneys, county prosecutors, state attorneys, and city attorneys.

public defender A government officer whose function is to act as counsel in defense of indigent defendants coming before the court.

release on recognizance Release from custody of an arrested person without bail on his promise to appear for trial at a later date.

response time The time that elapses between receipt of a call or alarm and the arrival of police units at the crime scene.

search warrant An order issued by the court upon application by law officers, directing that a particular location be searched for specified materials. Such a warrant is issued by a judge only upon a showing of probable cause that the specified materials are located in the designated location and were involved in the planning or commission of a crime.

sentence, definite A sentence for a specified period of time such as ten years. Also known as "straight" or "flat-time" sentence.

sentence, indefinite A sentence calling for the serving of a length of time somewhere between a minimum and maximum set by the court.

sentence, indeterminate Very much like an indefinite sentence but different in that the amount of time served is determined by some nonjudicial government agency such as a parole board.

sentence, suspended A sentence whose execution is withheld by the court, usually under specified conditions.

sentencing, concurrent A requirement that an offender serve multiple sentences simultaneously.

sentencing, consecutive A requirement that an offender serve multiple sentences one after the other or nonsimultaneously.

sequester, jury A process whereby jury members are kept isolated from the public during the course of a trial and/or verdict deliberations. Sequestered jury members are fed and housed by the court and are not allowed contact with outside persons.

status offense Acts that are illegal only when committed by juveniles; e.g., violation of curfew, truancy, and running away from home.

subpoena A court order directing that a witness appear in court or bring certain specified materials. Failure to do so could result in being charged with contempt of court.

summons A written order issued by a judicial officer requiring a person accused of a criminal offense to appear in a designated court at a specified time to answer to the charges. This term should not be confused with the term "citation" which is an order issued by police requiring a court appearance. (See *citation*.)

Uniform Crime Reports (UCR) Annual statistical reports compiled and published by the FBI on crime in the United States. (See *index crimes*.)

venire The jury panel from which trial jurors are selected.

venue The geographic area in which a case may properly be heard in court.

victimization surveys Surveys conducted for the LEAA by the Bureau of the Census, which attempts to gauge the extent to which persons of 12 and over, households, and businesses have been victims of various types of crime. The resultant National Crime Panel reports describe the nature of the criminal incidents and their victims.

voir dire An examination, through questioning, of prospective jurors in order to determine if they can be fair and impartial. While this is an accepted definition for some, others contend that voir dire aids both sides in the choosing of a jury as partial to their side as can be obtained.

Index

Acquittal, 259, 271-272, 272-273, 286
Adjudication, 70-73, 183-190, 209, 264-274, 289-290
Administration
    court, 246, 437-439
    police, 96
    prison, 324, 335
    public, 436
Affidavits, 173-174
Affirmative action, police, 430
Aftercare (parole), juvenile, 408
Aggressive patrol, 93
Alarms, 119
Alcohol, Tobacco, and Firearms, Bureau of, 108
Allen, Harry E., 352, 353, 360, 364-365, 375-376
Alternates, jury member, 281
American Corrections Association, 360-361, 440
American Judicature Society, 226, 437
American Law Institute Model Penal Code, 298-299
Analysis, police unit of, 96
Antitrust Division, Department of Justice, 158
Appeal(s)
    of court rulings, 72-73
    courts of, 160, 207, 217-218, 301-302
    jurisdiction of, 214-215
    sentence review, 299
    and Supreme Court, 218-219
Appearance. *See also* Bail; Binding over.
    court, 441
    defendant, 256-264
    initial, 182, 253-254
Appointment
    of defense counsel, 235
    judicial, 227-228
Apprehension, suspect, 124
Argument, closing, 190, 287
Arraignment, 70, 183-184, 264-265
Arrest, 68, 114-115, 252-264
Assignment, blind case, 438
Assistant attorney generals, U.S., 158, 159
Atonement, 205

Attorney(s)
    defense, 196, 233–239
    general, 158, 159–160
    sentence recommendations, 296–297
Auburn prison model, 313
Augustus, John, 316–317, 339

Backlogs, court, 186–187, 268
Bail, 69, 185, 213, 256–260, 269–270
Bailiffs, court, 245
Bail Reform Act of 1966, 263–264
Bargaining, plea. See Plea bargaining.
Barnes, Harry E., 312–313, 314
Battle, trial by, 205–206
Beats, police, 93–94
Behavior
    jurist, 240–241
    modification, 361
    police, 133–135, 135–136, 144–145
    prisoner, 368
    prosecutor's, 192–196
    and rehabilitation, 291
Bent, Alan E., 136, 138
Bercal, Thomas C., 89
Bill of Rights, 40–41, 42–45
Bills of attainder, 40
Binding over, 69–70, 254–255
Bird, Otto A., 37
Blackmun, Harry, 361
Blacks, 430
Black's Law Dictionary, 35
Blanchard, Robert E., 354
Bloch, Herbert A., 33
Block, Peter, 432
Blood feud, 205
Blumberg, Abraham S., 26–27, 234–235, 236
Blumberg crime classifications, 26–27
Bond. See Bail
Booking, 68
Book of the States, 1976–1977, 398–399
Border Patrol, U.S., 108
Brady v. *United States*, 272
Brennan, William, 394
Brown, Gerald, 424

Bugs, electronic, 123
Burger, Warren E., 45

Calls, citizen, 118–119
Caplan, Gerald, 423
Carlson, Norman, 323
Case
    assignment, 438
    flow, 438
    intake, 173
    loads of probation officers, 355–356
    preparation, 130–132
    presentation, 190, 286
    rejection of criminal, 69
    screening, 172–173, 173–174
Census, Bureau of, 29, 31
    and victimization surveys, 29, 31
Census of State Correctional Facilities, 331
Challenge of Crime in a Free Society, The (President's Commission on Law Enforcement and the Administration of Justice), 417
Challenges
    for cause, 189, 242–243
    peremptory, 189, 243, 281
Chamelin, Neil C., 18, 332, 333, 335, 341, 404–405, 407
Charge
    to jury, 288
    motion for dismissal of, 269
Charging, 68–69, 155–157, 186, 252–264. See also Arraignment.
    and arraignment, 264–265
    criteria, 174, 176–178
    and prosecutors, 172–174, 176–183, 194–195, 435–436
Children, 396
CIs (confidential informants), 122, 123, 128–129, 253
Citations, 115, 264
Civilians, police employment of, 430–431
Clare, Paul K., 313, 314, 316, 402, 430–431
Classification, prisoner, 358–359

Cleared crimes, 25-26
Clerk, court, 245
Closing argument, 190
Coconspirators, unindicted, 182
Codes
　revised criminal, 444-445
　state penal, 293-294
Coercion
　of confessions, 267
　and guilty pleas, 271, 272
Coffey, Alan R., 400, 407
Cogan, Morris L., 428
Cohn, Alvin W., 234, 279, 311, 312
Cole, George F.
　on bail, 258, 260
　on defense counsel, 239
　on juvenile justice system, 390, 395, 397, 400, 404
　on *mala prohibita*, 23
　on police culture, 144
　on rehabilitation, 323
　on trial cases, 209
Command, police, 90
Commonplace crime, 27
Complaint, citizen, 68, 118-119
Components, criminal justice system, 6, 9
Compulsory process, 212
Compurgation, trial by, 205-206
Computers, 438, 443
　and witnesses, 438
Concurrency, jurisdictional, 215
Conditions, probationary, 353-354
Conferences, pretrial, 269
Confessions, 211, 267
Confidential informants (CIs), 122, 123, 128-129, 253
Confinement, institutions of, 326-335
Congress, U.S., 18, 39-40, 208, 261, 331, 418
Constitution, U.S., 17, 39-41, 243, 256
Contempt of court, 181
Continuances, trial, 70, 185, 268
Control
　appellate superintending, 217-218
　crime, 52-53, 56

prisoner, 360-361
span of, 91
Convictions, 124, 186, 187, 259, 272, 300, 441
Corrections, 9, 61-64, 72, 310-344, 425-426, 439-442
　community, 371-374
　cost of standards of, 426-427
　Des Moines, 440-441, 442
　environmental influences on, 375-380
　juvenile, 74, 404-408
　officials, 378-379
Corwin, E. S., 42
Costs
　of incarceration, 259-260, 263, 321
　of NACCJSG recommendations, 426-427
Council of State Governments, 438, 444
Councils, sentencing, 299
Counsel, right of, 212, 233
Courtesy, senatorial, 228
Courts, 9, 60-61, 70, 204-219, 278-280, 289-290, 425. *See also* Supreme Court, U.S.
　appellate, 45-46, 61, 73, 160, 361, 377-378
　contempt of, 181
　innovations in, 437-439
　juvenile, 389-390, 396-397, 400-404
　participants, 244-246
　and plea bargaining, 186, 269-274
　and police, 142
　and probation, 353-354, 379
Creamer, J. Shane, 114
Cressey, Donald R., 187-188, 237-238, 268, 272, 297
Crime, 13, 22-29, 31-32, 423-424
Crime Control Act of 1973, 418
Crime Index, FBI, 24-25, 32
Criminal Division, Department of Justice, 158
Criminalistics, 85
Criminal Justice Coordinating Council, New York City, 262
Crofton, Walter, 316

Cross-examination, 190, 285–286
Culture, police, 144–145
Custody
    and jail, 326–327
    juvenile, 400
    and prisons, 360, 361. *See also* Corrections.
Custom vs. law, 33
Customs, Bureau of, 108, 159
Customs Service, 108
Czajkoski, Eugene, H., 353, 357

Darwick, Norman, 102, 103
DEA (Drug Enforcement Administration), 105, 106
Death penalty, 213, 311, 312–313, 315
"Declaration of Principles" (National Prison Association), 314
Defense, counsel for, 233–239, 282–283, 285–286, 287
Deliberations, jury, 288–289
Delinquency. *See* Juvenile justice system.
Demands, system, 7, 11
Depositions, 184
Deputy attorney general, U.S., 158
Des Moines (Iowa) project, 440–441, 442
Detection
    crime, 68, 122–124
    of delinquent acts, 399
Detectives, 95
Detention
    juvenile, 403, 408
    preventive, 260–262
Deterrence, crime, 52, 53, 54–55, 87, 291, 319–320
Detoxification, programs of alcohol, 264
Discharge for cause, 281
Discipline, judicial, 231–233, 437
Discovery, 183, 185, 266
Discretion
    judicial, 210, 295–296, 298, 444
    of juvenile officers, 402
    of parole boards, 444
    of police, 135–136, 399–400
    prosecutorial, 152–153, 178, 180, 193–194

Dismissal, case, 185, 255, 259, 269
Dispensation, justice of, 208
Disposal, motions of, 266
District attorneys, 158, 159, 161
District courts, U.S., 61
Districts, judicial, 206
Diversion
    from justice system, 69, 350–351, 400, 441
    programs for drugs, 264
Docket entry, 173
Double jeopardy, 212

Downing, Rondal, 230
Drug Enforcement Administration (DEA), 105, 106
Drugs, diversion programs for, 264
Dual system, courts', 207
Due process of law, 41, 54, 56, 73, 206, 210–213, 444
    and court administration, 438
    for juveniles, 390–396
    and plea bargaining, 209
    Supreme Court and, 42, 44, 45, 365–366, 417
Duffee, David, 313–314, 320, 342, 358–359, 360, 369
Duncan v. *Louisiana*, 280
Dynamics, system, 11–15

Eavesdropping, electronic, 123
Economic Crime Project Center, 435
Education
    corrections staff, 440
    of police, 428–429
    prison programs of, 362
    of prosecutors, 434
Eighth Amendment, 41, 45, 213, 315, 361, 367, 377
Elections, judicial, 225–226, 228–230, 300
Elitism, judicial, 228–230
Employment, police, 429, 430–431
Enforcement, law, 8–9, 52, 53–54, 56, 57–58, 87
    federal, 104–109
    government influence on, 141–142

Enforcement *(continued)*
    innovations in, 427-434
    and juveniles, 399-400
    and plea bargaining, 186
    state, 101-103
Entrapment, 122-123
Environment, 6, 14-15
    corrections, 375-380
    criminal court, 299-300
    law enforcement, 133-145
    prosecutor, 192-196
Equal Employment Opportunity Commission, 430
Escobedo v. *Illinois*, 267
Evidence, 127-128, 183, 185, 206, 266, 267, 282, 283-285
Examination, witness, 190, 285-286
Exclusive jurisdiction, 215
Exemplary Projects, 419
Expertise, witness with, 285
Ex post facto laws, 40
Extradition, 157

Facilities, correctional, 63, 323, 327-328, 329, 378, 441
Federal Bureau of Investigation (FBI), 24-25, 32, 104-106, 109, 119
Federal Bureau of Prisons, 64, 331
Federal Equal Opportunity Act, 430
Federal Office of Parole and Probation, 64
Fees, legal, 234, 243, 244
Felkenes, George T., 15, 96, 241
Felonies, 23-24, 328-329
Fences, 128
Fielding, Henry, 84
Fielding, John, 84
Fifth Amendment, 41, 181, 210, 211, 212, 286
Fines, 210, 213, 292-293
First Amendment, 366-367
Fitch, Robert, 313-314, 320, 342, 358, 359, 360, 369
Foreman, jury, 288
Fortas, Abe, 388-389, 390-392, 393-394
Fourteenth Amendment, 41, 42, 44, 45, 210-211

Fourth Amendment, 40-41, 43, 44, 123, 211, 253
Fox, Sanford J., 402
Fox, Vernon B., 18, 332, 333, 335, 341, 404-405, 407
Fragmentation, system, 16-17
Frankel, Marvin E., 298, 320-321
Frisks, 117, 121
Fuller, Lon L., 37
Functions
    civil, 157
    criminal justice, 8-9, 52-56
    defense attorney, 233-235
    investigative, 124-125
    municipal police, 86-89
    prosecutorial, 155-158
    sheriff, 99-100
    state enforcement agencies, 102-103
    system, 6, 8
    of trial courts, 208-213
Furloughs
    prison, 317, 363
    work, 363

Gault, Gerald, 390-394
Geis, Gilbert, 33
Georgetown University, 261
Gideon, Clarence, 233
Gideon v. *Wainwright*, 73, 233
Goldstein, Joseph, 35
Government
    and criminal courts, 300-301
    impact on prosecutors, 192-193
    influence on police, 140-144
    and prisons, 377-378
Grand juries, 69, 159, 180-182
Grants, government, 378, 418, 421, 442, 443
Guided-interaction programs (GIPs), 342, 374
Guilt, and pleas, 265, 271, 272

Habeas corpus, writ of, 40, 157, 218, 366
Halfway centers, 372-373
Halfway houses, 317, 342, 372-373, 406
Hand, Richard, 298

Hanging, 312
Hazard, Geoffrey C., Jr., 224-225
Healy, Patrick J., 166
Hearings
    adjudicatory, 74
    juvenile, 402, 403-404
    parole, 368-369
    precharge, 182-183
    preliminary, 69, 254-256
Hearsay evidence, 284-285
Heffernan, Esther, 365
Historical development
    of corrections, 310-317
    of criminal courts, 204-208
    of prosecution, 154-155
    of sheriff's office, 98-99
    of state law enforcement, 101-102
    of treatment of juvenile offenders, 388-396
Holt v. Sarver, 377
Homes, group, 406
Hoover, J. Edgar, 105-106
Houston, University of, 434

Identification, suspect, 124
Immigration and Naturalization Service (INS), 105, 107-108
Immunity, use, 181
Impeachment, judicial, 232, 437
Incapacitation, offender, 291, 320
Incarceration, 63, 259, 262, 292, 312-313, 320-321. See also Institutions, correctional; Institutions, juvenile.
Incorporation, selective, 211
Indictments, 69, 174, 212
Influences
    community, 138-140
    on police, 136, 140-144
Information
    charge for, 69, 174
    criminal justice systems of, 443-444
    police unit of, 96
Informer, confidential (CI), 122, 123, 128-129, 253
Initial appearance, 69

Inmates, correctional institution, 335, 360, 361, 365-367
Innocence, presumption of, 210
In re Gault, 390-394
In re Winship, 394
Insanity, not guilty by reason of, 265. See also Sanity, motion to determine.
Inspection, police, 96
Institute for Court Management, 437
Institute for Law and Social Research, 436
Institute of Criminal Law (Georgetown University), 261
Institutionalization, 357-367
Institutions
    correctional, 326-335, 337
    juvenile, 406-408
Intensive intervention, 374
Interdependence, component, 6, 9-10
Internal Revenue Service (IRS), 108, 109, 159
International Association of Chiefs of Police, 429
International Conference of City Managers, 87, 88
Interrogations, police, 120-122, 127
Intervention
    crisis, 433
    programs of intensive, 374
Investigation
    crime, 68, 94, 95, 124-130
    grand jury, 181
    police, 97, 131-132, 431
    preliminary, 120
    pre-sentence, 71, 296, 316, 351-352, 440
    report of pre-sentence, 340-341

Jackson, Donald D., 213, 225, 228, 230-231, 232, 233
Jacob, Herbert, 166, 209, 227
Jacoby, Joan E., 172, 180
Jails, 326-328
James, Howard, 230, 231, 259, 260
Jeopardy, 269
    once in, 265

Job actions, police, 430
Johnson, Frank, 378
Judges, 224-233, 266, 269, 286, 289, 441, 444
   and bail, 260, 263-264
   and juries, 279-280, 288
   jurisdictions of, 216, 217, 218
   and juvenile hearings, 403
   and pleas, 265, 269-274
   and probable cause, 252-253, 254
   and prosecutors, 196
   selection of, 300, 437
   and sentencing, 209-210, 295-296, 297, 357
Judgment, former, 265
Judicial districts, 206
Judicial Qualifications Commission (California), 232
Judicial review, 42
Judiciary Act of 1789, 155, 207-208
Juries, 69, 206-207, 212, 239-244, 279-282, 288-289, 394-395
   and prosecutors, 193, 194
   selection of, 189, 438
   and sentencing, 295, 296, 297
Jurisdictions, court, 61, 214-219
Justice, Department of, 64, 82, 104-108, 155, 158-159, 331, 418, 419
Justice Academy (Connecticut), 440
Juvenile Justice and Delinquency Prevention Act of 1974, 418-419
Juvenile justice system, 63, 73-74, 95, 396-408, 426

Kalmanoff, Alan G., 178, 180, 181, 291, 321
   on jails, 328
   on plea bargaining, 270, 273
   on police discretion, 124-125
   on pretrial release, 262
Kalven, Harry, 239-240, 280, 300
Kamisar, Yale, 254-255
Kaplan, John, 258-259, 260
Kerper, Hazel, 33, 35, 353-354, 356, 404, 405

Kerper, Janeen, 353-354, 356
Kessler, Joan B., 240
Kirkham, George F., 144-145
Klockars, Carl B., Jr., 354-355
Kramer, John H., 313, 314, 316, 402

Labor, police division of, 90
Ladinsky, Jack, 235-236
Lateral entry, professional, 429
Law, 14, 33-38, 40, 42-45, 72-73, 192. *See also* Enforcement, law.
Law Enforcement Assistance Administration (LEAA), 18, 328, 378, 418, 419, 421-424, 427, 443
   and corrections, 439-440, 441-442
   on judges, 224
   and police, 428, 429, 431
   and prosecutors, 434, 435, 436
   and victimization surveys, 29, 31
Law Enforcement Education Program, 422
Leadership, police, 135
Legal
   aid, 235
   justice, 208
   norms, 33
Legislation
   criminal code, 444-445
   federal, 417-419
London Metropolitan Police Department, 84, 85

McCartt, John M., 343
McColley, Robert, 323
McKeiver v. *Pennsylvania*, 394-395
Maconochie, Alexander, 315-316
Madison, James, 40
Magna Charta, 207
Maintenance, order, 104
Major Offense Bureau of the Office of the District Attorney for Bronx, New York, 434-435
Mala en se crimes, 23
Mala prohibita crimes, 23
Management, calendar, 438
Mandamus, writ of, 217-218

Mangogna, Thomas J., 343
Mapp v. *Ohio*, 43–44, 116, 267
Marshals, U.S., 105, 106–107
Martinson, Robert, 322
Mattick, Hans, 323
Merit system, judicial, 228–230, 437
Metropolitan Police Act of 1829 (British), 84
Miller, Frank, 293–294, 396–397
Minorities, and police, 430
Miranda v. *Arizona*, 233, 267
Miranda warning, 127
Misdemeanors, 23–24, 328–329
Missouri plan, 228–230, 437
Mistrial, 289
Mitchell, John, 181
Model Penal Code, American Law Institute's, 298–299
Modus operandi, criminal, 85
More, Harry W., 158, 403
Morgan, Loren, 90
Morris, Norval, 377
Motions
    defense, 265–269
    directed verdict, 286
    pretrial, 185
Myren, Richard A., 86, 89, 142–143

NACCJSG. *See* National Advisory Commission on Criminal Justice Standards and Goals.
Nagel, William, 324
National Advisory Commission on Criminal Justice Standards and Goals (NACCJSG), 119, 125, 126, 342, 352, 355, 362, 424–427, 435
    on community influence on police, 138–139
    on judicial election, 226
    on juvenile probation, 405
National Center for State Courts, 438
National College of District Attorneys, 434
National College of the State Judiciary, 231
National Council on Crime and Delinquency, 376–377, 398

National Crime Information Center, 105
National Crime Panel Surveys (NCPS), 31–32
National Criminal Justice Information and Statistics Service, 419, 421
National District Attorneys Association (NDAA), 166, 176, 177–178, 434, 435–436
National Institute of Law Enforcement and Criminal Justice, 419, 426–427
Nationalization, criminal justice, 416–427
National Prison Association, 314
National Training Institute, 106
National Welfare Fraud Association, 435
Neilson, Robert, 435
NeMoyer, Edgar C., 187
Neubauer, David W., 153, 195, 236, 238
Newman, Donald J., 187, 270, 273, 295, 351
    on corrections, 310, 325–326
    on probation, 352, 353, 354
New York City Police Department, 85
New York Street Crime Unit, 431
Nolle prosequi, 70, 186, 269, 289
Nolo contendere, 70, 184, 265
Nonsystem, criminal justice as, 15–17
Norms, legal, 33
No true bill, 69

Observation, police, 117–118
Offender-based tracking systems, 443
Offenses, known, 25
Office of Court Alternatives (Orlando, Florida), 441
Office of Law Enforcement Assistance (OLEA), 417–418
Office of Prosecution Management, 436
Officers, parole, 369–371
Omnibus Crime Control and Safe Streets Act of 1968, 417, 421, 443
Opening statements, 282–283
Operations, police, 142–143
Ordeal, trial by, 205–206
Order, maintenance of, 8, 9, 52, 53, 54, 56, 87, 104
Organization
    parole, 337–339

Organization *(continued)*
    police, 90–91, 93–98, 133–135, 136
    prison, 332–335
    of prosecutorial offices, 158–164, 166
    of sheriff's office, 100
    of state enforcement agencies, 103
Organized crime, 27
Organized Crime Strike Forces, Department of Justice, 158–159
Outdoor-style institutions, 406
Outlawry, 205

Packer, Herbert L., 56, 318–319
Palko v. *Connecticut*, 42
Palmer, John, 360
Parens patriae, 388, 389–390, 393
Parole, 63, 72, 314, 315–316, 337–339, 367–371, 408, 444
Pat downs, police, 116, 121
Patrol, U.S. Border, 108
Patrols
    highway, 101, 102–103
    police, 91, 93–95
Peel, Robert, 84
Penal Code, American Law Institute's Model, 298–299
Penal codes, state, 293–294
Penitentiaries, 313. *See also* Institutions, correctional.
Pennsylvania prison model, 313
Personnel
    court support, 245–246
    police unit of, 96
    prosecutor's office, 164, 166
Petition, filing of, 402
Platoons, police, 93
Plea bargaining, 70, 186–188, 209, 289, 425, 426, 445
    and court, 269–274
    jury influence on, 239–240
    and prosecutors, 194–195
    and public defenders, 238
    and sentencing, 273–274, 297
Pleas, defense, 265
Plebiscite, judicial, 228
Plotkin, Robert, 366, 367
Points of fact, 72–73

Police, 17, 57, 68, 133–136, 144–145, 194–195, 425
    authority, 114–117
    municipal, 82–98
    organization, 90–91, 93–98
    professionalization of, 428–431
    state, 101–103
Policing, team, 95, 432
Politics
    and judges, 226–228
    and prosecutors, 193, 194
Popper, Karl, 36
Populations
    of community correctional facilities, 343
    jail, 327
Power, doctrine of inherent, 301
Prassel, Frank R., 206, 327
Precincts, police, 93
Predictability, verdict, 241
Preferred position theory, 44
Preliminary hearing, 69
Preparation
    case, 130–132
    trial, 184–185, 268
Presentation, case, 283–286
Presentiment, 181
President's Commission on Law Enforcement and the Administration of Justice, 82, 243–244, 350–351, 417
    on bail, 261
    on courts, 216
    on judges, 226, 270
    on juvenile aftercare, 408
    on plea bargaining, 186–187
    on police, 91, 135, 429
Prevention, crime, 8–9, 52–53, 54–55, 87, 88
Prisonization, 364
Prisons, 213, 313–314, 323. *See also* Institutions, correctional.
Proactive tactics, 122–124
Probable cause, 114, 252–256
Probation, 191, 210, 292, 316–317, 339–341, 352–357, 379
    departments of, 379
    formal, 405–406

Probation (continued)
   Orlando program of, 441
   programs, 63
   violation of, 72
Procedure(s)
   court, 437
   laws of, 192
   rights of, 209, 212
   rules of, 219
   sentencing, 296-297
   trial, 282-290
Professional crime, 27
Professionalization
   of corrections staff, 439-440
   of police, 428-431
Prohibition, writ of, 218
Property, crimes against, 28
Prosecution, 9, 152-167, 172-196
   and closing arguments, 287
   examination of witnesses, 285-286
   and hung jury, 289
   and opening statements, 282-283
   vs. rehabilitation, 262
   standards, 435-436
Prosecution Management Information System, 436
Prosecutors, 58-60, 192-196, 266, 434-436
   local, 159-164, 166
   and plea bargaining, 186, 187
Psychiatry, 268, 362
Psychodrama, 361
Psychology, 268, 362
Public defenders, 235, 236-239
Public-order crime, 27
Pugh v. *Locke*, 377
Punishment, criminal, 213, 311-313, 315, 319-320, 360-361

Quakers, 322

Rand Corporation, 124, 125-126, 127-128, 129-130, 131-132
Rap sheets, police, 174
Reactive patrol, 94
Reality therapy, 361

Rebuttals, 287
Recall, judicial, 232
Reception, institutional, 358
Recidivism, 261, 322, 356, 407, 441
Records, criminal, 258, 259, 282, 329
Recreation, prison, 363
Redirect, 286
Reentry, inmate, 342, 441
Reform, prison, 314
Reformation, criminal, 313
Reformatories, 314
Rehabilitation, criminal, 291, 314, 321-324, 398
   programs of, 361-363
   vs. prosecution, 176, 262
   and reintegration, 325
Reintegration, inmate, 325
Release. *See also* Parole.
   inmate, 69, 253, 263, 269, 317, 371-372, 441
   pretrial, 262-264
Removal, judicial, 232
Report, social history, 404
Reporters, court, 245
Response time, 119
Resting of case, 286
Restitution, criminal, 291, 324-325
Retribution, criminal, 290-291, 317-319, 320. *See also* Punishment, criminal.
Review, judicial, 271-273
Roe v. *Wade*, 45
Rosenberg, Maurice, 224
Rosett, Arthur, 187-188, 237-238, 268, 272, 297
Rossum, Ralph A., 136, 138
Rubin, H. Ted, 395-396, 401-402, 437, 438
Ruchelman, Leonard, 141, 142

Sanctions, 35, 232, 290-293
San Francisco Committee on Crime, 270-271
Sanity, motion to determine, 268
Saxbe, William, 322
Schools, state training, 406-408
Screening, case, 68-69, 172-173, 173-174

Search and seizure, 115–117, 211, 267
Searches, police, 119, 120, 253, 267
Secrecy, grand jury, 182
Secret Service, 108
Sectors, police, 94
Selection
    defense counsel, 235–239
    judicial, 225–230, 437
    jury, 241–243, 281, 438
    parole, 368–369
Selective incorporation, 44
Self-government, prison, 362–363
Self-incrimination, 211, 286
Sentences, 273–274, 293–295, 329, 352–353, 357
Sentencing, 71–72, 191, 209, 259, 290–299, 444
Sequestering, jury, 281–282, 288
Serrill, Michael, 376–377, 421–422, 423
Services, police bureau of, 97
Severance, motions for, 267
Shelters, juvenile, 406
Sheriffs, 98–100
Shift, police, 94
Simonsen, Clifford E., 242, 343, 352, 353
    on juvenile justice system, 388, 407
    on prisons, 358, 360, 364–365, 375–376
Singer, Richard G., 298
Single, Eric W., 259
Sixth Amendment, 41, 212, 233, 278–279, 280
Solicitor general, U.S., 158
Solomon, Hassim M., 327, 328, 342–343, 372
Specht, David, 432
Staff
    custodial, 335
    jail, 327–328
    police, 91
    prison treatment, 335
Standards
    of criminal justice, 417
    prosecutorial, 435–436
Standards and Goals Commission, on inferior courts, 216

Standing mute, 265
Stanley, David T., 368–369, 371
State
    case presentation, 283–286
    correctional institutions, 328–332
    court systems, 215–218
    and jails, 328
    law enforcement agencies, 101–103
    prosecutors, 159–160
Statements, opening, 190, 282–283
Status offenses, 398
Statute of Westminster, 207
Stephan, Cookie, 240
Structure
    of court system, 213–219, 436–437
    of criminal justice system, 57–64
    jail organizational, 327–328
    of LEAA, 419–421
    of prosecutorial offices, 158–164, 166
    of sentencing, 444
Stuckey, Gilbert B., 205, 279–280, 285, 287, 294–295
Subculture, inmate, 365
Substantive, criminal law, 192
Summonses, 115, 264
Supervision
    of juvenile aftercare, 405, 408
    parole, 369–371
Suppression, evidential, 267
Supreme Court, U.S., 17–18, 41, 46, 61, 73, 207, 217, 297, 299
    on bail, 213
    and Bill of Rights, 211
    on capital punishment laws, 315
    and constitutional law, 42–45
    and criminal justice, 301–302, 416–417
    on due process, 41, 390–396
    and Eighth Amendment, 377
    on entrapment, 122–123
    on field interrogations, 121
    on fines, 293
    and illegally seized evidence, 116, 267
    influence on corrections, 377–378
    and juries, 181–182, 241–242, 243, 280, 288

Supreme Court *(continued)*
    on parole revocation hearings, 370–371
    on plea bargaining, 272
    and police, 428
    and prisoner rights, 365, 366, 367
    and probable cause, 253
    and probation reports, 352
    on right to counsel, 233
    and speedy trial, 212, 279
Surrebuttal, 287
"Swap shop," police, 431
Swaton, J. Norman, 90
Sykes, Gresham, 364
Synthetic officers, 355
Systems theory, 6–7, 11–15

Tax Divisions, Department of Justice, 158
Team policing, 95, 432
Technical violations, 356–357
Technology, 85–86. *See also* Eavesdropping, electronic.
Technology Transfer, office of, 419
Testimony, evidential, 283
Therapy, mental, 355, 361
Time servers, probationary, 355
Torts, 154
Traffic units, police, 95
Training
    of corrections staff, 439–440
    judicial, 231
    of police, 96, 428–429
    in prisons, 362
    of prosecutors, 434
Traynor, Roger, 232
Treasury, Department of, 108–109, 159
Treatment
    community, 341–344
    juvenile, 389
    prisoner, 359–363, 367
Trial
    advocacy, 157
    by battle, 205–206
    bench, 70
    by compurgation, 205–206
    courts of general, 216–217
    and juries, 206–207, 289
    de novo, 73, 217
    by ordeal, 205–206
    practice standards, 190
    preparation, 184–185, 268
    speedy and public, 212
Trimble, Preston, 188, 193
Turk, Austin, 33

Undercover agents, 122
"Uniform Crime Reports" (UCR), 24, 25–26, 28, 29, 31–32, 105
Unionization, police, 429–430
Upperworld crime, 27
U.S. News and World Report, 322

Velde, Richard, 424
Venire, 242
Venue
    motion for change of, 185, 212, 266
    trial, 215, 278
Vera Institute, 261, 263
Verdicts, 240–241, 286
Vetter, Harold J., 242, 343, 358, 388, 407
Vice, criminal, 122
Vice units, police, 95–96
Violence, crimes of, 28
Visitation, penal privileges of, 363
Vocabulary, juvenile justice, 390
Voir dire examination, 189, 281, 242–243

Waldron, Ronald J., 185
Wallace, George, 378
Waltz, Jon, 258–259
Warrants
    arrest, 115
    for electronic eavesdropping, 123
    issuing, 253
    search, 115
Warren, Earl, 44
Warren Court, 43–44
Watch programs, neighborhood, 433
Watson, Richard, 230
Weeks v. *United States*, 267
Weimar, David, 273
Westminster, statute of, 207

Wheeler, Stanton, 365
Whisenand, Paul M., 18, 54-55, 332, 333, 335, 341, 404-405, 407, 432
White, Byron Raymond, 272
Wicker, Tom, 376, 377
Wilson, James Q., 28-29, 133-134
Winters, Glenn R., 227

Witnesses, court, 188, 212, 244-245, 266, 284-286, 438
Wolff v. *McDonnell*, 366
Wolf v. *Colorado*, 43
Work release, 317

Zeisel, Hans, 239-240, 280, 300